# THE
# ROLAND AND OTUEL ROMANCES
# AND THE
# ANGLO-NORMAN *OTINEL*

# MIDDLE ENGLISH TEXTS SERIES

The Middle English Texts Series are scholarly texts designed for research and classroom use. Its goal is to make available to teachers, scholars, and students texts that occupy an important place in the literary and cultural canon but have not been readily available in print and online editions. The series does not include those authors, such as Chaucer, Langland, or Malory, whose English works are normally in print. The focus is, instead, upon Middle English literature adjacent to those authors that are needed for doing research or teaching. The editions maintain the linguistic integrity of the original work but within the parameters of modern reading conventions. The texts are printed in the modern alphabet and follow the practices of modern capitalization, word formation, and punctuation. Manuscript abbreviations are silently expanded, and *u/v* and *j/i* spellings are regularized according to modern orthography. Yogh (ȝ) is transcribed as *g, gh, y,* or *s,* according to the sound in Modern English spelling to which the medieval pronunciation corresponds; thorn (þ) and eth (ð) are transcribed as *th*. Hard words, difficult phrases, and unusual idioms are glossed either in the right margin or at the foot of the page. Explanatory and textual notes appear at the end of the text, often along with a glossary. The editions include short introductions on the history of the work, its merits, and points of topical interest.

# THE
# ROLAND AND OTUEL ROMANCES
# AND THE
# ANGLO-NORMAN *OTINEL*

Edited by
Elizabeth Melick, Susanna Fein, and David Raybin

A publication of the
ROSSELL HOPE ROBBINS RESEARCH LIBRARY
in collaboration with
the University of Rochester Department of English
and the Teaching Association for Medieval Studies

by

MEDIEVAL INSTITUTE PUBLICATIONS
Kalamazoo, Michigan
2019

Manufactured in the United States of America

## Library of Congress Cataloging-in-Publication Data

Names: Melick, Elizabeth, editor. | Fein, Susanna, 1950- editor,
    translator. | Raybin, David B., 1951- editor, translator.
Title: The Roland and Otuel romances and the Anglo-French Otinel / edited
    by Elizabeth Melick, Susanna Fein, David Raybin.
Other titles: Middle English texts (Kalamazoo, Mich.)
Description: Kalamazoo : Medieval Institute Publications, 2019. | Series:
    TEAMS Middle English texts series | Includes bibliographical references.
    | In Middle English and Old French with parallel English translation;
    introduction and commentary in modern English. | Summary: "This edition
    contains four Middle English Charlemagne romances from the Otuel cycle:
    Roland and Vernagu, Otuel a Knight, Otuel and Roland, and Duke Roland
    and Sir Otuel of Spain. A translation of the romances' source, the
    Anglo-French Otinel, is also included. The romances center on conflicts
    between Frankish Christians and various Saracen groups. In addition to
    Charlemagne and Roland, each romance features a Saracen character:
    either the kind but loathsome giant Vernagu or Otuel, Vernagu's handsome
    and sharp-tongued nephew. The romances deal with issues of racial and
    religious difference, conversion, and faith-based violence"-- Provided
    by publisher.
Identifiers: LCCN 2019044356 (print) | LCCN 2019044357 (ebook) | ISBN
    9781580443883 (paperback) | ISBN 9781580443890 (hardback) | ISBN
    9781580444125 (pdf)
Subjects: LCSH: Charlemagne, Emperor, 742-814--Romances. | Roland
    (Legendary character)--Romances. | Otinel (Legendary
    character)--Romances. | Romances, English. | Narrative poetry, English
    (Middle) | Romances, Anglo-Norman--Translations into English.
Classification: LCC PR2064 .R65 2019  (print) | LCC PR2064  (ebook) | DDC
    821/.108--dc23
LC record available at https://lccn.loc.gov/2019044356
LC ebook record available at https://lccn.loc.gov/2019044357


ISBN   9781580443883 (paperback)
ISBN   9781580443890 (hardback)
ISBN   9781580444125 (pdf)

Printed and bound by CPI Group (UK) Ltd, Croydon, CR0 4YY

# CONTENTS

# ACKNOWLEDGMENTS

In our joint work on this edition, Elizabeth Melick edited the four Middle English romances, while Susanna Fein and David Raybin edited and translated the Anglo-Norman *Otinel*. The introductions, notes, and bibliographical apparatus were created collaboratively.

Elizabeth is indebted to Kent State University's Graduate Student Senate for awarding her funds that allowed her to travel to London to consult manuscripts at the British Library. A Donald Howard Fellowship from the New Chaucer Society also supported her stay in London (which coincided with the 2016 NCS Biennial Congress in London). Elizabeth is grateful to the librarians at the British Library, who provided digitized images and helped to arrange her Manuscripts Room visit. She also thanks the many faculty of Kent State University who supported this project with guidance and encouragement, particularly Wesley Raabe, Christopher Roman, Robert Trogdon, Jennifer Larson, Judy Wakabayashi, Susanna, and also David (as guest faculty). Finally, she is grateful to her friends, family, and partner Tyler Ponder for cheering her on with tireless enthusiasm, making it possible for her to pursue and complete this project.

David acknowledges the influence of Robert Hanning, who first introduced him to the *Song of Roland* several decades ago, and the late Peter Haidu, with whom he discussed it at length. Susanna is deeply grateful for the research support she receives from the Institute of Bibliography and Editing, the English Department, and, especially, the Division of Research and Sponsored Programs (led by Vice President Paul DiCorleto), of Kent State University. A sabbatical leave in 2018 was an invaluable gift during the making of this edition. David and Susanna both wish to thank Elizabeth for perceiving the need and advocating for a modern edition of the Middle English Roland and Otuel poems. Her drive caused them to see the importance of enabling students to discover these romances alongside the *chanson de geste* of *Otinel*.

Together we acknowledge the generous support of the National Endowment for the Humanities, which has permitted the Middle English Texts Series to flourish in its prodigious production of more than ninety editions in hard and online versions. The support of the Rossell Hope Robbins Library, University of Rochester, directed by Anna Siebach-Larsen, and of the staff of Medieval Institute Publications, Western Michigan University — Marjorie Harrington, Tyler Cloherty, and Director Theresa Whitaker — is also very much appreciated. We are especially indebted to the sharp-eyed, dedicated, incomparable editorial team at the Robbins Library — Pamela Yee, Ashley Conklin, Steffi Delcourt, and Emily Lowman — who made this edition better than it would have been otherwise. And, not at all least, we are enormously grateful to Alan Lupack, emeritus director of the Robbins Library and himself the editor of the METS *Three Middle English Charlemagne Romances*, and to Russell A. Peck, Executive Editor *of pris*, for their enduring enthusiasm and good-sense feedback regarding this project.

For their generous, wide-ranging gifts to Middle English studies,
we dedicate this volume to

Russell Peck

and

Alan Lupack

# GENERAL INTRODUCTION

The legendary Frankish conqueror Charlemagne loomed large in the imaginations of medieval English Christians concerned with crusades, empires, and national legacy. Although feelings toward the French were less than friendly during the period of the Hundred Years' War (1337–1452), the English admired the illustrious exploits of Charlemagne (742–814), King of the Franks and the Lombards and First Emperor of the Romans, for his zealous dedication to the suppression of pagans. In this, he was regarded a proto-crusader. The renown of Charlemagne, last of the Nine Worthies, is often cited in Middle English writings, and, as shown by the surviving canon of ten romances featuring the exploits of Charlemagne and his knights, his legends were often adapted into adventures for the entertainment of English audiences. Of these, five belong to what is called the Otuel cycle: *The Siege of Milan*, *Roland and Vernagu*, *Otuel a Knight*, *Otuel and Roland*, and *Duke Roland and Sir Otuel of Spain*.[1]

## THE OTUEL CYCLE IN MIDDLE ENGLISH ROMANCE

The tales of the Saracen knight Otuel and his uncle Vernagu deserve to be better known because they offer important medieval literary models of the Saracen — that is, Muslim or other pagan — as either hero or anti-hero. Versions of their story are deeply grounded in the broader "Matter of France" tradition best known through the *Song of Roland* (*Chanson de Roland*), an Anglo-Norman *chanson de geste* composed in the late eleventh or early twelfth

---

[1] The remaining five Charlemagne verse romances are: *The Sultan of Babylon*, two versions of *Firumbras*, *The Tale of Ralph the Collier*, and the Middle English *Song of Roland* (*DIMEV* 1562, 1554, 972, 2596, 1819; *NIMEV* 950, 944.5, *593.8, 1541, 1132.5, respectively). The character Roland, Charlemagne's illustrious nephew, features prominently in eight of the ten Charlemagne romances, that is, all except *Siege* and *Ralph the Collier*. Despite some imprecision, the term *cycle* is retained in this volume because it is a recognized designator for the five romances that relate the Otuel narratives. On the English Charlemagne romances, see Smyser, "Charlemagne Legends"; Ailes and Hardman, "How English"; and Cowen, "English Charlemagne Romances." There are also some later English prose lives or romances that feature Charlemagne: Caxton's *Charles the Grete* (1485) and *The Foure Sonnes of Aymon* (c. 1489), and John Bourchier's *The Boke of Duke Huon of Burdeux* (printed by Wynkyn de Worde, c. 1534) (Smyser, "Charlemagne Legends," pp. 86–87, 98–100). There is also an early printed verse romance: *Capystranus* (Wynkyn de Worde, 1515). A useful resource for understanding the corpus of Middle English romance is the *Database of Middle English Romance*, ed. McDonald, Morgan, and Nall.

century.[2] Inspired by the *Song*'s tragic story of Roland's death while battling Saracens in Spain, French poets composed dozens of *chansons de geste* that feature Charlemagne as ruler of Christendom, that is, as conqueror and converter of non-Christians, leader of a band of courageous *dussepers* (twelve peers), and uncle of Roland, his preeminent knight. One of those *chansons de geste* is *Otinel*, a late-twelfth- or early-thirteenth-century poem that is the source for three Middle English romances: *Otuel a Knight*, *Otuel and Roland*, and *Duke Roland and Sir Otuel of Spain*.[3] The source for *Roland and Vernagu* is the *Chronicle of Pseudo-Turpin*, a history of Charlemagne's reign composed in the mid-twelfth century.[4] A chapter of the *Chronicle* tells of a combat between Roland and Ferragus (Vernagu in *Otinel* and the Middle English romances).

The Otuel-cycle romances have attracted little attention, probably because the corpus is small and their quality has been regarded as slight. Moreover, when the three *Otinel*-derived romances are mentioned in critical discussion, scholars often decide to conflate them even though they are distinctly different from one another.[5] In an overview of the cycle, H. M. Smyser's kindest comment is that the *Duke Roland* poet was "a competent versifier." More typical is his comment that "lines 909–58 [of *Otuel a Knight*] may serve as a convenient example of the banality all too frequently found in most of the English Charlemagne romances."[6] Still, while the poets who penned the Otuel-cycle romances may not have risen to the literary talents of Geoffrey Chaucer or the *Gawain* Poet, the romances

---

[2] For an edition and translation of the *Song of Roland*, see *The Song of Roland: An Analytical Edition*, ed. and trans. Brault. For an overview of the poem's critical tradition, see Raybin, "*The Song of Roland*."

[3] There are two largely complete manuscript witnesses of *Otinel*: an Old French version in Vatican City, Biblioteca Apostolica Vaticana MS Reg. Lat. 1616; and an Anglo-Norman version in Cologny, Fondation Martin Bodmer Cod. Bodmer 168. See Dean and Boulton, *Anglo-Norman Literature: A Guide*, p. 53n78; and the introduction to *Otinel* in this volume. The Old French version has been edited (with lacunae supplied from the Anglo-Norman version) in *Otinel*, ed. Guessard and Michelant. The Anglo-Norman version is edited and translated for the first time in this volume. *Otinel* has not been the subject of a large body of criticism, but see Aebischer, *Études sur Otinel*; and Hardman and Ailes, *Legend of Charlemagne*.

[4] The *Chronicle of Pseudo-Turpin* pretends to have been written by Turpin, Archbishop of Reims from c. 753 to c. 800. The historical Turpin is an obscure figure about whom little is known. The first appearance of the legendary Turpin is in the *Nota Emilianense* (c. 1060), a sixteen-line Latin text in an otherwise inconsequential manuscript that is the earliest document to suggest the existence of a *Song of Roland*: Madrid, Biblioteca de la Real Academia de la Historia, Codex 39, fol. 245r. Turpin's name appears in a list of famous heroes in *chansons de geste* said to have accompanied Charlemagne to Spain — Roland, Bertrand, Ogier Short-sword, William Short-nose, Oliver, and Bishop Turpin. For a Middle English translation of the *Chronicle*, see *Turpines Story*, ed. Shepherd. For editions of French versions, see *The Anglo-Norman 'Pseudo-Turpin Chronicle'*, ed. Short; *The Pseudo-Turpin*, ed. Smyser; and *An Anonymous Old French Translation*, ed. Walpole. On the *Nota Emilianense*, see Walpole, "The *Nota Emilianese*" (for a translation); and *The Chronicle of Pseudo-Turpin*, ed. Poole, pp. xxxii–xxxiii (for a photographic image of the page containing the note).

[5] A notable exception to scholars' tendency to conflate the three Otuel romances is Speed, who examines the prominence of the conversion theme in each of the three Middle English Otuel romances, and argues that *Duke Roland* foregrounds conversion much more than do the other two versions; see Speed, "Translation and Conversion."

[6] Smyser, "Charlemagne Legends," pp. 94, 92.

deserve attention, especially in the current social and political climate, given how curiously, suspiciously, and sometimes sympathetically they scrutinized — and sought to incorporate through conversion — the religious and racial Other.

In another volume in this series, *Three Middle English Charlemagne Romances*, Alan Lupack explains how Charlemagne was made the last of the Nine Worthies because he had, as Emperor, defended "Christianity — and thus, for most medieval western readers, the civilized world — from the advancing Saracens, a more imminent and proximate threat than that which was met by the other Christian Worthies."[7] Middle English Charlemagne romances imagine French Christians in legendary conflict against Saracens rather than against the enemy Charlemagne had in fact battled most often: the Saxons. Historical accounts like Einhard's *Life of Charlemagne* (dated 829–36) suggest that the Saxons were more prone to plague Charlemagne than were Muslims from the East, and that they were the group Charlemagne was most intent on subduing. But perhaps because the Saxons had been successfully converted, and also perhaps because they were ancestors of the English themselves, the poets of late medieval English romances followed French models and depicted Charlemagne at war with their own religious enemy — Saracens.

In this vein, the Otuel-cycle romances feature Charlemagne's Christian realm in conflict with non-Christians, and here some weighty questions of who can and cannot be converted come to the fore. In *Roland and Vernagu*, the chief philosophical and theological matter concerns how there are some human-like creatures that cannot ever be converted to Christianity, that is, how physical form, size, and racial coloring may define an individual as too monstrous to be saved. The same issue is presented and resolved differently in *Otuel a Knight*, *Otuel and Roland*, and *Duke Roland*. In those romances, the medieval audience meets a Saracen hero who rapidly becomes the narrative's most interesting character, and they are asked to consider the validity and efficacy of a forced conversion achieved by divine intervention. Alongside theological quandaries raised when a Saracen is the featured protagonist, the Otuel-cycle romances further invite reflection on a host of issues: Western conceptions of the non-Christian Other, attitudes toward intercultural exchange, and medieval prejudices that still affect modern attitudes of racism, religious division, and nationalist zealotry.

## THE MIDDLE ENGLISH OTUEL-CYCLE ROMANCES IN OVERVIEW

The five Otuel-cycle romances devolve from three sequential stories that center on a seemingly worldwide conflict between Charlemagne and the Saracen ruler Garcy.[8] The earliest story (about a war) is told in *The Siege of Milan*,[9] the next episode (about a second war) appears in *Roland and Vernagu*, and segments of the third story (about the coming of the messenger Otuel and a final war) surface in *Otuel a Knight*, *Otuel and Roland*, and *Duke Roland*. Brief summaries of the three narratives follow here.

---

[7] *Three Middle English Charlemagne Romances*, ed. Lupack, p. 1.

[8] Emperor Garcy resurfaces (without Charlemagne) in a different Middle English romance — *Le Bone Florence of Rome* (*DIMEV* 575; *NIMEV* 334), ed. Heffernan — where he rules Constantinople.

[9] For *The Siege of Milan*, see *DIMEV* 408; *NIMEV* 234. It is not included in this volume because it has already been edited for the Middle English Texts Series; see *The Siege of Milan*, ed. Lupack.

*Narrative 1: The Siege of Milan.* The romance treats a conflict between Christendom and a Saracen army led by Sultan Arabas, who has conquered many Christian cities and is currently occupying Lombardy and attacking Milan. Alantyne, lord of Milan, requests Charlemagne's help, but Ganelon, the infamous traitor of the *Song of Roland*, persuades Charlemagne to keep most of his forces in France and send forth only Roland.[10] There ensues a serious dispute between Charlemagne and Turpin, who scolds and then excommunicates Charlemagne for failing to aid a besieged Christian city. Charlemagne repents and joins Roland and Turpin in the siege of Milan. The romance's ending is unfortunately lost, but it likely concluded with a Christian victory over Arabas.

*Narrative 2: Roland and Vernagu.* The romance opens by explaining that Ebrahim, Spain's Saracen king, persecutes and kills Christians, and currently has Constantinople under attack. When Emperor Constantius begs Charlemagne for help, Charlemagne saves the city, and as a reward the emperor gives Charlemagne relics of Christ's Passion. Saint James then appears miraculously to Charlemagne, explaining that he must go to Galicia and recover the saint's bones. After experiencing this vision three times, the emperor resolves to invade Spain, the mission expanding beyond Galicia to include conquest of all of Islamic Spain. During each siege, Charlemagne prays for victory, and God always grants him success. With the Saracen faith conquered, Charlemagne establishes an episcopal structure throughout Spain.

The crucial Vernagu episode occurs after this set-up of conquest. While holding court in Pamplona, Charlemagne receives a challenge from Vernagu, a Saracen giant so loathsome that courtiers rush forward to gawk at him. Several *dussepers* try unsuccessfully to fight him, but before a *dusseper* can strike, Vernagu lifts him up, tucks him under his arm, carries him off, and sets him down unharmed but humiliated. Roland then begs for a chance to face the giant, and despite their size difference, they engage in an equally matched fight. After several grueling hours, Vernagu asks for a break and falls asleep on the bare ground (because he is too large to enter a building). Roland sets a stone under Vernagu's head to serve as a pillow, and when Vernagu wakes and discovers the "pillow," he is moved by Roland's kindness. With a new sense of goodwill, Vernagu questions Roland about Christian doctrine. Roland expounds Christianity's major tenets, answering each of Vernagu's incredulous questions about complicated concepts. After this surprising conversation, the fighters resume the duel to prove which faith is true. Vernagu prevails at first, but when Roland calls out to God for help, an angel appears, ordering him to kill Vernagu because he can neither be converted nor made virtuous. Roland immediately slays the giant and presents his head to Charlemagne as a trophy. The romance ends with a forecast of future conflict. Word of Vernagu's death spreads, reaching the ears of his nephew Otuel.

---

[10] Ganelon's treachery, frequently cited by medieval writers, has also often been examined in modern scholarship on medieval attitudes to violence and treason. For discussions of Ganelon and his betrayal in various literary texts, see Haidu, *Subject of Violence*, pp. 66–69; Leitch, *Romancing Treason*, pp. 149–54; and Mickel, *Ganelon, Treason*.

*Narrative 3: Otuel a Knight / Otuel and Roland / Duke Roland and Sir Otuel of Spain.* These romances tell versions of the story in the French *Otinel*.[11] The story of *Roland and Vernagu* lies in the background, as a prequel that the audience would evidently have known, and *Otuel and Roland* includes an ending based on the *Song of Roland* story. Each narrative opens with Otuel coming as a messenger to Charlemagne's court bearing a challenge from Garcy, the Saracen emperor: if Charlemagne converts, he may keep his lands; if he refuses, Garcy will attack. Otuel hurls insults at Charlemagne, Roland, and the *dussepers*, and he also reveals his personal motive: he hopes to avenge his uncle Vernagu's death. Enraged by Otuel's taunts, a French knight attacks and is immediately slain. With the knights crying out for Otuel's death, Charlemagne and Roland agree that Otuel must be protected, for he has come as a messenger, so the king grants him eight days' surety. Still angry, Otuel challenges Roland to a duel on the following day. Both knights are elaborately armed, with Otuel's arming assigned to Charlemagne's beautiful daughter Belesent and her maidens, who express concern for his welfare.[12] During a pause in the duel, Roland asks Otuel to convert and become a peer, offering him lands, titles, and Belesent as bride. Otuel refuses, however, and steadily gains an advantage over Roland. Charlemagne prays, and in response a dove alights on Otuel's helmet; the Saracen miraculously converts. Otuel is baptized and made a peer.

Charlemagne and the *dussepers* now consider how best to answer Garcy's threat. They agree to wait until spring and better weather before heading to Ataly, Garcy's capital city. Once spring arrives, they embark, set up camp across a river from Ataly, and build a bridge. Three *dussepers* — Roland, Oliver, and Ogier the Dane — decide to ride out in secret in search of adventure and soon encounter four Saracen kings, whom they overhear boasting about how they want to kill Roland.[13] The three knights meet the four kings and slay three, but the last king, the handsome Clarel, begs for his life. They start to take him back to camp as a prisoner but encounter a large force of Saracens. Realizing that their situation is dire, the knights release Clarel because they cannot simultaneously hold him and fight the Saracens. In the melee, Ogier is gravely injured. Clarel reappears, refuses to let his fellows kill Ogier, and instead sends Ogier to his paramour to be healed. Roland and Oliver flee the battlefield.

---

[11] See Ailes, "What's in a Name?," who discusses the terms "Anglo-Norman romance" and "*chanson de geste*" as they pertain to the three texts and *Otinel*. Ailes points out which elements of *Otinel* conform to *chanson de geste* tradition and which are characteristic of romance, ultimately concluding that *Otinel* is a *chanson de geste* that contains romance elements. For a discussion of how English authors adapted, resequenced, and remodeled narratives from *chansons de geste* so that they would suit romance conventions, see Hardman, "Roland in England."

[12] The character Belesent, Charlemagne's royal daughter, also appears as a strong-willed love interest (Belissant) in a wholly different French *chanson de geste*: *Ami et Amile* (c. 1200); see Jones, *Introduction to the Chansons de Geste*, pp. 113, 119–22. In the *chanson*'s Middle English descendent, *Amis and Amiloun*, the heroine is still named Belisaunt, but she is the daughter of the duke who is lord of both titular heroes. For the Middle English *Amis and Amiloun* (ed. Foster), see *DIMEV* 1350; *NIMEV* 821.

[13] Roland, Oliver, and Ogier the Dane are all well-known characters in French *chansons de geste*. Roland and his companion Oliver star, of course, in the Charlemagne legends and especially the *Song of Roland* retellings. Ogier the Dane, "one of the most popular epic heroes of the French Middle Ages," also has a separate legend of his own (Jones, *Introduction to the Chansons de Geste*, pp. 35–36).

Back at Charlemagne's camp, Otuel notes the knights' absence and chafes that they left without him. He assembles a legion and rides toward Ataly. On the way, he encounters Roland and Oliver fleeing and chides them for cowardice. Roland and Oliver join Otuel and return to the battle, now easily won. Otuel kills many former comrades, including family members. Clarel confronts him, and when Otuel reveals his identity and conversion, Clarel accuses him of treachery. They agree to duel the next day. Otuel wins the duel, killing Clarel, at which point a battle breaks out between the forces of Garcy and Charlemagne. When the Saracens are defeated, Garcy tries to flee but is quickly captured and conveyed to France, where he is forced to convert. Rewarded for his service with lands, Otuel marries Belesent.

*Otuel a Knight* ends with Garcy's capture. *Duke Roland* follows the French story by closing with the wedding and a celebration of total Christian victory.[14] *Otuel and Roland* continues, however, and from this point onward its plot embraces elements from the *Song of Roland*. Having defeated Garcy, Charlemagne conquers other Saracen rulers in Spain and establishes his court in Pamplona.[15] The sultan of Babylon dispatches two captains to overthrow Charlemagne by treachery. They communicate with Charlemagne through Ganelon, claiming that they wish to become Christians, but in fact they have bribed Ganelon to join their conspiracy. Ganelon convinces Charlemagne to return to France, and as the French host marches through Roncevaux in the Pyrenees Mountains, the Saracens attack and defeat the rearguard led by Roland. All are slain. Charlemagne mourns Roland and fights a final battle against the Saracens, defeating them decisively. After Ganelon is convicted of treason in a trial by combat, Charlemagne buries the knights who fell at Roncevaux and builds a church to commemorate them.

Taken together, the narratives embedded in the Otuel-cycle romances establish a basic pattern: a Saracen army attacks Christendom, Charlemagne is forced to quell the threat, and another Saracen army makes a strike in retribution. It could be that few medieval English readers had access to all three installments of the narrative sequence, but it is notable that every manuscript witness of an Otuel-cycle romance contains at least one other Charlemagne romance. The Auchinleck and the London Thornton manuscripts each hold two romances from the Otuel cycle. The compilers of these manuscripts appear to present purposefully the cyclical violence found in the broad narrative sweep of the Charlemagne-versus-Saracens story. It seems very likely that their English audiences would have been readily able to recognize and pick up on the character- and theme-based connections among the various Charlemagne romances.

A key issue in the Otuel cycle concerns how the theme of conversion is presented. *Roland and Vernagu* pits admirable Christian knights against an unconvertible Saracen of

---

[14] The wedding is described in the Vatican City text, but not in the Cologny text of *Otinel*.

[15] Here the plot of *Otuel and Roland* is connected to that of *Roland and Vernagu* in significant ways. While Charlemagne is preoccupied with converting Otuel and defeating Garcy, the Saracens have regained power in Spain; in *Roland and Vernagu*, Charlemagne has just conquered and converted Spain. Thus, his efforts in *Otuel and Roland* to reconquer Pamplona fit the "loss and recovery" pattern described by Manion, *Narrating the Crusades*, p. 8, as one of the central characteristics of Middle English crusading romances. The narrative choice to present the failed conquest mission as one of recovery rather than as an aggressively expansionist endeavor lessens somewhat a sense that Charlemagne might be partly culpable for the death of Roland.

monstrous appearance. The romance's remarkable pause to allow Roland to expound Christian theology to Vernagu, who exhibits an intelligent curiosity about the matter, may seem to leave the impression that Saracens are open to conversion, but for the giant Vernagu that is not to be. The contrast with the three Otuel romances is extreme. While Vernagu is ultimately exposed as an irredeemable pagan (and apparently not entirely human), his handsome nephew Otuel can be converted. The baptized Otuel will be welcomed as Charlemagne's son-in-law and incorporated into the ranks of Charlemagne's knights.

## THE FIVE ROMANCES BELONGING TO THE OTUEL CYCLE

Although scholars of Middle English romance now generally agree that the five romances form a coherent Otuel cycle, there was formerly a period of uncertainty over the inclusion of *The Siege of Milan* and *Roland and Vernagu*. With four of these romances appearing in this edition, the scholarly debate is worth summarizing and reviewing. The three Middle English translations of the French *Otinel* obviously stand at the heart of the cycle. *Roland and Vernagu* and *The Siege of Milan* share themes and characters but seem to be more at the margins. *Siege*'s connections by character (other than Charlemagne) are fairly weak: Otuel is never mentioned, and Garcy is mentioned only once, when, after the Sultan has been killed, Ganelon remarks:

| "All if the Sowdane thus be dede, | *Although* |
| Thay will have another newe, | |
| A more schrewe than was the tother, | *cruel; the other* |
| Garcy that is his awenn brothir, | *own* |
| That more barett will brewe." | *trouble* |
| (lines 590–94)[16] | |

Moreover, *Siege* does not share any sources with the other four romances; it may in fact be, as Dieter Mehl suggests, an original English composition.[17] Smyser explains how the grouping came about: "Gaston Paris and Gautier suggested that the *Sege of Melayne* forms a kind of introduction to *Otuel* in the same way as the *Destruction de Rome* is introductory to *Fierabras*, and the *Sege* has ever since been placed in the Otuel Group."[18] Nonetheless, there are some conceptual benefits to including *Siege* in the cycle. Like his Otuel counterparts, the *Siege* poet emphasizes how war against Saracens is divinely sanctioned, and the poem's scope is similar to the others: it covers a single conflict between Christians and Saracens consisting of two main battles. It also fits generally with the chronology of the other romances, which are clearly meant to have all occurred before the action in the *Song of Roland*.

The second outlier, *Roland and Vernagu*, has a stronger connection to the Otuel romances, but its place has been questioned as well. According to Fred Porcheddu, the idea of a cyclical link between *Roland and Vernagu* and the Otuel romances is based on a flawed "Charlemagne and Roland" theory. He argues that the "cycle" title is itself problematic: "in

---

[16] *The Siege of Milan*, ed. Lupack, p. 126.

[17] Mehl, *Middle English Romances*, p. 153.

[18] Smyser, "Charlemagne Legends," p. 93.

comparing 'Charlemagne and Roland' to collections like the Icelandic sagas, Paris intended the word 'cyclic' to be synonymous with 'collective,' like an anthology, and the result of a single directing hand."[19] As Porcheddu further argues, the central piece of evidence supporting the label — the "Charlemagne and Roland" theory — is in limbo, so it is difficult to justify the categorization in the way that Paris intended.

While Porcheddu's critique of the term "cycle" for the Otuel cycle carries some weight, *Roland and Vernagu*'s place among the Middle English Otuel romances is legitimate because it acts as prologue or prequel to the Otuel story: Otuel's entrance as a Saracen protagonist is said to have come about in direct response to the action in *Roland and Vernagu*. Indeed, understanding Otuel's full motive for coming to Charlemagne's court requires knowledge of Vernagu's earlier interaction with Charlemagne, Roland, and the *dussepers*; Otuel arrives as Garcy's messenger and as would-be avenger of his uncle's death at Roland's hand. Moreover, when *Roland and Vernagu* is taken into consideration, Otuel's story presents a clear second attempt at achieving two goals: conversion of a pagan and total conquest over the Saracens. Otuel himself is seeking a do-over: he comes to Paris to defeat the Christians and undo his uncle's failure. At the same time, Charlemagne and Roland seek to correct a past mistake; during the duel they employ new conversion tactics and are successful. Without *Roland and Vernagu*, the conversion thread in the Otuel romances would be incomplete. Insofar as conversion is a guiding theme in Otuel's story, *Roland and Vernagu* fits in the cycle.

A related subject is the contested relationship of the Auchinleck manuscript *Roland and Vernagu* with the Fillingham manuscript *Otuel and Roland*. Porcheddu explains the curious situation that so slight a romance, rarely lauded for its literary value, has brewed a noted debate:

> . . . its meter and rhyme are not unusual for the tail-rhyme genre; there are no plot elements (apart from the simultaneous duel and theological debate between Roland and the Saracen giant Vernagu) which strike the reader as extraordinary. Although it is a unique copy and has been edited three times, the poem has never been considered important to scholars or students by virtue of its poetic content. Surprisingly, however, this obscure romance lies at the center of an impressive theory of a lost Charlemagne epic. . .[20]

In the 1940s, Ronald N. Walpole and H. M. Smyser resuscitated a nineteenth-century theory, expounded by Gaston Paris, that *Roland and Vernagu* and *Otuel and Roland* are two halves of the same poem: a single lost source called "Charlemagne and Roland."[21] They noted in particular the poems' three shared stanzas, identical stanzaic forms, and related plots. Their ideas drew on Laura Hibbard Loomis' Auchinleck bookshop theory, which proposed that the Auchinleck manuscript was evidence of a "bookshop" — that is, a publication center devoted wholly to book production — that employed multiple scribes,

---

[19] Porcheddu, "Edited Text," p. 480, referring to Paris, *Histoire Poétique de Charlemagne*, p. 156.

[20] Porcheddu, "Edited Text," p. 478.

[21] Walpole, "Source Manuscript of Charlemagne and Roland"; Smyser, "Charlemagne and Roland and the Auchinleck MS"; Paris, *Histoire Poétique de Charlemagne*, p. 156; see also Walpole, *A Study of the Source*. Paris based his argument on George Ellis' description of *Otuel and Roland* because the Fillingham manuscript was at that time lost.

hence that *Roland and Vernagu* and *Otuel and Roland* are remnants of a lost unified text.[22] The bookshop theory has since been discredited, and given the state of manuscript evidence, the "Charlemagne and Roland" theory is a house built largely on sand.[23] It cannot be entirely dismissed, but barring discovery of a manuscript containing a "Charlemagne and Roland" poem, it remains speculative.

## CHARLEMAGNE, ROLAND, AND HISTORICAL ACCOUNTS

Although the events and almost all the characters named in *Roland and Vernagu* and the three Middle English Otuel romances are romance fictions, the idea that Charlemagne fought in Spain and Lombardy has some basis in historical records. For medieval English readers, the line between history and fiction was less sharply drawn than for modern audiences. Medieval audiences would have recognized historical events referenced in the Otuel-cycle romances and considered these occurrences significant to the history of Western Christianity. The events of Charlemagne's reign thus provide context for the Otuel-cycle romances.

The posthumous chronicle of Charlemagne's life composed by his advisor Einhard is an important near-contemporary source of information about the Frankish ruler.[24] Despite the many layers of transmission, translation, and adaptation between Einhard's chronicle and the Otuel-cycle romances, some details found in the romances seem to have roots in Einhard, such as the *Roland and Vernagu* poet's description of Charlemagne:

| | |
|---|---|
| Now late we be of this thing, | *set aside* |
| And speke of Charles the king | |
|    That michel was of might. | |
| Of his lengthe and his brede, | *breadth* |
| As the Latin ous sede, | *tells us* |
|    Ichil you rede aright. | |
| Tuenti fete he was o lengthe, | *of height* |
| And also of gret strengthe, | |
|    And of a stern sight. | *imposing appearance* |
| Blac of here and rede of face, | *hair; red* |
| Whare he com in ani place | *Wherever* |
|    He was a douhti knight. | |
| (lines 425–36) | |

While the notion that Charlemagne was a giant is of course absurd, this description follows Einhard's depiction of him as an exceptionally tall man with dark hair and ruddy cheeks.[25]

---

[22] Loomis, "Possible London Bookshop."

[23] On the discrediting of the bookshop theory, see Cannon, "Chaucer and the Auchinleck Manuscript Revisited," pp. 131–33.

[24] See Ganz, "Introduction," pp. 9–10. Einhard composed his *Life* between c. 820 and c. 830, some years after Charlemagne's death in 814.

[25] Einhard, *The Life of Charlemagne*, ed. and trans. Ganz, p. 34. See also *The Chronicle of Pseudo-Turpin*, ed. and trans. Poole, pp. 56–57.

Other aspects of the Otuel-cycle romances are also connected to historical accounts. Although there is no evidence of his involvement in Charlemagne's court, a contemporary Archbishop Turpin did exist, and though the documentation is late, there may have been a Roland. The continuing conflict with Saracens from Spain, central to *Roland and Vernagu* and *Otuel and Roland*, may reflect the many Carolingian treaties, territorial disputes, and battles with Muslim leaders in Spain. Prior to Charlemagne's ascension, Muslim groups occupied cities in France, but Charlemagne expelled most of them after a series of battles and sieges. Soon thereafter, the Muslim governor Suliman sought an alliance with Charlemagne in order to gain an upper hand in his power struggles with other Muslim leaders. In return for Charlemagne's support, Suliman offered him control of northern Spain. The acquisition appealed to Charlemagne for two reasons: first, it would create a barrier between France and the Spanish Muslims, and, second, it could lead to the conversion of non-Christian populations.

In 778, Charlemagne's forces proceeded through Spain as two armies. One army, led by Charlemagne himself, went through the Pyrenees and Pamplona in the west, and the other went through Septimania toward Barcelona. After seizing Pamplona, populated by Basques who were Christians but unwilling to be ruled by a foreign party, Charlemagne proceeded to Zaragoza, which had been promised to him, and there reunited with the other half of his army. The ruler refused to turn over the city, and Charlemagne was able to sustain a siege for only a short amount of time before a more proximate threat from the Saxons and waning supplies led him to return to France, taking Suliman with him as hostage. Charlemagne again passed through Pamplona, where he discovered that the conquered city had rebelled against his rule and the resident Basques had joined with the Muslims to resist him. Charlemagne destroyed the city and then proceeded homeward across the Pyrenees.

The greater importance of the Saxon threat is well documented. Einhard recounts the Saxon campaigns at much length, and even his account of Charlemagne's Spanish campaign begins with a note on Charlemagne's conflict with the Saxons: "While he was vigorously and almost constantly pursuing the war with the Saxons, and had placed garrisons at suitable points along the frontier, he attacked Spain with as large a force as he could."[26] Alessandro Barbero describes the cyclical nature of the conflict between the Franks and the Saxons:

> Time and again the Saxon chiefs, worn down by war with no quarter, sued for peace, offered hostages, accepted baptism, and undertook to allow missionaries to go about their work. But every time that vigilance slackened and Charles was engaged on some other front, rebellions broke out, Frankish garrisons were attacked and massacred, and monasteries were pillaged.[27]

Charlemagne surely was eager to subdue the Muslim threat in Spain and gain new territories, but, as Barbero explains, he viewed it as his spiritual duty to achieve a permanent conversion of the pagan Saxons, considering himself a new David facing a new Jericho.[28]

---

[26] Einhard, *The Life of Charlemagne*, ed. and trans. Ganz, p. 24.

[27] Barbero, *Father of a Continent*, p. 45.

[28] Barbero, *Father of a Continent*, p. 47.

THE *SONG OF ROLAND*

Circumstantial evidence for the existence of a popular story about Roland's heroic death dates back at least to the early eleventh century, when brothers began to be named Roland and Oliver.[29] The oldest extant version of a Roland poem is the 4002-line *chanson de geste* in Anglo-Norman bound in Oxford, Bodleian Library MS Digby 23. Dating to around 1100, this magnificent poem, composed in the assonanced stanzas of variable length known as *laisses*, is the oldest extant secular narrative in a modern European language.[30] An otherwise unknown Turoldus, named in the manuscript's final line, is in some way related to the poem's composition, be it as composer, scribe, or some mixture. The text in Digby 23 is untitled, the name *Chanson de Roland* assigned by the young French medievalist Francisque Michel, who in 1833 came to England in search of French manuscripts in British libraries, most especially the long-sought "Chanson de Roland" sung by the Norman poet Taillefer at the onset of the Battle of Hastings in 1066.[31] Almost all critical studies of the *Song of Roland* treat the Oxford text.

The action of the poem centers around two battles. The first takes place at Roncevaux, a pass through the Pyrenees Mountains that separate France and Spain. Charlemagne has spent seven years in Spain, conquering the entire land save one city, Zaragoza, ruled by the Saracen king Marsile. Hoping to convince Charlemagne to withdraw, Marsile offers to convert to Christianity. After an exchange between Roland, who opposes the offer, and his stepfather Ganelon, who favors it, Charlemagne agrees to negotiate. At Roland's urging, he sends Ganelon to Zaragoza as his emissary. Furious and threatening revenge, Ganelon plots with Marsile to have Roland killed: Ganelon will arrange that, as Charlemagne crosses the Pyrenees, Roland with 20,000 young Frenchmen, the pride of Charlemagne's army, will man the rearguard, which is then open to a treacherous attack by Marsile's army of 400,000 Saracens. As Roland proclaims, "Paien unt tort e chrestïens unt dreit" (Pagans are in the wrong and Christians are in the right; line 1015).[32] The battle is long and fierce, featuring dozens of intensely violent single combats between the French twelve peers and the foremost enemy warriors — battles that show off the brutishness of the pagans so as to demonstrate

[29] Lejeune, "La Naissance du Couple Littéraire."

[30] The *Chanson de Guillaume* and *Gormont et Isembart* (surviving only in a 661-line fragment) are thought to date from about the same time. For editions, see Bennett; and Bayot. An Old French spiritual drama, *La Vie de Saint Alexis*, ed. Hemming, survives from c. 1050.

[31] Michel discovered the Digby 23 text in July 1835. The improbable story of Taillefer's battlefield singing is recounted by the Norman poet Wace (c. 1110–after 1174) in the *Roman de Rou*, lines 8013–18: "Taillefer, qui mult bien chantout, / sor un cheval qui tost alout, / devant le duc alout chantant /de Karlemaigne e de Rollant, / e d'Oliver e des vassals / qui morurent en Rencevals" ("Taillefer, a very good singer, rode before the duke on a swift horse, singing of Charlemagne and of Roland, of Oliver and of the vassals who died at Rencesvals."). The text comes from Wace, *Roman de Rou*, ed. Holden, 2:183; the translation is from Wace, *History of the Norman People*, trans. Burgess, p. 181. On Digby 23 and the discovery of the *Song of Roland*, see Russell, "Admiring Ambivalence," pp. 243–45; and Taylor, *Textual Situations*, pp. 26–70.

[32] Citations of the text and translation of the *Song of Roland* are drawn from Brault.

the natural superiority of the French.[33] Scenes of action are punctuated by two debates among worthy Roland, wise Oliver, and mediatory Archbishop Turpin over whether the duties of a vassal allow that Roland summon Charlemagne to their defense.[34] When, eventually, the French forces dwindle and the immensity of their loss is revealed, Roland determines to blow his horn, not so that Charlemagne will save them, but so that the emperor may avenge their deaths. In the end, the Saracens are defeated, their few survivors abandoning the battlefield, but all the French are dead. Roland's flesh is untouched, but he bursts his temples when he blows his horn to call Charlemagne. God sends four angels to raise Roland's soul to paradise, and miraculously stops the sun to allow Charlemagne time to kill the fleeing Saracens.

The second battle takes place on the plains outside of Zaragoza, where Charlemagne leads his army against the immeasurably large battalions of Baligant, emir of Babylon, who has arrived in Spain a day too late to support Marsile. A battle between massed troops concludes with a one-on-one fight between Baligant and Charlemagne, who triumphs when God sends Saint Gabriel to encourage him. The poem closes with a judicial combat that determines Ganelon has betrayed not only his fellow warrior Roland — which he claims was justified by their mutual hatred — but the emperor as well, and Ganelon is drawn and quartered. The final *laisse* finds Charlemagne, summoned to yet another battle against pagans, bemoaning his weary life.[35]

There is no evidence of a large battle at Roncevaux, and the historicity of Roland's death in the Pyrenees is uncertain. In his *Life of Charlemagne*, Einhard recounts an incident in August 778 in which a group of local Basques ambushed Charlemagne's baggage train as the emperor returned from a Spanish campaign. Among those killed were "Eggihard, the overseer of the king's table, Anselm, the count of the palace and Roland, the prefect of the Breton March."[36] Einhard makes no mention of Oliver, twelve peers, or a battle against Muslims. As the earliest manuscripts of the *Life* do not mention Roland, it is possible that his name was added in response to a developing legend.[37]

The continuing popularity of the Roland story is evidenced during the centuries following the Oxford *Roland*, as adaptations, translations, and references abound across Europe. Important early witnesses to the story's popularity include a late-thirteenth-century narrative in mostly rhymed, Italian-inflected French verse, presumably adapted from an assonanced French version and more than twice the length of the Oxford text.[38] This poem

---

[33] On violence as central to the poem's ethos, see Haidu, *Subject of Violence*, pp. 66–84. On the poem's treatment of the Islamic Other, see Kinoshita, "Alterity, Gender, and Nation" and "Political Uses and Responses."

[34] Roland is called "proz" and Oliver is called "sage" (*Song of Roland*, line 1093).

[35] For a basic introduction to scholarship on the *Song of Roland*, see Vance, *Reading the Song*; and the essays in Kibler and Morgan, *Approaches to Teaching*.

[36] Einhard, *The Life of Charlemagne*, p. 25. Einhard composed his *Life* long after Charlemagne's death and half a century after the ambush.

[37] See Mandach, *Naissance et Développement*, especially pp. 21–32.

[38] *The Song of Roland: Translations of the Versions in Assonance and Rhyme*, ed. and trans. Duggan and Rejhon. The narrative survives in two exemplars: Châteauroux, Bibliothèque municipale ms. 1 (8201 lines); and Venice, Biblioteca Nazionale Marciana MS Fr. Z. 7 (251) (8880 lines). The translation of Châteauroux-Venice 7 is based on Duggan's 2005 edition, *La Chanson de Roland — The*

romanticizes and extends the story, creating a different tone (that of a romance epic), yet existing as fine verse in its own right. The principal extant Middle English witnesses are lines 1979–2790 of *Otuel and Roland*, which recount the entire Roncevaux story in abbreviated form, and the Middle English *Song of Roland*, a 1049-line fragment in alliterative couplets in London, British Library MS Lansdowne 388, fols. 381r–95v, with folios missing at the beginning and end. The text that remains tells the story from Ganelon's return from Zaragoza until shortly before Roland blows his horn.[39]

## CHANSONS DE GESTE

*Otinel*, like the *Song of Roland*, is a *chanson de geste*. *Chansons de geste*, which may be understood as "songs of deeds, feats of arms, or lineages," are narrative poems, usually in French, that recount the imagined military adventures of various historical and pseudo-historical barons, knights, and kings. The action frequently centers on conflict between Christians and Muslims (referred to as pagans and Saracens), but many *chansons* focus on power relationships among kings and barons — the two themes are often combined. The poems are typically characterized as *epics*, a loose term that suggests heroic behavior and perhaps mythic or historical significance. The earliest *chansons* appear to have been sung or chanted, as evidenced by the incorporation of the formulaic lines and half-lines typical of orally composed narrative poetry; later *chansons*, which tend to have fewer formulas, were recited or simply read aloud.[40]

Over one hundred *chansons de geste* survive from the twelfth through the fifteenth centuries in over three hundred complete and partial copies, including several in Anglo-Norman.[41] The verse in many twelfth-century *chansons* is rendered in assonanced decasyllabic *laisses*, with a caesura after the fourth or sixth syllable, but *chansons* also exist with alexandrine (twelve-syllable) and octosyllabic *laisses*.[42] Later *chansons* tend to be composed in rhymed *laisses* with alexandrines, though assonance and decasyllables are reasonably common and there are many mixed forms. A number of late-twelfth- and early-thirteenth-century *chansons* announce the close of *laisses* with six-syllable lines.[43] The poet

---

*Song of Roland: The French Corpus*. For a complete list of manuscripts containing French versions of the Roland story, alongside a *précis* of *Roland* scholarship, see Raybin, "*The Song of Roland*." For earlier scholarship, see Duggan, *A Guide to Studies*.

[39] On the Middle English *Song of Roland*, see Hardman, "Roland in England"; and *Fragment of the Song of Roland*, ed. Herrtage.

[40] The classic study of the oral quality of the *chansons* is Rychner, *Essai sur l'art Épique des Jongleurs*.

[41] Jones, *Introduction to the Chansons de Geste*, p. xi. The volume offers a useful introduction to the history and development of the *chansons*. Although there have been many studies of individual *chansons*, there are very few studies of the *chansons* as a group. Two books by William C. Calin are helpful: *The Epic Quest* and *A Muse for Heroes*. See also Kay, *Political Fictions*; and Hindley and Levy, *The Old French Epic*.

[42] The Cologny text of *Otinel* has two *laisses* in alexandrines with all the rest in decasyllabic lines; see the explanatory note to *Otinel*, lines 17–44.

[43] Jones, *Introduction to the Chansons de Geste*, lists the versification, number of lines, and approximate dates for seventy-eight *chansons* (pp. 149–52), along with a bibliography listing over 150 critical editions of *chansons de geste* and related works, including editions of over 80 *chansons de geste* (pp. 187–96).

and dramatist Jehan Bodel, writing toward the end of the twelfth century, divides the narrative poetry of his day into three *matières* (matters): "De France et de Bretaigne et de Rome la grant" (of France, of Britain, and of great Rome). The "Matter of France" refers to the *chansons*, which Bodel says may be distinguished from frivolous Breton tales and sage Roman texts by their observable veracity, "Cil de France de voir chascun jor aparant" (those of France are true, as is every day apparent).[44]

Composition in *laisses* — that is, variable-length stanzas of mono-assonanced or mono-rhymed lines that present either a single moment, scene, or discourse ("unified" *laisse*) or a transition or series of elements ("composite" *laisse*) — is a distinguishing characteristic of the *chansons de geste*. The use of assonance or rhyme as a structural marker was effective in distinguishing scenes and conversations at a time when punctuation was rare and direct discourse was not delineated by quotation marks. A switch in assonance or rhyme might announce that one thought had ended and another was begun. Poets sometimes took advantage of the *laisse* structure to compose a sequence of two or more *laisses* that present the same basic information with slight variation. By slowing down the narrative progression, these sequences highlight a moment's dramatic importance. In the *Song of Roland*, for example, one set of three successive *laisses* shows Roland blowing his horn (his *olifan*) and Charlemagne hearing it from a distance. It is unclear and perhaps unimportant whether Roland blows his horn three times or just once (though Charlemagne says in the third of these *laisses* that the horn has sounded for a long time). What the poet conveys tremendously effectively is the extent of Roland's agony:

> Li quens Rollant, par peine e par ahans,
> Par grant dulor sunet sun olifan.
> Par mi la buche en salt fors li cler sancs,
> De sun cervel le temple en est rumpant.
> (lines 1761–64)

> [Count Roland, with pain and suffering,
> With great agony sounds his oliphant.
> Bright blood comes gushing from his mouth,
> The temple of his brain has burst.]

Later poets may have modeled their use of what specialists call "parallel" and "similar" *laisses* on their famous appearance in the *Song of Roland* and other early poems such as *Gormont et Isembart* and the *Chanson de Guillaume*.

*Chansons de geste* are generally divided among loose groups highlighting characters and themes: Charlemagne and Roland, William of Orange and his family, Garin le Lorrain and his family, rebellious barons, and the first and second crusades. There are also many outliers. Anglophone readers who wish to get a glimpse of the range of *chansons de geste* are encouraged to consult Joan Ferrante's translations of four poems in the *Guillaume d'Orange* cycle; Michael Newth's translations of *chansons* including the *Chanson de Guillaume*, *Gormont et Isembart*, the *Voyage de Charlemagne*, *Raoul de Cambrai*, and *Aye of Avignon*; and Samuel

---

[44] Quoted from Bodel's *Chanson de Saisnes* in Jones, *Introduction to the Chansons de Geste*, p. 2.

Rosenberg and Samuel Danon's translation of *Ami et Amile*.[45] Over the course of the twelfth century, coincident with the advent of Arthurian romance, *chansons de geste* pay increasing attention to mixing scenes of love with the ever-present scenes of war, but the two tendencies may have been parallel rather than causal. Romance-like elements tend to be especially strong in fourteenth- and fifteenth-century *chansons*.

## SARACENS AND THE CONVERSION THEME

Imagining Christian armies soundly defeating Saracen foes appealed to medieval English Christian audiences, who were themselves frequently in the midst of, recovering from, or preparing for crusades. Nonetheless, depictions of Saracens were not always wholly negative. While Western Christians wanted to triumph over Saracens, they also wanted to convert them. A concept of the "noble Saracen," able to be converted and incorporated into Christian society, also fascinated Christian audiences. Given current interest in cross-cultural relations and understanding of the Other, it is not surprising that the body of scholarship on Saracens in Middle English literature, particularly romance, has grown substantially in recent years.[46] This section presents a brief overview of the subject, especially as it relates to the Otuel-cycle romances.

It is easy to think of medieval England and France in the Middle Ages as spaces occupied by a homogeneous group of white Christians. White Christians certainly made up the vast majority of the English populace, but the British Isles were far from monocultural. Travel was difficult, and information tended to circulate slowly, but in addition to journeying to the wilds of Wales, Scotland, and Ireland, many medieval English ventured beyond the Channel and even beyond Europe, and they interacted through trade with people who were neither white nor Christian. Moreover, the English, like continental Europeans, were eager for information about territories beyond their borders. Stories about other peoples and faiths were popular. The travel narrative *The Book of Sir John Mandeville* was translated into many European languages, and over two hundred manuscript witnesses survive,[47] evidence that medieval Europeans wanted to know about other occupants of the world, even if their interest was not always benevolent. As Iain Macleod Higgins argues in *Writing East: The "Travels" of Sir John Mandeville*, the Mandeville author and adapters have a clear and obvious purpose in their descriptions of foreign lands and people: to distinguish Western Christians from the Other, and to use this distinction to critique the shortcomings

---

[45] Ferrante, trans., *Guillaume d'Orange* (includes *Coronation of Louis*, *Conquest of Orange*, *Aliscans*, and *William in the Monastery*); Newth, trans., *Heroes of the French Epic* (includes *Gormont and Isembart*, *Song of William*, *Charlemagne's Pilgrimage*, *Raoul of Cambrai*, *Girart of Vienne*, and *Knights of Narbonne*); Newth, trans., *Heroines of the French Epic* (includes *Capture of Orange*, *Song of Floovant*, *Aye of Avignon*, *Song of Blancheflor*, and *Bertha Broad-foot*); and *Ami and Amile*, trans. Rosenberg and Danon.

[46] Recent studies include Akbari, *Idols in the East*; Calkin, *Saracens and the Making of English Identity*; Czarnowus, *Fantasies of the Other's Body*; Heng, *Empire of Magic* and *Invention of Race*; Huot, "Others and Alterity"; Metlitzki, *The Matter of Araby*; and Ramey, *Black Legacies*.

[47] The language of the book's original text is uncertain, but was most likely French. There were numerous medieval translations and adaptations, and manuscripts are extant in Czech, Danish, English (five versions), French (three versions), German/Dutch (four versions), Irish, Italian, Latin (five versions), and Spanish; see Introduction, *Book of John Mandeville*, ed. Kohanski and Benson.

of the former through "use of the Other as a Self-critical mirror."[48] As in *The Book of Sir John Mandeville*, depictions of the Other in literature were wildly fictionalized and often derogatory, with a steady focus not just on observing foreigners, but on converting, subduing, or obliterating those who followed non-Christian faiths.[49]

In England during the Middle Ages, Saracens made popular characters for romances, particularly after the crusades had begun. Geraldine Heng argues that the crusades and English romance were closely intertwined. According to Heng, the romance genre developed as a response to the trauma experienced during the crusades and was used to examine some of the central issues raised by crusading activity:

> . . . key historical developments in England — the idea of a medieval English nation, crises in knighthood and the encroachment of forms of modernity threatening chivalric feudalism, the rise of conversion and missionizing as alternative forms of conquest to military adventurism, and the expanding sense of an infinitely enlarging world in which England was located — found expressive voice by retelling the history and meaning of the crusades against the Saracens and Islam.[50]

English audiences enjoyed romances that depicted Saracens and conversion efforts because these romances bolstered their crusading fantasies. In later romances, once the success of past crusades and the viability of future crusades had become questionable, depictions of Saracens were sometimes used as thought experiments for authors considering whether crusades could be won, and whether Saracens could truly be converted.

Most English Christians did not have much firsthand experience with Muslims unless they had traveled extensively. However, they did have access to texts and stories that would have informed them about Muslims and their faith. For example, *The Book of Sir John Mandeville* mixes accurate and fanciful details about Islam, and properly characterizes Muslims as highly devout. Nonetheless, Saracens and their faith were most often depicted in romance as unholy inversions of Christians and Christianity. Thus Saracens are usually shown as having three or four gods, worshiped as idols. The gods' names vary by romance, but the most common are Mahounde (Muhammad), Apollin, Jovin, and Termagaunt. Less common are Jubiter and Platon, names adapted, like Apollin and Jovin, from Greco-Roman mythology and history. In the four romances in this edition, Mahounde is the god invoked most often by Saracen characters, but Saracens in *Roland and Vernagu* pray to Apollin (line 860) and Jubiter (lines 343, 852, 860); Saracens call upon Apollin in *Otuel a Knight* (line 1276) and *Duke Roland* ("Apparoun," line 1483); and, in *Otuel and Roland*, Saracens invoke the group of Mahounde, Apollin, Jovin, and Termagaunt three times (lines 1185–87, 1195–99, and 1534–35), Termagaunt two additional times (lines 127, 736), and Platon three times (lines 122, 1235, 1487).

While inaccuracies in the depiction of Saracens may seem fairly innocent, Heng explains that when "Romances in the English Charlemagne/Roland cycle, like the *Sultan of Babylon* and *Otuel and Roland*, . . . exuberantly feature a multiplicity of Saracen gods and idols," this

---

[48] Higgins, *Writing East*, p. 80.

[49] On the Other as monstrous, see Friedman, *Monstrous Races*; Huot, *Outsiders*; and Cohen, *Of Giants* and "Green Children."

[50] Heng, "Jews, Saracens," pp. 257–58. See also Strickland, *Saracens, Demons, and Jews*, pp. 165–70; Czarnowus, *Fantasies of the Other's Body*; and especially Heng, *Invention of Race*.

"depiction of Islam as a polytheistic pagan apparatus turning on idol worship and false gods . . . is an aggressive polemical stance of denigration and dismissal."[51] Saracen characters often exclaim to their gods in prayers that mimic Christian prayers, and when they swear oaths, they usually avow "bi Mahoun" (e.g., *Otuel a Knight*, line 220) and praise him as a mighty worker of miracles (*Otuel a Knight*, lines 1183–84). When Clarel confronts a converted Otuel, he advises him to "leef en Mahoun" (*Otuel a Knight*, line 1168) or "Giffe thi hert unto Mahoun" (*Duke Roland*, line 223). In *Otuel and Roland*, Saracens even offer up a cry of "Mahoun joye" (line 825) after a successful attack, an adaptation of the Christian exclamation "Mountjoy!" There are several references to idol worship and idols: "maumetes" (*Roland and Vernagu*, line 323) and "maumettrie" (*Otuel a Knight*, line 25).

Saracens are also portrayed as heavy drinkers and prone to lust. In *Saracens and the Making of English Identity: The Auchinleck Manuscript*, Siobhan Bly Calkin argues that these inaccuracies were probably not truly intended to spread misinformation about Muslims, but were instead a way for English authors to negotiate their own national and religious identities:

> Within the context of the early fourteenth-century Auchinleck manuscript, Saracens serve to define the "Inglisch" identity asserted so stridently therein, and to explore the processes and problems involved in asserting such an identity in the 1330s. The Saracens of Auchinleck thus decisively demonstrate the various ways in which figures of religious alterity offer crucial insights into cultural and political debates in which their audiences are directly engaged. The manuscript therefore explains, at least in part, the popularity of Saracens in the late medieval West: these characters provided their audiences with the opportunity to examine purportedly exotic realms and people, but simultaneously ensured, through their inaccuracies and resemblances to Westerners, that such examination provided their audiences with ideas about, and clarifications of, the audiences' own concerns.[52]

Calkin's observations about Saracen characters in the Auchinleck manuscript romances (which include *Roland and Vernagu* and *Otuel a Knight*) apply equally well to the other Otuel-cycle romances. Vernagu's courtesy and honorable comportment align him with Christian values, but his enormous size and dark skin color define him as Other.[53] Clarel's lover Enfamy suggests the type of "enamored Saracen princess" who converts to Christianity for love. Though Enfamy never actually betrays Clarel, she is undeniably intrigued by Ogier when she heals his wounds.[54]

While converted Saracen characters like Otuel were popular with audiences eager to consider the successful conversion and incorporation of Saracens into Christendom,

---

[51] Heng, "Jews, Saracens," p. 258.

[52] Calkin, *Saracens and the Making of English Identity*, p. 211. On similar trends in French literature of the same period, see Daniel, *Heroes and Saracens*; Kinoshita, "Pagans are Wrong," and "Political Uses and Responses"; and Ramey, *Christian, Saracen and Genre*, pp. 53–66.

[53] Vernagu contrasts with the titular hero of the Charlemagne romance *Firumbras*, who is also a giant but converts when he sees that Christianity is superior to his own faith. On exemplary Saracens in French and English medieval literature, see especially Ailes, "Chivalry and Conversion"; Armstrong, "Postcolonial Palomides" and "The (Non-)Christian Knight in Malory"; and Klein, *Romancing Islam*.

[54] A more fully developed example of this type is Firumbras' sister Floripas, who falls in love with Guy of Burgundy and then betrays her father to help him and other imprisoned French knights.

Saracen characters who do not convert are nearly as important to an understanding of how the non-Christian Other was received. Vernagu and Clarel are prominent Saracens who cannot be persuaded to convert. Characters like Vernagu are often seen as suggesting that some Saracens simply cannot be converted because they have an inherent quality that prevents them from changing their faith. Carolyn Dinshaw discusses this principle in relation to the Syrians massacred by the Sultaness in Chaucer's Man of Law's Tale, noting that even though they have converted, the Man of Law does not present them as true Christians:

> Christian *converts* from Islam in *The Man of Law's Tale* are treated in ways that are not so different from the ways *intransigent* infidels are treated. They all die, that is, and they die because they're still corporeally, racially, the same . . . . No one, not even the usually hyperbolic Man of Law as narrator, bewails the deaths of so many Christians: their everlasting lives are not even mentioned. . . . But a question arises from this narrative treatment: is there a difference between a real converted Saracen and a fake one, if each shares the same ugly narratorial fate?[55]

Likewise, anxieties about whether Saracens could actually be converted are expressed often in the Otuel romances. An angel reveals to Roland that Vernagu, notwithstanding his interest in Roland's explanation of Christian tenets, can never be converted, and commands Roland to kill him. Otuel's conversion is achieved through a miracle, against his will and refusal to abandon his faith. Even as Otuel's faith has nominally changed, not much about his character or behavior is different. It is reasonable to ask whether such a conversion is genuine.

A related concern in the romances was about which methods were likeliest to bring about genuine conversion. Calkin discusses how some popular conversion methods — marriage, preaching, trade, money — are used to varying success in the Man of Law's Tale. Though marriage was a "peaceful complement to traditional crusade warfare in endeavours to extend Christian control over Saracen territories," its use in the Man of Law's Tale

> is not really about conversion in any spiritual sense, wherein a process of theological instruction leads to a change of religious belief. Instead, Chaucer's depiction of this marriage eliminates suggestions of proselytizing efforts on Custance's part and emphasizes the role of trade and 'certein gold' in spreading the Christian faith.[56]

It is in some measure unsurprising that Custance's marriage to the Sultan — arranged by a mercantile exchange of a Christian emperor's daughter and her dowry for a Saracen ruler's conversion — ends in a massacre of both Christians and Saracens.

The Otuel-cycle romances show the utilization of multiple conversion tactics, with Roland employing a trial-and-error approach to finding the most effective method. In

---

[55] Dinshaw, "Pale Faces," p. 26, emphasis original. On the physical manifestations of faith and baptism, see Akbari, "Incorporation in the *Siege*" and *Idols in the East*; Best, "Monstrous Alterity"; Calkin, "Marking Religion on the Body" and "Romance Baptisms"; Kelly, "'Blue' Indians, Ethiopians"; and Rouse, "Expectation vs. Experience."

[56] Calkin, "The Man of Law's Tale and Crusade," p. 4.

*Roland and Vernagu*, Roland expounds Christian theology to Vernagu, answering all his questions and explaining the most paradoxical tenets. In the Otuel romances, Roland first offers lands, titles, wealth, and status to Otuel and then proffers marriage to Belesent. All of these solicitations fail, and the stubborn Saracen is converted only by an act of divine intervention in response to Charlemagne's prayers. Insofar as a miracle is the only effective solution, the Otuel-cycle romances paint a fairly bleak picture of the possibility of genuinely converting Saracens.

## BELESENT AND OTUEL: INTERFAITH DESIRE, CONVERSION, AND MARRIAGE

The treatment of Belesent and Otuel's relationship is one of the most intriguing and curious ways in which the three Otuel romances overlap and yet differ. *Otuel a Knight* minimizes the relationship and includes Belesent in the narrative only when necessary, while *Duke Roland* features a Belesent who is obviously attracted to Otuel even before he converts to Christianity. Romantic attraction between a Saracen and a Christian is common in Middle English romance and typically leads to the Saracen's conversion and subsequent marriage.[57] That a Saracen would willingly convert for love of a Christian thus became another part of the Western Christian crusading fantasy, particularly when the Saracen was in a ruling position and could peacefully convert his or her nation. It is possible even that the Otuel/Belesent romance served as a distant yet direct model for Shakespeare's Othello/Desdemona interracial pairing.[58] Still, some aspects of the relationship between Belesent and Otuel are unusual. Observing how the conversion-through-marriage theme typically works in Middle English romance helps us to understand how the Otuel story, and especially *Duke Roland*, departs from the tradition.

Calkin explains that the concept of using marriage to effect conversion was hardly a pure fantasy for medieval Western readers:

> The idea that Christian women might participate in peaceful efforts to expand the influence of Christianity was not as uncommon as one might think, and was a possibility raised in literature about crusade and crusading locales . . . . In romances, women might preach Christianity to their husbands and convert them within the context of inter-faith marriage.[59]

Although there was a sense that conversions achieved through monetary bribes or marriage contracts were less effective than were those achieved through proselytizing, the concept of being able to convert an entire nation of Muslims by means of a well-strategized marriage was attractive. Referencing the Man of Law's Tale and the romance *The King of Tars*, Dorothee Metlitzki explains how the fantasy makes its way into so many romances:

----

[57] Two notable exceptions to this pattern appear in *Floris and Blancheflour*, a romance in which a Christian and Saracen marry without either one converting, and in Malory's *Le Morte d'Arthur*, where Corsabroyne dies before he is able to marry King Baudas' daughter. See *Floris and Blancheflour*, ed. Kooper (*DIMEV* 3686; *NIMEV* *2288.8). For the episode in Malory's *Le Morte Arthure*, see Malory, *Complete Works*, ed. Vinaver, pp. 406–08. On Malory's treatment of Saracen conversion, see, e.g., Armstrong, "Postcolonial Palomides" and "The (Non-)Christian Knight in Malory"; Melick, "Saracens, Graves"; Cecire, "Barriers Unbroken"; and Goodrich, "Saracens and Islamic Alterity."

[58] Othello's name may be derived from Otuel's; see Guilfoyle, "Othello, Otuel," pp. 50–51.

[59] Calkin, "The Man of Law's Tale and Crusade," p. 3.

> In spite of the differences in treatment, the core of the Christian-Muslim marriage theme in the *King of Tars* and the story of Constance is the same as in . . . the Arabian story of Omar an-Nu'man: the importance of the interreligious and binational marriage. The child of such a marriage . . . will bring about the harmonious union of two warring peoples. The dream of oriental romance throughout the Middle Ages is the union of Christian and Saracen.[60]

Christians were drawn to the conversion-through-marriage method for two reasons: it was a less violent alternative to issuing "convert or die" ultimatums to non-Christian enemies, and it appealingly suggested that some non-Christians *wanted* to be converted and integrated into the Christian community.

While the depictions of conversion through marriage in such romances as *The King of Tars* and the Man of Law's Tale certainly question the validity of conversions rooted in a marriage agreement, many interfaith marriages depicted in Middle English romances result from genuine attraction and love. In these relationships, the Saracen character is typically enthusiastic about his or her conversion, even when it is made clear that conversion is a non-negotiable condition for the marriage. Love for the Christian paramour becomes the primary motivator for their change of faith. Examples of this trope are found in *Octavian* and *Firumbras*.[61]

In *Octavian*, a Saracen princess, Marsabelle, falls in love with a Christian knight, Florent. Florent does not tell Marsabelle that she must convert if she wants to marry him, but he strongly suggests it:

> "In alle this werlde es non so free          *noble*
> Forwhi that thow wolde cristenede be          *If only*
>          And sythen of herte be trewe."          *then*
> (lines 1511–13)

Marsabelle immediately understands Florent's meaning and offers to convert:

> "Sir, if that thou myghte me wyn,
> I wolde forsake all my kyn,
>          Als I them never knewe.          *As if*
> Sythen thou wolde wedde me to wyfe          *Since*
> I would lyve in Cristen lyfe;
>          My joye solde ever be newe."
> (lines 1514–19)

---

[60] Metlitzki, *The Matter of Araby*, p. 140; see *The King of Tars*, ed. Chandler (*DIMEV* 1789; *NIMEV* 1108). Another Middle English romance that invokes the fantasy of conversion and peace effected through intercultural marriage is *Bevis of Hampton*, ed. Herzman, Drake, and Salisbury, pp. 187–340 (*DIMEV* 3250; *NIMEV* 1993).

[61] For the two versions of *Octavian*, see *Octavian*, ed. Hudson, pp. 39–95 (northern version; *DIMEV* 3132; *NIMEV* 1918); and *Octovian Imperator*, ed. McSparran (southern version; *DIMEV* 2930; *NIMEV* 1774). For editions of *Firumbras*, see *Sir Ferumbras*, ed. Herrtage (Ashmole version); and *Firumbras*, ed. O'Sullivan, pp. 1–58 (Fillingham version). Quotations from *Octavian* are from Hudson's edition (Lincoln Thornton manuscript), and quotations from *Firumbras* are from Herrtage's edition.

That Marsabelle does not hesitate to abandon faith and family and willingly offers to become a Christian does indeed lead to a happy marriage.

A similar pattern occurs in *Firumbras* when the Saracen princess Floripas falls in love with Guy of Burgundy while he and the other *dussepers* are imprisoned by Floripas' father. Floripas, revealing that she is in love with Guy, describes seeing him in battle against her father:

> "Fro þat day in-to þys; myn herte haþ he yraft,
> Ne kepte y neuere more blys; were he to meward laft [honor me]
> Wolde he be my worldly make; & weddy me to wyue,
> For his loue wold y take; cristendom al so blyue."
> (lines 1420–23)

Floripas not only offers to convert in order to marry Guy; she purposefully acts against her father's interest. As Metlitzki explains, "the appeal of this type is instructive, not only as the popular image of a 'good' Muslim princess but also in conjunction with the theory that the aggressive and masterful nature of such heroines was foreign to the feminine ideal of the West."[62] After her conversion, Floripas has a few missteps with her new faith, at one point even suggesting that the *dussepers* pray to her Saracen idols and ask for aid (lines 2525–28). But once the French knights smash the idols and show them to be powerless, she fully embraces Christian belief. At the same time, her actions throughout the romance show that her greatest affection is for Guy, not God. When Guy is captured by her father's army, Floripas forces the other Christian knights to undertake a risky rescue mission to save him, showing no qualms about using nefarious methods to insure that she and her love have a future together.

This kind of love affair between female Saracen and male Christian is a fairly common trope in medieval romance.[63] The interfaith marriage in *Otuel and Roland* and *Duke Roland* switches the pattern, however, in that the relationship occurs between a Christian woman and a Saracen man. While Belesent never offers to become a Saracen in order to pursue a relationship with Otuel, the description of her first encounter with Otuel closely mirrors the moments in *Octavian* and *Firumbras* when a Saracen princess falls in love with a Christian knight.[64]

On the morning of the duel between Otuel and Roland, Charlemagne asks Belesent to arm Otuel. After performing this intimate task enthusiastically, Belesent warns Otuel to be careful of Roland's sword. Her fervent prayers during the duel indicate her attraction to Otuel, even as it means wishing for Roland's failure. After Otuel converts, Belesent continues to cross the line of Christian propriety for her lover. In *Duke Roland*, the narrator explains that the reason Otuel misses Roland, Oliver, and Ogier's adventurous foray is that he is with Belesent in her chamber. The poet does not state directly that the as-yet-unmarried couple are sexually engaged, but the implication is undeniable. The

---

[62] Metlitzki, *The Matter of Araby*, p. 169.

[63] The trope may draw upon a Western belief that Muslim women were exceptionally lascivious and bent on seducing Christian men.

[64] These comparisons refer only to *Otuel and Roland* and *Duke Roland*. The arming scene and Belesent's voiced acceptance of marriage to Otuel are not present in *Otuel a Knight*.

emphasis on Belesent's amorous behavior might be a twist on the typical Saracen princess's romantic tendencies, or it might simply be designed to titillate, but it might also be intended as an English criticism of French promiscuity. It is perhaps relevant that the romances that include these scenes, *Otuel and Roland* and *Duke Roland*, depict the French less favorably than does the earlier *Otuel a Knight*, which was copied before the start of the bitter French-English conflict in the Hundred Years' War.

While Belesent's attraction to Otuel is palpable, Otuel seems only peripherally aware of Belesent. He thanks her for his armor, but when Roland first offers Belesent in marriage in return for Otuel's conversion, the Saracen adamantly refuses. Otuel eventually will marry Belesent — and receive the titles and land that come with her — but nothing short of divine intervention is capable of converting the steadfast Saracen. At a time when Christians were concerned that interfaith marriage contracts could not effect true conversion, the inefficacy of Roland's attempt to convert Otuel might be a suggestion that would-be proselytizers should rely piously on earnest prayer and direct supplication to God.

## NOTE ON THE PRESENTATION OF TEXTS

### All texts

Medieval letter-forms are converted to modern forms in accordance with METS practice: *i/j*, *u/v*, *th* (for thorn), *g/gh/y* (for yogh). Abbreviations are silently expanded. Word breaks are modern. In Middle English texts, the second-person pronoun *the* is spelled *thee* to avoid confusion with *the*, and *of* is distinguished from *off*. Final *-e* pronounced as a syllable is given an accent mark (e.g., *cité*). Scribal corrections (inserted letters, canceled letters) are not noted in the Textual Notes. Rubbed-out, worn, or otherwise obscured letters are not noted except by dots wherever letters are unreadable. Emended letters are listed in the Textual Notes.

### Roland and Vernagu

*Roland and Vernagu* is composed wholly in twelve-line tail-rhyme stanzas, rhyming *aabccbddbeeb*. It lacks its opening lines in its sole copy, the Auchinleck manuscript. What survives are 880 lines (73¼ stanzas). Paraphs in alternating red and blue mark the opening of each stanza. They may be viewed in the digital facsimile. There are six large colored initials in the manuscript copy, which denote scribal or authorial points of transition. The transitions are indicated in this edition by a line of three asterisks between stanzas (to represent the large colored initials, which appear at lines 17, 269, 365, 425, 485, and 533). These initials may be viewed in the digital facsimile.[65]

---

[65] Burnley and Wiggins, eds., *The Auchinleck Manuscript*.

*Otuel a Knight*

*Otuel a Knight* survives in the Auchinleck manuscript as 1738 lines, with a gap of 8 lines after line 120. The lacuna is indicated in this edition by numbered dotted lines, and the poem is therefore numbered at 1746 lines. Its verse form is octosyllabic couplets, with the scribe regularly adding marginal paraphs in alternating red and blue. In this edition, a small indentation appears wherever the scribe has inserted a paraph. The paraphs may be viewed in the digital facsimile. There are four large colored initials in the manuscript. These authorial or scribal points of transition are indicated in this edition by double spacing and a line of three asterisks. Appearing at lines 1, 677, 1081, and 1627, the large colored initials may be viewed in the digital facsimile.

*Otuel and Roland*

*Otuel and Roland*, as it survives in its sole copy in the Fillingham manuscript, numbers 2790 lines. Seven detectably missing lines are counted in the total, and they are indicated in this edition by dotted lines (see lines 8, 1501, 1615–16, 1849, 2218, and 2266). The poem is composed predominately in twelve-line tail-rhyme stanzas, rhyming *aabccbddbeeb*, with a pronounced tendency to produce a four-rhyme variant, *aabaabccbddb*. Stanza length is, however, variable; there are many stanzas of six, nine, or fifteen lines, and one of eighteen lines (lines 1820–37). Six-line stanzas are sometimes deployed stylistically as a way to mark points of transition, with the poet explaining a shift in scene. There is also a single couplet (lines 1979–80), which introduces the portion of the poem that retells the *Song of Roland*. In total, in its surviving state, the poem has 241 stanzas of variable length, plus the internal couplet.

The Fillingham copy has twelve large red initials, eight of which clearly denote sections because they are prefaced by a six-line stanza of transition (sometimes copied in a larger, somewhat more formal script). When the large initial that opens the poem is added to these eight initials, a structure of nine sections becomes evident. This structure is indicated in this edition by the insertion of "fitt" numbers (1–9) before the prefatory stanzas. Large initials appear at lines 1, 232, 676, 871, 1165, 1567, 1700, 1981 (headed by the couplet), and 2593. The prefatory stanzas are represented in this edition by italic font.

The remaining three initials mark secondary transitions. They occur at lines 1039, 1859, and 2377, and each is marked by a line of three asterisks in this edition. Line 1039 marks the moment Otuel sees that Roland, Oliver, and Ogier have departed to seek adventures without him. Line 1859 marks the coming of a new messenger to Charlemagne's court. The large initial at line 2377 is noticeably odd because it begins a stanza's fourth line, but it is positioned with significance: a large *R* on *Rouland*, it marks Roland's death scene.

*Duke Roland and Sir Otuel of Spain*

*Duke Roland and Sir Otuel of Spain* is wholly composed in twelve-line tail-rhyme stanzas with three rhymes, *aabaabccbccb*. It has 1596 lines (133 stanzas). There are six large red initials in the manuscript copy, which denote sections. Each of these sections is indicated in this edition by the insertion of "fitt" numbers (1–6). Large colored initials occur at lines 1, 157, 337 (before this line, the scribe writes "A fitt"), 661, 1057, and 1345. Robert Thornton, the scribe, supplies this work with an incipit and explicit, which provide its title. Both are included in this edition.

## The Anglo-Norman *Otinel*

The Anglo-Norman *Otinel*, numbering 1907 lines, is composed in monorhyming *laisses* of variable length, the epic verse form used in many Old French *chansons de geste*, including the *Song of Roland*. In transcriptions of the Anglo-Norman text, modern apostrophes, cedilla on *c*, and accent on tonic *e* are editorially added. If missing words or letters appear in the Old French *Otinel*, they are supplied from that text and noted in the Textual Notes. *Laisse* breaks are indicated by rhyme change. Most *laisses* are headed with a large colored initial (red or blue, two to four lines in size). *Laisses* that lack a large initial are noted in the Textual Notes. The initials may be viewed in the digital facsimile.[66]

### THE CHARLEMAGNE ROMANCES

Verse Romances (14th–15th centuries)
    *Duke Roland and Sir Otuel of Spain*
    *Otuel a Knight*
    *Otuel and Roland*
    *Roland and Vernagu*
    *The Siege of Milan*
    *Firumbras* (Fillingham)
    *Firumbras* (Ashmole)
    *The Sultan of Babylon*[67]
    *The Tale of Ralph the Collier*[68]
    The Middle English *Song of Roland*

Later Prose Romances (15th–16th centuries)
    *Charles the Grete* (translated and printed by William Caxton, 1485)[69]
    *The Foure Sonnes of Aymon* (translated and printed by William Caxton, 1489)[70]
    John Bourchier, *The Boke of Duke Huon of Burdeux* (printed by Wynkyn de Worde, 1534)[71]

Later Verse Romance (16th century)
    *Capystranus* (printed by Wynkyn de Worde, 1515)[72]

---

[66] "Cologny, Fondation Martin Bodmer, Cod. Bodmer 168," e-codices.

[67] *The Sultan of Babylon*, ed. Lupack, pp. 1–103.

[68] *The Tale of Ralph the Collier*, ed. Lupack, pp. 151–204.

[69] See Smyser, "Charlemagne Legends," pp. 86–87, 262.

[70] See Smyser, "Charlemagne Legends," pp. 98, 266.

[71] See Smyser, "Charlemagne Legends," pp. 98–100, 266.

[72] See *Database of Middle English Romance*, ed. McDonald, Morgan, and Nall.

RECOMMENDED FURTHER READING

Akbari, Suzanne Conklin. *Idols in the East: European Representations of Islam and the Orient, 1100–1450*. Ithaca, NY: Cornell University Press, 2009.

Barbero, Alessandro. *Charlemagne: Father of a Continent*. Trans. Allan Cameron. Berkeley: University of California Press, 2004.

Calkin, Siobhan Bly. *Saracens and the Making of English Identity: The Auchinleck Manuscript*. New York: Routledge, 2005.

Cawsey, Kathy. "Disorienting Orientalism: Finding Saracens in Strange Places in Late Medieval English Manuscripts." *Exemplaria* 21.4 (2009), 380–97.

Cohen, Jeffrey Jerome. *Of Giants: Sex, Monsters, and the Middle Ages*. Minneapolis: University of Minnesota Press, 1999.

Cowen, Janet M. "The English Charlemagne Romances." In *Roland and Charlemagne in Europe: Essays on the Reception and Transformation of a Legend*. Ed. Karen Pratt. London: King's College Center for Late Antique and Medieval Studies, 1996. Pp. 149–68.

Friedman, John Block. *The Monstrous Races in Medieval Art and Thought*. Syracuse, NY: Syracuse University Press, 2000.

Haidu, Peter. *The Subject of Violence: The Song of Roland and the Birth of the State*. Bloomington: Indiana University Press, 1993.

Hardman, Phillipa, and Marianne Ailes. *The Legend of Charlemagne in Medieval England: The Matter of France in Middle English and Anglo-Norman Literature*. Cambridge: D. S. Brewer, 2017.

Heng, Geraldine. *The Invention of Race in the European Middle Ages*. Cambridge: Cambridge University Press, 2018.

Huot, Sylvia. *Outsiders: The Humanity and Inhumanity of Giants in Medieval French Prose Romance*. Notre Dame, IN: University of Notre Dame Press, 2016.

Jones, Catherine M. *An Introduction to the Chansons de Geste*. Gainesville: University Press of Florida, 2014.

Kibler, William W., and Leslie Zarker Morgan, eds. *Approaches to Teaching the Song of Roland*. New York: Modern Language Association of America, 2006.

Kinoshita, Sharon. *Medieval Boundaries: Rethinking Difference in Old French Literature*. Philadelphia: University of Pennsylvania Press, 2006.

Manion, Lee. *Narrating the Crusades: Loss and Recovery in Medieval and Early Modern English Literature*. Cambridge: Cambridge University Press, 2014.

Ramey, Lynn Tarte. *Black Legacies: Race and the European Middle Ages*. Gainesville: University Press of Florida, 2014.

Strickland, Debra Higgs. *Saracens, Demons, and Jews: Making Monsters in Medieval Art*. Princeton: Princeton University Press, 2003.

# ROLAND AND VERNAGU INTRODUCTION

The tail-rhyme romance *Roland and Vernagu* tells the story of Charlemagne's conquest of Spain and Roland's encounter with a giant Saracen foe, Vernagu. Based on an episode in the Middle English *Chronicle of Pseudo-Turpin*, the scenes involving the giant are significantly expanded.[1] The romance begins as Charlemagne sets out to conquer Spain after the apostle James commands him (through a vision) to recover his body from Galicia. Charlemagne fulfills this mission, but then a giant arrives to issue the court a challenge. Roland, Charlemagne's nephew, fights the giant in a duel, and Vernagu is defeated. This romance sets up the action for the three romances of Otuel, who is Vernagu's nephew.

The sole manuscript witness of *Roland and Vernagu* is the Auchinleck manuscript (Edinburgh, National Library of Scotland MS Advocates 19.2.1), fols. 263ra–67vb.[2] A major repository of early Middle English literature, Auchinleck contains numerous works, twenty-three of them unique.[3] It is most famous for its eighteen romances that extol adventures by English knights and *gestes* by French heroes, as in *Roland and Vernagu* and *Otuel a Knight*.[4] Auchinleck is believed to have been copied in the 1330s. The dialects of *Roland and Vernagu* and *Otuel a Knight* suggest that both were originally composed in the East Midlands.[5]

Approximately forty-four lines of *Roland and Vernagu* are missing at the beginning because of a lost folio. Examining the source allows one to guess at some of the lost content. The first surviving line is "For he it seiȝe wiþ siȝt" (fol. 263ra), followed by the poet's declaration that he will write about Charles. In the Middle English *Chronicle of Pseudo-Turpin*, the account of Charlemagne's dream of Saint James constitutes the prologue offered by the poet. In this section, "Bishop Turpin" explains his eyewitness qualification to chronicle Charlemagne's life: "I have tried to write promptly, sending to your fraternal hands the most important of his admirable deeds and laudable triumphs over the Spanish Saracens,

---

[1] See *The Chronicle of Pseudo-Turpin*, ed. Poole, pp. 40–48.

[2] For *Roland and Vernagu*, see *DIMEV* 1353; *NIMEV* 823.3; and Smyser, "Charlemagne Legends," pp. 90–91, 263–64. The poem has 880 lines in twelve-line tail-rhyme stanzas; it is imperfect at the beginning.

[3] For studies on the Auchinleck manuscript, see Calkin, *Saracens and the Making of English Identity*; Connolly and Edwards, "Evidence for the History"; and Fein, *New Perspectives*.

[4] See Wiggins, "Importance."

[5] Herrtage, *English Charlemagne Romances. Part VI*, pp. xii–xvi; and Wiggins, "Importance." Herrtage identifies "dialectical peculiarities," which led him to place the poet in the East Midlands (p. xiii).

which I saw with my own eyes."[6] Because both passages mention seeing with one's own eyes, and because *Roland and Vernagu* closely follows the *Chronicle* at this point, it seems likely that the missing lines introduced Turpin and explained how he had seen and recorded Charlemagne's deeds.

The colorful giant character in *Roland and Vernagu* endures as a source of interest for critics discussing the Otuel-cycle romances. Vernagu is one of many non-Christian giants in Middle English romance. Scholarly discussions of these giants provide good conceptual frameworks for reading about the encounter between Roland and Vernagu, helping to pinpoint how medieval English audiences tended to view giants, and also how Vernagu departs from the typical representation.

Though Vernagu is Otuel's uncle, they may differ in appearance. Vernagu is described as having dark skin, supernatural strength, and ugly features. While no extant version of Otuel's story depicts Otuel's appearance in detail, he is apparently pleasing and attractive.[7] Once the shock of his dramatic arrival at Charlemagne's court wears off, Charlemagne's men admire Otuel and want to see him converted. An exceptional fighter, Otuel has nearly defeated Roland when their battle is interrupted. He seems to be of normal height, and his skin color is never described.

Ugly as he may be, Vernagu's gigantic freakishness adds a complicating factor to *Roland and Vernagu*, because his intellect comes into play. A foe who is a giant is not unusual, but giants who behave intelligently and peacefully are. In *Of Giants: Sex, Monsters, and the Middle Ages*, Jeffrey Jerome Cohen articulates the bodily signification of giants:

> The giant appears at the moment when the boundaries of the body are being culturally demarcated. In the England of the Middle Ages, he signifies those dangerous excesses of the flesh that the process of masculine embodiment produces in order to forbid; he functions at the same time to celebrate the pleasures of the body, to indulge in wine and food and sex.[8]

Cohen encapsulates the nature of most giants in Middle English romance. In *The Sultan of Babylon*, a giant married couple, Astragote and Barrok, guard the Sultan's city of Mountrible, and they parent two giant sons. Although both Astragote and Barrok are scary and possess superhuman strength, they imitate human behavior by marrying and raising children as humans would. They do not converse with their French foes, but Astragote does pray to Mahounde for help when he is overcome, which indicates that he has the power of

---

[6] *The Chronicle of Pseudo-Turpin*, ed. Poole, p. 3. Turpin is purportedly writing down his account and delivering it to Luitprand, a fictional dean of the cathedral at Aachen (p. xix).

[7] But see Boscolo, "Two Otinel Frescoes," pp. 202 and 204 (fig. 2), who shows a northern Italian fresco that depicts Otinel as a black giant. See also the Introduction to the Anglo-Norman *Otinel*, p. 262, in this volume.

[8] Cohen, *Of Giants*, p. xiii. On monsters in medieval thought, see also Friedman, *Monstrous Races*. On the topic of English anxieties about cultural diversity, their nation's diverse history, and their ties to the East, see Best, "Monstrous Alterity"; Calkin "Anxieties of Encounter" and "Violence, Saracens"; Cawsey, "Disorienting Orientalism"; Cohen, "Green Children"; Houlik-Ritchey, "Rewriting Difference"; Wilcox, "Romancing the East"; and Williamsen, *Quest for Collective Identity*.

speech and understands the Saracen faith.[9] After the couple is defeated, King Charles baptizes their offspring, naming them after Roland and Oliver, and adds them to his entourage. A similar acceptance of a giant into human company occurs in *Sir Bevis of Hampton* (another Auchinleck romance), where the giant Ascopart serves as Bevis' page for a time. The giant in *Octavian* (also an Auchinleck romance) loves a Saracen princess, Marsabelle, and in pursuing her hand in marriage, he shows himself to be both a competent fighter and versed in the art of courtly love.[10]

While these are giants who can function in civilized society alongside humans (often assisting them), the giant in the alliterative *Morte Arthure* represents another type in romance: the giant who is subhuman, bloodthirsty, and rapacious.[11] The alliterative *Morte* giant is nonhuman, eats infants, and viciously rapes a duchess. He has animal features and shows no evidence of being able to speak. Regarding the famous confrontation between the giant of Mount St. Michel and Arthur, Rebecca S. Beal writes that it is "a battle between medieval versions of civilization and barbarism, for the poem has clothed Arthur with armor produced by his civilization and associated that armor with the feast that shows the king's preeminence."[12] Beal goes on to note that, while Arthur's armor is produced by a civilized society, and his feasts are likewise products of a regulated community, the giant is clothed in only a kirtle and feasts on human flesh, including babies. The type of giant found in the alliterative *Morte* serves a purpose quite different from that of the more humanlike giants found in the other romances. Yet there are similarities between Vernagu and the giant of Mount St. Michel. Both emerge as defenders of non-Christian empires. Both challenge kings who have to defeat them in order to continue the expansion of their realms. And, in both cases, defeating the giant becomes more than a coming-of-age test for a young knight or a demonstration of masculinity. The giant operates as a symbol: any failure to vanquish him will result in a loss of vital land and prestige.

While the narrative functions of Vernagu and the giant of Mount St. Michel are thus similar, there are significant differences in their character and behavior. Unlike the grotesque, nonverbal giant faced by Arthur, Vernagu is able to speak, reason, and debate. As Dorothee Metlitzki explains, Vernagu differs "from the Frankish knights in color and size, but not in kind."[13] In terms of behavior, Vernagu is rather like his partially socialized counterparts in *Octavian* or *Bevis of Hampton* because he understands the strictures of courtly behavior and can conform to social codes. However, in being a reasoning creature who can participate in society, Vernagu is distinguishable from these romance giants. In *Octavian*, the giant is driven by love (more accurately lust) for Marsabelle. In *Bevis*, the giant

---

[9] "Mahounde" is the main god worshipped by Saracens in romance. "Mahounde" is meant to be Muhammad — another example of the inaccurate representation of Muslims in Western medieval literature, as Muslims believe Muhammad is a prophet, not a god. See the section "Saracens and the Conversion Theme" in the General Introduction, pp. 15–19, especially pp. 16–17.

[10] For *The Sultan of Babylon*, see ed. Lupack, pp. 1–103; for *Octavian*, see ed. Hudson, pp. 39–95.

[11] For an edition of the alliterative *Morte Arthure* (*DIMEV* 3745; *NIMEV* 2322), see ed. Benson, pp. 129–284. The giant of Mount St. Michel possesses qualities that reflect features of romance Saracens, for example, a violent temper, predatory lust, and non-white skin; see Sikorska, "Malevolent Visitors," pp. 77–78.

[12] Beal, "Arthur as the Bearer of Civilization," p. 98.

[13] Metlitzki, *The Matter of Araby*, p. 193.

orchestrates a tragic betrayal of Bevis when he is let go as Bevis' page. Although capable of reason and language, these giants still display the bodily excesses and amorality that mark their grotesque type.

Vernagu, on the other hand, exhibits none of those excessive tendencies. After he arrives at Charlemagne's temporary court in Pamplona, he issues an official challenge in response to Charlemagne's conquest of Spain and faces Charlemagne's knights in fair duels. Even though he could kill the French knights, Vernagu chooses to spare their lives: he carries each one off the field and sets him down unharmed. Beyond his reluctance to commit violence, Vernagu exceeds his fellow giants in intellect. In *Black Legacies: Race and the European Middle Ages*, Lynne Tarte Ramey discusses the criterion of reason in the evaluation of a creature's humanity. She notes that when medieval Westerners read accounts of foreign lands and people in texts about travel to the East, they were faced with the question of what makes a being human. In most cases, if a group (even a fictional group like pygmies) could speak and reason, they were considered sufficiently human for the purpose of salvation.[14] While many romance giants do speak and act rationally, it is rare for a giant to be shown to have an in-depth, intellectually taxing conversation with a human. *Roland and Vernagu* contains a decidedly odd scene in which Roland and Vernagu debate Christian theology in the middle of the night. After Roland and Vernagu have been dueling for hours, the sunlight fades and Vernagu requests time to rest. Too large to fit inside a building, he falls asleep in the field, whereupon Roland places a stone beneath Vernagu's head to serve as a pillow. Upon waking, Vernagu, moved by Roland's gesture, asks the knight to explain his Christian faith. As Roland expounds Christianity's tenets, Vernagu voices astute objections, which Roland quickly answers with familiar, pat explanations.[15]

Despite Vernagu's curiosity about Christianity and capacity for rational thought, which should qualify him for salvation, his story ends much the same way that the other giants' stories end — with a beheading. After their conversation, Roland and Vernagu resume the fight, each agreeing that the outcome will prove which faith is true. Mid-duel, an angel appears to Roland and informs him that Vernagu can never be converted; the giant must be killed. After this revelation, the scene takes a familiar turn: Roland strikes down Vernagu, removes the giant's helmet, cuts off his head, and brings it to Charlemagne as a trophy. Vernagu's relatively nonviolent disposition and unusual intellect may separate him from other giants who populate the pages of Middle English romance, but his death resembles that faced by the others. Phillipa Hardman explains that part of the function of dark-skinned, frightening Saracens like Vernagu is to provide contrast for the fair-skinned Saracens who are desirable converts:

> one can see something of the same paired effect in the treatment of Saracen champions, where those worthy of conversion are fierce but fair, while the representatives of infidel evil are monstrous and black. Thus, Fierabras' size provides a physical referent for his status as alien, hostile outsider, linking him while in his unconverted state with monstrous Saracen giants such as the Giant of Mautrible and Vernagu — but without their ugliness and

---

[14] Ramey, *Black Legacies*, p. 95.

[15] On Roland and Vernagu's theological discussion, see Vincent, who argues that the conversation mirrors a scholastic debate more than religious instruction ("Reading a Christian-Saracen Debate," pp. 95–97).

grotesque features, so that upon his conversion it is not difficult for Fierabras to be re-presented as an ideal specimen of knighthood.[16]

Vernagu may be uncommon for a giant, but, in the end, he is made to fulfill the typical function of a giant in a Western European medieval narrative — that is, to represent the Other — and, in being defeated, to reinforce the supremacy of those belonging to dominant categories. This function is all the more important because of *Roland and Vernagu*'s connection to the Otuel storyline, where Otuel is presented as his uncle's opposite. Otuel's conversion is ardently sought and prayed for. In contrast, the angel's words in *Roland and Vernagu* confirm what Roland must have known from the first moment he laid eyes on a giant:

> "For he nas never gode
>     Bi lond no bi se.
> Thei alle prechours alive                          *Even if all preachers alive*
> To Cristen wald him schrive,                       *administer penance to him as a Christian*
>     Gode nold he never be."                         *He would never be good*
> (lines 810–14)

Having received this angelic word, Roland quickly refocuses his attention and kills the monstrous pagan.

MANUSCRIPT:
Edinburgh, National Library of Scotland MS Advocates 19.2.1 (Auchinleck MS), fols. 263ra–67vb.

FACSIMILES:
Pearsall, Derek, and I. C. Cunningham, eds. *The Auchinleck Manuscript: National Library of Scotland Advocates' MS. 19.2.1*. London: Scolar Press, 1979.
Burnley, David, and Alison Wiggins, eds. *The Auchinleck Manuscript*. National Library of Scotland, 2003. Online at https://auchinleck.nls.uk.

PREVIOUS EDITIONS (IN CHRONOLOGICAL ORDER):
*Rouland and Vernagu*. In *The English Charlemagne Romances. Part VI*. Ed. Sidney J. H. Herrtage. EETS e.s. 39. London: Oxford University Press, 1882. Rpt. 1969. Pp. 37–61.
*Roland and Vernagu*. In *The Auchinleck Manuscript*. Ed. David Burnley and Alison Wiggins. National Library of Scotland, 2003. Online at https://auchinleck.nls.uk.

---

[16] Hardman, "Dear Enemies," p. 68.

..........................................

| | | |
|---|---|---|
| fol. 263ra | For he it seighe with sight. | *saw* |
| | Now bigin ichil of him, | *I will* |
| | Of Charls that was stout and grim, | *Charles (Charlemagne)* |
| | And tel you al that right. | *properly* |

5    An hundred winter it was and thre
       Sethen God dyed opon the tre,        *Since*
           That Charls the king
       Hadde al Fraunce in his hond —     *under his control*
       Danmark and Inglond,

10        Withouten ani lesing,        *lying*
       Lorein and Lombardye,      *Lorraine; Lombardy*
       Gascoun, Bayoun, and Pikardye  *Gascony, Bayonne; Picardy*
           Was til his bidding.        *Were at*
       And emperour he was of Rome,

15        And lord of al Cristendome.
           Than was he an heighe lording.

      *       *      *

| | | |
|---|---|---|
| | In that time was an emperour | |
| | In Costentin, of gret honour, | *Constantinople* |
| | Constansious he hight. | *Constantius; was called* |
| 20 | God he loved and alle His, | |
| | And hated hem that dede amis | *them; sinned* |
| | With al his might. | |
| | In Speyn tho, ther was a king — | *then* |
| | A stern man, withouten lesing — | |
| 25 | That werred ogain the right. | *against* |
| | Ebrahim was his name, | |
| | Wide sprong his riche fame; | |
| | He was a douhti knight. | *valiant* |

| | | |
|---|---|---|
| | Alle that leved in Godes lawe, | *believed* |
| 30 | He lete hem bothe hong and drawe, | *had them* |
| | Tho that he might oftake. | *Those; capture* |

And the patriark of Jerusalem
Out of lond he dede him flem,        *put him [the patriarch] in exile*
    Al for Godes sake.
35   The patriarke was ful wiis,
And to th'emperour he went, ywis,        *indeed*
    His mone for to make:        *complaint*
Hou the King Ebrahim
Out of lond exiled him,
40     With michel wer and wrake.        *much war and destruction*

King Costance th'emperour
Made swithe gret dolour        *such; lamenting*
    For this tidinges.
Jhesu Crist bisought he,
fol. 263rb  Almighti God in Trinité,
46     King of al kinges,
He sende him grace him to slo        *[That] He would; slay*
That had ywrought so michel wo        *[He] who had caused*
    And slawe Godes ginges.        *slain; people*
50   And sone so he had the bon ybede,        *As soon as; prayed the prayer*
An angel light doun in that stede        *alit; place*
    And this bode him bringes.        *message*

The angel seyd to th'emperour,
"Wele thee greteth thi Saveour,        *Your Savior greets you favorably*
55     Jhesu ful of might,
And bit thee sende with michel anour        *bids; honor*
After Charls the conquerour;        *For*
    He is a douhti knight.
He schal thee help in batayl
60   And sle the Sarrazin, withouten fail,
    That doth ogain the right."        *Who acts against*
Th'emperour was glad and blithe        *joyful*
And thonked God fele sithe;        *many times*
    His hert nas never so light.        *had never been*

65   Four the best, he sent of hem,        *them*
That on hight David of Jerusalem,        *one was called*
    And Samuel also,
Jon of Naples was another,
Ysac hight the ferth brother.
70     Thider he gan go,        *To that place they*
He went to the palais of Rome        *They; palace*
And bifor Sir Charls come
    And told him of her wo.        *their*
Thai toke him the letter and kist his hand,        *brought; kissed*

| | | |
|---|---|---|
| 75 | Swiche was the lawe of the land | *Such* |
| | And schal ben evermo. | *forever more* |
| | | |
| | Charls wepe for that dede | *wept at that news* |
| | When he herd the letter rede, | |
| | And hete an heigheing: | *ordered at once* |
| 80 | Al that might armes bere, | |
| | Kniif or scheld, swerd or spere, | *Knife; shield* |
| | Men schuld bifor him bring. | |
| | Thai busked hem and made hem yare | *prepared themselves; ready* |
| | To Costentin for to fare, | *Constantinople; go* |
| 85 | Withouten ani lesing. | |
| | Th'emperour was glad, ywis, | |
| | And underfenge with miche blis | *received* |
| | Sir Charls the king. | |

| | | |
|---|---|---|
| fol. 263va | Riche juels withouten lesing, | *jewels* |
| 90 | Sir Costance the king | |
| | Bifor Sir Charls he brought. | |
| | Savage bestes for the nones, | *Wild animals for the occasion* |
| | Gold and silver and riche stones, | |
| | Ac therof nold he nought. | *But he [Charles] would have none of them* |
| 95 | He bisought him of more honour | *He asked of him [Constantine] a greater honor* |
| | Of Jhesu Our Saveour | *Regarding* |
| | That al this warld hath wrought: | *Who* |
| | That He on suffred passioun — | *The things by which he had suffered the Passion* |
| | Of the croice and of the croun, | *cross; crown* |
| 100 | Therof he him bisought. | *He asked him for those* |

| | | |
|---|---|---|
| | Th'emperour his wil dede, | *did* |
| | And ladde him to the holy stede | *place* |
| | There the relikes ware. | *Where* |
| | Ther com swiche a swete odour | |
| 105 | That never yete so swete savour | *scent* |
| | No feld thai never are. | *Never had they sensed before* |
| | Of the smal that was so swote, | *smell; sweet* |
| | Thre hundred sike hadde her bote | *sick people were healed* |
| | And cast were out of care. | |
| 110 | Than brought thai forth the holy croun | |
| | And the arme of Seyn Simoun | |
| | Biforn hem alle thare. | |

| | | |
|---|---|---|
| | And a parti of the holy crosse | *piece* |
| | That in a cristal was don in clos, | *enclosed* |
| 115 | And Godes clotheing, | |
| | Our Levedi smok that hye had on, | *Lady's (Virgin Mary's) smock; she* |
| | And the yerd of Araon, | *staff* |

    Forth thai gun bring.          *brought*
    And a spere long and smert        *sharp*
120   That Longys put to Godes hert     *Longinus*
      He yaf Charls the king,      *gave to*
    And a nail, long and gret,
    That was ydrive thurth Godes fet,    *driven*
      Withouten ani lesing.       *lying*

125   When Charls had reseived that thing,
    He bisought Jhesu, heven King,
      To sende him might and space
    For to wite the sothe there,     *learn; truth*
    Yif the relikes verray were,     *authentic*
130     Er he thennes pase.   *Before he left from there*
    Than decended a lightnesse     *ray of light*
    Dounrightes fram the heven blis    *Downward*
fol. 263vb  In that ich place,       *same*
    That thai wenden alle, ywis,   *So that; believed*
135   Thai hadde ben in paradys,
      So ful it was of grace.

    Thai tok leve at th'emperour    *departed from*
    And thonked him of gret honour,
      And to Aise in Gascoyn went,  *Auch; Gascony (see note)*
140   Ther he duelled, siker aplight.    *very truly*
    So he biheld opon a night      *Until*
      Up to the firmament;     *the heavens*
    A way of sterres he seighe, ywis,  *A path of stars*
    Out of Spaine into Galis,     *Galicia*
145     As red as brond that brent.   *flame; burned*
    He bisought God in Trinité
    To sende him grace wite wat it be  *to know what it meant*
      With wel gode entent.

    And in the thought that he was in,
150   Ther com a voice and spac to him    *spoke*
      With a milde steven,     *gentle tone*
    "James the apostel, bi Crist,     *[I am]*
    Jones brother th'Ewangelist,  *John the Evangelist's brother*
      Godes deciple of heven,
155   That God bad prechy on the se,   *Whom; preach*
    Forthi Herodes lete me sle,  *Because; ordered me slain*
      Therof Y thee neven.    *call upon you*
    Mi body lith in Galis,
    Biyond Speyne, forsothe ywis,
160     Jurnays mo than seven.  *More than a seven-day journey*

Forthi me wondreth, withouten fail,                    *Because of this I am puzzled*
That thou comest nought to do batayl
    That lond for to winne,
And yif thou winnes that lond, ywis,
165   Y schal thee bring into that blis
    Ther ich woni inne.                          *That I dwell in*
Al that me seketh, more and lesse,                     *of both high and low rank*
Schal have forgevenes
    Of her dedeli sinne.                         *their*
170   Now wende and do as Y thee sede,             *go; told you*
And in batayl thou schalt spede                        *have success*
    When thou it wil biginne.

The way of sterres bitokneth, ywis,                    *betokens*
That of Spaine and of Galis                            *Galicia*
175     Thou schalt be conquerer.
Lorain and Lombardye,
fol. 264ra  Gascoyne, Bayoun, and Pikardye
    Schal be in thi pouwer."
Thus com the apostel Jamis                             *came*
180   Thries to Charls and seyd this,              *Three times*
    That was so stoute and fer.                  *valiant; fierce*
Now wendeth Charls with his ost                        *army*
Into Speyne, with michel bost,                         *pride*
    As ye may forward here.                      *further*

185   The first cité was Pampiloun,               *Pamplona*
That was a swithe noble toun,
    That Charls gan asayl.                       *began to attack*
And sex monethes he it bilay, aplight,                 *besieged, truly*
That no thing winne he it no might             *But he could win nothing of it*
190    For alle his batayle.                        *Despite*
For the walles so strong were
He no might have non entré there,                      *any entry*
    Withouten ani fayl.
Ther were mani strong gines,                           *engines of war*
195   And fele thousand of Sarazines,              *many*
    Swithe heyghe of parail.                     *Of such high nobility*

Than praid Charls to God of heven.                     *prayed*
"Lord," he seyd, "Here mi steven!                      *prayer*
    As Tow art ful of might,                     *As Thou*
200   Sende me grace this cité to winne
And sle the Sarrazins herinne,
    That don ogain the right."                   *act against*
Tho felle the walles of the cité;
Charls entred with his meyné                           *company*

205        Als a douhti knight.
And thurth the miracle that was there,
Ten thousand Sarrazins cristned were              *baptized*
        In that ich night.                    *same*

And tho that nold nought cristned be,        *those; would not*
210        He lete hem hong opon a tre             *ordered*
        Er he thennes pase.
Thus Charls thurth Spayn gan gon,          *went*
And wan the cités, everichon,
        Al thurth Godes grace.
215        Where he com in ani erd,                *region*
Ich man was of him aferd                  *Each*
        That loked on his face.             *Who*
The names of everi cité
That he wan, Y schal tel ye
220         Er ich hennes pase.             *go further*

fol. 264rb  Visim, Lameche, and Sumy,
Colomuber, Luche, and Urry,         *Coimbra; Lucena*
        Brakare and Vimaraile,
Conpostel, a cité grete,             *Compostela*
225        Aurilian and Tullet,              *Toledo*
        That strong is to asayl,
Golddelfagar and Salamencha,    *Font de la Figuera; Salamanca*
Uline, Canayls, Madris alswa,         *Madrid also*
        Calatorie and Lestoyl,       *Calahorra; Estella*
230        Medinacel, an heighe cité,
Segovus the grete and Salamenche,       *Segovia*
        Gramie and Sturgel,

Godian and Emerite,
Bourg in Spaine that nis nought lite,      *Burgos; little*
235        A swithe noble toun,
Nasers and Mathed,               *Nazaré*
Carion and Urpaled,        *Carrión de los Condes*
        And Oche of gret renoun,           *Oca*
Burbagalle, a castel also,
240        Costant, Petros, and other mo,
        Bayet and Pampiloun,
Ventos in the grene vale,           *Ventosa*
Caparre, Eustorge, and Entale,     *Cáparra, Astorga*
        Gascoine and Bayoun,

245        Toutor, a strong castel,    *Villena [formerly Ad Turres]*
Landulif and Portingal,          *Portugal*
        Burnam and Saragouns,      *Bornos; Zaragoza*

|  | | |
|---|---|---|
| | Granad and Satyne, | *Granada* |
| | Costaunce and Deine, | *Denia* |
| 250 | Teragon and Valouns, | *Terragona; Valencia* |
| | Leride, Acoun, and Sivile, | *Lerida, Guadix [formerly Acci]; Seville* |
| | Charls wan in a while, | |
| | Agabie and Urens, | *Ureuña* |
| | Quara, Melide, Gibalderie, | *A Guarda, Melide, Gibralter* |
| 255 | Barbaster, Vice, and Almarie, | *Barbastro, San Vicente; Almería* |
| | Agabie and Sisens. | |

|  | | |
|---|---|---|
| | Acoun, that Y spak of ere, | *mentioned before* |
| | Seyn James deciple lith there | *A disciple of Saint James is buried there* |
| | That hat Seyn Torquas. | *Who is called Saint Torquatus* |
| 260 | A swithe fair oliif tre | |
| | Biside his toumbe men may se, | |
| | That springeth thurth Godes grace. | |
| | Opon his fest in mid May, | *feast* |
| | Theron is frout of gret noblay, | *fruit; goodness* |
| fol. 264va | Bothe more and lasse; | |
| 266 | And who that seketh hem, verrament, | *those who seek [the olives], truly* |
| | At the Day of Juggement | |
| | Schal se Godes face. | |

\*        \*        \*

|  | | |
|---|---|---|
| | Alle the londes that were in Spayne, | |
| 270 | With dint of swerd, wan Charlmain. | *conquered* |
| | Portingale and Lavers, | |
| | Landuluf and Chastel, | *Castile* |
| | Bigairs, Bastles, and londes fele, | *Bagá* |
| | Moys and Navers — | *Navarre* |
| 275 | Alle the londes he wan yern, | *eagerly* |
| | Til he com to Lucern. | |
| | So stout he was and fers, | *strong* |
| | And tuelmoneth he it bilay, aplight, | *twelve months; besieged* |
| | And no thing win he it might, | |
| 280 | For al his dussepers. | *Despite; twelve peers* |

|  | | |
|---|---|---|
| | Tho preyd Charls to God a bone | |
| | That he him sent grace sone | |
| | The cité forto winne; | |
| | Tho fel the walles adounrightes, | *When* |
| 285 | King Charls entred with his knightes | |
| | Thurth that ich ginne. | *By means of; that very device (see note)* |
| | Charls acurssed that cité, | |
| | And Ventos and Caparre and Deneye, | |
| | For her dedeli sinne. | *their* |

| | | |
|---|---|---|
| 290 | Deserd thai were after than, | *Deserted; after that* |
| | That never sethen no Cristen man | *afterwards* |
| | No durst com therinne. | *Ever dared* |
| | | |
| | For Charls cursSed tho Lucern, | *then* |
| | Also tite the toun Ganbern, | *quickly* |
| 295 | And schal don ever mo, | *continued* |
| | And of the smoc of that toun, | *because of the smoke* |
| | Mani taketh therof pusesoun | *poison* |
| | And dyeth in michel wo. | |
| | And ther the other thre cités stode, | *where* |
| 300 | Beth waters red of helle flode | *Are waters as red as hell's river* |
| | And fisches therin al blo. | *discolored* |
| | And who that wil nought leve me, | *whoever does not believe* |
| | In Spaine men may the sothe yse, | *One may see the truth* |
| | Who that wil thider go. | *Whoever* |
| | | |
| 305 | And while Charls was in that stede, | |
| | A fair miracle God for him dede | |
| | Er he gan thennes wende: | *Before he left that place* |
| | Braunches of vines Charls sett | *Grape vine branches; set out* |
| fol. 264vb | In Marche moneth, withouten lett, | *month of March; delay* |
| 310 | As was the right kende; | *proper custom* |
| | And amorwe grapes thai bere, | *in the morning they bore grapes* |
| | Red and ripe to kerve there; | *harvest* |
| | For paners thai gun sende. | *baskets* |
| | And for "paners!" thai crid tho, | *because* |
| 315 | Yete men clepeth the cité so | *Still; call* |
| | And schal to the warldes ende. | *end of the world* |
| | | |
| | Clodonius the first Cristen king, | *Clovis* |
| | And Clotayrs, withouten lesing, | *Clotaire* |
| | King Dagabers, and Pipin | *Dagobert; Pepin* |
| 320 | Won mani tounes in Spaine, | |
| | Ac the gode Charlmain | *But* |
| | Wan it al with gin. | *great skill* |
| | Alle the maumetes in Spaine were, | *idols* |
| | That were the Sarrazins leve and dere, | *dear and beloved to the Saracens* |
| 325 | King Charls and Turpin | *(see note)* |
| | Thai destroyd thurth Godes might — | *through* |
| | Sum thurth miracle and sum thurth fight, | |
| | So seyt the Latin. | *says* |
| | | |
| | And an image of gret pousté | *idol; power* |
| 330 | Stode on a roche bi the se | *rock by the sea* |
| | In the gilden lond. | *glorious* |
| | His name was Salanicodus, | |

|   |   |   |
|---|---|---|
|   | As a man yschapen he wes, | *shaped* |
|   | And held a glaive an hond. | *lance in his hand* |
| 335 | Mahoun maked him with gin | *trickery* |
|   | And dede mani fendes therin, | *put many demons inside* |
|   | As ich understond, | *I* |
|   | For to susten the ymage | *support; idol* |
|   | And sett him on heighe stage — |   |
| 340 | For no man nold he wond. | *he held back* |

|   |   |   |
|---|---|---|
|   | The face of him was turned southeright. | *southward* |
|   | In her lay the Sarrazins founde, aplight, | *their teachings; indeed* |
|   | Of Jubiter and Mahoun, | *According to* |
|   | That when yborn were the king | *the king was born* |
| 345 | That schuld Spaine to Cristen bring, | *christianize Spain* |
|   | The ymage schuld falle adoun. |   |
|   | Charls dede that ymage falle | *caused* |
|   | And wan in Spaine the cités alle, |   |
|   | Bothe tour and toun; | *castle* |
| 350 | And with the tresour that he wan there, | *treasure; won* |
|   | Mani a chirche he lete arere | *built* |
|   | That was of gret renoun. |   |

|   |   |   |
|---|---|---|
| fol. 265ra | The first chirche, forsoth ywis, |   |
|   | Was Seyn James in Galis |   |
| 355 | That he lete arere, |   |
|   | With an hundred chanouns and her priour, | *canons; their* |
|   | Of Seynt Ysador the confessour | *Isidore [of Seville]* |
|   | For to servi there. | *serve* |
|   | And in Aise a chapel |   |
| 360 | Of lim and ston, ywrought ful wel, | *limestone, made* |
|   | Of werk riche and dere; | *expensive* |
|   | And Seyn James at Burdewes, | *Bordeaux* |
|   | And on at Tolous, another at Anevaus, | *one; Toulouse* |
|   | And mo as ye may here. | *more* |

*          *          *

|   |   |   |
|---|---|---|
| 365 | Charls duelled, siker aplight, |   |
|   | Thre mones and fourten night | *months* |
|   | In Bayoun with his ost. |   |
|   | Ther fel a miracle of a knight | *befell; to* |
|   | Wiche that was to deth ydight, | *Who was prepared to die* |
| 370 | Thurth the Holy Gost. |   |
|   | Sir Romain, forsothe, he hight; | *was named* |
|   | Er he dyd he hadde his right, | *Before; died; last rites* |
|   | Withouten ani bost. |   |
|   | On of his frendes he cleped him to, | *One; called to him* |

| | | |
|---|---|---|
| 375 | "Y schal dye, it is so, | |
| | Ful wele thou it wost. | *you know it* |
| | | |
| | Mine clothes that ichave, | *I have* |
| | Therwith that Y be brought in grave, | *With them [may] I be* |
| | With mete and drink and light; | |
| 380 | And sel min hors on heigheing, | *sell; at once* |
| | Pover clerkes sauters to sing; | *[So that] poor clerks may sing psalms* |
| | Therto that it be dight." | *[See] that it be arranged* |
| | And when he hadde yseyd thus stille, | *softly* |
| | Al so it was Godes wille, | *Just as* |
| 385 | Than died the knight. | |
| | The hors was seld, withouten duelinges, | *sold; delay* |
| | For to hundred schillinges, | *two* |
| | And put it up, aplight. | *[the friend] kept it* |
| | | |
| | And at the nende of thritti night, | *end of thirty nights* |
| 390 | To his seketour com the ded knight, | *executor* |
| | And seyd in this maner: | |
| | "Mi soule is in heven blis | |
| | For the love of min almis | *charitable gifts* |
| | That Y sett here; | *established* |
| 395 | And for thou hast athold min, | *because; withheld [my gifts]* |
| | Thritti days ich ave ben in pin | *been in pains* |
| fol. 265rb | That wel strong were. | *terribly strong* |
| | Paradis is graunted me, | |
| | And in that pain, thou schalt be | |
| 400 | That ich was in ere." | *before* |
| | | |
| | The ded thus in his way went. | *dead one* |
| | And he awaked, verrament, | *[the executor]* |
| | And wonder hadde, aplight. | |
| | And amorwe his sweven he told | *dream vision* |
| 405 | To erls and to barouns bold, | |
| | To squiers and to knight. | |
| | And amonges hem alle | |
| | As thai stoden in the halle, | |
| | Ther com a windes flight | *gust of wind* |
| 410 | And fele fendes that were swift, | *many demons* |
| | And beren him up into the lift, | *[they] bore him up into the sky* |
| | And held him there four night. | |
| | | |
| | Serjaunce the bodi sought, | *Soldiers* |
| | Ac thai no might it finde nought, | *But* |
| 415 | Four dayes, no more. | |
| | Fro Bayoun he went with his ost, | *From; they; their* |
| | And thurth Navern with miche bost; | *Navarre* |

The bodi than founde thore *[They] found there*
Ther the fendes had let him felle, *Where; fall*
420 And bere his soule into helle, *bore his soul to hell*
To hard paines sore. *harsh, sorrowful pains*
So schal everi sekatour *Thus shall every executor*
The dedes gode abigge wel sour *Bitterly pay for the dead man's wealth*
That hye binimeth the pore. *That he steals from the poor*

                *        *        *

425 Now late we be of this thing, *set aside*
And speke of Charles the king
That michel was of might.
Of his lengthe and his brede, *breadth*
As the Latin ous sede, *tells us*
430 Ichil you rede aright.
Tuenti fete he was o lengthe, *of height*
And also of gret strengthe,
And of a stern sight.
Blac of here and rede of face, *imposing appearance*
435 Whare he com in ani place *hair; red*
He was a douhti knight. *Wherever*

Four times in the yere *per year*
On his heued he bere *head; bore*
The holy croun of thorn:
440 At Ester, at Wissontide, *Easter; Whitsuntide*
fol. 265va And at Seyn James Day with pride, *[25 July]*
And in Yole as God was born; *Christmas*
And atte the mete in the halle, *feast*
Among his knightes alle
445 A drawe swerd him biforn. *drawn sword*
This was the maner ay *always*
And schal be til Domesday
Of emperour ycorn. *divinely chosen*

And whare he slepe anight,
450 Wel wise he was and wight *powerful*
And douted of tresoun; *was anxious about*
An hundred knightes him kept *[about him]*
That non of hem no slept,
That were of gret renoun.
455 And everi dughti knight *brave*
Held a torche light *lighted torch*
And a naked fauchoun. *drawn falchion*
Thus King Charls lay

|  | | |
|---|---|---|
| | With his ost, mani a dai | |
| 460 |     In the cité of Pampiloun. | |
| | | |
| | And on a day com tiding | *came news* |
| | Unto Charls the king | |
| |     Al of a douhti knight | *Entirely about* |
| | Was comen to Nasers. | *Nazaré* |
| 465 | Stout he was and fers, | *Large; ferocious* |
| |     Vernagu he hight. | *was called* |
| | Of Babiloun the soudan | *From; sultan* |
| | Thider him sende gan | |
| |     With King Charls to fight. | |
| 470 | So hard he was to fond | *challenge* |
| | That no dint of brond | *blow of a sword* |
| |     No greved him, aplight. | *injured* |
| | | |
| | He hadde tuenti men strengthe, | *twenty men's strength* |
| | And fourti fet of lengthe | *forty feet tall* |
| 475 |     Thilke panim hede, | *This pagan had* |
| | And four fet in the face | |
| | Ymeten in the place, | *Measured* |
| |     And fiften in brede. | *fifteen feet across* |
| | His nose was a fot and more, | *longer than a foot* |
| 480 | His browe as brestles wore, | *brows were like bristles* |
| |     He that it seighe it sede. | *Anyone who saw it said* |
| | He loked lotheliche | *loathly* |
| | And was swart as piche — | *swarthy as pitch* |
| |     Of him men might adrede! | *be afraid* |

*       *       *

|  | | |
|---|---|---|
| fol. 265vb | Charls com to Nasers | *came* |
| 486 | With his dussepers | |
| |     To se that painim. | |
| | He asked, withouten fayl, | |
| | Of King Charls batayl | *For a battle with* |
| 490 |     To fight ogaines him. | |
| | Charls wonderd tho | |
| | When he seighe him go, | *saw him move* |
| |     He biheld him ich a lim. | *in every limb* |
| | For seththen he was ybore, | *ever since he was born* |
| 495 | He no hadde ysen bifore | |
| |     Non that was so grim. | *Anyone so terrifying* |
| | | |
| | Sir Oger the Danais, | *Ogier the Dane* |
| | A knight ful curtays, | *exceedingly courteous* |
| |     To him first was ysent. | *sent to [Vernagu] first* |

| | | |
|---|---|---|
| 500 | And at his coming, | *when he attacked* |
| | Vernagu an heygheing | *hurriedly* |
| |     Under his arm him hent. | *picked him up* |
| | Yarmed as he was, | *Even though he was fully armed* |
| | He toke him in the plas | *place* |
| 505 |     And to the castel he went. | |
| | Sir Oger schamed sore, | *was sorely ashamed* |
| | Him o thought that com thore | *recalled what had happened there* |
| |     And held him foule yschent. | *felt himself foully disgraced* |
| | | |
| | Reynald de Aubethpine | |
| 510 | Was sent to that Sarrazin. | |
| |     He served him al so, | *He treated him the same way* |
| | And seyd to Charlmain, | |
| | "Sir, tho thou won Spain, | *given that you* |
| |     Hadestow non better tho? | *Have you no better knights then* |
| 515 | So Mahoun me give rest, | *As may Mahoun grant me peace* |
| | Ogain ten swiche the best | *Against* |
| |     To fight ich wold go!" | |
| | Sir Costentin of Rome | |
| | And th'erl of Nauntes come | *Nantes* |
| 520 |     To fight with bothe to. | *To fight with [him] together* |
| | | |
| | And Vernagu bar bothe — | *carried* |
| | No were thai never so wrothe — | *Never were they so angry* |
| |     To Nassers castel. | |
| | Under aither arm on, | *One under each arm* |
| 525 | As stille as ani ston, | *silent as any stone* |
| |     Might thai nought with him mele. | *engage* |
| | Tho Charls sent ten; | *Then* |
| | Al so he served his men; | |
| fol. 266ra |     Might no man with him dele! | *fight* |
| 530 | Charls bithought tho, | |
| | Yif he sent mo, | *more* |
| |     It were him wrotherhele. | *It would be his misfortune* |

    \*       \*       \*

| | | |
|---|---|---|
| | Roland the gode knight | |
| | Tho bad leve to fight | *Then asked permission to fight* |
| 535 |     Ogain that painim. | *Against* |
| | King Charls seyd, "Nay! | |
| | Thou no schalt nought, bi this day! | |
| |     He is to stout and grim." | *too large and fierce* |
| | So long he him bad | *[Roland]; pleaded* |
| 540 | That leve of him he hadde. | *got his permission* |
| |     Rouland armed him | *himself* |

|   |   |   |
|---|---|---|
| | And com anonright | *immediately* |
| | Into the feld to fight | |
| |     Ogain that Sarrazin. | |
| | | |
| 545 | And at his coming thare | |
| | Sir Vernagu was ware, | |
| |     And tok him under his hond. | *took him in his hand* |
| | Out of his sadel he gan him bere, | *bore him* |
| | And on his hors swere | *neck* |
| 550 |     He set Roulond. | |
| | And Rouland smot him so | *struck* |
| | That Vernagu tho | *then* |
| |     Unto the grounde wond. | *fell to the ground* |
| | And when the Cristen seighe this, | *Christians saw* |
| 555 | That Vernau fallen is, | |
| |     Thai thonked Godes sond. | *gift* |
| | | |
| | Thai lopen opon her stede | *leapt; their steeds* |
| | And swerdes out thai brede | |
| |     And fight thai gun tho. | *then they began to fight* |
| 560 | Rouland, with Durindale, | *(see note)* |
| | Brewe him miche bale, | *Caused him much harm* |
| |     And carf his hors ato. | *cut [Vernagu's] horse in half* |
| | When Vernagu was o fot, | |
| | He no couthe no better bot, | *remedy* |
| 565 |     To Rouland he gan go. | |
| | In the heued he smot his stede, | *struck Roland's steed on the head* |
| | That ded to grounde he yede. | *fell down dead* |
| |     O fot than were thai bo. | *both on foot* |
| | | |
| | A fot thai tok the fight, | *On foot* |
| 570 | And Vernagu anonright | |
| |     His swerd he had ylore. | *lost* |
| | Rouland, with al his might, | |
| fol. 266rb | He stired him as a knight | *sprang into action* |
| |     And yaf him dintes sore | *gave; blows* |
| 575 | Til it was ogain the none; | *nearly noon* |
| | Thus thai layd opon | *continued fighting* |
| |     Ay til thai weri wore. | *became weary* |
| | Douk Rouland sone he fond | *quickly realized* |
| | That with no dint of brond | *sword stroke* |
| 580 |     He slough him nevermore. | *Might he ever slay [Vernagu]* |
| | | |
| | When it com to the neve, | *evening* |
| | Vernagu bad leve | *requested permission* |
| |     To resten of that fight. | *cease fighting* |
| | Rouland him trewthe yaf | *gave him his promise* |

585 So he most bring a staf                          *So long as he might bring*
    After his wil ydight.                     *Prepared as he wishes*
  Vernagu graunted wel,                               *agreed*
  And went to her hostel                       *their lodgings*
    When that was night.
590 Amorwe, withouten fail,
  Thai com to the batayl,
    Aither as douhti knight.                            *Each*

  Sir Rouland brought a staf
  That King Charls him yaf,                     *had given him*
595     That was long and newe —
  The bodi of a yong oke                *trunk of a young oak tree*
  To yif therwith a stroke.                            *give*
    He was tough and trewe,
  And with that gode staf
600 Wel mani dintes he yaf                   *many strokes he gave*
    Vernagu the schrewe.                  *[To]; wicked*
  And at the non, aplight,
  Thai gun another fight
    And stones togider threwe.        *threw stones at each other*

605 Gode rappes for the nones          *Strong strokes for the occasion*
  Thai gaven with the stones,
    That sete swithe sore                    *struck so hard*
  That helme and heye targe                *helmet; shield*
  Thurth her strokes large                      *great buffets*
610     Therwith thai broken wore.               *were broken*
  And Vernagu at that cas                       *moment*
  So sore asleped was                            *exhausted*
    He no might fight no more.         *could no longer fight*
  At Rouland leve he toke               *Of Roland he asked permission*
615 That time, so seyt the boke,
    For to slepe thore.                          *To sleep there*

fol. 266va Roland yaf leve him                        *gave him leave*
  For to slepe wele afin,                   *sleep soundly at last*
    And rest him in that stounde,                *for a time*
620 And seyd that he nold                    *said that he would not*
  For the cité ful of gold                   *a city full of gold*
    Be therwith yfounde                      *Be ever caught*
  Slepeand to slen a knight,          *Having slain a sleeping knight*
  Thei that he had in fight                        *Even if*
625     Yif him dethes wounde.                        *Given*
  Tho Vernagu lay adoun,                          *Then*
  To slepe he was boun                        *ready to sleep*
    There opon the grounde.

|  |  |  |
|---|---|---|
|  | And Vernagu rout thore | *snores* |
| 630 | As a wild bore | *Like* |
|  | Tho he on slepe was. | *While; asleep* |
|  | To him Rouland gan gon | *went* |
|  | And tok the gretest ston | *largest* |
|  | That lay in that place; |  |
| 635 | He leyd under his heued, ywis, |  |
|  | For him thought it lay amis, |  |
|  | To lowe at that cas. | *Too low in that state* |
|  | And Vernagu up stode, |  |
|  | He stard as he were wode | *stared in amazement* |
| 640 | When he awaked was. |  |

|  |  |  |
|---|---|---|
|  | Vernagu asked anon, |  |
|  | "Who leyd this gret ston |  |
|  | Under min heued so? |  |
|  | It no might never be, | *It could never be* |
| 645 | Bot yif he were a knight fre; | *Unless it were a noble knight* |
|  | .................................. |  |
|  | Wist ich who it were. | *I'd like to know who* |
|  | He schuld be me leve and dere, | *close and dear to me* |
|  | Thei that he were mi fo." | *Even if he were my foe* |
| 650 | Quath Rouland sikerly, |  |
|  | "Certes, it was Y, | *Truly; I* |
|  | For that thou rot so. | *Because you snored so much* |

|  |  |  |
|---|---|---|
|  | And when tho me lovest miche, | *now that you love me* |
|  | Now tel me, sikerliche, |  |
| 655 | Whi thou art so hard | *Why you are so hard* |
|  | That no thing may thee dere, | *injure* |
|  | Knif, no ax, no spere, |  |
|  | No no dint of sward?" | *Nor no* |
|  | Quath Vernagu sikerly, |  |
| 660 | "No man is harder than Y |  |
|  | Fram the navel upward. |  |
| fol. 266vb | Forthi Y com hider, ywis, | *This is why; to this place* |
|  | To fight with King Charlis |  |
|  | With the hore bard." | *white beard* |

|  |  |  |
|---|---|---|
| 665 | Vernagu to Rouland sede, |  |
|  | "Al so thi God thee spede, | *May your God help you* |
|  | Whare were thou yborn?" |  |
|  | "In Fraunce, bi Seynt Austin, | *Augustine* |
|  | King Charls cosyn, |  |
| 670 | Our kinde lord ycorn. | *chosen* |
|  | We leveth opon Jhesu | *believe in* |
|  | That is ful of vertu, | *virtuous* |

That bare the croun of thorn.
And ye leveth in the fende,                            *believe in the devil*
675  Forthi withouten ende                             *For which reason*
Ye schul be forlorn."                                 *lost*

And when that Vernagu
Yherd speke of Jhesu,                                 *Heard mention*
He asked wat man he was.
680  Sir Rouland seyd, "He is
The King of paradys
And Lord ful of gras;                                 *grace*
In a maiden He was bore                               *From a virgin; born*
To bigge that was forlore,                            *redeem those who were lost*
685  As sonne passeth thurth the glas,                *As the sun passes through glass*
And dyed opon the rode                                *died upon the cross*
For our alder gode                                    *the good of us all*
And nought for His gilt it nas.                       *not for His own guilt*

And suffred woundes five
690  And ros fram ded to live                         *death to life*
Than thridde day,                                     *on the third day*
And fet out Adam and Eve,                             *fetched out*
And mo that were Him leve,                            *more souls that were dear to Him*
Fram helle, forsothe to say,
695  And sitt in Trinité,                             *sits in Trinity*
O God in Persones Thre,
Swiche is our lay."                                   *Such is our belief*
Vernagu seyd tho,                                     *then*
"It no might never be so!                             *cannot be so*
700  Therof Y sigge nay!                              *I deny it*

Hou might it ever be
That he were on and thre?                             *one*
Tel me now thee skille."                              *how it works*
Rouland than sede,
705  "Al so God me spede,                             *As*
fol. 267ra  Yis, with a gode wille.
As the harp has thre thinges,                         *parts*
Wode and soun and strenges,                           *wood and sound and strings*
And mirthe is thertille,                              *inheres in it*
710  So is God Persones Thre
And holeliche on in unité,                            *wholly one in unity*
Al thing to fulfille.

And as the sonne hath thinges thre,                   *sun*
Hete and white on to se,                              *heat; brightness*
715  And is ful of light,

So is God in Trinité,
Unité and magesté
  And Lord ful of might."
Quath Vernagu, "Now Y se
720 Hou He is God in Persones Thre.
  Now ich wot that right,         *understand that well*
Ac hou that He bicom man —       *But how*
The Lord that this world wan —      *who*
  Therof no have Y no sight."    *I do not understand this*

725 Quath Rouland, "He that ous bought    *saved us*
And al thing maked of nought,    *made all from nothing*
  Wele might He be so hende      *courteous*
That He wald sende His Sone
In a maiden for to wone,       *To dwell in a virgin*
730  Withouten mannes hende."     *involvement*
Quath Vernagu, "Saun fayl,      *without fail*
Therof ichave gret mervail.      *astonishment*
  Hou might he fram hir wende?    *come from her*
Hou might he of hir be bore,     *be born of her*
735 That was a maiden bifore?      *virgin*
  Y no may nought have in mende."  *cannot understand*

Rouland seyd to Vernagu,
"Mi Lordes Fader Jhesu      *My Lord Jesus' Father*
  Is so michel of might        *so powerful*
740 That He made sonne and se     *sun and sea*
And fisches in the flod to be,
  Bothe day and night.
Wele may He than, as Y thee er seyd,   *before*
Ben ybore of a maide
745  Withouten wem, aplight."     *blemish*
Quath Vernagu, "It may wele be.
Ac hou He dyed, Y no can nought se.   *But*
  Tel me now that right,

For I nist never no man       *have never known*
fol. 267rb That aros after than        *arose*
751  When that he ded was.     *After he had died*
And yif He Godes Sone were,     *God's Son*
He no might nought dye there.     *could not die*
  Tel me now that cas."       *Explain*
755 Quath Rouland, "Y schal tel thee:
His bodi slepe opon the tre,     *died; cross*
  And the thridde day aras.     *arose*
His Godhed waked ever and ay    *Divinity awoke*

|     |                              |                              |
|-----|------------------------------|------------------------------|
|     | And to helle tok the way,    | *traveled to hell*           |
| 760 | And bond Satanas.            | *bound Satan*                |

|     |                              |                              |
|-----|------------------------------|------------------------------|
|     | So schul we al arise         |                              |
|     | And of the dome agrise       | *tremble with fear of the doom* |
|     | Atte Day of Juggement,       | *Upon the Day of Judgment*   |
|     | And answerey for our dede,   | *answer for our deeds*       |
| 765 | The gode and the quede,      | *sinful*                     |
|     | Hou we our liif have spent." | *lives*                      |
|     | Quath Vernagu, "Now ichot wel | *I understand*              |
|     | Hou He aros ichadel,         | *in every way*               |
|     | And have in min entent.      | *understanding*              |
| 770 | Ac hou He steyghe to heven,  | *ascended*                   |
|     | Y no can nought neven        | *explain*                    |
|     | No wite, verrament."         |                              |

|     |                              |                              |
|-----|------------------------------|------------------------------|
|     | Than seyd Rouland,           |                              |
|     | "O Vernagu, understand,      |                              |
| 775 | Herken now to me.            | *Listen to me now*           |
|     | That ich Lord that with His might | *same; who*             |
|     | In a maiden alight,          | *alighted*                   |
|     | Yborn for to be,             |                              |
|     | As the sonne aros in the est | *Just as sun arose in the east* |
| 780 | And decended in the west,    | *set*                        |
|     | As tow might now se,         | *As you can see*             |
|     | Right so dede God Almight:   | *Just so did*                |
|     | Mounted into heven light     | *[He] arose*                 |
|     | And sit in Trinité."         | *sits*                       |

|     |                              |                              |
|-----|------------------------------|------------------------------|
| 785 | Quath Vernagu, "Now ich wot  | *understand*                 |
|     | Your Cristen lawe, everi grot. | *every part*               |
|     | Now we wil fight!            |                              |
|     | Whether lawe better be       | *Whichever; is better*       |
|     | Sone we schul yse,           | *We shall soon see*          |
| 790 | Long ar it be night."        | *before*                     |
|     | Rouland a dint him yaf       | *gave him a stroke*          |
|     | With his gode staf           | *good staff*                 |
|     | That he kneled, aplight,     | *was forced to his knees*    |
| fol. 267va | And Vernagu to him smot |                            |
| 795 | And carf his staf fothot,    | *broke his staff suddenly*   |
|     | Even ato aright.             | *Evenly in two*              |

|     |                              |                              |
|-----|------------------------------|------------------------------|
|     | Tho Rouland kneld adoun      | *knelt down*                 |
|     | And maked an orisoun         | *uttered a prayer*           |
|     | To God in heven light,       |                              |
| 800 | And seyd, "Lord, understond  |                              |
|     | Y no fight for no lond,      | *I do not fight for land*    |

|  |  |  |
|---|---|---|
|  | Bot for to save Thi right. | *preserve Your law* |
|  | Sende me now might and grace |  |
|  | Here in this ich place | *same* |
| 805 | To sle that foule wight." | *creature* |
|  | An angel com ful sone, | *came quickly* |
|  | And seyd, "Herd is thi bone; | *Your request was heard* |
|  | Arise, Rouland, and fight! |  |
|  |  |  |
|  | And sched the schrewes blod, | *shed the scoundrel's blood* |
| 810 | For he nas never gode |  |
|  | Bi lond no bi se. |  |
|  | Thei alle prechours alive | *Even if all preachers alive* |
|  | To Cristen wald him schrive, | *administer penance to him as a Christian* |
|  | Gode nold he never be." | *He would never be good* |
| 815 | When Rouland herd that steven, | *message* |
|  | He stirt him up ful even | *started up straight* |
|  | And faught with hert fre. | *noble* |
|  | Strokes bi sex and seven | *continuously* |
|  | Togider this knightes yeven | *these; gave* |
| 820 | That mani man might yse. |  |
|  |  |  |
|  | Rouland, withouten dueling, | *any hesitation* |
|  | Thurth might of heven King, |  |
|  | Vernagu he smot, |  |
|  | That the left arm and the scheld | *So that* |
| 825 | Fel forth into the feld | *Fell severed on the ground* |
|  | Fram that painim fothot. | *at once* |
|  | His arm tho he had lore, | *when; lost* |
|  | Swithe wo him was therfore, | *Such woe he felt* |
|  | And fast he faught, Y wot. | *he fought hard, I say* |
| 830 | He smot Rouland on the croun | *head* |
|  | A strok with his fauchoun |  |
|  | That thurth the helme it bot. | *through the helmet it bit* |
|  |  |  |
|  | No hadde ben the bacinet | *Had not the helmet* |
|  | That the strok withsett, | *Withstood that stroke* |
| 835 | Rouland hadde ben aqueld. | *would have been slain* |
|  | The Sarrazin sayd aswithe, | *quickly* |
|  | "Smite ich eft on sithe, | *If I could strike one more time* |
| fol. 267vb | Thi liif is bought and seld." | *Your life is bought and sold* |
|  | Rouland answerd, "Nay! |  |
| 840 | Mine worth thee rather pay, | *I'd rather that you pay* |
|  | Bi God that al thing weld." | *By God who wields all things* |
|  | With a strok ful large |  |
|  | He clef the Sarrazins targe | *split; shield* |
|  | That half fel in the feld. | *So that half fell* |

| | | |
|---|---|---|
| 845 | And at another venou | *by; attack* |
| | Roland smot Vernagu | |
| | That he fel doun to grounde; | |
| | And Rouland with Durindale | |
| | Yaf him strokes fale | *many* |
| 850 | And his dethes wounde. | *fatal wound* |
| | The paynem crid, "Help, Mahoun! | |
| | And Jubiter, of gret renoun, | |
| | That beth so michel of mounde. | *great on earth* |
| | As ye beth mightful, helpeth me, | |
| 855 | That ich might yvenged be | *avenged* |
| | Of this Cristen hounde." | *On this Christian dog* |
| | | |
| | Rouland lough for that cri, | *laughed at that plea* |
| | And seyd, "Mahoun, sikerly, | |
| | No may thee help nought, | *Cannot help you* |
| 860 | No Jubiter, no Apolin, | *Nor Jupiter, nor Apollo* |
| | No is worth the brust of a swin, | *Neither; a swine's bristle* |
| | In hert no in thought." | *In heart or in thought* |
| | His ventail he gan unlace | *neck-covering chain mail* |
| | And smot off his heued in the place, | *cut off his head* |
| 865 | And to Charls it brought. | |
| | Tho thonked he God in heven, | *Then* |
| | And Mari, with milde steven, | |
| | That he so hadde ywrought. | |
| | | |
| | And al the folk of the lond | |
| 870 | For onour of Roulond | *honor* |
| | Thonked God, old and yong, | |
| | And yede a procesioun | *held a procession* |
| | With croice and goinfaynoun, | *cross and banner* |
| | And "Salve" miri song. | *sweetly sang* |
| 875 | Bothe widowe and wiif in place | |
| | Thus thonked Godes grace, | |
| | Alle tho that speke with tong. | *those* |
| | To Otuel, al so yern, | *just as eager* |
| | That was a Sarrazin stern, | |
| 880 | Ful sone this word sprong. | *Soon word of this arrived* |

**EXPLANATORY NOTES TO ROLAND AND VERNAGU**

ABBREVIATIONS: **DR**: *Duke Roland and Sir Otuel of Spain*; **MED**: *Middle English Dictionary*; **OK**: *Otuel a Knight*; **OR**: *Otuel and Roland*; **Otinel**: Anglo-Norman *Otinel*; **Pseudo-Turpin**: *The Chronicle of Pseudo-Turpin*, ed. and trans. Poole; **RV**: *Roland and Vernagu*; **Whiting**: Whiting, *Proverbs, Sentences, and Proverbial Phrases*.

1        *For he it seighe with sight.* Approximately forty-four opening lines are missing because of damage to fol. 263 of the Auchinleck manuscript. See the discussion in the *RV* Introduction, pp. 27–28. The damaged leaf may by viewed in either of the facsimiles (listed on p. 31).

10       *Withouten ani lesing.* "without any lying." The *RV* poet uses this line frequently as a tag and metrical filler; he also tends to favor phrases that assert his honesty and the tale's veracity. His source, *Pseudo-Turpin*, purports to be an eyewitness account; see the discussion in the *RV* Introduction, pp. 27–28.

11–12    *Lorein and Lombardye, / Gascoun, Bayoun, and Pikardye.* Except for Lombardy, these are all regions in France that were strong principalities during the Middle Ages. Lombardy, a region in north Italy, figures prominently in many of the Otuel-cycle romances. Medieval Lombardy bordered on France. In *The Siege of Milan*, the central conflict between Saracens and Christians is over the city of Milan and the surrounding Lombard region. In *OK*, *OR*, *DR*, and *Otinel*, the Saracen Emperor Garcy has conquered many key Christian cities and made Lombardy his command center.

19       *Constansious.* Constantius VI (771–c. 805), a Byzantine emperor.

110–24   *the holy croun . . . . Withouten ani lesing.* The list of relics presented by Emperor Constantius to Charlemagne is most impressive. It includes the Crown of Thorns ("the holy croun"), the arm of St. Simon (on whom, see the note to line 111 below), a portion of the Cross set in crystal, a scrap of Jesus' robe, all (or a portion) of Mary's smock, the rod of Aaron, the spear of Longinus, and a nail driven through Jesus' feet at the Crucifixion. The relics, which give off a sweet odor, are largely (but not all) clustered around devotion to Christ's Passion. The presentation of the Crown of Thorns to Charlemagne helps to codify his role as divine ruler — follower and worldly successor to Christ.

111      *arme of Seyn Simoun.* The owner of this arm could be either Simon the Apostle or Simon of Cyrene. The former was one of the original twelve disciples of Jesus, Simon the Cananean (Matthew 10:4), also called Simon Zelotes (Acts 1:13), reputed to have been martyred by being sawn in half, longwise through his torso

and head. It is not clear that his arm held any special significance, but arm-and-hand-shaped reliquaries, fashioned of gold or silver, were not uncommon. See, for example, Klein, "Arm Reliquary of the Apostles" (c. 1190, Lower Saxony), Cleveland Museum of Art, viewable at http://projects.mcah.columbia.edu/treasuresofheaven/relics/Arm-Reliquary-of-the-Apostles.php. This identification would complement the appearance of James because Simon is another original apostle. However, it seems also possible, amid the other relics of the Crucifixion, that "Seyn Simoun" refers to Simon of Cyrene, never canonized but famous for being named as the one who "took up the Cross" and bore it for Jesus (Matthew 27:32; Mark 15:21, echoing Christ's command at Mark 8:34). Simon of Cyrene's service to Jesus is integral to the Stations of the Cross. A relic of his Cross-bearing arm would be extremely meaningful, representing the missionary zeal of the crusaders themselves, who figuratively took up the Cross to fight infidels.

117       *Araon.* Despite the unusual spelling, it is clear that the poet means Aaron, the brother of Moses, whose staff was transformed into a serpent in Egypt. The tale comes from Exodus 7:8–10.

120       *Longys.* According to legend, Longinus was the unnamed Roman soldier who pierced Jesus' side with a spear during the Crucifixion. The spear came to be regarded as a precious relic because of its association with Jesus' heart blood. In *RV*, Constantius possesses the Spear of Longinus and presents it to Charlemagne.

129       *Yif the relikes verray were.* On the treatment of relics in the literature of late medieval England, see Malo, *Relics and Writing*.

139       *Aise in Gascoyn.* Auch, a city in southwestern France, was the capital of the province of Gascony on the Spanish border. The Via Tolosona, one of the four traditional routes for pilgrims to Santiago de Compostela in Galicia, passed through Auch. The scribe's spelling may reflect the influence of Aix-la-Chapelle (Aachen) in Germany, where Charlemagne had an imperial residence and where he was buried in 814, or of Aix-en-Provence, a major center in Roman and late medieval France that Charles Martel (Charlemagne's grandfather) captured from Saracen occupiers in 737.

140       *siker aplight.* "in faith, truly." This is another phrase the poet uses frequently as both a metrical filler and a claim that the events being told are true.

144       *Galis.* Galicia is a region in northwestern Spain. Santiago de Compostela is located in Galicia and originated as a cathedral where Saint James' remains were buried. It was a popular pilgrims' destination during the Middle Ages, and remains so today.

152–56    *James the apostel . . . . lete me sle.* The speaker in Charlemagne's dream is St. James of Compostela, one of Jesus' twelve apostles, who was killed by Herod (the only martyrdom of a disciple cited in the Bible; see Acts 12:2). James was thus venerated as the first martyred disciple. As the poet says, James' brother was the apostle St. John the Evangelist (Matthew 10:3). James is the patron saint of

Spain, his remains enshrined (according to legend) in Santiago de Compostela in Galicia. In *RV*, his appearance before Charlemagne in a dream further verifies that the king's campaign into Muslim Spain has divine sanction.

185    *Pampiloun.* Pamplona is a city located near the border of Spain and France. According to historical accounts of Charlemagne's failed campaign in Spain, Pamplona was the first city he conquered.

206–08    *And thurth the miracle . . . . that ich night.* Mass conversion of Muslims is shown to occur first through prayer, then crushing warfare, and then "miracle." The poet does not reflect upon the compulsory nature of such conversion, and instead seems buoyed by the fact that this method works so well for the conqueror Charlemagne. Mass conversion of this kind, of ordinary citizenry, seems to be desirable, as opposed to the obdurate nature that sets the Saracen giant Vernagu, later in the poem, outside the scheme of salvation (see note to line 813 below). On the convertibility of desirable versus undesirable Muslims, see the discussion in the *RV* Introduction, pp. 28–30.

221–56    *Visim, Lameche . . . . Agabie and Sisens.* This long list of cities in Spain conquered by Charlemagne may combine names of real cities with fictional place-names that fit the meter and rhyme. It is impossible to identify every place as being a real locale that is still in existence, but enough do match up to suggest that the *RV* poet attempts to detail a sweeping swath of true geography. The list's extreme length also magnifies the success of Charlemagne's Spanish campaign. Discussing the use of journeys and unfamiliar locations in romances, Robert Rouse argues that romance authors may have included names and descriptions of places that the audience will never visit but would have heard of in other narratives ("Walking (Between) the Lines," pp. 137–39). The Latin, Old French, and Middle English versions of *Pseudo-Turpin* (the source for *RV*) all include similar lists of cities in Spain. See especially the long, helpful list in the translation of the Latin version (*Pseudo-Turpin*, pp. 10–13); and the abbreviated list in the edition of the Middle English *Turpine's Story* (ed. Shepherd, pp. 8–9, 44–46).

259–68    *That hat Seyn Torquas . . . . se Godes face.* This passage refers to a medieval legend of St. Torquatus of Acci, patron saint of Guadix, Spain. It would appear that pilgrims to his shrine, upon his feast day (May 15), could enjoy the miraculous fruit of his special, sanctified olive tree, and thereby be promised a vision of God's beatific face at the Last Judgment. St. Torquatus was a first-century missionary who evangelized the town of Acci (present-day Guadix).

280    *dussepers.* "Twelve peers." According to legend, Charlemagne recognized twelve knights — his *dussepers* — as his greatest, noblest warriors. Their likeness to the twelve apostles is noticeable, and perhaps even more so in the plot of *RV*, which is based upon a military campaign made in St. James the Apostle's honor.

286    *ginne.* "strategy, device, tactic, ingenious trick." See *MED ginne* (n.), senses 2a and 2b. It is unusual to apply this term to a prayer, which would normally be considered a miraculous intervention rather than a war strategy. The word *ginne* is also commonly used as a military term for a machine designed to besiege a city

(*MED ginne* (n.), sense 4a). Its use here may thus carry an ironic reference to that meaning, because Charlemagne is able to enter the city through a different kind of device.

309–16    *In Marche moneth . . . . to the warldes ende.* The site for this legend of a city's naming as "Paners" after the French word for "basket" is unknown. It was apparently a medieval origin story with strong local resonance, reaching even an English poet, but the exact place cannot be known. A historic district within Marseille, France, is called "Le Paniers," but its origin is post-medieval, and it is also too remotely located for it to have any bearing on the geography of *RV*.

317–19    *Clodonius the first . . . . and Pipin.* Clovis, Clotaire, Dagobert, and Pepin were kings who preceded Charlemagne in ruling the Franks. The first three names denote the Merovingian dynasty. Pepin refers to either Charlemagne's father or grandfather.

323       *maumetes.* "idols." Muslims, as Saracens, are inaccurately depicted as worshiping idols.

325       *Turpin.* Archbishop Turpin is an important military and ecclesiastical character in the *Song of Roland* and the Middle English Charlemagne romances. In *Otinel*, *RV*, and the three Otuel romances, Turpin's role is limited to episcopal duties: performing Mass and baptizing converts. In the fifth Otuel-cycle romance, *The Siege of Milan*, Turpin plays a central role.

328       *the Latin.* The phrase most likely refers to *Pseudo-Turpin*. See also line 429.

343       *Jubiter and Mahoun.* Middle English romances often misrepresent Muslims as polytheists who worship idols, naming three or four gods as central to their fictionalized faith: Mahoun, Jubiter, Apollin, and Termagaunt. See the discussion in the General Introduction, p. 16.

357       *Seynt Ysador the confessour.* Saint Isidore of Seville, famous as the last of the Church Fathers, was Archbishop of Seville from c. 600 until his death in 636. In c. 1063, his remains were translated from Seville, in what was then Islamic southern Spain, to the newly rededicated Basilica of San Isidoro in León, an important city in northwest Spain. Like the other locations mentioned in lines 353–64, León lies on a pilgrimage route to Compostela.

359       *in Aise a chapel.* On this location in Gascony, see the explanatory note to line 139 above.

363       *Anevaus.* This city has not been identified. The reading agrees with all prior editors. The minims of *n, v, u* invite other readings, but no possibility provides a viable clue. The city of Avignon is not situated in the right geographical area.

368–424   *Ther fel a miracle . . . . binimeth the pore.* Here the poet departs from the main narrative to offer a pious exemplum taken from a separate chapter in *Pseudo-Turpin* (pp. 17–18; and *Turpines Story*, ed. Shepherd, pp. 10–11). While Charlemagne and his host are sojourning in Bayonne, one of his knights, Sir Romain, is condemned to die. The condemned man asks a friend to prepare for his funeral, showing him the clothes he wants to be buried in and asking that his horse be sold and the profits donated to poor clerks so that they will sing psalms on his behalf. The friend, however, keeps the profit for himself. After thirty nights, the executed man appears to his friend in a dream and explains that, although he is now in heaven, he suffered excruciating pain for the past thirty days because his intended charity to the clerks was withheld. The man tells his dishonest friend that now *he* will suffer for his duplicity. The friend recounts his dream to the court, and then a strong wind fills the hall. Foul demons fly in, lift up the thief, and carry him away. Charlemagne's soldiers search for four days without finding him. Later when Charlemagne's host passes through Naverne, they find the dead executor's body where it was dropped by the demons. The poet closes the exemplum with a warning to other executors: anyone who withholds charity from the needy will experience the same punishment. Subsequent versions of this tale continue its association with the Charlemagne legend. In Etienne de Besancon's eleventh-century *Alphabetum narrationum* and its Middle English translation, the *Alphabet of Tales* #314, it is explicitly linked to Charlemagne. (For a modern edition, see *An Alphabet of Tales*, ed. Banks, 1:216–17, where tale 314 is titled "A Tale from Turpin.") The *Database of Middle English Romances* attributes the English romance to either *Pseudo-Turpin* or the *Estoire de Charlemagne*, so it seems likely that Etienne collected this anecdote and its connection to Charlemagne from one of these sources. A few centuries later, the exemplum appears in John Mirk's late-fourteenth-century *Festial* (see *John Mirk's Festial*, ed. Powell, 2:243). We are grateful to Thomas Hahn for pointing out some of the analogues of this exemplum.

380      *on heigheing.* "at once, hurriedly." The phrase is common in this romance.

425–60   *Now late . . . . cité of Pampiloun.* These lines are also found (with slight variations in wording) in *OR*, lines 1981–2016. The overlap contributed to the now-discarded "Charlemagne and Roland" theory of a lost romance. See the discussion in the General Introduction, pp. 7–8.

426–36   *And speke of Charles . . . . a douhti knight.* On Charlemagne's portrait, borrowed in part from Einhard's *Life of Charlemagne*, see the General Introduction, p. 9, and the note to lines 474–83 below.

429      *As the Latin ous sede.* See the note to line 328 above.

439–42   *The holy croun . . . . God was born.* There are no records of medieval kings wearing a crown of thorns in procession. A bas-relief reliquary shrine in Aachen Cathedral (dated to c. 1215) depicts Emperor Constantius presenting Charlemagne with the Crown of Thorns (compare note to lines 110–24 above). A pictorial window in Chartres Cathedral (c. 1225) shows Charlemagne offering relics he received from Constantius to his chapel in Aix-la-Chapelle (Aachen). See Pastan, "Charlemagne as Saint?," pp. 105–08, especially Figures 6.6 and 6.7.

440      *Wissontide.* Whitsuntide is the feast of Pentecost, which occurs fifty days after Easter.

474–83   *And fourti fet . . . . swart as piche.* Vernagu the giant is seen as remarkable for both his gargantuan size and his racialized Otherness (having dark not light skin, unlike the French, and unlike the English audience). His appearance contrasts with that of Charlemagne at lines 425–36 — a description borrowing from that found in Einhard's *Life of Charlemagne* (ed. and trans. Ganz, p. 34). See the discussion in the General Introduction, p. 9. Both portraits follow a pattern, however, in how they stress size, strength, and facial coloring (red face with black hair, in Charlemagne's case).

560      *Durindale.* Durendal is the name of Roland's famous sword. In Rocamadour, France, one may see a chapel with a sword embedded in its outside wall. By local legend, this sword is Durendal. De Veyrières notes the claim (found in l'abbé Cheval's 1862 guidebook, *Guide du Pèlerin à Roc-Amadour*) that the real Durendal was stolen in 1183 when Henry II pillaged the chapel, and he includes a drawing of the current sword ("L'Épée de Roland," pp. 139–41).

578–86   *Douk Rouland sone . . . . his wil ydight.* As Roland fights Vernagu, he finds that the impenetrability of Vernagu's skin from his navel upward makes it impossible for him to kill the giant with a sword. When they take a break from dueling, Roland requests a staff with which to fight Vernagu, hoping to have more success with this weapon. See also lines 660–61.

581      *the neve.* "the evening." See *MED even* (n.). The initial *n* comes from a false sense of elision after *the.* A common phrase was *on eve,* "in the evening," sometimes spelled or pronounced *o neve.*

660–61   *No man is harder than Y / Fram the navel upward.* On Vernagu's monstrous impenetrability, see the note to lines 578–86 above.

663–64   *King Charlis . . . . hore bard.* The reference here is to Charlemagne's iconic white beardedness. In *Otinel,* lines 36–37, Charlemagne has a "fluri gernun" (white moustache) and "grant barbe" (great beard). See, too, *OR,* line 71 ("hore berde"); and *DR,* line 80 ("white berde large and lange").

668      *Seynt Austin.* The St. Augustine sworn by here is probably the great Church Father, Augustine of Hippo (354–430). A more distant possibility is Augustine of Canterbury (d. 604), a Benedictine monk who became the first Archbishop of Canterbury. As a missionary to the pagan Anglo-Saxons, arriving in 597, he is considered England's "First Apostle." If Roland is swearing here by the English saint as he avows to his birth in France, then the English poet has inserted an odd bit of incongruity, consciously or not.

685      *As sonne passeth thurth the glas.* Roland is expounding the doctrine of the Immaculate Conception, wherein Jesus was conceived via Gabriel's annunciation of God's Word to the Virgin Mary (compare Luke 1:26–38). In medieval artistic depictions, the Word shines as light upon Mary, entering through her ear, without changing her state as a virgin. A very common verbal formulation of this event is repeated here: "as the sun passes through the glass," that is, just as light passes though glass without breaking it. The simile appears in a Harley lyric (contemporary with the Auchinleck manuscript): "Thourh hyre side he shon / Ase sonne doth thourh the glas" (*The Poet's Repentance,* lines 21–22). See *The Complete Harley 2253 Manuscript,* ed. and trans. Fein, 2:142–43.

695–712    *And sitt in Trinité . . . . to fulfille*. Roland expounds here the basic tenets of Christianity, as recited in the Athanasian Creed, which priests were enjoined to teach regularly to the laity, following the edicts of the Fourth Lateran Council (1215). Jesus died on the Cross, where he suffered five wounds; then he rose from death to life on the third day (the Resurrection, on Easter Day). During his time on the Cross, he harrowed hell (the Harrowing of Hell) and fetched out the virtuous souls of the patriarchs (from Adam and Eve, to John the Baptist). Jesus Christ now sits in heaven (the Ascension), as one of the Three Persons of the Trinity (God, Son, and Holy Ghost). God is indivisibly, mysteriously, and miraculously Three in One and One in Three.

756–60    *His bodi slepe . . . . bond Satanas*. Christ's Crucifixion, Resurrection, and Harrowing of Hell. By doctrine, Jesus died in the flesh, but his godhead merely slept. In his apparent passivity on the Cross, he actually descended with great triumphal energy to hell, bearing the Cross and breaking open the gates of hell, in order to vanquish and bind the Devil and release the virtuous biblical patriarchs from hell, where they had to dwell before his coming. The Harrowing of Hell was an extremely popular motif in medieval Christian culture, disseminated widely through the apocryphal Gospel of Nicodemus and appearing ubiquitously in art and literature. A copy of the Middle English verse *Harrowing of Hell* appears in the manuscript of *RV*, the Auchinleck manuscript, fols. 35vb–37ra. It also survives in two forms in MS Harley 2253 (c. 1340): an Anglo-Norman version of the Gospel of Nicodemus and the same Middle English poem found in Auchinleck; see *The Complete Harley 2253 Manuscript*, ed. and trans. Fein, 1:342–59 and 2:66–79.

795    *fothot*. "quickly, suddenly, in haste." See *MED, fot-hot* (adv.). The idiom survives into present day slang.

813    *wald him schrive*. "would administer penance to him." See *MED shriven* (v.), sense 2a, and *shrift* (n.). The sacrament of confession before a priest — an action known as "shrift" — was expected at least annually of every Christian. It was seen as necessary for cleansing the soul of sin and then receiving God's forgiveness. The doctrine is that God's mercy is available to all Christians who earnestly repent and orally confess. The angel speaks in hyperbole here, saying that even if every living priest were to shrive Vernagu, his soul would never by cleansed; he can never be "good." He is, therefore, outside the sphere of God's mercy. The angel verifies that the giant Vernagu can be killed by Roland without regret, for he is more devil than human. For a modern reader, this level of cold, divine judgment against a character who has been given affective, sympathetic attributes of reason, feeling, and emotion is troubling and disconcerting.

818    *bi sex and seven*. Proverbial. See *MED six* (num.), sense 2d: "bix six or seven" means "in large quantities in great numbers." See also Whiting S359.

861    *No is worth the brust of a swin*. Proverbial. See Whiting B552.

874    *Salve*. The song being sung triumphantly here is probably the popular liturgical hymn *Salve Regina* (Hail Holy Queen), because Roland has just thanked Mary for his victory over Vernagu (see lines 866–67). This hymn was sung during

processionals for Marian feasts, and often chanted in the evening by monks and university students as they headed off to their sleeping quarters.

878–80     *To Otuel . . . . this word sprong*. These final lines of *RV* establish a chronological transition to the events narrated in *OK*, the next romance copied in the Auchinleck manuscript. *RV* is copied by Scribe 1 in Quire 37, and *OK* by Scribe 6 in a new gathering (Quire 38). It has been recently proposed that these two seemingly different scribes are in fact the same scribe; see Hanna, "Auchinleck 'Scribe 6.'" Scribe 1 (the Auchinleck compiler) wrote the catchphrase found in the right bottom of fol. 267v — the opening line of *OK* — which shows that he intended *OK* to follow *RV*. To view the catchphrase, see *The Auchinleck Manuscript*, ed. Burnley and Wiggins, fol. 267v.

TEXTUAL NOTES TO ROLAND AND VERNAGU

**ABBREVIATIONS: BW**: *The Auchinleck Manuscript*, ed. Burnley and Wiggins; **H**: *Rouland and Vernagu*, ed. Herrtage, in *The English Charlemagne Romances. Part VI*, pp. 37–61; **MS**: Edinburgh, National Library of Scotland MS Advocates 19.2.1 (the Auchinleck MS), fols. 263ra–267vb.

| | |
|---|---|
| 1 | Romance begins incomplete. See *RV* Introduction, pp. 27–28, for estimated number of lost lines and their narrative content. |
| 17 | *was an emperour*. So BW, H. MS: *he* is written between *time* and *was*, omitted with three dots below the word. |
| 28 | *douhti*. So MS, BW. H: *douȝti*. |
| 65 | *of*. MS: *of* inserted above the line between *sent* and *hem*. |
| 123 | *thurth*. So MS, BW. H: *þurch*. |
| 162 | *nought*. MS: *nouȝt* written in superscript over *comest*. |
| 172 | *wil*. So MS, BW. H: *will*. |
| 175 | *schalt*. So MS, BW. H: *shalt*. |
| 179 | *Jamis*. So BW. H: *Iames*. MS: Scribe initially wrote *James*, then cancels *e* and inserts *i* above the word. |
| 206 | *thurth*. So MS, BW. H: *þurch*. |
| 213 | *everichon*. So MS, BW. H: *eurichon*. |
| 214 | *thurth*. So MS, BW. H: *þurch*. |
| 242 | *grene*. MS: final *e* in *grene* is superscripted. |
| 261 | *Biside*. So MS, BW. H: *Beside*. |
| 262 | *thurth*. So MS, BW. H: *þurch*. |
| 264 | *frout*. So MS, BW. H: *front*. |
| 282 | *him*. So BW, H. MS: *hm*. |
| 326 | *thurth*. So MS, BW. H: *þurch*. |
| 327 | *thurth*$_{1,2}$. So MS, BW. H: *þurch*$_{1,2}$. |
| 338 | *susten*. So H, BW. MS: *suiten*. |
| 370 | *Thurth*. So MS, BW. H: *þurch*. |
| 417 | *thurth*. So MS, BW. H: *þurch*. |
| 425 | *Now*. So BW, H. MS: *No*. |
| 609 | *Thurth*. So MS, BW. H: *þurch*. |
| 646 | Ellipses have been added because the rhyme scheme indicates that a line is missing. There is no break in the MS. |
| 653 | *tho*. So MS, H. BW: *þou*. |
| 685 | *thurth*. So MS, BW. H: *þurch*. |
| 742 | *day*. So MS, BW. H: *daye*. |
| 756 | *opon*. So MS. BW, H: *vpon*. |

814       *he*. So MS, BW. H: *be*.

822       *Thurth*. So MS, BW. H: *þurch*.

832       *thurth*. So MS, BW. H: *þurch*.

855       *be*. So BW. MS, H: *me*.

858       *seyd*. MS, BW, H: *syd*.

           *sikerly*. So MS, BW. H: *fikerly*.

880       Lower right margin of fol. 267vb: catchphrase *herkneþ boþe ȝing & old* (the first line of *Otuel a Knight*, the next poem in the Auchinleck MS).

# ⚜ OTUEL A KNIGHT INTRODUCTION

Of the surviving Middle English romances featuring the Saracen Otuel, *Otuel a Knight* is the oldest. It is also the only one written in couplets rather than tail-rhyme stanzas.[1] Its sole manuscript witness is the Auchinleck manuscript (Edinburgh, National Library of Scotland MS Advocates 19.2.1; c. 1330–40), fols. 268ra–77vb, where it is immediately preceded by *Roland and Vernagu*.[2] For a long time *Otuel a Knight* had only one edition — Sidney J. H. Herrtage's 1882 *The English Charlemagne Romances. Part VI* — where it is edited in the same volume as *Roland and Vernagu*. A second edition appeared in 2003 when the facsimile of the Auchinleck manuscript, edited by David Burnley and Alison Wiggins, was made available online. Accompanying the full-color digital images of the scribal copies of both *Roland and Vernagu* and *Otuel a Knight* are accurate transcriptions that provide some degree of emendation, but without any editorial punctuation, glossary, or commentary.

Like all of the Middle English versions of the French *Otinel*, *Otuel a Knight* tells the story of the Saracen knight Otuel who battles Roland on behalf of the Emperor Garcy and is miraculously converted to Christianity during the duel. After Otuel's conversion, he is incorporated into Charlemagne's court and fights on his behalf against Garcy. The three Otuel romances — *Otuel a Knight*, *Otuel and Roland*, and *Duke Roland and Sir Otuel of Spain* — are frequently treated by critics as a single poem because each contains portions of the same essential plot, with *Otuel and Roland* extended to include Ganelon's treason and Roland's fall at Roncevaux. In fact, the Otuel romances are distinct poems, with differences in rhyme scheme, stanza form, and treatments of the plot details. To illustrate the distinctions, the introduction to each poem focuses on four scenes. How these scenes are adapted contributes to the general tone of each poem.

The first scene comes directly before Otuel and Roland's duel. Otuel has to borrow armor from Charlemagne, who asks his daughter Belesent to arm the young knight. She is romantically attracted to him. The second scene occurs as Roland and Oliver flee the Saracens and encounter Otuel riding with his host to meet them. In each version, Otuel scolds Roland and Oliver for fleeing, but the poets have him express a different reprimand in each version, some harsher than the others. The third scene, like the first one, deals with a potential love interest. When Ogier is injured in battle, Clarel sends him to his paramour for healing; in the meeting between Ogier and Enfamy, there may be a suggestion of desire or the encounter may remain innocent. The fourth scene is Otuel and Clarel's duel: as Otuel

---

[1] For *Otuel a Knight*, see *DIMEV* 1784; *NIMEV* 1103; and Smyser, "Charlemagne Legends," pp. 92, 264. The romance in couplets has 1746 lines, counting an eight-line lacuna; lines 121–28 are missing due to damage to the manuscript.

[2] For studies on the Auchinleck manuscript, see Calkin, *Saracens and the Making of English Identity*; Connolly and Edwards, "Evidence for the History"; and Fein, *New Perspectives*.

and Clarel fight, Otuel slices off Clarel's cheek, leaving his teeth exposed; Otuel always mocks Clarel's injury, but the nature of the joke correlates to the tone set by the other three scenes. Here we will discuss the casting of the four scenes in *Otuel a Knight*, using the French *Otinel* as the standard for comparison.

Overall, the *Otuel a Knight* poet offers a sanitized version of the narrative: sexual desire between Otuel and Belesent is never specified or hinted at, and Otuel's reprimand of Roland and Oliver lacks the sarcastic bite it carries in the other versions. As a result of these choices, *Otuel a Knight* offers a straightforward celebration of Christians and condemnation of Saracens. Most notably, Belesent is virtually absent in *Otuel a Knight*; the poet seems to have decided either to eliminate scenes in which she was featured, such as the arming scene, or to minimize her role. In the French *Otinel*, a sexual tension between Belisant and the still-unconverted Saracen is palpable, lending credence to Belisant's enthusiastic acceptance of Otinel as her betrothed after his conversion.[3] Also removed is Belesent's eager acceptance of the marriage arrangement. Instead, the marriage is simply discussed by Charlemagne and Otuel, with Charlemagne praising Otuel's decision to defer his nuptials:

| | |
|---|---|
| Tho Otuwel hadde follaught nome | *When; taken baptism* |
| And to the kingges pees was come, | *peace* |
| The king beed him his doughter anon | *offered* |
| And feire londes mani on. | |
| Otuwel to the king saide, | |
| "Sire, keep me wel that maide. | *watch over for me* |
| Forsothe, ich nele hire nevere wedde, | |
| No nevere with hire goo to bedde, | |
| Er thi werre to the ende be brought | |
| And sumwhat of thi wille wrought. | *done deeds according to your will* |
| Whan King Garsie is slawe or take, | |
| Thanne is time mariage to make!" | |
| (lines 647–58) | |

Here, Otuel is depicted as the perfect Christian convert, and he seems almost indifferent to Belesent and marriage until he has proven himself in battle against the Saracens. The poet similarly removes mention of Belesent later in the poem, when the Christian host stages its siege of Ataly. In the French *Otinel*, Belisant is in attendance during the siege and involved in the care of knights in the camp (*Otinel*, lines 1240–47). No such references appear in *Otuel a Knight*. Belesent is not even mentioned again.

The author of this romance likewise removes any references to Saracen women. In the French source, the injured Ogier is taken to Clarel's lover for care, and Alfamie and her maidservants disarm and disrobe Ogier so that they can tend his wounds. Alfamie questions Ogier about his identity before she heals him (*Otinel*, lines 972–87). This scene of conversation and care is omitted in *Otuel a Knight*, replaced by a focus on Ogier's escape from imprisonment, particularly his spectacular performance in fighting off jailers and his clever scheme to convince the porter to open the gate.

*Otuel a Knight* tends to minimize the sarcastic tone that Otinel uses in the French source. The joke disappears from the scene in which Otuel comes to save Roland and Oliver, as

---

[3] Belisant's attraction to Otinel is evident in *Otinel*, lines 361–63, 397–98, 437–41, and 564–86.

Otuel simply encourages Roland and Oliver to turn back toward the battle:

> "Turneth agein anon,
> And helpeth to wreke you on youre fon!   *avenge yourselves; foes*
> Thei sschulle abugge, so mote ich thee,   *pay*
> That maketh you so faste fle!"
> (lines 1061–64)

A rallying cry has replaced the French source's sarcastic jab. The sharp-tongued, swaggering Otuel who arrived in Charlemagne's court at the beginning of the romance is now subdued and replaced by a more mundane, less imaginative killer of Saracens.

When Otuel faces Clarel in a duel near the end of the romance, a glimmer of his acerbic wit surfaces, though once again the poet changes the scene to remove any reference to women or lovemaking. In *Otinel*, when Otinel slices off Clarel's cheek, he sarcastically taunts Clarel that he is now so ugly his paramour will not want to have anything to do with him (*Otinel*, lines 1455–56). When this moment is translated in *Otuel a Knight*, Otuel comments on Clarel's strength and jokes twice about his exposed teeth:

> "Clarel, so mote thou thee,
> Whi scheuwestou thi teth to me?   *Why do you show your teeth to me*
> I nam no toth-drawere!   *tooth-puller*
> Thou ne sest me no cheine bere."   *You don't see me carrying a chain*
> (lines 1325–28)

> "Bi Godes ore,   *mercy*
> Sarazin, thou smitest fol sore!
> Suthen thi berd was ischave,   *Now that your beard has been shaved*
> Thou art woxen a strong knave."   *You have become; young man*
> (lines 1337–40)

Otuel's comment is still mocking, but it omits mention of Clarel's love relationship. As is his wont, the *Otuel a Knight* poet prefers to depict societies, Christian and Saracen, where women are marginal and have negligible roles in anything important.

*Otuel a Knight* is an earnest if slightly clumsy Middle English retelling of the French source. The poet who composed this version makes changes to characters' dialogue, broadly adapts or omits scenes, and shifts the narrative focus to a straightforward report of the events in the romance. He seems reluctant to include anything that might suggest that a Christian could feel unseemly desires or behave in a cowardly manner, focusing instead on glorifying Christians and promoting conversion efforts.

MANUSCRIPT:

Edinburgh, National Library of Scotland MS Advocates 19.2.1 (Auchinleck MS), fols. 268ra–77vb.

FACSIMILES:

Pearsall, Derek, and I. C. Cunningham, eds. *The Auchinleck Manuscript: National Library of Scotland Advocates' MS. 19.2.1*. London: Scolar Press, 1979.

Burnley, David, and Alison Wiggins, eds. *The Auchinleck Manuscript*. National Library of Scotland, 2003. Online at https://auchinleck.nls.uk.

PREVIOUS EDITIONS (IN CHRONOLOGICAL ORDER):
*Otuel*. In *The English Charlemagne Romances. Part VI*. Ed. Sidney J. H. Herrtage. EETS e.s. 39. London: Oxford University Press, 1882. Rpt. 1969. Pp. 65–116.
*Otuel a Kniʒt*. In *The Auchinleck Manuscript*. Ed. David Burnley and Alison Wiggins. National Library of Scotland, 2003. Online at https://auchinleck.nls.uk.

| | | |
|---|---|---|
| fol. 268ra | Herkneth, bothe yinge and olde | |
| | That willen heren of batailles bolde; | *Who; wish to hear* |
| | And ye wolle a while duelle, | *If; abide* |
| | Of bolde batailles ich wole you telle | |
| 5 | That was sumtime bitwene | *once* |
| | Cristine men and Sarazins kene. | *fierce* |
| | There was sumtime a king in France, | |
| | A doughty man with spere and launce, | *valiant* |
| | And made Sarazins ful tame — | |
| 10 | King Charles was his name, | |
| | And was born in Seint-Denys | *Saint-Denis* |
| | Nought bote a litel fram Parys, | *Not far from* |
| | And was a wol treu knight | *well* |
| | And meintenede Cristendom aright. | |
| 15 | In his time, a king ther was, | *During [Charles's] reign* |
| | An hethene that uncristned was, | |
| | That was king of Lumbardie, | *Lombardy* |
| | And was yhoten King Garsie. | *named* |
| | Marsile was his also, | *Marseilles* |
| 20 | And manie other londes mo. | |
| | A swithe gret lord he was; | *such* |
| | In his time non suych ther nas. | *there was none such as him* |
| | On Jhesu Crist ne levede he nought | *did not believe* |
| | That him hadde so dere abought. | |
| 25 | He levede al in maumettrie | *idolatry* |
| | And forsok God and Seinte Marie. | |
| | In alle londes there he wente | *where* |
| | He slough al that evere he hente | *slew; captured* |
| | That wolde on Jhesu Crist bileve, | |
| 30 | And tok the lond to his byheve. | *benefit* |
| | Night and day it was his thout | *intent* |
| | To bringe Cristendom to nout. | |
| | In hethenesse ther nas no king | |
| | That ne hel of him sum thing | *didn't hold some property from him [Garcy]* |
| fol. 268rb | Or dude him omage or feuté. | *paid him tribute; fealty* |
| 36 | Suich a mighty king was he, | *Such* |
| | Alle thei scholden to him bouwe. | *They all had to bow to him* |

|    |                                        |                                    |
|----|----------------------------------------|------------------------------------|
|    | He was lord of londes ynowe,           | *many*                             |
|    | And yit he thoughte wit maistrie       | *yet; with force*                  |
| 40 | Habben al Cristendom to gye.           | *rule all Christendom*             |
|    | Al Cristendom, more and lasse,         | *those both high and low*          |
|    | He thoughte to maken hethennesse.      | *wanted to turn into heathen lands*|
|    |    Whan he wolde haven a parlement, | *hold a council*         |
|    | There com to his comaundement          | *came at his command*              |
| 45 | To helpen hym wit alle thinges         |                                    |
|    | Fiftene hethene kinges,                |                                    |
|    | And alle thei were togidere sworn      | *they all swore together*          |
|    | That Cristendom scholde be lorn,       | *conquered*                        |
|    | And maden alle here ordenaunce         | *made their declaration*           |
| 50 | To werren uppon the king of Fraunce,   | *make war on*                      |
|    | For thei herden alle tidinges          |                                    |
|    | That he was chef of Cristene gynges,   | *people*                           |
|    | And the king wiste it wel.             | *understood*                       |
|    | Nou schulle ye here hou it bifel.      |                                    |
| 55 |    Hit was on Childermasse Day, | *(see note)*               |
|    | Soth to segge withouten nay,           | *True to say*                      |
|    | That King Charles of Sein-Denys        |                                    |
|    | Wente him toward Parys;                |                                    |
|    | Hise duzzeperes with him he nam,       | *His twelve peers; took*           |
| 60 | And muche poeple to him kam.           |                                    |
|    | And token alle here consail thare      | *[they] decided together*          |
|    | That thei wolden withalle fare         | *they would travel at once*        |
|    | Into Marsile riden and gon             |                                    |
|    | And werren there with Godes foon,      | *make war; foes*                   |
| 65 | And hadden set a certein day           |                                    |
|    | To wenden thider withouten delay.      | *go there*                         |
|    | Bote ar thei thiderward ferden,        | *But before they went that way*    |
|    | Suiche tydinges thei herden            | *Such news they heard*             |
|    | Of a Sarasin, doughti and good,        | *From*                             |
| 70 | That amoevede al here blod.            | *stirred their wrath*              |
|    |    There com a Sarazin ful of rage | *came*                  |
|    | Fram King Garsie in message;           | *as a messenger*                   |
|    | Into Paris the wei he nam              |                                    |
|    | And to the kinges paleis he kam.       | *palace*                           |
| 75 | Otuwel his name was,                   |                                    |
|    | Of no man afered he nas.               | *was not afraid of any man*        |
| fol. 268va | Into the paleis tho he cam,      | *then*                             |
|    | A skwier be the hon he nam,            | *He took a squire by the hand*     |
|    | And seide, "Ich am comen her,          |                                    |
| 80 | Kyng Garsies messager,                 |                                    |
|    | To speke with Charles, king of this lond, |                                 |
|    | And with a knight that heet Roulond,   | *is called*                        |
|    | And another hatte Oliver,              |                                    |
|    | Knightes holden withouten peer.        |                                    |

85 Those thre, ich biseche thee,
That thou telle me whiche thei be."
    The skwier thoughte wel by sight          *knew by looking*
That Otuwel was a doughti knight,
And for he was in message come,
90 Bi the hond he haveth him nome          *He took him by the hand*
And ladde him into the halle
Among the grete lordes alle.
And there thei stoden oppon her feet,          *where; their*
He schewede him where the king seet,          *showed; sat*
95 And taughte him hou he scholde knowe,          *told*
There thei seten oppon a rowe,          *Where*
Roulond and Olyver
And the gode knight Ogger.          *Ogier*
    Anon as Otuwel hadde a sight
100 Of Charles that was king and knight,
For eye of no man he ne leet,          *awe; would he hesitate*
Bote wente to him there he seet.
Hit was the boldeste Sarazin          *He*
That evere thorte drinke win,          *dared drink wine*
105 And that was sene, withoute lesing,
Tho he spak with Charles the king.          *When*
He seide to him amydde his halle,
"Sire King, foule mote thee falle!          *may destruction fall upon you*
Thou art aboute for to greve          *enrage*
110 Mahoun that we onne byleve.
Therefore, have thou maugré!          *shame*
So thee greteth Garsie, bi me,          *Thus does Garcy greet you*
That me haveth in message sent
To seggen his comaundement.          *deliver*
115 And thou, Roulond, that art his knight,
Nou ich knowe thee be sight,
May ich mete thee in the feeld
With thi spere and with thi scheld,
Ich wole wyte, so mote ich thee,          *know, as I may thrive*
120 Right bytwene me and te,          *you*
fol. 268vb .........................................
.........................................
.........................................
.........................................
125 .........................................
.........................................
.........................................
.........................................
"That thou makest off this bost,          *[Roland is speaking]; What*
130 Tel me nou, yef thou wost."
Quath Otuwel, "So mote ich thee,

Inelle nought hele for eie of thee.     *I will not hide it; fear*

It was oppon a Weddenesdai

In Averil, before the May,     *April*

135    King Garsie the weie nam,     *took the way*

To the cité of Rome he cam;

Twenti thousende was the sawe     *number*

That were thare of Sarazin lawe.

Corsouse, mi swerde, ful harde fel

140    And bot there Freinche flechs fol wel."     *pierced their French flesh*

    Estught of Leggers, a Freinshe knight,

He sterte op anonright

And kypte anon in his hond     *picked up*

A gret muche fir-brond,     *very large firebrand*

145    And to Otuwel a strok hadde ment,     *intended*

And Roulond bynam him the dent.     *But Roland stopped the blow*

    Thanne seide Charles the king,

"Ich forbede, oppen alle thing,     *upon*

That no man be so wood     *rash*

150    For to don hym other than good!     *anything but*

A kinges messager for he is,     *because*

He ne schal habbe non harm, iwis."     *should not be harmed, certainly*

    "Sire King," quath Otuwel, "be mi blod,

And ani of hem be so wod     *If; them*

155    To drawe to me swerd or knif,

Certes, he schal lesen his lif!"

    The kinges knightes hadden tene     *were enraged*

Of Otuwel wordes kene.

With that word, anonright

160    Op starte a Freinsche knight.     *Up stood*

Bihinden Otuwel he cam,     *came up behind*

And be the hod Otuwel nam     *seized Otuel by the hood*

And braid with so gret might,     *jerked*

And braid adon that hethene knight,     *down*

fol. 269ra    And anon out with a knif,

166    And wolde have reved him his lif.     *taken his life*

And that Sarazin Otuwel

Was iarmed swithe wel

That he ne dede him nought bote good,     *[the French knight] didn't harm [Otuel]*

170    Ne drough of his bodi no blood.

    He starte op and was wroth,

To ligge longe him was loth,     *To hesitate; unwilling*

And Corsouze his brond he drough     *sword*

And the kinges knight he slough,

175    And amang hem alle he stood     *among them*

And lokede as he were wood.     *furious*

The kinges knightes were agramed,     *outraged*

And summe of hem were asschamed     *ashamed*

|     | That Otuwel in the halle |                            |
|-----|--------------------------|----------------------------|
| 180 | Slough a knight among hem alle, |                     |
|     | And bigunnen op to stonden |                          |
|     | And thoughte to leggen on him honden. | *lay hands [i.e., seize]* |
|     | Otuwel therof was war |                                |
|     | And in his herte it him bar | *it seemed to him*          |
| 185 | That thei nere aboute no good, |                      |
|     | And seide to hem, there he stod, | *where*              |
|     | "Bi the louerd, Sire Mahoun, | *lord*                  |
|     | Knightes I rede ye sitten a doun! | *advise*           |
|     | For yef ani of you so hardi be | *if; audacious*        |
| 190 | That any strok munteth to me, | *raise a blow*          |
|     | Mahoun mi God ich here forsake |                       |
|     | Yef he sschal evere ordres take | *holy orders*         |
|     | Of ani other bisschopes hond |                         |
|     | Bot of Corsouze, mi gode brond." | *Except; sword*      |
| 195 | Thei behelden Otuwel alle, |                           |
|     | Knightes and skwieres in the halle; |                  |
|     | Ther nas non that there stood | *were none*             |
|     | That ne wende Otuel were wod. | *failed to understand*  |
|     | And evere he held his swerd ydrawe |                   |
| 200 | And gaf nought of hem alle an hawe. | *held them in contempt* |
|     | King Charles stood upright |                           |
|     | And comaundede anonright |                             |
|     | That no man sscholde be so wod | *foolhardy*            |
|     | To do the messager nought bote good. |               |
| 205 | Knightes and sweines in the halle | *men*              |
|     | Were wol glade therof alle |                           |
|     | That the king so bad, |                                |
|     | For mani of hem was sore adrad, | *sorely afraid*       |
| fol. 269rb | And thei withdrowen hem echone. |                 |
| 210 | And evere stod Otuwel alone |                          |
|     | And biheld hem as thei yede | *walked away*            |
|     | Yef ani him wolde strok dede. | *In case any would strike him dead* |
|     | Thanne seide Charles the king, |                       |
|     | "Bi God that made alle thing, |                        |
| 215 | Sarasin, nere thou messager, | *if you were not*       |
|     | Wrother hele come thou her. | *No good would come to you here* |
|     | I rede thou yeld op thi brond |                        |
|     | And take't out of thin hond." | *give it up*           |
|     | Quath Otuwel that Sarazin, |                           |
| 220 | "Bi Mahoun that is louerd myn, | *my lord*            |
|     | I nelle take it out of min hond | *will not*          |
|     | To no man of al thi lond |                            |
|     | That is therinne geten and bore! | *That is begotten and born therein* |
|     | That wind thou havest ilore." | *You have wasted your breath* |
| 225 | "Sarasin," quath Roulond, |                            |

|  |  |  |
|---|---|---|
|  | "Tak me thi swerd in myn hond, | *Give me* |
|  | And iche wole save thee, bi mi blod — |  |
|  | Sschal no man do thee nought bote good. |  |
|  | And whan thou art redi to fare, | *ready to depart* |
| 230 | Forsothe, thi swerd sschal be yare." | *In truth; ready* |
|  | Quath Otuwel the Sarazin, |  |
|  | "Bi Mahoun that is louerd min, |  |
|  | Thaugh ich hadde skwieres twelve, | *Even if* |
|  | Ich wole bere myn swerd miselve! |  |
| 235 | Holte o roum, ich wolde rede, | *Stand back* |
|  | And thanne dostou a god dede." | *You'll have done a good deed* |
|  | "Sarazin," quath Charles the King, |  |
|  | "Let ben al thi thretning. | *Stop* |
|  | Tel me nou, alle and some, |  |
| 240 | In what message artou come." |  |
|  | Otuwel that noble knight |  |
|  | Answerede anonright, |  |
|  | "Hider me sente King Garsie. |  |
|  | Spaine is his, an Lumbardie, |  |
| 245 | And manye londes name couthe | *well renowned lands* |
|  | That I ne mai nought nemne with mouthe. | *name* |
|  | Bi me he sente thee to segge, |  |
|  | Thou sscholdest Cristendom alegge | *denounce* |
|  | And maken thine men in eche toun |  |
| 250 | For to leven on Sire Mahoun, | *believe in* |
|  | And thou and alle thine barons bolde. |  |
|  | Of him ye sschulle youre londes holde, |  |
| fol. 269va | Thanne mightou amenden, yif thou wilt, | *make amends* |
|  | That thou havest Mahoun agult. | *wronged* |
| 255 | And, certes, bote it so bifalle, | *if you do not do this* |
|  | Garsie wele give thine londes alle | *will* |
|  | To Olecent of Esclavenye, | *Slovenia* |
|  | The kinges sone of Ermenie, | *Armenia* |
|  | That haveth his o doughter to wif, | *own* |
| 260 | That he loveth as his lif. |  |
|  | Thous sschal al thi murthe adoun, | *happiness decline* |
|  | Bote thou leve on Sire Mahoun." | *Unless; believe* |
|  | The duzzepieres answerede tho, | *then* |
|  | "Certes, while we moun ride and go, | *can ride and walk* |
| 265 | Fraunse sschal he nevere give |  |
|  | To no man while we moun live. |  |
|  | Sire King, his wille nou thou wost, | *know* |
|  | Let asemblen al thin ost, | *army* |
|  | And let us oppon Garsie wenden, | *attack* |
| 270 | Alle hise londes for to sschenden, | *ruin* |
|  | Of wordes that he haveth ispeke. | *[Because] of* |
|  | Forsothe, we reden thou be awreke!" | *advise you to seek revenge* |

   "Certes, Sire King," quath Otuwel,

   "Thine Freinsche knightes kune yelpe wel,      *can yelp*

275 And whan thei beth to werre ibrought,

   Thanne be thei right nought.        *are worthless*

    Thaugh thou bringe with sscheld and spere   *Even if*

   Al that evere may wepene bere

   To werren upon King Garsie,

280 Certes, alle thei sscholden deie.

   And thou art king and old knight,      *Because*

   And havest iloren al thi might,

   And in thi yiukthe, tak god hede,       *youth*

   Thou nere nevere doughti of dede!"   *You were never brave in battle*

285   Tho was the king agramed,        *outraged*

   And alle hise duzzeperes asschamed

   That Otuwel, that hethene knight,

   Tolde of hem alle so light.       *Belittled all of them*

    Roulond bi the king stood

290 And amevede al his blod,        *became enraged*

   And seide in wrathe anonright

   To Otuwel that hethene knight,

   "To werren on Garsie, yef we fare

   In bataille, and I mete thee thare

295 And I may mete thee aright,

   Bi Jhesu that is ful of might,

fol. 269vb Thou ne sschalt nevere after that day

   Despice Freinchsman, yef ich may."   *Disparage Frenchmen*

    "Ough," quath Otuwel, and lough,     *laughed*

300 "Wherto makestou it so tough

   To threte me in another lond?

   Nam ich here at thin hond?       *Am I not here*

   Yef thou havest wille to fighte,

   Whanevere thou wolt let thee dighte,     *make ready*

305 And thou sschalt finde me redi dight,     *prepared*

   In the feld to bide fight."       *waiting for*

    "Bi God," quath Roulond, "Ich wolde be yare,

   Whan ich wiste to finde thee thare,

   And evele mote he thrive and thee    *may he have bad luck*

310 That ferst failleth of me and te."     *between me and you*

    "Ye leve ya," quath Otuwel tho,      *As you say*

   "Whether so failleth of us two,       *Whoever*

   Ich wole finde Mahoun to borwe.    *Mahoun will be my surety*

   Ich wile be redi erliche tomorwe."

315   Quath Roulond thar he stod on grounde,

   "S'elpe me Gode, feere ifounde!"   *So help me God, I've found a match*

   Right before the kinges eien,       *eyes*

   That alle the kinges knightes seien,     *see*

   Either other his trewthe plighte     *swear an oath*

| | | |
|---|---|---|
| 320 | Uppon morwen for to fighte. | |
| | King Charles stod al stille | |
| | And biheld his gode wille, | *[Otuel's] resolve* |
| | And seide, "It is harm, iwis, | *truly a shame* |
| | That thou nost what follaut is. | *do not know; baptism* |
| 325 | Yef thou woldes follaut take | |
| | And thine false godes forsake, | *false* |
| | Ichc wolle maketh, so mote ihc thee — | *as I may thrive* |
| | And tou wille bleve with me — | *If you* |
| | A riche man in mi lond. | |
| 330 | That ich wille sikere thee on hond." | *promise* |
| | Otuwel that hardi knight | |
| | Answerede anonright, | |
| | "Cristes cors uppon his heued | *Christ's curse upon his head* |
| | That me radde such a red, | *Who advises me such a thing* |
| 335 | To forsake mi god Mahun! | |
| | Inelle nought leve thi false sarmon." | *I will not* |
| | Thaugh Otuwel speke outrage, | *spoke outrageously* |
| | For he was comen on message, | *Because* |
| | King Charles, that was heende and god, | *noble and good* |
| 340 | Nolde soffre him habbe nought bote god, | *Would not allow him to be harmed* |
| | Bote seide to him anonright, | |
| | "Be thou skwier? Be thou knight? | *Are you* |
| fol. 270ra | Tel me, yef thi conseil is nome, | *message is finished* |
| | Of what linage thou art come." | |
| 345 | Otuwel answerede this, | |
| | "A kinges sone ich am, iwis, | *truly* |
| | Soth to segge and nought to lye. | *True to say; it is no lie* |
| | Ich am the kinges cosin, Garsie. | *(see note)* |
| | Fernagu myn eem was, | *uncle* |
| 350 | That nevere overcomen nas. | *Who had never been overcome* |
| | Sir Roulond, thi cosin, him slough. | |
| | Therefore wole rise wo inough. | *Because of this, there will be woe* |
| | Therefore ich desire so moche | |
| | To fighte with Roulond sikerliche. | |
| 355 | Ich wille tomorewen, in the day, | |
| | Awreken his deth yef ich may. | *Avenge [Fernagu's] death* |
| | Nou he haveth iseid his sawe, | *has promised* |
| | That he ne mai him nought withdrawe | |
| | That we schule bothe fighten ifeere, | |
| 360 | Nou ich wille that thou it here: | *hear* |
| | Min emes deth ich awreke, | *I will avenge my uncle's death* |
| | Or myn herte sschal tobreke!" | *break* |
| | King Charle gan to meven his blod, | *grew enraged* |
| | Bot natheles he was hende and good, | *nonetheless* |
| 365 | And nolde for hise wordes heghe | *would not because of; haughty* |
| | Don Otuel no vileinie, | |

Bote comaundede anon a swein                                  *attendant*
Gon fechen him his chaumberlein,                    *To fetch his attendant*
A ying knight ant nought old,                                     *young*
370    That was wel norssched and bold,                      *nourished*
And seide to him, "Sire Reiner,
Tak here this messeger
And to his in saveliche him lede,                             *inn safely*
That for no word ne for no dede
375    That he haveth don and seid
That non hond be on him leid;
And loke that he be wel idight                              *well cared for*
And onoured als a knight."                                   *honored as*
        The chamberlein anon dede
380    Als the king him hadde ibede,                           *bidden*
And ladde him hom to his in.
And whan he was icomen in,                                *had come in*
He tok his leve the chamberlein                     *The chamberlain left*
And wente to the king agein.
385    Littel slep the king that night,
For ferd of Roulant that gode knight
fol. 270rb    Of the bataille he hadde inome                *agreed to*
Leste he were overcome.
For the king hadde sein fol wel                             *Because*
390    The kuntenaunse of Otuel,                  *appearance (countenance)*
The king wiste wel afin                               *knew completely*
Hit was a bold Sarazin,                                          *He*
For he saugh hit wel by sight
Tho he saugh him slen his knight.                            *When*
395        On morwe tho the dai sprong,                   *In the morning*
And the larke bigan hire song,                                   *its*
King Charles wente to cherche                               *church*
Godes werkes for to werche.                            *To do God's work*
Roulond his cosin with him yede,
400    Of Godes help that hadde nede.
Thei wenten anon to here masse                            *hear mass*
For here sinnen sscholde be the lasse.            *To lessen their sin*
        Tho the masse was iseid                                *Then*
And the vestement doun ileid,
405    The king and Roulond ifere                           *together*
Wente forth, as ye moun here,
Right to the paleis gate,                                      *palace*
And founde hovinge therate                            *standing there*
Otuel, armed and idight,
410    Al redi to bide fight.
Tho seide that Sarazin,                                         *Then*
"Sire King, where is thi cosin
Roulond, that his truthe plighte

|     |                                           |                                  |
|-----|-------------------------------------------|----------------------------------|
|     | That he wolde with me fighte?             |                                  |
| 415 | He was tho fol heie of mod,               | *very haughty*                   |
|     | Is he nou ilete blod?"                    | *feeling weak*                   |
|     | Roulond stod al and herde                 |                                  |
|     | Hou Otuel toward him ferde,               | *acted toward him*               |
|     | And answerede anonright:                  |                                  |
| 420 | "By Jhesu that is fol of might,           |                                  |
|     | Thin heued sschal fele under thin hood    | *Your head will feel under your hood* |
|     | That I nam nought laten blood."           |                                  |
|     | "Welcome be thou," quath Otuwel tho,      | *then*                           |
|     | And turnde his stede and made him go,     |                                  |
| 425 | And to the place tho rod he               |                                  |
|     | There the bataille sscholde be.           | *Where; would*                   |
|     | Al aboute the water ran.                  | *The river flowed all around [it]* |
|     | Ther nas nother man ne wimman             | *woman*                          |
|     | That mighte in riden no gon               | *ride in nor leave*              |
| 430 | At no stede bote at on.                   | *one [entry]*                    |
| fol. 270va | And there Otuwel in rood,          |                                  |
|     | No lengere he ne abood.                    |                                  |
|     | Roulond that doughti knight                |                                  |
|     | Was fol hasteliche idight                  | *hastily prepared*               |
| 435 | And his stede he bistrod,                  | *mounted his steed*              |
|     | And no lengere he ne abood.                |                                  |
|     | Er the dai idon it were,                   |                                  |
|     | Ther thei sschollen fighten ifere.         | *each other*                     |
|     | Anon als Roulond beheeld                   |                                  |
| 440 | Otuwel hovede in the feel,                 | *mounted; field*                 |
|     | Roulond was so egre to fighte              |                                  |
|     | That for al the world he ne mighte         |                                  |
|     | Abide to riden in at the gate              |                                  |
|     | There Otuwel rod in ate.                   | *To where Otuel rode*            |
| 445 | He thoute the nekste weie to ride          | *chose; closest path*            |
|     | And no lengere he nolde abide.             |                                  |
|     | He smot his stede with spores brighte,     | *struck; spurs*                  |
|     | And with help of Godes mighte,             |                                  |
|     | Over the water the stede swam,             |                                  |
| 450 | And to londe saf he cam.                    |                                  |
|     | Anonright, als Roulond                      |                                  |
|     | Hadde ikaught the druye lond,               | *achieved; dry land*             |
|     | Gret envye was ham betwene.                 | *enmity*                         |
|     | Thei riden togidere with speres kene,       | *sharp*                          |
| 455 | That were sterne and nought longe,          | *sturdy*                         |
|     | And the knightes were bothe stronge,        |                                  |
|     | And smyten either in otheres sscheld        | *hit each other*                 |
|     | That bothe hors fellen in the feld,         | *[So that]*                      |
|     | And risen agein op fram the grounde;        | *[When they had]*                |
| 460 | And bothe knightes were hole and sounde.    | *uninjured*                      |

|  |  |  |
|---|---|---|
| | Tho the stedes were risen bothe, | *When the steeds were both standing* |
| | The knightes woxen bothe fol wrothe | |
| | And drowen swerdes ate laste, | |
| | And either hugh on other faste. | *cut each other* |
| 465 | Roulond to Otuwel smot | |
| | A strok that fol sore bot. | *bit hard* |
| | He wolde have smiten Otuwel, | |
| | And he blenkte swithe wel. | *But; dodged it well* |
| | And Roulond smot the stede broun | |
| 470 | And clef the heued al adoun, | *cut off its head* |
| | And the stede fel to grounde, | |
| | Bote Otuwel was hol and sounde. | |
| | Roulond was hende and good of wille | |
| | And hovede oppon his stede stille. | *remained* |
| fol. 270vb | To smiten made he semblant non | *He made no move to strike* |
| 476 | Er Otuwel was risen and gon. | *Before* |
| | "Roulond," quath Otuwel, "What was thee? | *What are you* |
| | Art tou blynd? Mightou nought se? | |
| | Wil ich oppon mi stede sat, | *While; sat upon my steed* |
| 480 | Whi sscholde mi stede habbe that? | *have this treatment* |
| | It hadde be more honour to thee, | |
| | Forsothe, to habbe ismite me." | |
| | "Ough," quath Roulond, "Blame me nought! | |
| | Bi Sen Geme, ich habbe isought, | *James, that's what I intended* |
| 485 | Otuwel, ich hadde yment | |
| | That thou sscholdest have ifeled that dent. | *felt; blow* |
| | Ich hadde wel levere, so mote ich thee, | *I would rather, so I may thrive* |
| | Otuwel, habbe yoven it thee." | *had it hit you* |
| | Otuwel was wroth his stede was slawe, | |
| 490 | And with his swerd he bar idrawe, | |
| | He smot to Roulond with good wille | |
| | That ovede oppon his stede stille. | *remained* |
| | That he hadde Roulond ment, | *He had intended that for Roland* |
| | And he failede of his dent | *But* |
| 495 | And smot Roulondes gode stede, | |
| | That nevere eft on erthe hene yede. | *never after walked the earth* |
| | Otuwel thoute, on errore deede, | *upon his mistake* |
| | Tho he hadde slawe his stede, | *When* |
| | Hou Roulond hovede stille as ston | |
| 500 | Til he was risen and gon; | *Until he [Otuel]* |
| | And he stod al stille | *And [therefore]* |
| | And leet Roulond risen at wille, | |
| | And seide, "Roulond, so mote ich thee, | |
| | That strok ich mente to thee, | |
| 505 | And nou it is on thi stede istunt. | *it fell on your steed* |
| | Let nou stonde, dunt for dunt!" | |
| | Tho thei sien non other bote, | *Then; no other option* |

Thei wenten togidere al on fote

And strokes yeden bitwene ham so kene        *exchanged*

510    That the fer sprong out bitwene.        *sparks flew*

      King Charles with hise knightes bolde

Was come the bataille to biholde,

And bisoughte God, fol of might,

He sscholde save Roulond his knight.

515       Bothe knightes were gode and stronge

And foughten togidere swithe longe.

Roulond was a hende knight,        *skilled*

And feled that Otuwel smot aright        *felt*

fol. 271ra   And that myght was in his arm,        *strength*

520    And thoute to saven him fram harm,        *himself*

And seide, "Otuwel, let thi fight!        *halt*

And leve on Jhesu, ful of might,        *believe in*

And ich wele ben at acent        *in assent*

That thou sschalt wedde Belecent,

525    The kinges doughter, mi nese, that is.        *niece*

I rede, Otuwel, that thou do this."

      Quath Otuwel to Roulond,

"Whil my swerd is in min hond,

Al thi preching is for nought;

530    Hit ne cam nevere in my thout.

Me ne stant nought of thee swich awe        *I do not fear you so much*

That thou sschalt make me reneie mi lawe        *abandon my faith*

For to wedde Belecent.

So nis nought mi wille iwent."        *This is not what I want*

535       Tho thei ne mighte nought acente,        *Because; agree*

Agein to bataille thei wente,

And foughten harde togidere beie;        *both*

Never on of other ne stod eie.        *had any fear*

      Roulond bigan to meven his blood

540    That Otuwel so longe stood,

And fortene up with the brond        *thrust*

That he bar in his hond,

And in the heued he thoute to redde        *head; planned to strike*

Otuwel, bote nought he ne spedde.        *did not succeed*

545    Otuwel starte o side        *shifted to the side*

And lette the swerd bi him glide.

And Roulond with the swerdes ende

Reighte Otuwel oppon the lende.        *Struck; hip*

Als he wolde the dent fle,        *Because he wished to avoid*

550    Otuwel fel on kne.

      Otuwel asschamed was

That he knelede oppon the gras,

And for anger his herte gan sswelle

And thoughte Roulond for to quelle.        *kill*

| | | |
|---|---|---|
| 555 | In the heued he hadde him ment, | |
| | Bote Roulond bleinte for the dent, | *swerved away from* |
| | As swete Jhesu Crist wolde | |
| | That Roulond there deie ne sscholde. | |
| | Biside the heued the dent wente, | |
| 560 | And the hauberk he torente | *chain mail coat; tore* |
| | Fram the hepebon an heigh, | *hip bone at once* |
| | That alle the pece out fleigh. | *pieces flew apart* |
| fol. 271rb | King Charles saugh there he stood, | *from where* |
| | And was fol dreri in his mood, | *apprehensive* |
| 565 | And was swithe sore afright | |
| | To lese Roulond his gode knight. | |
| | For Otuwel smot so heterliche, | *hotly* |
| | The king wende sikerliche | *thought certainly* |
| | That Roulond sscholde been ylore, | *would be lost* |
| 570 | And was a sori man therefore. | |
| | As the king stod in doute, | *doubt* |
| | He spak to his folk aboute, | |
| | And seide to alle that there were, | |
| | "Lordinges, doth as ich you lere: | *do as I ask* |
| 575 | Sitte eche man oppon his kne | *Kneel* |
| | And biddeth to God in Trinité, | *pray* |
| | For His grace and for Hise mightes, | |
| | Sende seightnesse bitwene tho knightes, | *reconciliation; those* |
| | And give Otuwel wille today | *desire* |
| 580 | For to reneien his lay. | *renounce his faith* |
| | Everichone thei token here red, | *obeyed their command* |
| | And deden as the king ham bed. | |
| | To Jhesu Crist thei deden here bone, | *made their request* |
| | And swete Jhesu herde ham sone. | *them straightaway* |
| 585 | A whit colvere ther cam fle | *white dove* |
| | That al the peple mighten se, | |
| | On Otuweles heued he lighte, | *alighted* |
| | Thoru the vertu of Godes mighte. | |
| | And Otuwel, that doughti knight, | |
| 590 | Withdrough him anoonright | |
| | Fram Roulond, and stod al stille; | |
| | To fighte more he ne hadde wille, | |
| | And seide, "Roulond, thou smitest fol sore. | |
| | Withdrau thin hond and smight namore. | |
| 595 | Yef thou wolt holden that thou me het, | *to what you promised* |
| | That I sschal wedde that maiden swet, | |
| | The kinges doughter Belesent, | |
| | Forsothe, than is mi wille went. | |
| | Yef I sschal wedden that faire may, | *maiden* |
| 600 | Ich wille bileven oppon thi lay, | |
| | And alle myne godes forsake, | |

|        | And to youre God ich wille take." | *accept* |
|--------|--------|--------|
|        | Roulond likede that word fol wel, | |
|        | And answerede Otuwel, | |
| 605    | "I thonke it Jhesu ful of might, | |
|        | Thorou wham that grace is in thee light!" | *Through whom; entered* |
| fol. 271va | Otuel caste of his hond | *out of* |
|        | Corsouse, his gode brond, | |
|        | And Roulond his also, | |
| 610    | And togidere thei gune go. | |
|        | Eyther forgaf other his loth, | *hatred* |
|        | Nas non of hem with other wroth, | *angry* |
|        | Bote clippe and kusse eyther other | *embraced; kissed* |
|        | As either hedde been otheres brother. | |
| 615    | King Charles rood thidere anon, | |
|        | And knightes with him many on. | *many a one* |
|        | Anon as he thider cam | |
|        | Bi the hon Roulond he nam, | *hand; took* |
|        | And seide, "Roulond, for Godes erthe, | |
| 620    | Hou is thee and this man iwurthe? | *reconciled* |
|        | So harde strokes as ye habben give, | |
|        | Hit is wunder that ye live!" | |
|        | "Sire," quath Roulond, "We beth al sounde, | |
|        | Nother of us ne haveth wounde. | |
| 625    | Otuwel haveth his conseil nome | *taken* |
|        | That he wile Cristene bycome, | |
|        | And ich habbe granted, bi youre acent, | |
|        | That he sschal wedde Belecent." | |
|        | "Certes!" quath Charles tho, | |
| 630    | "Nou thou wolt that it be so, | |
|        | I grante wel that it so be. | |
|        | Forwhi that he wille dwelle with me, | *If* |
|        | Thanne hadde ich thee and Oliver, | *I have* |
|        | Otuwel and gode Ogger; | |
| 635    | In al the world in lenkthe and brede | *length and breadth* |
|        | Ther nis king that nolde me drede." | |
|        | The king took Otuwel anon | |
|        | And to his paleis made him gon, | |
|        | And makeden murthe and meloudie | |
| 640    | Of alle maner of menestrausie | *minstrelsy* |
|        | For the miracle that was wrought: | |
|        | That Otuwel hadde iturnd his thought. | *changed* |
|        | On moruen tho the day was bright, | *morning when* |
|        | Thei ladden to churche that noble knight. | |
| 645    | Bisschop Turpin was bisschop tho, | *then* |
|        | He follede him that day, and nammo. | *baptized; no others* |
|        | Tho Otuwel hadde follaught nome | *When; taken baptism* |
|        | And to the kingges pees was come, | *peace* |

|   |   |   |
|---|---|---|
|  | The king beed him his doughter anon | *offered* |
| 650 | And feire londes mani on. | |
| fol. 271vb |     Otuwel to the king saide, | |
|  | "Sire, keep me wel that maide. | *watch over for me* |
|  | Forsothe, ich nele hire nevere wedde, | |
|  | No nevere with hire goo to bedde, | |
| 655 | Er thi werre to the ende be brought | |
|  | And sumwhat of thi wille wrought. | *done deeds according to your will* |
|  | Whan King Garsie is slawe or take, | |
|  | Thanne is time mariage to make!" | |
|  |     Quath King Charles to Otuwel, | |
| 660 | "Nou I se thou lovest me wel, | |
|  | And yef I leve, so mote I thee, | *as I believe* |
|  | Thou ne sschalt nought lese thi love on me." | *waste* |
|  |     Tho leet the king asemblen anon | *ordered to be assembled* |
|  | Alle hise duzzeperes, echon. | |
| 665 | "Lordinges," he seide, "What is youre red? | *advice* |
|  | King Garsie seith I sschal be ded, | |
|  | And as ye habbeth iherd segge, | *heard spoken* |
|  | He thenketh Cristendam to legge — | *conquer* |
|  | Whether wole we wenden oppon him anon, | *ought to* |
| 670 | Other abide til winter be gon?" | *Or* |
|  | The duzzeperes acentenden therto | *agreed* |
|  | To bide til winter were ido. | |
|  | And alle winter the king of Fraunce | |
|  | Lette maken his purveianse. | *preparations* |
| 675 | Al that winter at hom he bod, | |
|  | And in somer to werre he rod. | |

*        *        *

|   |   |   |
|---|---|---|
|  | Lordinges, bothe yinge and olde, | |
|  | Herneth as we formest tolde, | *Listen; first* |
|  | Hou the werre was fol hyghe | *intense* |
| 680 | Bitwene King Charles and King Garsie. | |
|  | Anon as winter was ygon, | *As soon as* |
|  | The king asemblede his host anon, | |
|  | And mochel peple cam to his bond | *many; because of their pledge to him* |
|  | Out of mani diverse lond. | |
| 685 | Averil was comen an winter gon, | *April* |
|  | And Charles tok the weie anon | |
|  | And drough him toward Lumbardie | *went towards* |
|  | To werren oppon King Garsie. | |
|  | There was set, withouten faille, | |
| 690 | Certein day of bataille. | |
|  |     Anoon as Charles was icome | |
|  | Nigh honde thar the bataille was nome, | *Near at hand; to be undertaken* |

|              | In a mede anonright | *meadow* |
|---|---|---|
|              | The kinges pavilons were ipight | *pavilions; pitched* |
| fol. 272ra   | Under an hul bisides a rivere; | *hill* |
| 696          | And bifel as ye moun here. | *[it] happened* |
|              | Fol nygh the water the king lay | *Close to* |
|              | Of bataille forto abide his day, | *To await the day of battle* |
|              | And uppon that other side | |
| 700          | He mighte seen hise enemis ride, | |
|              | And there nas brugge ne forde non | *bridge; ford* |
|              | That man mighte over riden ne gon. | |
|              | King Charles that gode knight | |
|              | Tok carpenters anonright | |
| 705          | And lette make a brugge anon | |
|              | That men mighten over gon. | |
|              | Tho the brugge was al yare | *When; ready* |
|              | That men mighten over fare, | |
|              | Hit bitidde uppon a day | |
| 710          | Wil Charles in his bed lay, | *While* |
|              | That Roulond an Oliver | |
|              | And the gode knight Oger | |
|              | Over the brugge thei wenten ifeere | |
|              | Auntres for to sen and here. | *Adventures* |
| 715          | And tho thei over passed were, | *when* |
|              | Suche auntres thei funden there | |
|              | For al the good under sonne | |
|              | Thei nolde habben the gamen bigonne. | *That they would not have begun the game* |
|              | Of Garsies ost, foure hethene kinges | |
| 720          | Wenten forte here tidinges | |
|              | For alle cas that mighte bitide, | *what might be happening* |
|              | Wel iarmed bataille to bide. | |
|              | Here foure names ye moun wite | *Their; know* |
|              | As we finden in romaunse write: | |
| 725          | Curabeles hatte thet o king, | *was called the first king* |
|              | A stout Sarazin withouten lesing; | |
|              | That other Balsamun het, | *was called* |
|              | A werse man yede non on fet; | *walked never on foot* |
|              | Astaward was the thriddes name, | *third's* |
| 730          | He lovede werre and hatede game; | *merriment* |
|              | The ferthe king highte Clarel, | |
|              | That nevere yite ne dede wel. | *had done a good deed* |
|              | As thei riden alle yfere, | |
|              | That on seide as ye moun here, | |
| 735          | "Mahoun, leeve ous yit abide | *let it happen to us* |
|              | Into Fraunce that we moun ride | |
|              | And ich mighte Roulond mete; | *If* |
|              | Al with wrathe ich wolde him grete. | |
| fol. 272rb   | That traitour he slough mi brother, | |

| | | |
|---|---|---|
| 740 | Ne gete ich neve eft such another." | *I'll never have* |
| | Roulond herde, and Oliver | |
| | And the gode knight Ogger, | |
| | Hou thei speken hare wordes highe | *proud* |
| | And thratten Roulond to die; | *threatened* |
| 745 | And Roulond was so nygh | *near* |
| | That alle foure kinges he sygh. | *saw* |
| | "Felawes," quath Roulond anon, | *Fellows* |
| | "Yich am war of oure fon. | *aware; foes* |
| | Thei beth foure, and we bote thre. | |
| 750 | Datheit habbe that hem fle! | *Curses* |
| | Nou we habben founden game; | |
| | Ga we to hem, a Godes name." | *Let's go* |
| | Anon as Clarel ham sygh, | *saw them* |
| | He seide, "Oure enemys beth nygh. | |
| 755 | Ich se bi here cuntenaunse | *appearance* |
| | Thei beth Cristene men of Fraunce. | |
| | Charles ost lith here biside | *host* |
| | In pavilons, bataille to bide, | |
| | And these beth of hise men, iwis; | |
| 760 | Therfore mi reed is tis — | *advice* |
| | That we hasteliche to ham ride | |
| | And loke whether thei wole abide." | *meet* |
| | With that word the kinges anon | |
| | Touchede here stedes and made hem gon, | *Spurred their* |
| 765 | And toward the Cristene knightes thei riden, | |
| | And thei doughtiliche abiden. | |
| | Astaward with Roulond mette, | |
| | Nought he ne spak, ne him ne grette, | *greeted* |
| | Bot smot him with his spere anon, | |
| 770 | Thorou the sscheld he made hit gon. | |
| | And Roulondes spere, ywis, | |
| | Was wel betere than was his; | *[Astaward's]* |
| | To Astawardes herte hit yede, | *heart it went* |
| | And caste him doun off his stede. | |
| 775 | "Aris," quath Roulond, "and tak thee bet; | *accept your defeat* |
| | At this time thou art ilet." | *defeated* |
| | Curabeles no lengere ne abood; | |
| | To god Ogger anon he rod. | |
| | Ogger was a strong knight | |
| 780 | And rod to him with gret might, | |
| | And bar adon hors and pak | *packsaddle* |
| | And the Sarazins nekke tobrak. | *broke* |
| fol. 272va | Balsamum and Oliver, | |
| | Eyther neighede other ner. | |
| 785 | Tho Balsamun bigan to ride, | *When* |
| | Oliver nolde no lengere abide. | |

He pingde his stede with spores kene,                    *pricked; sharp spurs*
And smot a strok that was sene;
He ne mighte tho no bette do,                    *could not have done better*
790    Bote gurde the nekke bon otwo.                    *cut; in two*
        Thus Roulond and Oliver
And the gode knight Ogger
Slouwen the hethene kinges thre,
And yit nolde nought Clarel fle.
795    To the Duk Roulond he rood,
And Roulond his strok abod.
For wrathe hise felaus were islein,                    *[Clarel's]*
He rood to Roulond with gret mayn,                    *force*
And bar a spere, greet and long.
800    And the Sarazin was strong
And in the sadel sat faste,
And Roulond to grounde he kaste.
With the fal the steede anoon,
Tobarst that o sschanke bon.                    *one leg bone*
805    Roulond uppon his feet stood,
And ne hadde nought bote good.                    *was unharmed*
        Ogger saugh fol wel tho                    *then*
That Roulondes hors was ago.                    *gone*
Ogger that was doughti of dede
810    Smot doun Clarel off his stede.
Oliver tok the stede anon
And to Roulond he gan gon.
"Roulond, have this," quath Oliver,
"This thee sente good Ogger,
815    And Clarel he haveth to grounde ithrowe
For he broughte thee so lowe."
        Roulond that hadde his stede ilore                    *lost*
Thonkede hem bothe therfore,
And was the gladdeste man under sonne
820    That he hadde an hors iwonne.
        Clarel uppon his feet stood
And faught as he were wood.
On none maner he nolde fle,
Bot faught agein hem alle thre.
825    The thre knightes were fol strong;
He ne mighte nought dure agein ham longe,
fol. 272vb And seide to hem alle thre,
"Lordinges, let me olive be!                    *alive*
To you it were lutel honour
830    To sle me that nabbe no socour!"                    *has no aid*
To fighte more he forsook,                    *refused*
And Roulond his swerd tok.
Roulond was hende and nought forsok,                    *did not refuse*

And of Clarel his swerd he tok.

835       "King Clarel," quath Ogger,

"Worth up bihinden me her."                  *Mount up behind*

Tho was King Clarel glad

For to do that Ogger bad,

And was staleworthe and light           *able-bodied; agile*

840    And lep up anonright.                      *leapt up*

Tho wenten thei forth withouten targing,          *delay*

And thoute presente Charles the king

With Clarel that thei hadden inome,            *captured*

And hopeden to ben welcome.              *hoped to be*

845    And of here weie thei were let,          *But; hindered*

And swithe harde thei were met.

Thei sien of Garsies men afeerd,           *were afraid of*

Bothe with spere and with swerd,

Bitwen hem and the paviloun,

850    There thei sscholden wenden adoun.     *Where they had to go*

Thei ne mighte skapen in nevere a side;    *escape by either side*

Thoruout hem thei mosten ride.     *But had to ride through them*

       "Felawes," quath Ogger tho               *then*

To Roulond and Oliver bo,                    *both*

855    "Ich wene er we hom come,            *before; home*

Clarel ous worth bynome,         *will cause us to be seized*

Lordinges, what is nou youre red?           *opinion*

Wole we smiten of his hed?"           *Should we; off*

       Quath Roulond, "So mote ich thee,

860    At that red nel ich nought be."    *I would not be guilty of that*

"No, ich nother," quat Oliver,

"Bi the Louerd Sein Richer,           *Saint Richerus*

On live I rede we leten him go,            *Alive*

And ne do we him nammore wo.          *no more woe*

865    Such cas may fallen in sum neede,       *It may occur*

He mai quiten us oure mede."        *repay; kindness*

       "Bi God," quath Ogger, "that is soth,      *true*

And where he do or he ne doth,    *But whether he does or he does not*

Hit were sschame to ous, iwis,

870    To sslen a man that yolden him is.    *slay; has yielded himself*

fol. 273ra  I rede we leten him gon his wey,

For we mot entenden to another pley."   *must attend; matter*

       Alle thre thei were at on,          *in agreement*

And leten Clarel on live gon.

875    Clarel nolde no lengere abide,

He ne askede non hors onne to ride,

Bote on fote dede him go

And levede hem thare in muchel wo.        *left*

       "Nou, lordinges," quath Ogger

880    To Roulond and to Oliver,

"Ich wole triste to my sswerd
And fonde forto passe this ferd.                                      *attempt; escape this danger*
Ich hope thoru help of Godes might
To se mi lord Charles this night.
885    Yef ani Sarazin with eie                                             *If; wrath*
Cometh to lette me of mi weie,                                    *stop me on my way*
S'elp me God and this day,                                               *So help me*
He sschal abugge, yef ich may!"                                          *pay for it*
            "Nou," quath Roulond, that doughti knight,
890    "And ich wille helpe thee, bi mi might!
I nele today, bi Sein Martin,                                           *I will not*
Yilde me to no Sarazin."                                              *Yield; any*
            Quath Oliver, "So mote ich thee,
In mani peril ich habbe ibe,
895    And yef ich faille at this nede,
God ne lete me nevere eft spede.                            *never give me success again*
I nele, yef God halt me sound,                                          *uninjured*
Today yelde me to non hound!"
            Thei markeden hem alle thre                               *crossed themselves*
900    To Him that tho lede deth on tre,                             *once suffered*
And no lengere thei ne abiden;
Anon into the ferde thei riden.                                          *battle*
            A Sarazin with Roulond mette,
And of his weie Roulond lette.
905    He cam out of al the here,                                           *host*
And bar to Roulond a gret spere.
A bold knight that hatte Byoun,                                        *was named*
An Roulond bar him adoun.
            Oliver that was his brother,
910    He mette with another,
A doughti knight, an hethene man,
A strong thef that heet Bassan.                                           *thief*
Oliver was horsed wel
And bar a spere, kene and fel,                                    *sharp and fierce*
fol. 273rb    And smot him right under the sscheld,
916    That there he lay amidde the feld.                                   *So that*
            And the gode knight Ogger
Mette with on that heet Moter                                              *one*
And wolde him habbe doun ibore;
920    And Ogger was wroth tharfore,
And smot the Sarazin so sore
That he ne spak neveremore.
            Oliver, Ogger, and Roulond
Among the Sarazins stureden here hond                          *wielded their hands*
925    Thoru help of God that is above,
That ham hadde that grace iyove,                                         *given*
Thorou the ferd as thei riden,

|       | Alle that here strokes abiden | received |
|       | Thei were maimed foreveremore; |
| 930   | The doughti knightes thei smiten so sore |
|       | That withinne a litel stounde | short time |
|       | Thei felden mani on to grounde. |
|       | Tho cam a soudan, stout and firs, | Then; sultan; fierce |
|       | On of Garsies duzzepeers | One |
| 935   | That hatte Karmel of Tabarie. |
|       | Oppon the Sarasins he gan crie, |
|       | "Recreiede knightes, whi nele ye fighte? | Cowardly |
|       | Traitours, theves, where youre mighte? | where [is] |
|       | It is sschame, bi god Mahon, |
| 940   | That oure folk goon thus adoun." |
|       | With this word Carmel anon |
|       | Pingde his stede and made him gon, | Pricked |
|       | And rood to Ogger in that hete | heat [of battle] |
|       | And thoute he sscholde his lif forlete, | [Ogger's]; destroy |
| 945   | And was strong and ful of tene | anger |
|       | And smot sore, and that was sene. |
|       | He smot Ogger in the sscheld, |
|       | That Ogger lay amidde the feld. |
|       | Sore he fel oppon the grounde |
| 950   | And hadde a fol luther wonde. | grievous |
|       | The Duk Roulond that seygh; |
|       | For wrathe he was wod wel nygh, | nearly insane |
|       | And for wrathe smot him so sore | [Carmel] |
|       | That he ne spak nevere eft more. |
| 955   | Tho cam Anwe of Nubie, | Then |
|       | On of kinges knightes Garsie, | King Garcy's knights |
|       | And felde Oliver to grounde, |
|       | Bote he ne gaf him nevere a wounde. |
| fol. 273va | Roulond was fol wroth withalle | indeed |
| 960   | Tho he saugh Oliver falle, | When |
|       | And Anawe of Nubie he smot |
|       | That nevere eft crouste he ne bot. | So that he never again bit a crust |
|       | Oliver ros op fram the grounde |
|       | Al hol withouten wonde, | whole; wounde |
| 965   | And anon his stede he nam | took |
|       | And to Roulond sone he cam. |
|       | Tho was Roulond fol fawe | Then; glad |
|       | That Oliver nas nought isslauwe. | slain |
|       | Tho thei were togidere imet, | When |
| 970   | Tho were thei harde biset | Then |
|       | Amang Sarasins that were kene, |
|       | And thei smiten sore for tene. | anger |
|       | Whil Roulond faught and Oliver, |
|       | Hevere stod the gode Ogger, | Still |

975     And hadde lorn his gode stede,
        And his wounde gan faste blede,
        And yit he faught there he stod,
        And leide on as he were wod.
            Whil Ogger that doughti knight
980     Agenes Sarazins stod in fight,                          *Against*
        Oppon a stede Clarel com drive,                         *came riding*
        That Ogger halp to saven olive                          *helped*
        Thorou cunseil of Roulond and Oliver,
        And anon he knugh Ogger.                                *recognized*
985     "Ogger," he seide, "hit is my red,                      *advice*
        Yilte come ore thou art ded;                            *Come yield yourself before*
        Thou holpe to save mi lif a day;                        *today*
        Ich wole saven thin gef I may."                         *if*
            Ogger saugh wel with his eye
990     That he was in point to deye,                           *on the verge of death*
        And to Clarel he gan gon
        And tok him his swerd anon.
            Clarel nas no wedded man;
        Clarel hadde a fair lemman                              *paramour*
995     That was hoten Aufanye
        And was born in Ermenie.                                *Armenia*
            Clarel anonrightes
        Clepede to him two knightes,                            *Called*
        And seide to hem anon,
1000    "To mi lemman ye schulle gon,
        And segge that ich sente hire this knight,              *say; her*
        And that his wounde be heled aright,                    *healed*
fol. 273vb  And god hede to him nome                            *give good care to him*
        To saven him til mi tocome."                            *protect him until I return*
1005        The knightes deden as he hem bad.
        To his lemman he was lad,
        That was hoten Aufanye,
        That was kinges doughter Garsie,
        And yo was glad of that present,                        *she*
1010    To do Clareles comaundement.
        Roulond and Oliver foughten
        That of here lives nought ne roughten.                  *be ruined*
        Thei hadden foughten overmyghte;                        *excessively*
        Thei ne mighte no lengere dure to fighte,
1015    An anon turnden here steeden                             *turned around*
        And flowen, for thei ne myghten nought speden.          *fled; succeed*
            To Otuwel it was told
        That Roulond, that was bold,
        Oliver and Ogger bo                                     *both*
1020    Were over the water go.
            Otuwel anonrightes

|      | | |
|------|---|---|
| | Leet armen him and alle hise knightes. | *Had himself armed* |
| | Tho he was armed and wel idight, | *When* |
| | He wente to the king anonright, | |
| 1025 | And seide, "Sire, I dwelle to longe! | *waited* |
| | Roulond, Oliver, an Ogger the stronge, | |
| | Ove the water alle thre | *Over* |
| | Beth went for envie of me, | *Have gone; spite* |
| | To loke wher thei mighten spede | |
| 1030 | To don any doughti deede | |
| | Among the Sarazins bolde, | |
| | And I sscholde be couward hoolde. | *considered a coward* |
| | Therfore I nele no lengere abide; | |
| | To sechen hem ich wole ride. | |
| 1035 | Thaugh thei habben envie to me, | |
| | Ich wille for the love of thee | |
| | Fonden whother I mighte comen | *Discover whether* |
| | Te helpen hem ar thei weren inomen, | *before; captured* |
| | And yif hem any harm bytit, | *has occurred* |
| 1040 | Let ham witen hare oune wit." | *It will be their own fault* |
| |     Quath the king, "Par charité! | |
| | Otuwel, ich biseche thee, | |
| | For Godes love, highe thee blive, | *go quickly* |
| | And fonde to saven hem olive | *try to; alive* |
| 1045 | Er thei be slawe or nome, | *Before; taken* |
| | And thee sschal sone socour come." | *aid shall soon come to you* |
| fol. 274ra |     Otuwel no lengere ne abood; | |
| | Anon his stede he bistrood | *mounted* |
| | And alle hise knightes bi his side, | |
| 1050 | And toward the ferd he gan to ride. | *battlefield* |
| |     Anon as Otuwel was goon, | |
| | The king leet dighte his host anon | *ordered this army to prepare to ride* |
| | After Otuwel to wende, | |
| | As a god king and hende. | |
| 1055 |     As Otuwel bigan to ride, | |
| | He lokede abouten in eche side | *each* |
| | And he saugh ate laste | *saw* |
| | Where Roulond fleygh and Oliver faste. | *fled* |
| | Otuwel touchede his stedes side | *spurred* |
| 1060 | An agein hem he gan ride, | *towards* |
| | And seide, "Turneth agein anon, | |
| | And helpeth to wreke you on youre fon! | *avenge yourselves; foes* |
| | Thei sschulle abugge, so mote ich thee, | *pay* |
| | That maketh you so faste fle!" | |
| 1065 |     Tho thei herden Otuwel speken | *When* |
| | That thei sscholden ben awreken, | *be avenged* |
| | Tho were thei ferchs to fighte, | *fierce* |
| | And tournden agein and were fol lighte. | *light-hearted* |

|       | "Lordinges," quath Otuel tho, | |
|-------|-------------------------------|---|
| 1070  | "Whuder is god Ogger go?" | *Where* |
|       | And thei answereden, sikinge sore, | *sighing heavily* |
|       | "Forsothe, we ne sien him nought yore, | *recently* |
|       | We ne witen where he is bycome, | |
|       | Whether he is islawe other nome." | |
| 1075  | "Allas, allas!" quath Otuwel, | |
|       | "This tiding liketh me nout wel. | |
|       | Sire Charles, my lord the king, | |
|       | Wole be sori for this tiding. | |
|       | For Godes love, hie we blive, | *let us go quickly* |
| 1080  | And loke we whother Ogger be alive." | |

*        *        *

|       | Otuwel and Oliver | |
|-------|-------------------|---|
|       | And Roulond, that doughti bacheler, | *young man* |
|       | With a feir compaignye | |
|       | Thei bigunnen for to hie | |
| 1085  | Toward King Garsies host, | |
|       | For to abaten of hare bost. | *In order to deflate their boast* |
|       | There was a Sarazin strong, | |
|       | That bar a brod swerd and a long, | |
|       | And was hoten Encumbrer, | |
| 1090  | And bigan to neighen hem ner | *come near* |
| fol. 274rb | Oppon a muche blak stede. | *dark black* |
|       | And Otuwel took of him hede, | *was wary* |
|       | And of his armes hadde a sight | *coat of arms* |
|       | And knugh him anonright, | |
| 1095  | And no lengere he ne abod. | |
|       | Otuwel to him rood | |
|       | And bar him doun, hors and man — | |
|       | Thus Otuwel gamen bigan! | *the game (i.e., battle)* |
|       | Estught of Legers, a noble knight | |
| 1100  | That with Otuwel cam to fight, | |
|       | Bar a spere of tre fol fin | *fine wooden spear* |
|       | And smot a bold Sarazin | |
|       | Into the bodi, thoru the sscheld, | |
|       | And there he lay det in the feld. | *dead* |
| 1105  | Oliver ho slough another, | *he slew* |
|       | And the ferthe, Roulond, his brother. | |
|       | Tho the Freinche knightes seien | *When* |
|       | The Sarasins fallen with hare eien, | *their eyes* |
|       | Thei nolden tho no lengere abide. | |
| 1110  | Thei smiten to in eche side | *(see note)* |
|       | And felden Sarazins faste, | *defeated* |
|       | And thei flowen ate laste. | *[the Saracens] fled* |

|  | King Clarel made hem torne agein | *turn around* |
|---|---|---|
|  | Oppon Cristene men to lein; | *destroy* |
| 1115 | And he leide on faste, | |
|  | And the thef ate laste | |
|  | Slou Dromer of Alemaine — | |
|  | That reu fol sore the King Charlemaine. | *rued* |
|  | Erpater King of Ynde was; | |
| 1120 | He cam with a mase of bras, | *brass mace* |
|  | And Otuwel on the helm he reighte | *struck* |
|  | So harde that al the heued toqueighte. | *shook* |
|  | Quath Otuwel, "So mote Y thee, | |
|  | Ich ne thoute naught boruwe that strok of thee;[1] | |
| 1125 | Bi min heued, under myn hat, | |
|  | I nele nought longe ouwe thee that." | *owe you* |
|  | Otuwel with a fauchoun | *sword* |
|  | Cleef him al the heued adoun, | *Split* |
|  | And he fil under his horse feet; | *fell* |
| 1130 | Quath Otuwel, "That ich thee biheet!" | *[Here is] what I promised you* |
|  | Tho was Otuwel fol of mood, | *full of courage* |
|  | And faught as he were wood. | |
|  | Al the kinges ost anon | |
|  | Foleuweden Otuwel echon, | |
| fol. 274va | Roulond and Oliver, | |
| 1136 | And maden a foul larder. | *carnage* |
|  | The knightes leiden on so faste, | |
|  | The Sarazins flouwen ate laste. | *fled* |
|  | Tho neighede it toward eve, | *evening was near* |
| 1140 | Tho moste the ost bileve | *the host must depart* |
|  | And dwellen there al that night, | |
|  | Til on morwe the dai was bright. | |
|  | Tho the ost was withdrawe, | *When* |
|  | To resten hem as is the lawe, | *custom* |
| 1145 | King Clarel kam in fourme of pees | *appearance of peace* |
|  | With tweie felawes, mo ne lees, | *two fellows, no more or less* |
|  | Toward Charles ost the king | |
|  | For to wyten a tiding. | *hear news* |
|  | And Otuwel agein him wente | *towards* |
| 1150 | To wite who him thidere sente. | |
|  | Thanne seide King Clarel | |
|  | To the doughti Otuwel, | |
|  | "Knight," he seide, "so mote thou thee, | |
|  | Tel me what thi name be. | |
| 1155 | Thou art so doughti man of dede, | |
|  | And mani a knight havest maked blede, | |

---

[1] *I hadn't planned to receive that stroke from you*

Ich wolde fol fain, bi myn eye,                          *am very eager*
Bringe thi name to the King Garsie."
  "Bi God, felawe," quath Otuwel,
1160  "Er this, thou kneuwe my name fol wel,                  *Before now*
So God sschilde me fram sschame.                  *shield me from shame*
Otuel is my Cristine name —
Mahun ich habbe forsake,
And to Jhesu ich habbe me take."
1165    "Allas," quath Clarel, "whi destou so?
So wrecheliche havestou do?                             *wretchedly*
Yit I rede thou turne thi mood,                            *advise*
And leef on Mahoun ore thou art wod,                    *believe in*
And ich wole pese, yef thou wilt,                        *make peace*
1170  That thou havest Garsie agult."              *For how you have wronged*
  "Figh!" quath Otuel tho,
"On Mahoun and on Garsie bo!
Bi Him that maude Adam and Eve,
Y nele nevere oppon you leve;                           *trust you*
1175  Bi Jhesu that is fol of might,
And ich may mete him aright,                                  *If*
There sschal no Sarazin skape olive                  *escape alive*
That ich may hente, so mote ich thrive."                    *seize*
fol. 274vb    "Otuwel," quath Clarel tho,
1180  "Were we sumware bitwene us two,               *If we were just us two*
Bi Mahoun that ich onne bileve,
Oppon thi bodi ich wolde preve
That Mahoun may mo miracles make                            *more*
Than He that thou art to itake —                        *have chosen*
1185  He nis nought half, be mi croun,
So mighty as is Sire Mahoun!"
  Quath Otuwel, "Bi Godes mighte,
Clarel, mi truthe ich thee plighte:                     *I promise you*
Whanevere thou wolt hit schal be —
1190  Evele mote he thrive that fle."             *Evil befall him who flees*
  Quath Clarel anonright,
"Bi Mahoun that is fol of might,
Woltou sikere me on hond                           *If you will promise me*
That no man of King Charles lond
1195  Schal do me no vileynie,
By the deth that I sschal deye,                    *By the death I shall die*
Mi conseil is anon inome;                               *oath; pledged*
Tomorue erliche ich wille come."                             *early*
  Quath Otuwel, "Ne doute thee nought.
1200  Bi God that al the world haveth wrought
And the deth that I schal deie,
Thou ne sschalt hente no vileinie
Of no man of King Charles lond,                               *By*

|  | Bote right of myn oune hond. | *Except* |
| 1205 | Bi Him that made leef and bough, | |
| | Theroffe thee sschal thinken ynough." | *You should see this is sufficient* |
| | Quath Clarel, "Tho do thi best; | |
| | Tomorwe thou sschalt finde me prest." | *ready for battle* |
| | Thus the were there bothe at on. | *they; in agreement* |
| 1210 | Er thei wolden otwinne gon, | *go separately* |
| | Eyther other his trewethe plighte | |
| | Oppon morwen for to fighte. | |
| | On moruwen tho the day sprong, | *when* |
| | Clarel the king thoughte long | *It seemed a long time [to]* |
| 1215 | To the paviloun til he cam | |
| | To holde the day that he nam. | |
| | Oppon a stede wel idight | |
| | He cam fol redi to bide fight. | |
| | King Charles with hise knightes bolde | |
| 1220 | Comen out Clarel to biholde, | |
| | Hou becom al redi dight, | |
| | Boldeliche to bide fight. | |
| fol. 275ra | Clarel was bold on his hond, | *brave on his side* |
| | For Otuwel sikerede him on hond | *had promised him* |
| 1225 | That no man of flechs and blood | |
| | Ne sscholde doon him nought bote good, | |
| | Bot hemselve tweien fighte, | *Only the two of them would fight* |
| | And habbe the maistrie who so mighte. | |
| | Tho was Clarel for trist | *confident* |
| 1230 | Forto segge what him lust. | *That he could say what he liked* |
| | King Charles was an old man, | |
| | And Clarel hede theroffe nam, | *took heed thereof* |
| | And seide, "Charles, thou art old, | |
| | Who made thee nou so bold | |
| 1235 | To werren oppon King Garsie, | |
| | That is cheef of al painie? | *heathendom* |
| | Al paynime he haved in wold; | *He has command of all pagans* |
| | Thou dotest for thou art so hold." | *behave feeble-mindedly; old* |
| | King Charles warythede anonright | *became enraged immediately* |
| 1240 | That Clarel tolde of him so light, | *had mocked* |
| | And hadde iment tho fol wel | *wanted then very much* |
| | To habben ifoughten with Clarel; | *To fight* |
| | And bad fetten his armure bright | *fetch* |
| | And wolde armen him anonright, | |
| 1245 | And seide in wrathe, "By Godes mighte, | |
| | Ich miself wole with him fighte!" | |
| | Roulond bi the king stood | |
| | And bigan to meven his mood, | |
| | And sede to the king anon, | |
| 1250 | "Thou havest, Sire King, mani on | *many* |

Gode doughti knightes of deede;
To fighte thiself thou ne havest no nede!"                    *you have no need to fight*

    "God sschilde, Sire," quath Oliver,                    *God forbid*
"Hit sscholde springe, fer or ner,                    *That it should happen, far or near*
1255     To putte thin oune bodi to fight                    *put your own body in a fight*
And havest so mani a doughti knight."                    *While you*
    King Charles swor his oth
And bigan to wexe wroth,
And seide, "For ought that man may speke,
1260     Miself ich wile ben on him wreke."                    *I will seek revenge myself*
    "A, Sire," quath Otuwel tho,
"For Godes love, sei nought so!
Ich and he beth truthe plighte                    *swore an oath*
That we sschole togidere fighte,
1265     And ich wole telle thee, withoute faille,
Wherefore we habbe taken bataille.                    *Why*
fol. 275rb   He wolde habbe maked me yusterday
To habbe reneied my lay,                    *renounced my faith*
And seide that ich was ilore,                    *damned*
1270     And God nas nought of Marie bore,                    *born*
And seide algate he wolde preve                    *definitively*
That ich am in misbeleve.                    *believe a false faith*
Therefore he profreth him to fight                    *offered himself*
To wite whether is more of might:                    *learn which [faith]*
1275     Jhesu that is Louerd min,                    *Lord*
Or Mahoun and Apolyn.
Thous we habbeth the bataille inome,
And bothe we beth iswore to come."
    Quath the King Charles tho,
1280     "Otuwel, whan it is so,                    *if*
Tak the bataille, a Godes name,                    *in*
And Jhesu schilde thee fram sschame."
Otuwel that noble knight
Lette armen him anonright,
1285     And his gode stede bistrod,                    *mounted*
And no lengere he ne abood,
Bote to the stede he rood fol right,                    *place*
There Clarel hovede to bide fight.                    *Where; stood waiting*
    Anon as Otuwel was icome,                    *As soon as*
1290     Here conseil was anon inome.                    *They quickly came to a decision*
No lengere thei ne abiden;
Anonright togidere thei riden.
Noon other nas ham bitwene
Bote gode stronge speres and kene;
1295     Nas never nother of other agast,                    *afraid*
And either sat in his sadel fast,                    *saddle steadily*

That bothe stedes yeden to grounde, *fell*
And the knightes weren al sounde;
And bothe stedes wenten forth,
1300 That on south, that other north. *one*
The knighte on fote togidere yede, *went*
An drowen hare swerdes gode at nede;
Ne sparede thei nought the swerdes egge; *edge*
Eyther on other bigan to legge. *strike*
1305 Thei were bothe swithe stronge
And foughten togidere swithe longe.
King Clarel was wel negh wood *quite amazed*
That Otuwel so longe stood.
In gret wrathe Otuwel he smot,
1310 And his swerd felliche bot, *bit ruthlessly*
fol. 275va And thau the swerd nevere so good,
The gode helm it withstood, *helmet*
Bote Otuwel astoneied was *stunned*
There he stood up on the gras.
1315 Quath Otuwel, "So mote ich go,
He ne lovede me nought that smot me so! *He loves me not who hits me so*
Ich warne thee wel, so mote ich thee,
Thou sschalt habbe as good of me." *You will have the same from me*
Otuwel for wrathe anon
1320 Areighte him on the chekebon *Struck directly*
Al the fel of that was thare, *flesh*
And made his teth al bare. *exposed*
Tho Otuwel saugh is chekebon, *When; saw his*
He gaf Clarel a skorn anon, *mocked*
1325 And seide, "Clarel, so mote thou thee, *as you may thrive*
Whi scheuwestou thi teth to me? *Why do you show your teeth to me*
I nam no toth-drawere! *tooth-puller*
Thou ne sest me no cheine bere." *You don't see me carrying a chain*
Clarel felede him wounded sore *felt himself to be*
1330 And was maimed for everemore,
An smot to Otuwel with al his might.
And Otuwel that doughti knight
With his swerd kepte the dent *deflected*
That Clarel him hadde iment,
1335 And yit the dent glood adoun *glided*
And smot Otuwel oppon the croun. *on the head*
Quath Otuwel, "Bi Godes ore, *mercy*
Sarazin, thou smitest fol sore!
Suthen thi berd was ischave, *Now that your beard has been shaved*
1340 Thou art woxen a strong knave." *You have become; young man*
Otuwel smot Clarel tho
O strok and nammo, *One; no more*
That never eft word he ne spak, *again*

|      |                                            |                                 |
|------|--------------------------------------------|---------------------------------|
|      | And so Otuwel his tene wrak.               | *avenged his anger*             |
| 1345 | Tho was Charles glad ynough                |                                 |
|      | That Otuwel King Clarel slough,            |                                 |
|      | And gaf Otuwel that doughti knight         |                                 |
|      | A god erldam that selve night.             | *good earldom; same*            |
|      | Al that in the ost was                     |                                 |
| 1350 | Maden murthe and solas                     | *merriment and joy*             |
|      | That Otuwel hadde so bigunne,              |                                 |
|      | And hadde so the maistri wonne.            |                                 |
|      | Al that night over al the ost,             |                                 |
|      | Thei maden alther joye most.               | *exceeding joy*                 |

|            |                                          |                                    |
|------------|------------------------------------------|------------------------------------|
| fol. 275rb | Ther cam a messager and browghte tiding  |                                    |
| 1356       | To Garsie that riche king                |                                    |
|            | That Otuwel, his cosin in lawe,          |                                    |
|            | Hadde King Clarel islawe.                |                                    |
|            | Tho Garsie it undergat,                  | *When; realized*                   |
| 1360       | He was swithe sori for that,             | *so dismayed*                      |
|            | And for wrathe there he stood,           |                                    |
|            | Corsede hise godes as he were wood,      | *Cursed*                           |
|            | And seide, "Allas, and walawo!           |                                    |
|            | Nou is gode Clarel go!                    |                                    |
| 1365       | Certes, myn herte it wile tobreke         |                                    |
|            | Bote ich mowe Clarel awreke."            | *Unless; avenge*                   |
|            | Tho lette Garsie asemlen anon            | *ordered to be assembled*          |
|            | Alle hise Sarazins echon,                |                                    |
|            | And thoughte thoruout alle thing         | *above all*                        |
| 1370       | To ben awreken on Charles King,           |                                    |
|            | And on his cosin Otuwel,                 |                                    |
|            | And on himself the wreche fel.           | *achieve the vengeance himself*    |
|            | King Charles herde be a spye             | *from*                             |
|            | That Garsie thratte him to die,          |                                    |
| 1375       | And he asemblede hise knightes echon     |                                    |
|            | And sede to hem alle anon,               |                                    |
|            | "Lordinges, Garsie thinketh to ride;     |                                    |
|            | Forsothe, I nele no lengere abide!"      | *I will*                           |
|            | The king armede him anon                 |                                    |
| 1380       | And alle hise knightes echon.            |                                    |
|            | The king gurde him with his swerd        | *armed*                            |
|            | And wente himself with his ferd.         | *army*                             |
|            | The king cam stilleliche with his ost,   | *silently*                         |
|            | And Garsie cam with gret bost.           |                                    |
| 1385       | Tho the ostes neigheden niegh            | *When; came near*                  |
|            | That either ost other siegh,            |                                    |
|            | Out of Garsies ost cam ride              |                                    |
|            | A Turkein that was ful of prude.         | *Turkish knight; pride*            |
|            | Roulond was good and hende,              |                                    |
| 1390       | And agenes him gan wende.                |                                    |

The Tourkein no lengere nabod;                          *held back*
To Roulond anon he rood
And gurde Roulond with a spere,
That wel couthe a strok bere,
1395   And as doughti as he was,                          *But*
His o stirop he las.                                     *lost one of his stirrups*
    Roulond was aschamed tharfore
That he hadde his stirop lore,
fol. 276ra  And with Dorendal that was good
1400   He smot the Tourkein oppon the hood,
And he sey doun of his stede,                            *fell down off*
So Rowlond quitte him his mede.                          *paid him his reward*
Quath Roulond, "That ich thee biheet —                   *promise*
Thou nult na more stonden on thi feet!
1405   Min o stirop thou madest me tine,                  *lose*
Nou havestou lose bothe thine!"
    Ther cam another stout Sarazin
That was armed wel afin,                                 *completely*
That highte Myafle of Bagounde.
1410   And with a litel stounde                           *short time*
He made his stede swithe to goon,                        *quickly*
And smot Oliver anoon;
Thorouout al his armure bright,
He woundede sore that gode knight.
1415     Roulond saugh be contenaunse            *by his appearance*
His brother was hurt with le launce;
His warde-cors anon he fond                              *attendant*
And tok a spere out of his hond,
And made his hors make a sturt                           *advance*
1420   To him that hadde his brother hurt,               *Toward*
And touchede him with the speres ord                     *point*
That nevere eft he ne spak word,
And tok Myafles stede anon
And sette Oliver theron.
1425     There was a noble Sarazin,
A king that heet Galatyn,
And cam with a compainie,
And bigan faste to hie.
    Otuwel was war of that,                   *aware*
1430   Oppon his stede there he sat,
Hou King Galatin cam with wille
Cristene men forto spille.                               *kill*
With the spores the steede he nam,                       *goaded (applied)*
To Galatyn the king he kam;
1435   Thorou the bodi he him bar,
And bad he scholde eft be war                            *next time be wary*
Of such a strok whan it kam.

Non other hede of him he ne nam,
Bote rood forth oppon his stede,
1440          And leet the Sarazin ligge and blede.          *lie and bleed*
          Tho smiten tho ostes togidere anon
And foughten faste and good won,          *gained success*
fol. 276rb          And todaschten many a scheld;          *broke apart*
Mani a bodi lay in the feld.
1445          Tho cam over the donne ride          *hill riding*
An hethene king fol of prude,
And browghte with him al ferche tho          *fiercely*
A thousende Sarazins and mo,
And foughten faste a good stounde,
1450          And felden Cristene men to grounde.
          A doughti bacheler cam ride
Oppon King Charles side,
A yong knight that sprong furst berd,          *growing his first beard*
Of no man he nas aferd.
1455          Five hundred men with him he broughte
That of hare lif litel thei thoughte;          *Who cared little for their lives*
Nas non twenti winter old,
And echon was doughti man and bold;
He hadde ichosen hem fol wide,
1460          Bolde men bataille to bide.
Thei foughten faste withinne a stounde          *for a time*
And broughten Sarazins to grounde.
Thei were bolde and foughten faste;
The Sarazins flouwen ate laste.          *fled*
1465          Roulond and Oliver hulpen wel,
And the doughty Otuwel.
          Coursabex the king cam tho
And mette fleinde a thousend and mo;          *fleeing*
"Traitours!" quath Coursabex the king,
1470          "Certes, this is a foul thing
That ye schule fle for ferd!          *flee in fear*
Traitours, tourneth agein the berd!          *turn your faces around*
Tourneth agein, alle with me,
And we wole make the Freinche fle!"
1475          Thous Coursabex himself allone
Made tourne hem agein echone.
          The yinge knight that was so bold,
Right nou that ich of habbe told,
With Coursabex wel sone he mette,          *soon*
1480          And with his swerd anon he sette
Such a strok oppon his croun
That of his stede he fel adoun.
The yinge knight to him cam,
And Coursabex olive nam,          *took alive*

| | | |
|---|---|---|
| 1485 | And sente him Charles the king — | *[Coursabex to]* |
| | Tho was he glad of that tiding. | |
| fol. 276va | Tho the Tourkeins seien alle | *When* |
| | That Coursabex was falle, | *had fallen* |
| | And Cristene men smite sore, | |
| 1490 | Thei flouwen and nolde fighte namore; | *fled* |
| | And the gode yinge knight | |
| | Suwede and leid on doun right. | *Pursued* |
| | There ne halp nough Sire Mahoun, | |
| | The Tourkeins yeden faste adoun. | *fell* |
| 1495 | Tho kam Poidras of Barbarin, | *Then came* |
| | And with him mani a Sarazin. | |
| | Poidras oppon the yunge knight | |
| | Leid on with al his might, | *Attacked* |
| | And here men togidere huwen, | *slashed* |
| 1500 | And hethene hornes faste blewen. | |
| | Poidras and the yinge knight, | |
| | Bitwene hem was strong fight; | |
| | Poidras hadde the more mayn | *strength* |
| | And hadde wel neigh the knight slain. | *very nearly* |
| 1505 | Otuwel that doughti knight | |
| | Was war of that anonright; | |
| | Otuwel no lengere na bood, | |
| | To Poidras anoon he rood, | |
| | And smot Poidras of Barbarin | |
| 1510 | That there he lay as a stiked swin. | *stuck pig* |
| | Otuwel rood into the feerd, | |
| | And leide on faste mid his swerd. | |
| | Roulond and Oliver | |
| | Negheden Otuwel ner | |
| 1515 | And the berdles knight, | |
| | And slowen Sarazins adounright. | |
| | King Garsie herde withinne a stounde | |
| | Hou hise men yeden to grounde. | |
| | King Garsie hadde a conseiler, | |
| 1520 | And anon he took him neer, | |
| | And seide to him, "Sire Arperaunt, | |
| | Agenes Otuwel myn herte stant, | *remains opposed* |
| | That thous haveth reneied his lay | *thus; repudiated his faith* |
| | And sleth mine men, night and day. | |
| 1525 | Sire Arperant, what is thi reed | *advice* |
| | That the thef traitour nere ded? | *is not dead* |
| | Certes, Fraunce hadde be wonnen | *would have been conquered* |
| | Ne hadde his tresoun be bigunnen!" | *Had not his treason begun* |
| | "King Garsie," quath Arperaunt, | |
| 1530 | "Bi Mahoun that yonder stant, | *stands there* |
| fol. 276vb | Al the while that Roulond | |

Mai bere Durendal in his hond,
And Oliver rit by his side,
For no thing that may betide,                          *Not for anything that may occur*
1535    Thou ne schalt nevere Otuwel winne                        *conquer*
For nought that evere thou kans biginne."
Tho was Garsie wel nygh wood
For wrathe on molde there he stood.                      *the ground*
      There was an Affrikan gent                             *nobleman*
1540    That hatte Baldolf of Aquilent.
King Garsie seide to him anoon,
"Certes, Baldoff, thou most goon,
And take with thee knight an swein,                     *knights and men*
And tourne the Cristene men agein;                       *turn around*
1545    And ich miself wole after come
And helpe that Otuwel were nome."
      Quath Baldolf, "Bi Sire Mahun,
Louerd, we wole don what we moun,
And com thou after and tak hede
1550    Wuche maner that we spede;
And yef thou sest that nede be,
Com and help us er we fle,                                 *before*
For whan an ost to flight is went,
Bote socour come, it is schent."              *Unless help comes, it will end in ruin*
1555      Baldolf took his compainie
And to the bataille he gan heye,                          *hastened*
And withinne a litel stounde,
Hard bataille thei habben ifounde.
      Otuwel doughti of dede,
1560    Where thei comen he took hede,
And no lengere he ne bood,
Bote hasteliche to ham he rood.
Roulond and Oliver
Neigheden Otuwel ner                                     *Appeared*
1565    And the gode yinge knight
That was so doughti man in fight.
Tho thei foure weren ifere,                                  *When*
Tho mighte men seen and here
Harde strokes dele and dighte,
1570    And with Sarazins boldeliche fighte.
      Ther cam out of Garsies ost
A man that made muche bost,
A king that hatte Karnifees,
And muchel onour there he les.                               *lost*
fol. 277ra    Ther kam a knight of Agineis,                      *Agen*
1576    A bold man and a courteis,
And with Carnifees he mette,
And wende Carnifees to lette;                        *intended to stop*

|      |                                         |                     |
|------|-----------------------------------------|---------------------|
|      | King Karnifees him haveth istunt        | *has stopped*       |
| 1580 | And slough him ate forme dunt.          | *with the first blow* |
|      | Tho Karnifees hadde thous do,           | *When*              |
|      | He wende to serven ham alle so.         |                     |
|      | Otuwel no lengere na bood,              | *waited*            |
|      | To Karnifees anon he rood;              |                     |
| 1585 | Karnifees knugh Otuwel                  | *knew*              |
|      | By hise armes swithe wel,               |                     |
|      | And seide to the gode gome,             | *man*               |
|      | "Forsworne, thef, artou come!           |                     |
|      | Bi Mahoun," quath Karnifees,            |                     |
| 1590 | Thou schalt hoppen heuedles!"           | *go about headless* |
|      | Otuwel, withoute targing,               | *delay*             |
|      | Answerede Karnifees the king:           |                     |
|      | "Bi Sein Geme, ich ne habbe nought munt | *James; don't intend* |
|      | Tha thou schalt give me that dunt!"     | *blow*              |
| 1595 | Thei nolden no lengere abide            |                     |
|      | Anon togidere thei gunde ride.          |                     |
|      | Karnifees smot Otuwel;                  |                     |
|      | Biside the heued the strok fel.         |                     |
|      | A corner of Otuweles scheld             |                     |
| 1600 | He gurde out amidde the feld.           | *carved out*        |
|      | Quath Otuwel, "Good it wite,            | *God knows*         |
|      | That strok was wel ismite!              |                     |
|      | Nou thou schalt, bi Seint Martyn,       |                     |
|      | Preven a strok of myn!"                 | *Test*              |
| 1605 | Otuwel Karnifees smot                   |                     |
|      | With Corsouse that wel boot             | *so well cut*       |
|      | That Karnifees soughte the ground;      |                     |
|      | Ros he nevere eft hol ne sound.         |                     |
|      | Tho the Sarazins wisten alle            | *When*              |
| 1610 | That Karnifees was ifalle,              |                     |
|      | And that he nolde namore arise,         |                     |
|      | Tho bigan ham alle to agrise,           | *shudder with fear* |
|      | For in al Garsies feerd                 | *army*              |
|      | Nas such a man to handle a swerd.       | *There was never*   |
| 1615 | Tho tournde thei to flight,             |                     |
|      | The Sarazins, anonright.                |                     |
| fol. 277rb | Thous the gode Otuwel             |                     |
|      | And Roulond that was good and snel,     | *valiant*           |
|      | Thoru the help of Godes might,          |                     |
| 1620 | Maden the Sarazins tourne to flight,    |                     |
|      | Thorou swete Jhesu Cristes grace;       |                     |
|      | And thei suweden faste the chasse.      | *made a quick pursuit* |
|      | The Sarazins were so adredde            |                     |
|      | Into the water manye fledde;            |                     |

1625    Summe swumme and summe sunke,                                      *swam*
        And coold water ynough thei drunke.

                    *          *          *

        Til Roulond and Oliver the gode                                     *While*
        In manie harde stoures stode,                                       *battles*
        Godde Ogger in prisoun lay,                                         *[who] in*
1630    Bothe bi night and eke be day.                                      *also*
        Herkneth what hede good to him nam                     *Listen; good luck to him*
        And hou he out of prisoun kam.
            Sevene hethene knightes bolde
        Ogger was bitaken to holde,                          *were assigned to guard Ogier*
1635    And the foure Ogger slough,
        And yit he skapede wel inough.                                *then; escaped*
            There was a noble skuier
        That with queintize halp Ogger;                                     *cunning*
        Swithe priveliche and stille,                            *secretly and quietly*
1640    He broughte Ogger, to his wille,                           *as he requested*
        His swerd and his armure bright,
        And Ogger armede him anonright.                                    *himself*
        Tho he hadde on his gode wede,                              *When; clothing*
        The squier broughte him a good stede.
1645    Ogger no lengere ne abood;
        The goodde stede he bistrood.
        The squier was armed and wel idight,
        And hadde a good hors and a light;                        *good, swift horse*
        And al so stille as a ston,                               *just as quietly*
1650    The squier lep to horse anon,
        And to the porteres windou he kam,
        And in his hond his mase he nam,                                    *mace*
        And oppon the windou he schof                                     *struck*
        That the windou al todrof.                                      *shattered*
1655        Hit was abouten midnight
        And the porter was afright,
        And askede anon who was thare,
        And who makede al that fare.                                       *noise*
fol. 277va      "Porter," quath the squier tho,
1660    "Undo the gate, and let us go!
        We here tellen, bi Sire Mahoun,                                *have heard*
        That Cristene men goon alle adoun,
        And ich and mi felawes, iwis,
        We wole witen hou it is,
1665    And yef we ani good winne,                                        *goods*
        Forsothe, thou schalt parten therinne!"                  *have a part of it*
        And he dude op the gate wide                                      *opened*
        And lette ham bothe out ride,

| | | |
|---|---|---|
| | And steek agein the gate fast, | *closed* |
| 1670 | And there thei sien Ogger last. | *they last saw Ogier* |
| | Ogger rood al that night, | |
| | Til on the morewen the day was bright, | |
| | That nevere his feet comen on grounde | |
| | Er he hadde his felawes founde. | |
| 1675 | Tho Roulond and Oliver | *When* |
| | Weren war of gode Ogger, | |
| | Thei were fol glad of that sight | |
| | And thonkeden Jhesu fol of might. | |
| | Tho Roulond and Oliver | *When* |
| 1680 | Adden imet with gode Ogger, | *Had met* |
| | Thei were also fous to fight | *eager* |
| | As evere was a foul to flight, | *bird* |
| | And wenten into the bataile anon, | |
| | And foughten faste and good won, | |
| 1685 | And made the Sarazins agaste, | |
| | And Otuwel nas nought the laste. | *least [of them]* |
| | Tho alle foure weren ifere, | *When* |
| | Thar nere none strokes dere; | *There were never any harsher strokes* |
| | Tho doughti knightes smiten so sore | *Then* |
| 1690 | As thaugh thei ne hadden nought foughten yore, | *before* |
| | That withinne a litel stounde | |
| | Sarazins yeden alle to grounde. | |
| | King Garsie took god hede | |
| | Hou his folk to grounde yede, | |
| 1695 | And no lengere he ne abood; | |
| | Toward his pavilons he rood. | |
| | And Otuwel anoon byheld | |
| | There he rod in the feld, | *Where* |
| | And warende fore anon tho | *immediately warned in advance* |
| 1700 | Roulond and Oliver bo, | |
| | And Ogger that douhty knight | |
| | That King Garsie was tornd to flight. | |
| fol. 277vb | Tho Roulond and Oliver | *When* |
| | And the gode knight Ogger | |
| 1705 | Sien where King Garsie rood, | |
| | Ther nas non that lengere abood; | |
| | Hasteliche the wey thei nomen, | *took* |
| | And to King Garsie thei comen. | |
| | King Garsie was afered to deye | |
| 1710 | And bigan mersi to crie, | |
| | And seide, forsothe, that he wolde | |
| | Of King Charles his lond holde, | *Under* |
| | And ben at eche perlement, | *attend each council* |
| | Redi at his comaundement. | *Obedient to Charles's command* |
| 1715 | King Garsie seide this, | |

"For His love that youre Good is,
Taketh me on live and sle me nought!
Leet mi lif be forbought,                                                     *ransomed*
And let me as a prisoun goon                                                  *prisoner*
1720   Bifore King Charles anoon,
And don him omage with myn hon                                                *hand*
To holden of him al mi lond!"
       Thanne seide Otuwel,
That was doughti knight and snel,                                             *brave*
1725   To Roulond and to Oliver
And to the gode knight Ogger:
"Nou he haveth this gift igive,
I rede that we laten him live.
Bifore the king he schal be brought,
1730   For Gode, we nulle slen him nought."
An thei acenteden therto,
And seiden, "It wile be wel ido."
And withouten any targing,                                                    *delay*
Thei ladden him bifore the king.
1735        Thanne seide Otuwel that gode knight
To King Charles anonright,
"Sire," he seide, "Her is Garsie,
That sumtime thratte thee to die.                                             *once threatened*
He wile nou, yif thi wille be,
1740   Do thee omage and feauté                                               *homage and fealty*
And ben at thi comaundement,
And at eche parlement
Al redi at thin hond;
And holden of thee al his lond,
1745   And for his lond rente give,
With thee noue, he mote live."                                                *so might he live*

## EXPLANATORY NOTES TO OTUEL A KNIGHT

**ABBREVIATIONS**: *DR*: *Duke Roland and Sir Otuel of Spain*; **MED**: *Middle English Dictionary*; **OK**: *Otuel a Knight*; **OR**: *Otuel and Roland*; **Otinel**: Anglo-Norman *Otinel*; **Pseudo-Turpin**: *The Chronicle of Pseudo-Turpin*, ed. and trans. Poole; **RV**: *Roland and Vernagu*; **Whiting**: Whiting, *Proverbs, Sentences, and Proverbial Phrases*.

11       *Seint-Denys*. Saint-Denis, located near Paris, is the site of the Basilica of Saint-Denis, housing the relics of the martyred first bishop of Paris. It has long been connected to the royal line, and was the burial site for almost all French kings from the tenth century until the French Revolution. Charlemagne's parents — Pepin le Bref and Bertrada of Laon — were interred in the basilica at Saint-Denis, the construction of which was begun by Pepin and completed by Charlemagne. There is, however, no evidence to credit the poet's statement that Charlemagne was born in Saint-Denis.

17       *Lumbardie*. Lombardy, a region in north Italy, figures prominently in many of the Otuel-cycle romances. Medieval Lombardy bordered on France. In *The Siege of Milan*, the central conflict between Saracens and Christians is over the city of Milan and the surrounding Lombard region. In *Otinel*, *OK*, *OR*, and *DR*, the Saracen Emperor Garcy has conquered many key Christian cities and made Lombardy his command center.

34       *hel*. See *MED holden* (v.1), sense 7a(b): "to hold (an estate, a manor, land, etc., from a feudal lord)."

55       *Childermasse Day*. Holy Innocents' Day (December 28). See *MED childermasse-dai* (n.), "the feast day commemorating Herod's slaughter of the infants." See Matthew 2:16. This detail is borrowed from the source; see *Otinel*, line 17, and compare *OR*, line 48.

58       *Parys*. Charlemagne arrives from Saint-Denis and holds court in Paris. The other Otuel narratives also set this scene in or near Paris. In *Otinel*, Charlemagne holds court in Paris, having come from Clermont Ferrand (line 18). In *OR*, he appears to live in Paris and hold court in Saint-Denis (lines 50–51). In *DR*, Charlemagne dwells in Paris (line 39). These settings are historically inaccurate. The Roman town of Lutetia Parisiorum did not develop into the administrative center of France until the eleventh and twelfth centuries. Hugh Capet, count of Paris and duke of the Franks, was elected king of the Franks in 987, and subsequent Capetian kings expanded the city's size and influence. During the Carolingian age, Aix-la-Chapelle, also called Aachen, was where Charlemagne lived and ruled.

59          *duzzeperes.* "Twelve peers." According to legend, Charlemagne recognized twelve knights — his *dussepers* — as his greatest, noblest warriors.

70          *amoevede . . . blod.* To stir one's blood with anger. See *MED ameven* (v.), sense 1a. The phrase recurs at lines 290, 363, and 539.

71–120      *There com a Sarazin . . . . me and te.* Compare *Otinel*, lines 27–58.

104         *thorte drinke win.* The comment that Otuel would drink wine illustrates one of many inaccuracies in the depiction of Muslim behavior.

119         *so mote ich thee.* "so may I thrive," an idiomatic phrase used frequently in *OK*, where it occurs more than a dozen times. See *MED thriven* (v.), sense 1c. For a negative variation ("evele mote he thrive [and thee]"), see lines 309 and 1190. For a variation in second person ("so mote thou thee"), see line 1325.

136         *Rome. OK* is unique among the Otuel poems in placing Garcy in Rome and having Charlemagne travel to meet him in Lombardy (lines 687–88). In *Otinel*, *OR*, and *DR*, Garcy's headquarters is in Atelie/Ataly, the name the poets give to Pavia, the capital of Lombardy that the historical Charlemagne conquered in 773–74. See the explanatory notes to *Otinel*, lines 165–67 and 664–68.

139         *Corsouse.* Corsouse is Otuel's named sword. In *Otinel*, it is called Curçuse; in *OR*, it is Cursins; in *DR*, it is Corsu. Compare the explanatory note to *OR*, line 106.

141–76      *Estught of Leggers . . . . he were wood.* Compare *Otinel*, lines 83–99.

192         *ordres.* Otuel puns as he tells the knights that if any be so bold as to strike him, the only "ordres" (holy orders/blows) they will take are from his sword, Corsouse, not a bishop.

200         *gaf nought of . . . an hawe.* A "hawe" is literally the fruit of a hawthorn, and idiomatically "a thing of little worth." See *MED haue* (n.2), sense 1b; and Whiting H190.

224         *wind . . . havest ilore.* Proverbial. See Whiting W329.

255–57      *And certes . . . . Olecent of Esclavenye.* Compare *Otinel*, lines 130–36.

313         *Ich wole finde Mahoun to borwe.* The phrase has a legal valence: "I will have Mahoun as my surety, or guarantor," as if for a pledge or loan. For the idiom *finden to borwe*, see *MED borgh* (n.), sense 3a.

325         *follaut.* This Middle English word for the sacrament of baptism is derived from Old English *fulluht, fulwiht.* Both this word and the Latin/French-derived *bapteme* were widely used in English. See *MED fulloght* (n.) and *bapteme* (n.).

346–49      *A kinges sone . . . . myn eem was.* Compare *Otinel*, lines 204–08.

348         *cosin.* A general term for any blood relation or relative by marriage. See *MED cosine* (n.), sense 1a (general sense) and 2a (a nephew or niece, specifically). See also *OK*, lines 352 and 412; and compare *Otinel*, line 207.

349         *Fernagu.* Otuel's reference is to his uncle "Fernagu" (or "Vernagu," as the name is spelled in *RV*), who was slain by Roland in a duel. Vernagu is the well-mannered

giant Saracen who arrives at Charlemagne's court as a messenger in *RV*, the romance that directly precedes *OK* in the Auchinleck manuscript.

416     *ilete blod.* "feeling weak," that is, as one would feel after having been medically treated for an illness by the letting of blood. The taunting insult given here by Otuel to Roland is what medieval readers and listeners would have most expected and enjoyed about this character. The French *Otinel* tradition brands him for his talent in verbal wit and comic insult.

521–34     *And seide . . . . mi wille iwent.* Compare *Otinel*, lines 456–65.

578     *seightnesse.* "reconciliation, peace, accord." See *MED saughtnesse* (n.), where this line is cited.

585     *whit colver.* A white dove is a traditional sign for the presence of the Holy Spirit (one of the Three Persons of the Trinity), which is associated with God's grace (see Luke 3:22). The symbol is very common in medieval art and literature, and the audience of *OK* would have readily caught this meaning. Here, the Holy Spirit is referenced as "the vertu of Godes mighte" (line 588). Compare *Otinel*, lines 516–18; *OR*, lines 568–73; and *DR*, lines 578–79.

645     *Bisschop Turpin.* Archbishop Turpin is an important military and ecclesiastical character in the *Song of Roland* and the Middle English Charlemagne romances. In *Otinel*, *RV*, and the three Otuel romances, Turpin's role is limited to episcopal duties: performing Mass and baptizing converts. In the fifth Otuel-cycle romance, *The Siege of Milan*, Turpin plays a central role.

697–706     *Fol nygh . . . . over gon.* The construction of a bridge is common to all the Otuel poems. *OK* is unique in having Charlemagne observe enemy soldiers riding on the other side of the river and in not specifying the name or location of the river, nor mentioning a city (which is named Ataly in the other poems). Compare *OR*, lines 695–701; *DR*, lines 754–56; and *Otinel*, lines 674–80.

724     *As we finden in romaunse write.* It is a common trope for romance authors to refer to a source for their works, lending credibility to their tales. The *OK* poet most likely did work with a version of the French *Otinel* before him.

725–31     *Curabeles hatte . . . . highte Clarel.* Compare *Otinel*, lines 696–702.

834     *his swerd he tok.* The gesture of taking Clarel's sword, that is, disarming him with his consent, denotes that Clarel is now the Frenchmen's prisoner of war, under the safekeeping of his captors. Compare line 992, where Ogier the Dane allows Clarel to take his sword. See also the corresponding scene in *Otinel*, lines 814–17.

853–60     *Felawes . . . . ich nought be.* Compare *Otinel*, lines 843–50.

862     *Sein Richer.* Saint Richerus (or Richer) of Reims, was a tenth-century monk and historian of France. His naming by Oliver is an anachronism, for he lived later than Charlemagne. His four-part *Historiae* begins with the reign of Charles the Fat (839–88), grandson of Charlemagne, so this mention of Saint Richerus may be meant to evoke an association with the Carolingian Empire. It may also be

relevant that Turpin, the ecclesiastical authority in the Charlemagne romances (and purported author of *Pseudo-Turpin*, the source for *RV*), was himself archbishop of Reims. Throughout the Middle Ages, Reims was the traditional site for the coronation of kings of France.

882      *ferd*. "danger, something inspiring fear." See *MED ferde* (n.1), sense 2.

891      *Sein Martin*. Saint Martin of Tours, a bishop and martyred saint (316–397). The oath may convey a patriotic French air to English readers; it is said that Saint Martin's relics were sometimes carried by French kings into battle. The veneration of Saint Martin was widespread in medieval Europe, especially in French regions. See also line 1603.

962      *nevere eft crouste he ne bot*. Proverbial. See Whiting C583 and B520.

992      *tok him his swerd anon*. On this formal gesture of capture, compare the note to line 834 above.

1013      *overmyghte*. "Beyond endurance"; see *MED, over-might* (adv.), where this instance is cited as the only appearance of the word.

1017–40      *To Otuwel . . . . hare oune wit*. Compare *Otinel*, lines 1000–17.

1040      *Let ham witen hare oune wit*. "Let them blame their own wits," or, as is commonly said in modern English, "It will be their own fault." See *MED witen* (v.3), sense 1a(c), "lay the blame on, hold accountable," where this line is cited.

1061–64      *And seide . . . . so faste fle*. Compare *Otinel*, lines 1043–47.

1110      *smiten to in eche side*. "struck about in every direction." The phrase *smiten to* would normally have an object; see *MED smiten* (v.), sense 1b(c), "strike at (somebody or something)." Here, modified adverbially by "in eche side," it denotes the wild actions of many knights striking everywhere.

1124      *boruwe*. "receive (a blow) with the intention of returning it." See *MED borwen* (v.), sense 1b.

1136      *maden a . . . larder*. Proverbial. See *MED larder* (n.), sense 3a: "make a slaughter."

1151–212      *Thanne seide . . . . for to fighte*. Compare *Otinel*, lines 1195–1233.

1231–82      *King Charles . . . . fram sschame*. Compare *Otinel*, lines 1311–52.

1276      *Mahoun and Apolyn*. Middle English romances often misrepresent Muslims as polytheists who worship idols, naming three or four gods as central to their fictionalized faith: Mahoun, Jubiter, Apollin, and Termagaunt. See the discussion in the General Introduction, p. 16.

1328      *cheine*. Otuel taunts Clarel that he is not a tooth-puller because he does not carry the chain used to pull out teeth. This vivid scene of the handsome Clarel's facial disfigurement is present in all three Roland and Otuel romances, although how Otuel mocks Clarel takes a different form in each one. Compare *Otinel*, lines 1452–56.

1337–40    *Quath Otuwel . . . . a strong knave.* Normally a beard is a sign of strength, as in the biblical story of Samson (Judges 16:17). Here, according to Otuel's sarcastic insult, the reverse seems to be the case: being so brutally "shaven" makes Clarel "strong." The joke may also imply that Clarel's Muslim identity has been marred.

1399       *Dorendal.* Durendal is the name of Roland's famous sword. In Rocamadour, France, one may see a chapel with a sword embedded in its outside wall. By local legend, this sword is Durendal. De Veyrières notes the claim (found in l'abbé Cheval's 1862 guidebook, *Guide du Pèlerin à Roc-Amadour*) that the real Durendal was stolen in 1183 when Henry II pillaged the chapel, and he includes a drawing of the current sword ("L'Épée de Roland," pp. 139–41).

1472       *tourneth agein the berd.* Proverbial. See Whiting B120.

1510       *lay as a stiked swin.* Proverbial. See Whiting S966. The phrase is especially insulting because Muslims consider pigs dirty; pork is prohibited from their diet.

1530       *Bi Mahoun that yonder stant.* Arperaunt refers to a nearby idol.

1575       *of Agineis.* "of Agen." The French knight is from the city of Agen, located in southwest France in the Aquitaine region.

1603       *Seint Martyn.* See the note to line 891 above.

1629–78    *Godde Ogger . . . . fol of might.* In the penultimate scene of the romance, just before the capture of King Garcy, Ogier the Dane breaks out of prison and rejoins his comrades. In this version, he is aided in his escape by a cunning squire, who brings Ogier his horse and armor and then convinces the porter to open the gate. For alternate scenarios, see *Otinel*, lines 1836–69; *OR*, lines 1616–36; and *DR*, lines 1543–60.

1681–82    *fous . . . As . . . a foul to flight.* Proverbial. See Whiting F564.

1697–746   *And Otuwel . . . . he mote live.* Compare *Otinel*, lines 1876–1901. On the different endings among the French and Middle English accounts of Otuel/Otinel, see the explanatory note to *Otinel*, lines 1899–904.

# TEXTUAL NOTES TO OTUEL A KNIGHT

**ABBREVIATIONS: BW**: *The Auchinleck Manuscript*, ed. Burnley and Wiggins; **H**: *Otuel*, ed. Herrtage, in *The English Charlemagne Romances. Part VI*, pp. 65–116; **MS**: Edinburgh, National Library of Scotland MS Advocates 19.2.1 (the Auchinleck MS), fols. 268ra–77vb.

| | |
|---|---|
| 6 | *Sarazins*. So MS, H. BW: *Sarrazins*. |
| 34 | *hel*. So MS. BW, H: *held*. |
| 59 | *with*. MS, BW, H: *wit*. |
| | *he*. So H. MS, BW: *ne*. |
| 69 | *Sarasin*. So H, BW. MS: *sazasin*. |
| 71 | *There*. So MS, BW. H: *þer*. |
| 77 | *Into the paleis tho he cam*. MS repeats the line at bottom of fol. 268r at the top of 268v, spelling *palais* in second copying. BW, H also omit repeated line. |
| 78 | *hon*. So MS. H, BW: *hond*. |
| 98 | *gode*. So MS, BW. H: *godde*. |
| 121–28 | MS: eight lines missing where a miniature has been removed. A blue paraph marks missing line 127. |
| 139 | *mi swerde ful*. So BW, H. MS: Text is rubbed away. |
| 178 | *asschamed*. So MS, BW. H: *aschamed*. |
| 187 | *Sire*. So MS, BW. H: *fire*. |
| 244 | *an*. So MS, BW. H: *and*. |
| 249 | *thine*. So MS, H. BW: *þin*. |
| 250 | *Sire*. So MS, BW. H: *fire*. |
| 261 | *sschal al*. So MS, BW. H: *sschall all*. |
| 269 | *oppon*. So MS, BW. H: *upon*. |
| 272 | *thou*. So MS, BW. H: *you*. |
| 279 | *King*. So BW, H. MS: *k* rubbed from page. |
| 283 | *yiukthe*. So MS. BW, H: *ʒinkþe*. |
| 285 | *was the king agramed*. So BW, MS. H: *was the king was a gramed*. |
| 287 | *Otuwel*. So BW, H. MS: *otuwet*. |
| 302 | *ich here*. So MS. BW, H: *ich nought here*. |
| 327 | *Ichc wolle maketh, so mote ihc thee*. MS: line written in the margin, inserted between lines 326 and 328. |
| | *maketh*. So MS. BW, H: *make þe*. |
| 345 | *answerede*. So MS, BW. H: *answerde*. |
| 351 | *Sir*. So BW, H. MS: *sr*. |
| 357 | *Nou*. So MS, H. BW: *ʒou*. |
| 361 | *awreke*. So MS. BW emends to *will wreke*. H: *ich wille a-wreke*. |
| 363 | *Charle*. So MS. BW, H: *Charles*. |

| | |
|---|---|
| 368 | *fechen*. So MS, BW. H: *sechen*. |
| 428 | *nas*. So MS, BW. H: *was*. |
| 440 | *feel*. So MS. BW, H: *feeld*. |
| 452 | *druye*. So MS, BW. H: *druþe*. |
| 455 | *sterne*. So BW. MS: *stene*. H: *steue*. |
| 456 | *bothe*. So MS, BW. H: *boþ*. |
| 462 | *bothe*. So MS, BW. H: *boþ*. |
| 468 | *blenkte*. So MS. BW, H: *blenkt*. |
| 472 | *Bote*. So MS. BW, H: *Bot*. |
| 476 | *gon*. So MS, H. BW: *gan*. |
| 484 | *ich*. MS, BW, H: *Ihc*. |
| | *isought*. So MS, BW. H: *ifouȝt*. |
| 490 | *idrawe*. So MS, BW. H: *idraue*. |
| 492 | *ovede*. So MS. BW, H: *houede*. |
| 516 | *togidere*. So MS, BW. H: *to gider*. |
| 518 | *feled*. So BW, H. MS: *d* is superscripted, inserted with caret. |
| 528 | *my*. So BW, MS. H: *mi*. |
| 547 | *ende*. So BW, MS. H: *end*. |
| 554 | *Roulond*. So BW, MS. H: *roulonde*. |
| 574 | *you*. So BW, H. MS: *wou*. |
| 603 | *likede*. So MS, BW. H: *likete*. |
| 612 | *wroth*. So BW, H. MS: *worþ*. |
| 618 | *hon*. So MS. BW, H: *hond*. |
| 633 | *thee*. BW, H: *þe*. MS: *þe* is superscripted, inserted with caret. |
| 635 | *al*. So MS, BW. H: *all*. |
| 654 | *goo*. So MS. BW, H: *go*. |
| 669–70 | *Whether wole we wenden oppon him anon, / Other abide til winter be gon*. So BW, H. MS: Scribe initially omitted line 670. The line is copied at the bottom of the column, and scribe uses marginal *a* and *b* to note the proper placement of the line. |
| 683 | *bond*. So MS, BW. H: *hond*. |
| 685 | *an*. So MS, H. BW emends to *and*. |
| 695 | *bisides*. So MS, BW. H: *besides*. |
| 697 | *nygh*. So MS, BW. H: *niȝ*. |
| 711 | *an*. So MS. BW, H: *and*. |
| 716 | *Suche*. So MS. BW, H: *Such*. |
| 719 | *ost*. So MS, BW. H: *oft*. |
| 720 | *forte*. So MS, BW. H: *for to*. |
| 725 | *Curabeles*. MS, BW, H: *Turabeles*. |
| 740 | *neve*. So MS. BW, H: *neuer*. |
| 741 | *Roulond*. So MS. BW, H: *Roulonde*. |
| 747 | *Roulond*. So MS. BW, H: *Rouland*. |
| 748 | *Yich*. So MS. BW: *Iich*. H: *Ich*. |
| 751 | *founden*. So MS, BW. H: *fonnden*. |
| 760 | *is tis*. So MS, BW. H: *is þis*. |
| 781 | *adon*. So MS, H. BW: *a doun*. |
| 785 | *Balsamun*. So MS, BW. H: *balsamum*. |

| | |
|---|---|
| 789 | *He ne.* So H. BW: *he ne (ne).* MS includes a second *ne*, which I have omitted. BW puts second *ne* in parenthesis, likely to preserve meter. |
| 817 | *Roulond.* So MS. BW, H: *Rouland.* |
| 823 | *maner.* So MS, BW. H: *manner.* |
| 832 | *swerd tok.* So MS, BW. H: *swerd he tok.* |
| 840 | *up.* So H, BW. MS: *vt.* |
| 869 | *were.* So MS. BW, H: *where.* |
| 872 | *mot entenden.* So MS, BW. H: *moten tenden.* |
| 908 | *An.* So MS. BW, H: *and.* |
| 914 | *bar.* So MS, BW. H: *bare.* |
| 938 | *where youre.* So MS. BW, H: *where is ʒoure.* |
| 958 | *he.* So H, BW. MS: *be.* |
| 963 | *op.* So MS, BW. H: *ap.* |
| 964 | *wonde.* So MS, H. BW: *wounde.* |
| 968 | *nas.* So MS, BW. H: *was.* |
| 970 | *thei.* So BW, H. MS: *rei.* |
| 981 | *com.* So MS, BW, H: *come.* |
| 986 | *come.* So MS, BW, H: *to me.* |
| 1015 | *An.* So MS, BW, H: *and.* |
| 1022 | *hise.* So BW, H. MS: *hise* is superscripted, inserted with caret. |
| 1026 | *an.* So MS, H. BW: *and.* |
| 1027 | *Ove.* So MS, BW, H: *Ouer.* |
| 1038 | *Te.* So MS. BW, H: *To.* |
| 1060 | *An.* So MS. BW: *and.* H: *&.* |
| 1069 | *Otuel.* So MS, BW. H: *otuwel.* |
| 1149 | *And.* So MS, H. BW omits word. |
| 1167 | *rede.* So BW, H. MS: *rere.* |
| 1196 | *deth.* So MS, BW. H: *deap.* |
| 1206 | *sschal.* So MS, BW. H: *sschall.* |
| 1208 | *Tomorwe.* So BW, H. MS: *r* is superscripted, inserted with caret. |
| 1209 | *the.* So MS, H. BW: *þei.* |
| 1221 | *becom.* So MS, BW. H: *he com.* |
| 1223 | *hond.* So MS, BW. H: *bond.* |
| 1224 | *Otuwel.* So BW, H. MS: *tuwel.* |
| 1229 | *for.* So BW. H: *fol.* MS: scribe initially copied *for* and then wrote an *l* over the *r*. |
| 1238 | *hold.* So MS, H. BW: *bold.* BW notes that the *h* has been altered to form a *b* in the manuscript. |
| 1302 | *An.* So MS, H. BW: *and.* |
| 1311 | *swerd nevere so.* So MS. BW: *swerd neuere nere so.* H: *swerd nere neuere so.* |
| 1323 | *is.* So MS, H. BW: *his.* |
| 1326 | *thi.* So MS, BW. H: *þe.* |
| 1331 | *An.* So MS, H. BW: *and.* |
| 1350 | *Maden.* So BW, H. MS: *Aaden.* |
| 1353 | *night.* So MS. BW, H: *miʒt.* |
| 1367 | *asemlen.* So MS, H. BW: *asemblen.* |
| 1404 | *stonden.* So MS, BW, H: *stenden.* |
| 1416 | *le.* So MS. BW, H: *þe.* |

| | |
|---|---|
| 1433 | *steede*. So MS, BW. H: *stede*. |
| 1445 | *donne*. So MS. BW, H: *doune*. |
| 1456 | *thoughte*. So MS, BW. H: *rouʒte*. |
| 1472 | *berd*. So MS, BW. H: *herd*. |
| 1493 | *nough*. So MS. BW, H: *nouʒt*. |
| 1514 | *Negheden*. So MS. BW, H: *Neiʒeden*. |
| 1523 | *reneied*. So MS, BW. H: *reneid*. |
| 1536 | *kans*. So MS, H. BW: *kanst*. |
| 1543 | *an*. So MS. BW, H: *and*. |
| 1594 | *Tha*. So MS, H. BW: *Þat*. |
| 1621 | *Thorou*. So MS, BW. H: *Þrou*. |
| 1625 | *swumme*. So BW, H. MS: *smumme*. |
| 1628 | *manie*. So BW, H. MS: *mananie*. |
| 1680 | *Adden imet with gode Ogger*. So H. MS: *adden imet wiþ gode*. BW: *hadden imet wiþ gode Ogger*. |
| 1683 | *bataile*. So MS, BW. H: *bataille*. |
| 1693 | *took god*. So MS, BW. H: *toke god*. |
| 1713 | *perlement*. So MS, BW. H: *parlement*. |
| 1721 | *hon*. So MS. BW, H: *hond*. |
| 1729 | *schal*. So MS, BW. H: *schall*. |
| 1731 | *An*. So MS, H. BW: *and*. |

# ❧ OTUEL AND ROLAND INTRODUCTION

*Otuel and Roland* is a Middle English tail-rhyme romance found in the Fillingham manuscript (London, British Library MS Additional 37492), fols. 30v–76r.[1] *Otuel and Roland* has two halves: the first, which tells the story of the Saracen Otuel's conversion and deeds of valor (lines 1–1978); and the second, which covers the plot of the *Song of Roland*, in which Charlemagne's ill-fated attempt to conquer Zaragoza leads to Roland's death (lines 1979–2790). *Otuel and Roland* is notable not only for its inclusion of Roland's death, but also for its mention of Vernagu, the slain giant of *Roland and Vernagu* (line 16).

Copied in the second half of the fifteenth century, Fillingham contains four other English texts: *Firumbras*, *The Hermit and the Outlaw*, *The Devil's Parliament*, and *The Mirror of Mankind*.[2] Three of these — *Otuel and Roland*, *Firumbras*, and *The Hermit and the Outlaw* — are unique to the manuscript. Fillingham was lost for many years after George Ellis borrowed it in 1801 from its owner William Fillingham so that he could add a description of *Otuel and Roland* to his *Specimens of Early English Metrical Romances*. A surviving letter from Ellis to Fillingham, now stored with the manuscript in the British Library, details Ellis' early observations about differences between *Otuel and Roland* and the Auchinleck romance *Otuel a Knight*, as well as an assurance that he is caring for the manuscript. According to Mary O'Sullivan, editor of *Otuel and Roland* and *Firumbras*, the manuscript was unavailable from the time that Ellis borrowed it until 1907, when the British Museum acquired it.[3] Several folios are missing from the Fillingham copy of *Otuel and Roland*, and a portion of text is gone due to a tear. Despite these losses, the plot can be filled in by means of *Otinel* and Ellis' summary in *Specimens*, which appears to have been made before the damage occurred.[4]

Three scribal hands are present in the Fillingham manuscript, and there is notable variation in dialect among them. In particular, O'Sullivan finds that the scribe who copied *Otuel and Roland* tends to use forms belonging to a Southern dialect, while Northern forms are more common in *Firumbras*.[5] Despite Fillingham's fifteenth-century date, *Otuel and Roland* is usually assigned to the mid-fourteenth century, setting its composition soon after *Roland and Vernagu*. Textual links between the romances are strong: they share a passage

---

[1] For *Otuel and Roland*, see *DIMEV* 1787; *NIMEV* 1106; and Smyser 1967, pp. 91–92, 264. On its stanza form, see the General Introduction, p. 23.

[2] For the other contents of Fillingham, see *DIMEV* 1554, 440, 6376, 2084; *NIMEV* 944.5, 260, 3992, 1259.

[3] *Firumbras and Otuel and Roland*, ed. O'Sullivan, p. xiii. For Ellis' letter, see *Firumbras and Otuel and Roland*, ed. O'Sullivan, pp. xi–xii.

[4] Ellis, *Specimens*, pp 357–79.

[5] *Firumbras and Otuel and Roland*, ed. O'Sullivan, p. xv.

that describes Charlemagne, and they employ the same stanza form. These connections form the basis of the now mostly discarded "Charlemagne and Roland" theory discussed in the General Introduction, pp. 7–8. The similarities may, however, be taken as evidence in favor of a composition date for *Otuel and Roland* that is close to those of the Auchinleck *Roland and Vernagu* and *Otuel a Knight*.

In judging this romance against the other Middle English Otuel romances, in terms of the four touchstone scenes,[6] one finds that *Otuel and Roland* retains the French *Otinel*'s amorous attraction between Otuel and Belesent as well as Otuel's characteristic sarcasm and derision. While the virtually woman-less *Otuel a Knight* removes Belesent's arming of Otuel, *Otuel and Roland* keeps the scene and gives Belesent a front-row seat for Otuel's duel with Roland. During her cousin's fight with the Saracen, Belesent prays for Otuel's safety and adds commentary on the duel for her father (lines 442–44, 499–504). Belesent is also present for Otuel's miraculous conversion and baptism, during which Charlemagne offers her as wife to Otuel (lines 598–606). In *Otuel and Roland*, Belesent is not allowed to choose whether she will marry Otuel, but she does speak up and express love for her betrothed (lines 611–15). Equally delighted, Otuel promises to protect Belesent and asks that she be able to accompany the army at the siege of Ataly (lines 616–27).

Likewise, another scene involving women's agency — the *Otinel* scene with Saracen women in which Alfamie heals Ogier the Dane — is replayed in *Otuel and Roland*, where the intimacy of Enfamy's care for Ogier is emphasized:

| | |
|---|---|
| Bothe by day and eke by nyght, | |
| Hereself hys woundys gan dyght | *tended to* |
| And gaf hym drynkes der. | *precious potions* |
| Sche made hym salves soft, | |
| And as Oger lay in loft | |
| He feld hym bothe hole and fer. | *felt himself grow; strong* |
| (lines 1018–23) | |

Enfamy, who has already expressed curiosity about Ogier's identity, tends to his wounds herself. Bits of the *chanson de geste* describing Ogier's escape are missing, but a farewell to Enfamy is added. Having just broken his chains, stolen a horse, and thus made ready to flee Ataly, Ogier takes an improbable moment to shout to Enfamy that he is leaving, promising to speak with her tomorrow (lines 1628–33). Ogier's plan to return to Enfamy is not mentioned again, but his parting words suggest desire, and perhaps love. In general, the author of *Otuel and Roland* seems happy to include the *Otinel* scenes that feature strong women, and is even prone to increase their influential roles.

Similarly, Otuel's penchant for derisive jokes is presented every bit as humorously as in the French *Otinel*. The *Otuel and Roland* poet retains Otuel's comic chiding of Roland and Oliver when they flee the battle, and his mockery of Clarel's exposed teeth during their duel is mordantly witty. As Roland and Oliver gallop away from the Saracens, Otuel reprimands them but also encourages their return to battle, demonstrating an eagerness to help the knights regain honor:

---

[6] These scenes, which feature women or Otuel's insults, are named in the introduction to *Otuel a Knight*, pp. 65–66.

| | |
|---|---|
| "Lese thou schalt thy swete!" | *lifeblood* |
| Syr Otuel gan to chyde, | |
| And sayde, "Roulond, for thy pryde | |
| Thy lyfe thou wylt forlete! | *give up* |
| What wenes tou and Olyver alone | *presume* |
| To sle the Sarysyns everchon, | |
| And thus to grounde hem bete? | |
| | |
| Nay, though thou and Y and Olyver | |
| Hadde ben ther al in fer | |
| Ageyns the hedyn lawe — | *heathen* |
| And ek Charles the conquerour, | |
| Though he brought alle hys power — | |
| Yet schuld they be nought alle slawe. | |
| Ac turne ageyn with me anone, | |
| And venge we ous of Godys fone, | *foes* |
| And gynne we a new plawe. | *let us begin a new battle* |
| Ther schulle a thousand, for thys thyng, | |
| Thys day of hem have here enthyng | *ending* |
| Withinne a lytel thrawe." | *short time* |

(lines 1056–74)

Although judging that the two knights' pursuit of the Saracens is foolhardy and rash, Otuel seems not to want to wholly discredit their valor. While he cannot resist giving them a scolding, he reserves the brunt of his derision for Saracens, his former fellows.

Otuel and Clarel's duel in *Otuel and Roland* contains the longest and most cutting jokes about Clarel's exposed teeth found in any version, including even the French *Otinel*. In *Otuel and Roland*, Otuel makes a joke about the close shave he has given Clarel with his sword, and he then enumerates the ways the injury will damage Clarel's reputation and love life:

| | |
|---|---|
| Tho lowe Otuel, and sayd, | *laughed* |
| "Y sawe never, so God me rede, | |
| Sythe that Y was bore, | |
| Never man in knyghtys wede, | |
| Al so fer as Y have rede, | |
| A berd so clene yschore! | *shaved* |
| So God me save and sent savour, | *send salvation* |
| Now ys Cursins a good rasour! | *razor* |
| Hyt were harm that it were lore, | *It would be a shame if it were lost* |
| Hyt ys scharp, and that ys sene! | |
| Hyt had yschave thy berd ful clene | |
| That ther nys laft no more! | |
| | |
| Now be thou syker in alle thyng: | |
| Nyl never Garcy the Kyng | |
| Byleve on thee after thys, | |
| Neyther Enfamé, that fayrer thyng, | |
| Sche nyl namore of thy playyng, | |
| Ne ffor no love thee kysse. | |
| Now thy behoveth to grenne, | *grin* |
| And to make thee to mowe on menne, | *grimace* |

> For thy mouth syttyth alle onmys.                    *amiss*
> Now ne helpth ne nought thy god Mahound,
> Jubiter, ne that breythen Platoun,                   *worthless*
>     That thou ne art syker of thys."                 *be protected from this*
> (lines 1465–88)

Along with the jokes about how Clarel's appearance will repulse his lover, the poet adds more insult to Otuel's speech: Clarel has now lost his emperor's trust, and his gods will no longer aid him.

Overall, *Otuel and Roland* provides the closest translation of *Otinel* among the three Middle English Otuel romances, adding some details but generally staying true to the action and tone of the French text.[7] Where *Otuel and Roland* differs most from both *Otinel* and the other Middle English versions is in its addition of an 812-line retelling of the events in the *Song of Roland* (lines 1979–2790). Composed in the same stanza form as *Otuel and Roland*'s first 1978 lines, this long addendum is in effect a summary of the Roland story, designed to place the Otuel episode in the broader context of Roland's and Charlemagne's lives.

MANUSCRIPT:
London, British Library MS Additional 37492 (Fillingham MS), fols. 30v–76r.

PREVIOUS EDITION:
*Otuel and Roland*. In *Firumbras and Otuel and Roland*. Ed. Mary I. O'Sullivan. EETS o.s. 198.
    London: Oxford University Press, 1935. Rpt. 2007. Pp. 59–146.

---

[7] *Otuel and Roland* is unique in including a brief scene in which Emperor Garcy is christened: "The Erchebyschop Syre Turpyn, / A swythe good clerk of dyvyn, / Crystened hym that day; / The soule of that Sarsin / Forto save fro helle pyn, / He lered hym Goddys lawe" (lines 1682–87).

# OTUEL AND ROLAND

### Fitt 1

| | | |
|---|---|---|
| fol. 30v | *Herkenyth, lordynges, and gevyth lyst,* | *Listen* |
| | *In the worchyp of Jhesu Cryst,* | |
| | *Of a conquerour* | |
| | *That was yhote Sir Charlemayn,* | *called* |
| 5 | *Howe he wan Galys of Spayne* | *Galicia* |
| | *With ful grete honour,* | |
| | *And how that he overcam* | |
| | ......................................... | |
| | *With full grete vygour,* | |
| 10 | *And howe Rowland and othyr knytys to* | *two* |
| | *Ageyn four knytys foughtyn do,* | *Against; then* |
| | *And ever was a grete warryour.* | |
| | | |
| | *And the Kyng Ebryan* | *Ebrahim* |
| | *Helde werre ageynes ham,* | *them* |
| 15 | *And greved hem ful sore;* | *aggrieved them* |
| | *And howe Rowlond slowe Vernagu* | *slew* |
| | *Thorugh the myght of Jhesu,* | |
| | *That leved in false lore;* | *believed; false beliefs* |
| | *And the caytyf Emon* | *wicked* |
| 20 | *Helde werre agens Charlyon* | |
| | *Thrytty wyntyr and more,* | *Thirty winters* |
| | *And magre hym and al hys* | *in spite of* |
| | *Thorugh the myght of Jhesu* | |
| | *In the Mount Albene thay wore.* | *Mount Alben (in Lombardy); were* |
| | | |
| 25 | *And ther Rouland the gode knyght* | |
| | *Overcom Otuell in fyght —* | |
| | *Nowe ye schulle yhuyre —* | *hear* |
| | *And was cristenyd withoute fayle,* | *[Otuel] was baptized* |
| | *And helpe Charles in many a batayle,* | |
| 30 | *And was hym lef and dere.* | *beloved and dear* |
| | | |
| | *And all the dussyperys with hym,* | *twelve peers* |
| fol. 31r | *Bothe Gwynes and Sir Turpyn,* | *Ganelon* |

121

|  | *That was stoute in fyght;* | *strong* |
|---|---|---|
|  | *And howe Charles aftyr than* |  |
| 35 | *All hys fomen overcam* | *enemies* |
|  | *Thorowe the grace of God Almyght;* |  |
|  | *With swerdys dynt, withouten les,* | *lies [i.e., truly]* |
|  | *Hys lond he held in grythe and pes,* | *order and peace* |
|  | *Withoute warre and fyght.* |  |
| 40 | *The Ercheboschope Syr Turpyn* |  |
|  | *Alle those dedys wrote in Latyn* | *deeds* |
|  | *Whiles he hem saugh in syght.* | *As; witnessed them* |
|  | *Of Charles that was so grym,* | *stern* |
|  | *Nowe y wolle begynne of hym* |  |
| 45 | *To tell you aryght.* |  |

|  | Nought longe theraftyr yt was, |  |
|---|---|---|
|  | That ther byfel a wondyr cas | *marvel* |
|  | On Chyldermasse Day. | *(see note)* |
|  | Charlys, thorugh Goddys grace, |  |
| 50 | Out of Parys toke the pas | *path* |
|  | To Seynd-Denys, the ryght way. | *Saint-Denis* |
|  | Hys dussypers with hym he ladde, |  |
|  | And other men, also goode and sadde, | *trustworthy* |
|  | And knytys stoute and gay. | *mighty and merry* |
| 55 | Thenne came there a messynger |  |
|  | That was bothe stout and fer, | *fierce* |
|  | And made grete deray. | *trouble* |

|  | Syr Otuell he hyght, | *was called* |
|---|---|---|
|  | A man of moche myght, |  |
| 60 | To batayll he was boun. | *ready* |
|  | To hym he clepyd a knyght | *called* |
|  | That was curteys and wyght, | *brave* |
|  | Gawter of Amoun, |  |
|  | And sayd, "Syr, Y thee beseke | *beseech* |
| fol. 31v | That thou woldyst me teche | *show* |
| 66 | To Kyng Charlyon, |  |
|  | And to Roulond hys nevewe | *nephew* |
|  | That hath many a vertu |  |
|  | And grete of renon." | *renown* |
| 70 | And tho Gawter answered, | *then* |
|  | And sayde, "He with the hore berde, | *white* |
|  | That ys Charlyon. |  |

|  | And the dussipers that sitten hym next, |  |
|---|---|---|
|  | Tho arne the twelf that thou syxt, | *Those are; see* |
| 75 | Curteysly, withoute lesyng." | *lying [i.e., truly]* |
|  | Otuel yede the kyng nere | *went* |

And hym myssayde, as ye now here,                          *insulted*
    And bade hym sytte stylle
  And sayde, "Y am Garcies messanger —
80  In alle thys world nys hys peer.                        *none is*
    He hath me sent thee tylle.                         *to you*
  The wylde fyre, that ys so sterne,           *wild fire [of battle]; savage*
  Thyn hore lokkys there schulle berne                *white locks; burn*
    For thyn dedes ylle.                                *wicked*
85  And Roulond that Y be thee se,                     *see beside you*
  And alle tho that be wyght thee,                       *those; with*
    Yut Y hope to spylle."                               *slay*

Roulond sayde, "Do nought ylle,
  But thou haddyst eny skylle,                    *If you have any sense*
90    To none that ys hereinne.
  But yf thou haddyst spylt                         *Unless; cause harm*
fol. 32r  Ere eny thyng more mysgylt,                     *Before; offends*
    Harm schal tou none wynne."               *No harm will come to you*
  Charlemayn the conquerour
95  Comaunde to every dussiper,
    What tale that he bygynne,                     *Whatever his message be*
  That no man leye on hym none hond
  To to the messanger no schond —                   *To do; disgrace*
    Hys wyt hys ful thynne.                          *He has a dim wit*

100  "Ye, Charles, ne care thou nought therefore —     *don't worry about that*
  That ylke man nys nought ybore                 *No one has yet been born*
    That durst me abyde.                           *dares; fight*
  Though he hadde my deth yswore,
  Al hys oth schulde be forlore                       *oath; broken*
105    Whylys that Y have by my syde
  Cursins my goode swerde,                            *Corsouse*
  Wherwith Y was fyrst gerde                           *armed*
    Of Kyng Garcy with pride."                        *By*
  Roulond sayde, "Styfly thou standyst               *Proudly*
110  And ful yelpe wel thou canst,                       *boast*
    And wel canst chyde.                            *insult*
  Yf thou wylt thyn erande bede,                 *carry on your errand*
  Tel on and wende hom in thy nede —                  *go home*
    No lenger that thou ne abyde!"                     *stay*

115  Tho were the Frenche stylle,                        *silent*
  And Otuel gan to carpe grylle                   *speak fiercely*
    To Syre Charlemayn,
  And sayde, "Garcy sent me thee tylle,
  And sayde that he wyl thy body spylle                *kill*
120    For the wynnyng of Spayne.

| fol. 32v | Byleve on hys god Mahon, | |
| | Jubiter, and Syre Platon, | |
| | Thou mayst be ful fayn." | *You must [do so] eagerly* |
| | Charles sayde, "So mote Y thee, | *thrive* |
| 125 | That ylke thay schal thou never se, | *very day* |
| | I telle thee for certayn, | |
| | | |
| | That Y schal byleve on Termagaunt, | *[never] believe* |
| | Ne on mametrye that yow by stant, | *idolatry; adhere to* |
| | Whyle me lastyd my lyf. | |
| 130 | But by the Kyng in Trinité, | |
| | Al so sone as Y may Garcé se, | |
| | Out of londe Y schal hym dryve." | |
| | "Ye, so thynketh me," quod Otuel, | |
| | "The Frenche konne yelpe wel — | *boast* |
| 135 | Ful evyl mote they thryve! | |
| | Faynte men thay gonne agaste, | *They frighten cowards* |
| | And of here dedys thay best unwraste, | *are worthless* |
| | Suche maystrye to kythe." | *proclaim* |
| | | |
| | Tho sayde Syre Charlyon, | |
| 140 | "Sarsin, so helpe thee Mahon, | *Saracen* |
| | Wyl Garcye with me fyght?" | |
| | "Ye, Syre," he sayde, "By my croune, | |
| | Alle the Frenche to fylle adoun, | *conquer* |
| | Be thay never so wyght. | *mighty* |
| 145 | I wote he haght redy thare | *know; has commanded* |
| | An houndred thousand men and mare, | |
| | By day and be nyght; | |
| | For nothyng wel he flen, | *flee* |
| fol. 33r | Though he wyste yslaw to ben, | *knows he will be slain* |
| 150 | For no maner syght. | |
| | | |
| | And yut hath my Lord Garcy | *recently* |
| | Has don arered in Lumbardy | *raised* |
| | A burgh that ys ryche, | *city* |
| | Ful wel hyt ys walled uyterly. | *completely* |
| 155 | The bourgh hys hote Utaly — | *called; Ataly* |
| | There nys none so ryche! | |
| | Two wateres rennen there abowte | *rivers* |
| | That hym bytrenten, san doute, | *encircle it* |
| | With many a dep dyche. | |
| 160 | Yf thow wylt, Charles, undyrfare, | *journey [to Ataly]* |
| | Men schulle se thy sydes bare | |
| | With many a sory tyche. | *wound* |

Thow olde cherl," Otuel sayde,

"Come nought there, Y thee rede,                    *advise you*

165         But go and make a flyng                    *start*

To throwe aboute in ferhede                        *armed combat*

Pies and crowes to don to deth,                    *Magpies*

       And other foules, olde and yong!           *birds*

For age ys stolen thee uppon,

170   And thy lyf dayes beght ny don,              *are nearly done*

       And don hys alle thy werryng.              *is; warring*

Thou nart nought wordy at nede                     *worthy*

Ageynes a knyght to prike a stede,

       And thynne arn al yong."                   *your [knights] are all young*


175   "Schrew Sarsin," Roulond sayde,

"Were thow al so doughty in thede                  *as; deed*

       As tou nowe seist with worde,

Alle thys lond in lengthe and brede

fol. 33v Myght have of thy body drede,

180         Withouten speres orde.                *point*

And thou unto Lumbardy fare,                       *If*

And Y may mete thee there

       With Dorundale my brond,                   *Durendal*

I schall wyte howe hyt can byte                    *teach [you]*

185   For thy wordys and thy dyspyte,              *insults*

       By Jhesu Crist my Lorde."


"Ye," sayd Otuel, and lowe,                         *laughed*

"The brydde that syttyth on the bowe,              *bird; bough*

       For drede of thee fle he wyl fonde,        *be tempted to flee*

190   And Y schall wete wel ynowe                  *know; enough*

Why thou makyst hyt sa towe                        *How tough you will make it*

       Yf thou wylt come to honde.                *to fight*

The wylde best in the fryth                         *wild beast; forest*

Ther ne may no man make hys gryth                  *protect him*

195        Where thou hom fynde in londe.        *If you were to find him*


Yf thou wylt with me fyght,

Do arme thee anoneryght                            *immediately*

       And go we pley in same.                    *together*

Y am redy, syker Y thee plyght,                    *truly; promise*

200   Have Y helme and hauberk bryght

       To layke with thee a game.                 *play*

Men schull wyte be lyte                            *know in a short time*

Wetheres swerde can bettyr byte,                   *Which*

       And that ys levest to grame,               *which is most eager to harm*

205   Wethyr swyrd bettyr byte schall,

Of Cursins and of Dorundale,
  By Mahon swete name!"

Rouland sayd, "Y wyl thee nought spare,
And Y wyst to fynde thee thare,                                    *Should I happen*
210   Forthe with thee wolde Y fyght."
And Otuel sayd, "Have thou no care,
fol. 34r  Into a medowe we schull fare,
  By Mahon ful of myght!
And wethur of us hym withdrawe,
215  Men schull deme the ryght sawe                         *judge; verdict*
  Longe er hyt be nyght."                               *before*
And Rouland sayd with wordys bolde,
"That ilke covenaunt Y schall holde                              *very same*
  Thorugh grace of God Almyght."

220  Gauter of Amoun and Oger,                               *Ogier*
And Olyver and hys fadyr Reyner,
  Charles comaunded in fere,                            *together*
And hys chamberleyn Reyner,
And yfynde the messanger                                         *supply to*
225   All that nede were.                               *All that he needs*

**Fitt 2**

*Here bygynnyth a batayle snelle*                               *fierce*
*Of Rowland and of Otuel,*
  *That wondyrlyche was in syght,*
*And howe Otuel ycristened was.*
230  *Herkenyth nowe a mery pas*                            *story*
  *And of a stronge fyght!*

Amorwe er it were daylyght                                       *In the morning before*
And er the sonne schon bryght,
  Charles to chyrche yede,                              *went*
235  To byseche God Almyght
For Roulond that noble knyght,
  To helpe hym at nede,
With alle the dussypers,
And the abbot of Seynt-Omeres,                                  *Saint-Omer*
240   In ryme as Y rede.
fol. 34v  The abbot song the masse
With ful moche mekenesse                                         *piety*
  And bad Roulond that God schulde hym spede.       *prayed*

Kyng Charles brought a basyn
245  With florens of gold fyn,                              *fine gold coins*

And yede to the offryng.
That he wan of a Sarsin                                    *Whatever*
In the lond of Appolyn,
        Withoute eny lesyng,                              *lying*
250   Charles offrede the basyn al;
And Roulond offred Dorundal,
        ..............n to honouryng,
...n pound of florens, Y undyrstonde.
...Dorundale that good bronde
255         ...........yn gaf Charles the kyng.

...whenne the masse was don everydel,                     *completely*
....com the Sarsin Otuel
        ...........ay al in hyghyng:                       *haste*
...ys Roulond he ys nought lel!                           *loyal*
260   ...trouth nys neveradel!                            *nothing at all*
        ........deth of hys endynge.
......ale yesterday there he stode,
.........................was lete blod,
........................wenyng,
265   .....................ough so byhyd,
...................chal out be kyd,
        ...........nge dwellyng.

...............kneled in a schapel
.....................e Sarsin Otuel,                       *(see t-note)*
fol. 35r        What bost he gan blowe.
271   He yede to hym with hert lel,
And sayde, "Dogge, thou lyest by Seynt Mychel,
        And that schal thou ben knowe!
For Y was never pale ne wan,                              *[i.e., afraid]*
275   For Sarsin ne for no man,
        So God my soule owe."                             *owns*
Tho Charles the conquerour                               *Then*
Comandyd to every dussyper
        To arme Roulond arowe.                           *one by one*

280   The dussypers everychone
Yede to arme Roulond anone,                              *Came*
        Alle withoute fayle.
On hym an haketon thay gonne done                         *padded jacket*
Over hys hauberk, that bryght schon,                     *coat of mail*
285         That ryche was of mayle —
And it made, ywys,                                        *was made, truly*
That was whylom Denys prentys —                           *By one who was once an apprentice of Denis*
        Of a trewe entayle,                              *beautiful design*
Estre of Langares, that was lel,

290          Brought hym an helm of steel
                    Ful strong to assayle.

             The helm was grene as glas
             Tha whylome hit aught Galyas,                              *once was owned by*
                    And sythe Kyng Barbatyan.                           *afterwards*
295          Hym gert in that plas                                      *armed*
             With Dorundale that good was,
                    That he byfore wanne.
             Duk Reyner hym brought a schyld,
             A fayrer myght have be non in feld,
fol. 35v            And that wel many a man telle can,
301          With a lyon thereinne raumpande,                           *reared up*
             That whylome aught a geante                                *was once owned by a giant*
                    That was a doughty man.

             Tho Olyver hym brought a spere,                            *Then*
305          As good as any man myght bere
                    In feld to batayle;
             Kyng, knyght, ere any ryder                                *or*
             Myght it ful wel were,
                    Hys enymye to assayle.
310          The Duk Terry sette anone                                  *Then*
             The spores that of gold schon,                             *spurs; shone*
                    Forsothe withoute fayle.

             Oger hym brought hys stede,
             As good as any man myght lede —
315                 Hyt was wonne in Hongery.
             Hit ne bar never knyght at nede
             But he schulde wel spede                                   *have success*
                    And wynne the maystery.
             The sadyl was wel dere-worth,                              *splendid*
320          The beste aboven erthe
                    That eny man myght aspeye.                          *find*
             Roulond into the sodel sprong,
             And rod hym to Charles the kyng,
                    Hys mercy forto crye.                               *To seek his blessing*

325          Kyng Charles hef up hys hond                               *held*
             And blessyd hys cosyn Roulond,
                    And at hym leve he tok,                             *he [Roland] took his leave [of Charles]*
             And into the medewe he gan ryde.
             There ran a water by that syde,
fol. 36r            That was a wel dep brok.                            *brook*
331          That on Leire ycleped ys,                                  *Loire*

And that other Some, ywys,                                    *Somme*
      Also sayth sure the bok.


Anone com Otuel to the kyng,
335   And bysought hym in hyyng                          *at once*
      That he hym lente armur:                    *should lend*
Spere and schyld atte bygynnyng,                              *first*
Helm, hauberk, and other thyng
      That myght dyntes endure.                   *blows*
340   Kyng Charles called Belysent,
Hys doughter, so fayre and gent,
      Curtayse, cler, and pure.                   *beautiful*
"Doughter, tak to the messanger                              *receive*
Into thy chaumber ryght now here,
345      And arme hym wel and sure."


The mayde hym answared with hert lel,
"Y schal hym arme swythe wel,                                 *very*
      As ye han me bede."                         *bidden*
Sche toke Laumbr de Mouble,
350   And mayde Resonet de Rowenele,
      To fette forthe hys wede.                   *garments*
Sche went to the kynges cheste
And tok armur of the beste
      That eny knyght myght lede,                 *wear*
355   And gan to arme that hethen knyght,
That in batayle ne in fyght                                  *So that*
      Of no man hym ne drede.          *He might fear no man*


Fyrst an haketon of fyn styl,                                *padded jacket*
And an hauberk ywrought ful wel,                             *coat of mail*
fol. 36v      She dude on that knyght.               *put*
361   Mayde Rosynet de Rowenel
An helme brought to Syre Otuel,
      And on hys heued hyt dyghte.                *head; placed*
The helme was riche, for the nonys,
365   Of sylver, gold, and precious stones
      That schone ful bryghtt.
The Belysent hym gyrde                                       *Then*
With Cursins hys gode swerde                                 *Corsouse*
      That felon was in fyght.                    *fierce*


370   The burde Belysent hym brought                   *lady*
A schylde, no bettyr myght be wrought,                       *shield*
      Forsothe withoute fable.
Hyt was so wel ywrought
That none myght bettyr be thought,

375    With thre Sarisins heuedys of sabyl         *black*
   In syghte of hys schylde, to lede.       *on the front of; carry*
   Thay broughten to hym Mygades stede       *(see note)*
     Out of the kyngys stable;

   Anon the stede wyst wel
380  That hys maystyr Otuel
     Schuld to batayle.
   The mayde Rosenet de Rouenel
   Thoo spores fettyn hym, good and lel,     *Then; trustworthy*
     Wythouten ony fayle.
385  The Sarisin spronge into the sadyl anone,
   And priked the stede and let hym gone,
     That was of fayre entayle.        *appearance*
   Agen to Belysent he rode;
   The mayde stode and abode,
390     That was of hye parayle.        *high nobility*

fol. 37r "Damysel, gramercy!" sayde Otuel,
   "Myn armure ys good and lel,
     By that Y se in syght;
   And that schal Rouland fynde wel,
395  With my swerde yground of stel,       *sharpened*
     That Y am a man of myght."
   "Syre Otuel," quod that mayd smale,       *young*
   "I rede thee that thou kepe fro Dorundale,     *advise*
     For Rowland ys a man ful wyght;     *powerful*
400  And but thou kepe wel thyne heued,      *Unless*
   Ellys hyt worthe sone astoned      *become; smashed*
     Ful longe ere hyt be nyght.       *before*

   Ac thyke Lorde, that best may,       *But this same*
   Fro schame schylde thee today,
405     Yf yt be Hys wylle."
   Otuel went forthe hys way
   Into the medewe as hyt lay;
     Rowland he thought to spylle.       *kill*
   Kyng Charles the conquerour
410  Went up into hys toure,
     An gan to crye schrylle:        *loudly*
   "Now, lordyngys al!" he sayde,
   "Gothe nowe fast oute of the mede,      *meadow*
     That no man come hem tylle!"      *near them*

415  And the knyghtes with sperys tho
   Smyten her horsys and let hem go,
     As men of moche myght.

In the felde to fyght thay were tho,
For eythyr was other foo —
420         That was a sely syght! *remarkable*
The gonne to ryden with grete raundon *They; speed*
fol. 37v Eyther to bere other adown,
        With strengthe and fyght.
The speres were scharp and gode,
425 And thorugh the schyldes they wode, *pierced*
        Into here bryny bryght. *coats of mail*

Yperced was eyther scheld
That the speres al toschyvered, *splintered*
        That were so gret and long.
430 Off here stedys they fellyn adoun,
So dude eyther gomphanon — *banners*
        No game was hem among!
Tho sone thay wyste that thay were sounde *As soon as*
And neyther of hem hadden wounde,
435         Anone ageyn to hors they sprong;
Ful faste they gonne togedyr smyte
Ful sterne strokys and stryte, *violent*
        The fyr therafter outsprong. *sparks*

"Now," quod Belysent, "Y am sure
440 That good and trewe ys Otuels armure;
        The sothe Y se everydele.
To God Y make my prayer,
As He hys Lord and brought ous dere, *is; redeemed (bought)*
        Leve hym to spede wel." *Allow*
445 The knyghtes eft togyder gonne ryde
And foughten as they were wode,
        With good hert and lel;
Duk Roulond with Dorundale,
He gaf strokys many and fele,
450         And spared neveradel. *not a bit*

Roulond with Dorundale so fel
fol. 38r A sterne stroke gaf Otuel
        Uppon the helm so schene, *bright*
That god and stonys and crystall *god [i.e., depiction of Mahoun]*
455 Tobrokyn and into the foeld fel,
        To wetyn and nought to wene. *To know and not to guess*
Hys honde he withdrowe, aplyght, *certainly*
And smote a dynte of muche myght *so much*
        That thay myghten it sene.
460 The hors byfore the knyght *in front of*

By the schuldrys anoneryght,
    He smote on the grene.         *field*

Otuel fyl to grounde
And felt hym hole and sounde,        *himself to be*
465       And sayd to Rouland in sede,     *in his seat*
"Yut am Y hole and sounde,
And thou worse than ony hounde,
    So Mahon me spede!
Thou hast don grete vylonye
470   Wenne thou sparest my bodye
    And hast slayn my stede.
And er we departe atto,
Y schall do thee moche wo
    And do thy sydes to blede."      *make*

475   Anon Sir Otuel with hys honde
A strok gaf Sir Roulande,
    A ful styrne dynt of myght.
He forcarfe, Y understande,      *sliced off*
A grete pese with hys honde
480     Off hys hauberk, ful ryght.
The stede he carf even ato,      *in half*
Bytwene the schuldrys, anoneryght tho,
    Even into the erthe ryght.
fol. 38v  Roulond fel to the grounde,
485   But he ne hadde no wounde,
    He thonkyth God Almyght.

Tho was Rouland sore agramyd;    *enraged*
Was he never so sore aschamed
    Byfore in no batayle.
490   Eft they foughten in samen,    *Once again; together*
Ne was ther no chyldys game,
    So harde gan eythyr othyr assayle.
The medewe quok of her dynt,    *quaked with their strokes*
The fyr outsprang as spark of flynt,
495     Oute of helme, hauberk, and mayle.
Tho Roulond hastylyche anone
Dronke to hym wel good wone    *good fortune*
    Of strokys, withouten fayle.

Quod Belysent to the kyng tho,
500   "Thy batayle worthe sone ydo,    *will soon be done*
    By that Y se in syght.
The swete worchyth hem to wo,    *sweat stirs; woe*
That here hertys bothe to    *two*

Bene astonyed of fyght." *dazed*

505 Kyng Charles felle don on knees tho,
And an oryson to God he gan do, *prayer*
That ys in hevyn lyght,
That He sende pes hem bytwene,
And the Sarisin to be cristen, *baptized*
510 As He ys ful of myght.

Roulond to Otuel tho sayd,
"Sarisin, do by my rede, *advice*
And leve on God Almyght! *believe in*
And to the kyng Y woll thee lede,
515 And he woll geve thee to mede *as a reward*
Hys doughtyr so bryght.

fol. 39r And thou and I and Oliver
Mowen wende togedyr in fere *May go; as companions*
Into batayle and into fyght.
520 Ne schulle we fynde in no londe
None that schall us withstonde,
Neythyr kyng ne knyght."

Quod Otuel, "So mote Y thee, *thrive*
That ne schaltou never se —
525 To forsake Mahon,
Ne Tormegaunt that ys so fre,
Ne Jovyn, the goddys thre,
That beth goddys of grete renown!
By that I have yment *Instead I intend that*
530 Erst Y schall geve thee a dynt *First*
With Cursins my fauchon!" *sword*
Efte togedyr they smyten, aplyght, *Again*
Eythyr of hem was so lyght *agile*
And wode as eny lyon. *mad*

535 Duk Roulond the gode knyght
Smote a dynt of moche myght
Anone to the paynym.
Therof the Sarisin hadde a syght
And that strok he flye, aplyght, *dodged*
540 That hyt fel bysyde hym.
The hauberk fro the schuldyr bone,
Rouland carf yt down anone —
That was a stroke ful grym!
"Allas!" he sayde, "unworthy in hape." *luck*
545 For ther ne fel out no blodys drepe *drops of blood*
Out there at none lym. *any limb*

The Frenche cryed anonryght,
"Nowe overcome ys thys fyght,

fol. 39v          Thorughe helpe of God and Marye!"
550    At lyte they knewe that hethyn knyght,                          *Little did they know*
By God that thys world had dyght,
Ne nothyng of hys felonye.                              *Nor anything of his violent temper*
Roulond on the holme he smote
With Cursins that bytter bote                                      *bitterly struck*
555          A strok with grete envye.                                *malice*
Yf the swerde ne hadde ywenyd,                                      *slipped*
Rouland hys lyf ther hadde lenyd,                                   *lost*
And Otuel wonne the maystrye.

Tho was Rouland swythe wo                                   *very dismayed*
560    That he ne myght that Sarisin slo
That was so ful of pryde.
The Sarisin smote efte so                                   *once again*
Hys hauberk evene ato,                                      *evenly in half*
Evene alonge by the syde.
565    The Frenche seyen that all,                                     *saw*
And to Jhesu Cryst they gonne calle,
And alle to God helpe they cryede.
With that ther come a colvyr bryght                                 *dove*
That fro hevene tho lyght,                                  *alighted*
570          In that ilke tyde.                                *very moment*

The Holy Gost thorugh here alder prayer                     *of them all*
Alyght apon that Sarisin there
Thorugh Goddys holy myght.
Tho sayd the messanger,
575    "Leve Roulond, come me ner.                                     *Dear*
Y have forlorne my fyght.                                   *given up*
Mahon and Jovyn Y wyl forsake,
And to Jhesu Crist Y wyl me take
To bene Hys knyght."
580    The Sarisin drewe awey hys bronde,                              *threw*
And so dude Duk Roulond,

fol. 40r          And kust hem anonryght.                           *they kissed*

And Charles went thyder anone,
And so dud the barons echon
585          That weren in that cyté.
Quod Charles, "How ys thys ydon?"
And Rouland sayd to hym anon,
"Thys Sarisin cristen wyl be,
But thou most sese in hys hond                                      *grant*
590    Belysent, with muche londe,

    Thy doughtyr, fayr and fre."
  Tho sayd Charles the kynge,
  "Y am glad of thys tythyng         *tiding*
    That Y hem so schal se."

595 To chyrche they went anonryght,
  And Turpyn cristened that knyght
    That couthe Goddys lawe.       *learned*
  The kyng toke her by the hond;
  "Doughtyr," he sayd, "to me thou undyrstond  *from me*
600   Nowe a lyte throwe      *in a short while*
  Thou schalt be weddyd to thys knyght."
  "Syr," sche sayd, "syker aplyght,     *very truly*
    Therof Y am ful fawe."      *willing*
  Tho sayd Charles to Sir Otuel,
605 "Thou schalt have thys damysel
    Ryght as for thyn awe."      *own*

  Quod Otuel, "Yf ye love me wel,
  Ye ne dur drede neveradel    *need never endure dread at all*
    Of Garcins grete power."
610 The mayde yaf agen an answere,
  "Syr," sche sayd, "Have thou no care,
    By Goddys moder dere,
  Y love thee more in hert myn
fol. 40v Thanne Y do my fadyr and al my kyn
615   That me to woman bere."   *Who raised me to womanhood*

  Syr Otuel to the kyng sayde,
  "Thou most lede with thee thys mayde   *must take*
    Withouten eny vylonye,
  With knyghtys gode, doughty in dede,
620 With schyld, and spere, and many a chylde,  *person (i.e., man)*
    Ferre into Lumbardye.
  Whenne thou hast that londe ynome   *taken*
  And all the Sarisins overcom
    And yslowe Kynge Garcye,    *slain*
625 Thenne woll we be spousyd, ywys,   *married*
  And holde fest with joye and blysse
    In the burugh of Utalye."    *city*

  The kyng with hys knyghtys alle
  Wenten to Parys into hys halle
630   With moche melodye.
  He held fest ryche and ryall,     *feast*
  Forsothe, in the kyngys halle,
    With myrthe and mynstrelsye.

|        | At the fourtenyghtys ende,                | *two weeks'* |
| 635    | He asked yf he wolde wende                | *should* |
|        | Forthe into Lumbardye,                    |  |
|        | Or ellys byleve styl thare                | *remain* |
|        | Tyl the wynter passed were                |  |
|        | And the wethyr were drye.                 |  |

| 640    | Kyng Charles of Seynt-Denys               |  |
|        | In that same cyté of Parys,               |  |
|        | Somer he ther gan byde.                   | *Summer; await* |
|        | And whenne the fowlys songon on the rys,  | *birds; branch* |
|        | The kyng sent aftyr knyghtys of prys;     | *excellence* |
| 645    | To a mownteyn gan he ryde.                |  |
|        | Forsothe, the left the kyng,              | *then departed* |
|        | And with hym many a gret lordyng,         |  |
| fol. 41r | With ladyes ful gret in pryde.          |  |
|        | Ther was Rowland and Olyver               |  |
| 650    | And Syr Otuel and Oger —                  |  |
|        | In hert ys nought to huyde!               | *hold back* |

|        | Esteryche of Langares and Sir Turpyn,     |  |
|        | Archel, Etus, and Syr Geryn,              |  |
|        | Nemes and Sir Reyner,                     |  |
| 655    | Tho thay were in the kyngys inne,         | *When; lodgings* |
|        | They say many a paynym                    | *saw* |
|        | Comyng with grete power:                  |  |
|        | Lemosyns, Bretons, and Lumbardye,         | *Limousins (i.e., inhabitants of Limoges)* |
|        | Bayons, Gaskoynes, and Pycardye,          |  |
| 660    | Of londys bothe ferre and ner;            |  |
|        | Provynciales and Almaynes,                |  |
|        | That couthen wel fyght on the playnes,    |  |
|        | Of Normans bothe stoute and fere.         | *And* |

## Fitt 3

|        | *Nowe here bygynnyth a batayle*           |  |
| 665    | *Ful fel to founde, sam fayle,*           | *violent to relate, without fail* |
|        | *Of thre goode dussypers —*               |  |
|        | *Rowlond, Olyver, and Oger.*              |  |
|        | *Forsothe, yt were knyghtes sam pyr,*     | *without peer* |
|        | *Ypreved in many contrés.*                |  |

| 670    | *Howe they slowe undyr a forest*          |  |
|        | *Kynges thre that were full prest*        | *ready* |
|        | *To fyght in mede othyr in felde,*        |  |
|        | *And the furthe kynge they toke,*         | *fourth; captured* |

|  | *As hyt ys fownd in the boke,* |  |
|---|---|---|
| 675 | *And slowen all that with hym helde.* |  |

| fol. 41v | In Averel the thyrdde thay, | *April; day* |
|---|---|---|
|  | Whenne foules synge on the spray, | *branch* |
|  | Thay wentyn fro Seynt-Denys. |  |
|  | Syre Otuel with muche pryde |  |
| 680 | Sette Belysent by hys syde |  |
|  | Uppon a mule a prys. | *of worth* |
|  | And sone after thay forlete | *departed* |
|  | The lond that hem thought swete, |  |
|  | And leftyn Parys. |  |
| 685 | Forth to Burgoyne the wente, | *Burgundy they* |
|  | Two ferdales, verement, | *furlongs, truly (see note)* |
|  | That Otuellys was, ywys. | *belonged to Otuel* |

|  | And forth they wente into Lumbardye, |  |
|---|---|---|
|  | To that mount swythe hey | *very high hill* |
| 690 | That men callyn Poyne. |  |
|  | And there the Frensche myghten se |  |
|  | The borwgh that men calle Utalé, |  |
|  | Bysyde the water of Coyne. |  |
|  | In a mede that grene was |  |
| 695 | Charles chese a fayre plas | *chose* |
|  | To telden on hys pavylon. | *pitch his tent* |
|  | Sevene dayes he sojourned there, |  |
|  | And over the water he dude rere | *build* |
|  | A fayre brygge, withoute assoyne, | *bridge; delay* |

|  | That the Frenche men myghten tho |  |
|---|---|---|
| 700 | Over that brygge come and go, |  |
|  | To fleen here enymyes. |  |
|  | Uppon a day it byfylle so, |  |
|  | The Duk Roulond and knyghtes to | *two* |
| fol. 42r | Spokyn wordys unwys; | *Spoke unwise words [i.e., acted foolishly]* |
| 706 | And armeden hem in goode wede, | *clothing (i.e., armor)* |
|  | And uche of hem tok a gode stede | *each* |
|  | That was of gret prys; |  |
|  | Thay bysaughtyn God Almyght |  |
| 710 | That he schulde hem fynde here fylle of fyght, | *find for them abundant fighting* |
|  | For the love of Sent Denys. |  |

|  | Kynges foure withouten fayle, |  |
|---|---|---|
|  | Were went out to seche batayle, | *seek* |
|  | Of hedynesse thay were, | *heathenness* |
| 715 | Wel yarmyd, syker sam fayle. |  |
|  | Ye mowe yhere grete mervayle. | *might* |

Lordynges, wyl ye now here?

Here names Y wylle that yow wyte,                                    *Their*

As in Frensche it ys ywrete,                                        *written*

720          Now lesteneth to lere —                                   *learn*

Curables and Askeward

And Balsomon strong and hard;

Clarel was here fere.                                              *companion*


The knyghtes seyden as they gonne ryde,

725     Yf thay myght that tyme abyde                        *If it were to happen*

That thay myght with Roulond mete,

Thay wolde hym make blody syde,                      *bloody his sides*

And Olyver that was so ful of pride,

With grymly woundes and grete.

730     Tho sayde Clarel that ryche kyng,

"Suche res nyl helpe no thyng,                                    *rashness*

Ne no bale vyl it bote.                              *It won't cure any misfortune*

Ye han herd here byfore,

That Roulond as a knyght ycore,                               *is; special*

fol. 42v          Curtays be way or strete.                         *everywhere*


736     At wolde my lord Termagaunt,                          *By the will of*

That Y myght mete with Roulond,

With hym wolde Y fyght.

Hyt scholde hym rewe, with myn hond,                    *He will regret*

740     The doughty eyres of Agelond                              *heirs*

That he slow with unryght."

The knyghtes undyr the forest were,

And herden the kynges alle there,

And of hem haddyn a syght.

745     The place was called Forestent,

That the knyghtes were in went,

That weren of muche myght.


Roulond to hys felawes sayde,

"Now we have that we bede —                                   *prayed for*

750          God ous save hole and sounde —

But we ben doughty in dede                                        *If*

And styf syttyng on stede

Whenne we hem haven founde."

He smot hys hors and let hym gon,

755     And Kyng Clarel sey hym anone,                              *saw*

By hys lord Mahound,

"Thre knyghtes Cristen Y se!

We beth foure, and thay but thre.

Go we felle hem to grounde."

760 Alle foure knyghtes with muche pride
   Smyten here hors and gonne to ryde                         *Spurred*
      Ageynes the knyghtes kene.                          *fierce*
   And Askeward, nought to hyde,
   He gaf Roulond a wounde wyde
fol. 43r       With a spere that was ful kene,                *sharp*
766 That thorugh hys schylde yt wode,               *penetrated*
   And at hys hauberk hyt withstode,                 *But*
      Wel Y wote, withowtyn wene;                     *lie*
   And Rowland thoughth that strok to yelde,      *return*
770 An karfe ato the kyngys schelde,                 *in two*
      Anonryght uppon that grene.

   The stroke was scharp that Rouland sprong,
   And thorugh the kynges hert hyt stonge
      And thorughoute hys syde.
775 Kyng Corable so egre smot                     *eagerly*
   With a spere that bytter bote               *bit bitterly*
      Bytwene hauberk and hyde.                  *skin*
   Tho was the spere byhynde fast,      *When; stuck behind*
   The knyght sat the sadyl brast,     *[on] the broken saddle*
780       With yre and muche pryde.             *anger*

   Oger Denys hys swerde out brayde,     *Ogier the Dane; drew*
   And to the kynge fast he leyde —
      He couthe ful wel hys craft.               *knew*
   A wownde he made swythe wyde,
785 The armur fyl down by hys syde,
      The helme conne outbrast.               *shattered*
   Balsamon, a kyng unhende,                *ignoble*
   To Olyver he wolde wende
      And quelle hym with hys craft.    *overcome; strength*
790 Oliver he smot with hys schelde,
   The launce brast in the felde —
      That was a wel gode schaft.

   Olyver withouten abode                     *delay*
   With that cours to hym rode,             *Forcefully*
795       And in the schylde hym hytte.
fol. 43v The schaft was strong and the heued brod,     *spearhead*
   And thorugh the kynges body hyt glod,
      And made a wel brod flytte.              *wound*
   Doun he fyl dede to grounde,
800 Ne was he never afterward sonde,
      Non lenger myght he sytte.
   Slaw weren the kynges thre,

|  |  |  |
|---|---|---|
| | But yet nolde nought the ferthe fle, | |
| | So wod he was of wytte. | *maddened* |
| | | |
| 805 | Hym thought hys hert brast ato | |
| | But yf he myght Olyver slo | *Unless* |
| | Ere he thennes wende. | *from there* |
| | He smot hys stede and let hym go. | *gallop* |
| | In hys herte hym was ful wo, | |
| 810 | For slawe were al hys kynde. | *slain; people* |
| | But Roulond tho bytwyne rode | |
| | And the kynges strok he abode, | |
| | He kydde that he was hende. | *showed; noble* |
| | Ac though the strok weren ful grete, | *But even though* |
| 815 | In the schelde he it sette, | |
| | He nolde no lenger lende. | *delay* |
| | | |
| | The schaft was bothe gret and long, | |
| | And the kyng was wondyr strong, | |
| | And schof as he wolde awede. | *charged; enraged* |
| 820 | Theren nas no game hem among, | *between them* |
| | The schaft was styf and nought outsprong | *flexible* |
| | And overdrew hys stede. | *extended beyond* |
| | Hors and man of Roulonde ryght | *Roland's horse and body directly* |
| fol. 44r | The kyng threw doun, aplyght. | *truly* |
| 825 | "Mahoun joye!" he gredde. | *cried* |
| | That was the maner of the lawe, | *custom* |
| | Whenne a knyght were overthrowe | |
| | That doughty were of dede. | |
| | | |
| | Kyng Clarel wolde awey have rede, | *ridden* |
| 830 | Ac Oger com by that other syde | |
| | And smot hym with a spere. | |
| | Hys hynder arson gan out glyde, | *uptilted back of a saddle* |
| | Over the sadyl, it nys nought to hyde, | |
| | There Oger gan hym bere. | |
| 835 | Oger tok the kynges stede, | |
| | And to Roulond gan hym lede, | |
| | And sayd, "Here ys on thee to bare! | *one for* |
| | Thys ys an hors good an fyn | |
| | And moche bettyr thanne was thyn, | |
| 840 | And with gayer gere!" | *more colorful* |
| | | |
| | Rowland up stert and nought ne lay, | *didn't lie down* |
| | And into the sadyl that was so gay | |
| | Smertilyche gan he sprynge. | *Skillfully* |
| | Ryght to the place they token the way, | |
| 845 | Ther that they fought, sothe to say, | |

With Sir Clarell the kyng.
The Duk Roulond and Olyver,
Wyghthly they wente the kyng ner,                              *Valiantly*
    Withouten more dwellyng,
850  But Kyng Clarel toke that fyght
Agens hem thre with al hys myght,                              *the three of them*
    Forsothe withoute lesynge.

Tyl hys swerd was brost atto,                                 *When*
fol. 44v  No wondyr thowe hym were wo,                        *if*
855      Nedes he most hym yelde.                             *He had to surrender*
He bysought Rowlond do,                                       *then*
He schulde hym save from hys fo,
    And from alle harme hym schylde.
That broke swerd hym bytok                                    *broken*
860  The good Rowland, so seyth my boke,
    Ther he yt fonde in felde.
They setten the kyng uppon a stede,
And to Charles they thought hym lede,
    To Mount Paynt that ys teld.

**Fitt 4**

865  *Nowe here bygynneth a batayle*
*Of these thre knyghtes, sam fayle,*
    *That wondyr it ys to telle!*
*For Cristendom they foughten ful sore*
*With vi milers and vii sckore*                               *six thousand and seven score [i.e., 6,140]*
870      *Off Sarisins stronge and felle.*

And as they yendyrward weren,                                 *headed in that direction (yonder)*
The sey an host hem byforn                                    *They saw*
    Of Kyng Garcions knyghtys,
With vi milers and vii skore,
875  The strengyst Sarisins that ower were;                   *ever*
    Alle they were redy to fyght.
Ther-thorugh thay most hym lede,
Or ellys lese her manhede                                     *reputation for valor*
    Yf that they flowyn, aplyght.                             *Were they to flee*
880  He herde trumpes and tabeures,                           *They; drums*
Hornes, chymbys, and chynoures.                               *chimes; cymbals*
    Somdel they were afryght.                                 *They were quite afraid*

The good Oger sayd tho,
fol. 45r  "Good hyt ys to lete hym go,
885      Clarelle the kene kyng —
Yut he may save ous fro wo;

Among the Sarisins altho                                                          *because*
    He ys a grete lordyng."
Where he wolde, thay lat hym passe.                                               *Wherever he wished*
890    And these knyghtys with Goddys grace
    Assaylethen bothe elthe and yong.                         *Assailed; old*
Roulond made a grysly wounde
In Kyng Bremer, forsothe, that stounde                                           *soon after*
    That he hadde hys endyng.

895    Tho Syre Olyver after thanne
Slow a kyng that hyght Blasan,
    That ful strong was in fyght.
Syre Oger, that doughty man,
Slow another that hyght Morgan
900    With Cursable so bryght.                              *(see note)*
And Roulond with Dorundale,
Deled strokes gret and smale —
    Forsothe, there was a semly syght!                      *splendid*
Olyver with Haunchecler
905    Slow many a Sarsin there
    With swerd that schon ful bryght.

Over alle, where these knyghtes rod
There was ymad a way ful brod
    That waynes myghten mete.                               *carts; pass [i.e., broad as a two-way street]*
910    For there that Dorundale glod,                       *Wherever*
There was no Sarsin that abod                                                    *encountered [it]*
    That he ne lese hys swete.                              *lifeblood*
There come Carmele de Taborye
Uppon a stede of Lumbardye,
fol. 45v    And grymlyche gan to grede.                      *lament*
916    "Fyghteth," he sayde, "better wone,                  *for better luck*
Or ellys we beyth dede uchone!                                                   *each one*
    Who schal ouren bale bete?                              *relieve our suffering*

Fy, a devlys! How may thys be
920    That these Crysten knyghtes thre
    Schulle bryng ous alle to grounde?
Ryght ful sone ye schullyn se
Myn owyn hond schal you sle
    Wythin a lytyl stounde."
925    He smot Oger on the schylde
That he felle into the fylde
    And in hys body a wounde.
Oger do off hys stede felle,                                                     *then*
And the blod of hys body outwelle —
930    Such hap he hath there founde!                       *ill luck*

Tho Roulond that syght sey,                                  *When*
For wrath he was wood wel neyghe
    And priked tho to Carmele.
He smot hym on the helm in hye,
935    That in to the sadyl the swerd fley —
    No leche ne myght hym hele.                          *surgeon*
Tho come Syre Aufer of Daubery,
The strengest with Garcy,
    He thought with hym to mele.                         *fight*
940    With hys spere he smot hys schylde,
    That the hede at the haubrek feld,            *spearhead; broke*
    So myche was that steole.                 *strong; steel armor*

Tho Roulond worthy on wede,                              *in armor*
He dude dere a welle good dede:                              *there*
945    That Sarisin there he slow.
fol. 46r  These knyghtes bothe, for certayn,
Ere they wenten out of the playn,
    Fyghtyng they hadde ynowe.                         *enough*
As Olyver sat on hys stede,
950    Rowlond tho to hym yede,
    "Here bygynneth a sory plawe!"                      *plight*
Therof sayd Olyver, "Thou ne drede!                      *Do not fear*
My strenghthe ys good and nothyng gnede —               *not lacking*
    Of hem Y ne yeve nought an hawe!"       *Of them I care not a bit*

955    Tho thay bothe gonne to ryde,
And slowe adown ucche syde                               *slew; each*
    Alle that they before hem stode.
Of gode Oger in that tyde,
That blod ranne oute of hys wounde wyde,
960    And he syked sore unsounde.                      *groaned*
Tho the Sarisins hym throng                       *Then; bombarded*
With sperys and swyrdys strong,
    And made hym many a wounde.
So fast hys body gan blede
965    That he forgate hys gode stede —             *abandoned*
    Wel wo was hym that stowunde!                    *moment*

With that come ryde an amerel                        *Saracen lord*
Bysydes the Kyng Clarel
    That Roulond feld adown;
970    For Oger savede hym that tyde,          *Because Ogier had saved him once*
Amonge the Sarisins of muche pryde
    Dude Oger grete renon.            *[He] did Ogier a great honor*
"Come to me!" Clarel seyde,

"Of nothyng ne schaltou drede,

fol. 46v  Ne of no Sarsins treson.

976       Forsothe, there schal no man de drede                          *make you afraid*
          Whyles my body may thee were,                                  *guard*
                By my god Mahon."

          The ameraunt sayde, "So mote Y thee,

980       Thou ne schalt nought hys waraunt be,                          *guarantor*
                That he ne schal be todrawe."                            *dismembered*
          The kyng wel wroth tho was he,
          He hewed the ameraunt in peces thre,
                And so he hath hym slawe.

985       "Lo," he sayde, "Syre Ameral,
          Thus men thee teche schall
                To sygge wycked sawe,                                    *say; statement*
          Now may Oger Denys
          Ever more have pes                                             *peace*

990             In ernest and eke in plawe."                            *play*

          He dude knyghtes come hym ner,                                 *commanded*
          And bytok hem Denys Oger                                       *entrusted to them*
                To hys lemman hym to lede.                               *sweetheart*
          Forth they went alle yfere,                                    *together*

995       And fond that mayde in on erbere,                             *garden*
                And thus to here thay sayde:                             *her*
          "Kyng Clarel, thyn owyn lemman,
          Swythe wel thee grete can,
                And for hys love he thee bede                            *prays*

1000      Thou scholdyst kepe thys Cristen knyght.
          Today he had wonne in fyght
                Many goode knyghtes in dede.

          Twey other and thys knyght
          Thys day haveth slaw in fyght

1005            A thousand of oure mayné."                               *troops*
          Thenne lowe that mayde so bryght,                              *laughed*
fol. 47r  And sayde to hym anoneryght,                                   *them*
                "Why ne hadde ye brought al thre?"
          Tho sayde to here a knyght doughty,

1010      "Good damysel Enfamy,
                Ous ne lyketh syker no gle!                              *We really don't like your mockery*
          Fyrst mote somer come
          Ere thay tweye wyl be ynome,                                  *Before those two; taken*
                And more batayle schal be."

1015      The damysel do anoneryght                                      *then*
          Cleped sevene of here knyght,                                  *Called for*

                    And bytok hem Syre Oger.
          Bothe by day and eke by nyght,
          Hereself hys woundys gan dyght                          *tended to*
1020            And gaf hym drynkes der.                          *precious potions*
          Sche made hym salves soft,
          And as Oger lay in loft
                    He feld hym bothe hole and fer.               *felt himself grow; strong*
          Whenne he waked, he hadde no wounde,
1025      But felt hys body hole and sounde.
                    To God he made hys prayer.


          And ever Roulond and Olyver
          Ageynes the Sarsins foughte there,
                    That were so ful of pryde.
1030      Tho that they sey that Garcy com there                  *When*
          With helm bryght and many spere
                    Uppon here ryght syde,
          Ful loth hem was to ben ytake do.                       *captured then*
          They smyten here hors and letten hem go,                *spurred; gallop*
1035                Away gonne thay to ryde.
          An houndred Sarsins and wel mo
          Faste redyn after tho
                    To take hem in that tyde.


                    *         *          *


fol. 47v  Otuel aspyede wel there                                 *noticed*
1040      How Oger, Roulond, and Olyver
                    Weren out yfare,                              *gone away*
          And with hem never a dussyper.
          Charlys the coquerour
                    Therfor was in care.                          *anxious*
1045      Otuel let crye thorow the oste,
          "In the name of the Holy Gost,
                    As armes, lordynges, yare!"                   *To arms; make ready*
          Florys, hys stede, he bestrod,
          And Samon by hym rode
1050                And hys baner bare.


          Toward the batayle he gan ryde
          With hys knyghtes by hys syde;
                    With Roulond he gan mete.
          Many a Sarisin in that tyde
1055      Sayden to Roulond, and cryde,
                    "Lese thou schalt thy swete!"                 *lifeblood*
          Syr Otuel gan to chyde,
          And sayde, "Roulond, for thy pryde

Thy lyfe thou wylt forlete! *give up*
1060 What wenes tou and Olyver alone *presume*
To sle the Sarysyns everchon,
And thus to grounde hem bete?

Nay, though thou and Y and Olyver
Hadde ben ther al in fer
1065 Ageyns the hedyn lawe — *heathen*
And ek Charles the conquerour,
fol. 48r Though he brought alle hys power —
Yet schuld they be nought alle slawe.
Ac turne ageyn with me anone,
1070 And venge we ous of Godys fone, *foes*
And gynne we a new plawe. *let us begin a new battle*
Ther schulle a thousand, for thys thyng,
Thys day of hem have here enthyng *ending*
Withinne a lytel thrawe." *short time*

1075 A knyght there was swythe fre, *noble*
He was cleped Emptybré,
In the foward of the batayle. *vanguard*
He come dryvyng to Syr Olyvere,
Allemost he com hym to ner,
1080 Forsothe without fayle.
Olyver with a good spere
Thorugh the hert gan hym bere
Ryght over at hys hors tayle,
That the Sarisin overdrew — *fell over*
1085 That the soth men wel knewe,
That weren at that assayle.

Esterych of Langares, a dussyper,
Slow a Sarysin stoute and fer
That was of Turkye.
1090 He smot hym thorugh the lyver,
That he ne flycted, fer ne ner. *couldn't escape*
"Mahon, help!" he gan crye.
Many an helme was ofwenyde, *flew off*
And many a bassinet al tocleved
1095 Of the Sarsin companye.
Many a spere and many a schyld,
fol. 48v Were dryven adown into the feld,
And many a sadyl made empty.

Olmadas of Aschomoyne
1100 He gaf Charles chamberleyne *struck*
That bar Duk Reyner adoun,

And toke the stede by the reyne
To wynnen at he was ful fayne                                    *eager*
    And lepe into the arson.                              *saddle*
1105  But Emoleres, a strong knyght,
Hym to sle he dud hys myght
    With hys gode fawchon.
He smote the Sarisin in the schyld,
That helm and heued flye into fylde,
1110      And wanne hym grete renoun.

Tho come Galyan, that hethen knyght
That erst hadde slayn in fyght                                   *previously*
    Many a Crysten man.
He smote Emoleres aplyght,
1115  That to grownde he fyl ryght.
    Hys stede of hym he wan.
Wel nyghe he hadde hym slawe
And brought hym of lyf dawe,                     *to the end of his life days*
    Ac Sire Artok tho cam                               *But*
1120  And savyd hym fro vylonye,
That unnethe he myght crye                *So that scarcely might he cry out*
    That the Sarisins flowen echon.         *Before all the Saracens fled*

And as the Sarisins flowyn in that tyde,
The Cristen swed and gan to ryde,                               *pursued*
1125    And tho com Kyng Clarel the kyng,
And slowe by every syde.
Whoso wolde strokys abyde
    Hadde there hys endyng.
fol. 49r  He slewe the Emperour of Almayne —
1130  Sore hyt rwed Charlemayne          *Sorely did Charlemagne mourn for*
    That heye lordyng.
Empater ther come byhynde,
A kyng ycome of grete kynde,
    And oute of many a bekeryng.                       *battle*

1135  Syr Bernard of Orlyaunse,                           *Orléans*
Empater gaf hym myschawnce                                       *injury*
    With dynt of dethys wownde.
Among the dussypers of Frawnce,
Empater gaf hym myschaunce,
1140    And gan to ryde to Otuel in that stounde.
Ac Otuel of hym was ware,
And with Cursins he smote hym thare
    On hys helme that was rownde.
He clef hys heued into the teth,

| | | |
|---|---|---|
| 1145 | So that all men wel seth | *might see* |
| | He grenned as an hownde. | *grinned* |

Syr Otuel tho made alle
The dukes adown falle,
        That he myght hytte aryght.
1150 To Mahon they gonne crye and calle,
To Jovyn and to her goddys all,
        That schulde hem help in fyght.
Tho thay flowyn with a careful crye,
Tyl they com to Kyng Garcy,
1155        As fast as they ever fle myght.
Duk Rouland and Syr Otuel
And Olyver that was gode and lel                    *loyal*
        The Sarisins slowen down ryght.

## Fitt 5

Here bygynnyth a batayll felle                      *fierce*
1160 Of Kynk Clarell and Otuel,                      *Between*
fol. 49v        And wondurlyche strong;
How they fouten for the lawe,                       *faith*
Lystenyth to my sawe,                               *words*
        And thynketh nought to long.        *don't consider it too long*

1165 Anone Clarel to Otuel sede,
"Sey me, knyght, so God thee spede,                 *Tell*
        What that thy name now be?
Thou hast yslaw in length and brede
An c knyghtes of oure ferede,                       *hundred; army*
1170        Sethe Y fyrst saw thee.
Wel fayn Y wolde thyn name bryng
To Garcy, the ryche kyng
        That ys so fayre and fre."
"O, thou coward!" sayde Otuel,
1175 Thou oughtest my name know well,
        By God that ys in Trinité,

Forsothe, my name Otul ys;
Thou hast yknowe or thys.                           *before*
        Now Mahound Y have forsake.
1180 Kyng Charles of Seynt-Denys
Me hath ygeve hys doughter of prys,
        And Crystendom Y have take."
"O," quod Clarel the fayre kyng,
"Now Y here a wondour thyng.
1185        Mahound geve thee wrake                 *ruin*

But thou byleve on Jovyn,                                          *Unless*
Termagaunt, and Appolyn,
fol. 50r         And hem amendys make."

"Cursed be," Otuel seyde,
1190   "Mahound and alle hys felawrede —                    *fellowship*
              Forsothe, thay beyth alle unwrest!              *wicked*
       Whoso hem loveth, thay mowe drede;         *Whoever; ought to fear*
       Of goodnesse here lawe ys gnede,                        *lacking*
              And schal be whyle it last."
1195   Sayde Clarel, "So Mahound thee spede,
       Were we yend in that mede,                          *Were we to go*
              We selve to alle prest,          *Ourselves to battle together*
       Y wolde thee teche that Appolyn,
       Termagaunt, and Jovyn
1200          Were goddys of the best."                     *the best gods*

       "Ye," sayde Otuel the good gome,                         *man*
       "Tomorwe Y wyl thyder come,
              My treuthe Y thee plyght."                     *promise*
       The glove of that kyng he had ynome
1205   Among the knyghtes alle and som,                        *Before*
              With Kyng Clarel to ffyght.
       Tho the sonne to rest was gonne,                        *When*
       The kyng yede to bedde anone                            *went*
              As sone as it was nyght.
1210   On morwe whanne the larke song
       And the lyght day it sprong,
              There rose bothe baron and knyght.

       Clarel of hys bedde awoke,                              *from*
       And cleped hys knyghtes fotehote,                     *quickly*
1215          Hys wyll to don in dede.
       Gamor, Melyn, and Memorok,
fol. 50v None of hem hys heste forsok,                        *orders*
              But duden as he hem bede.
       An haketon they duden hem uppon                 *padded jacket*
1220   And an haberjon that bryght schon              *coat of armor*
              That lyght was forto lete.                *reflected light*
       And thereon a corset, san fayle —                  *body armor*
       What man so it bare in batayle,
              The lasse thrust hym drede.

1225   Men brought hym an helm bryght
       That Barnard the gode knyght
              Was went forto be were.                    *Had once worn*
       Thereon an adderes heued, aplyght —              *snake's head*

|  | | |
|---|---|---|
| | Forsothe, it was a sely syght | *marvelous* |
| 1230 | In eche batayle to bere. | |
| | And a schyld that was unryde, | *fearsome* |
| | Of warlok that sayntes hyde, | *Of a demon that scares saints* |
| | He was a greselyche fere. | *It was grisly in appearance* |
| | Ypaynted it was with Mahoun | |
| 1235 | Of gold, Jubiter and yk Platon, | *also* |
| | And yche ymad with a spere. | *each bearing* |
| | | |
| | Forth they fettan hym a schaft — | *fetched* |
| | He that it made couthe hys craft; | *knew* |
| | Hyt was of a trew tre. | *sturdy* |
| 1240 | Hys swerd Melyn was hym betaught; | *brought to him* |
| | Therwith he hadde heuedes ykaught | |
| | Of kynges, two or thre. | |
| | Hys stede forth was fette, | |
| | And Kyng Clarel thereon set, | |
| 1245 | That semely was to se. | |
| | Twe hethe knyghtes also sket | *heathen; quickly* |
| fol. 51r | Two spores of gold duden on hys fet, | *fastened* |
| | And eyther sat on hys kne. | |
| | | |
| | Tho thay fette here god Mahound, | *brought [the idol of]* |
| 1250 | And alle the Sarsins of renoun, | |
| | And settyn hym amyd the toun of Utalye. | |
| | That uppon here knees thay seten adown, | *kneeled* |
| | With alle the lordys of that toun, | |
| | And also Kyng Garcye. | |
| 1255 | Thay sayden, "Mahound, we thee byseche, | |
| | Today thou be oure alder leche, | *healer of us all* |
| | And on Clarel have mercy. | |
| | As thou art god ful o muche myght, | |
| | That he mowe sle Otuel in fyght, | |
| 1260 | That doyth thee so muche vylonye." | |
| | | |
| | Over that water Clarel gan to ryde, | |
| | And tho sey he come, on hys ryght syde, | *saw* |
| | Charlys the Kyng of Fraunce. | |
| | The dussypers comen that tyde, | |
| 1265 | And alle here ost with muche pride, | |
| | With schyld, spere, and launce. | |
| | "Thou, olde Charlys," Clarel sayde, | |
| | "Swythe long thou hast ous anyede, | *annoyed us* |
| | Kyng Garcy with disturbaunce, | |
| 1270 | And now thyn dayes ben agoon, | |
| | And age ys fallyn thee uppon, | |
| | Thou mayst doute of myschaunce. | *fear* |

Old wrecche, what dost thou here?
Thou ne art nought worth, fer ne ner,
1275         Schaftys forto schake,
Hors to stryde, ne armour to bere,
fol. 51v  A kyng to assayle with no spere,
        Crounes forto crake,                   *crack*
Ne emp no sadyl, ne wynne no stede,        *empty any*
1280 Ne do no knyghtes sydes to blede;
        Thyn handys gynnen to quake.
Fy, a devylys, for vylony,
That thou dretest Kyng Garcy          *threaten*
        Suche maystryes to make!"

1285 Tho byspake he that was wys,
Charlys of Sent-Denys,
        To the Kyng Clarel ful ryght,
"Thrytty kynges of prys
Y have yslaw or thys
1290         In hedynesse with fyght.         *heathenness*
Thorugh grace of Almyghty God in Trinité,
Thys day thou schalt on of hem be
        Ful longe ere it be nyght.
Make thee redy, that thou were dare,     *if you dare*
1295 For myn olde body schal be yare,         *ready*
        Thorugh grace of God Almyght!"

Duk Roulond stood the kyng by,
"Mercy, Lord!" he gan to crye,
        "Ne com nought in batayle!
1300 Thou hast knyghtes ful hardy,
Bothe Otuel, Neymes, and Y,
        Kyng Garcy to assayle.
Y wyl fyght with hym, ywys,
That hath sayde to thee amys.
1305         Hyt ne schal hym nought avayle!"
fol. 52r  The dussypers everychon,
Profreden thus anone,         *Proffered [themselves]*
        That weren hye of parayle.    *noble without peer*

Charlys was swythe wroth,
1310 And to Sent Denys made hys oth
        That to deth he schulde be dyght.   *he [Clarel]*
"He schall wete the certayn soth        *learn*
That he is to Jhesu Crist loth,        *hateful*
        Yff he wylle kythe hys myght."   *show*
1315 Otuel gan to Charles crye,

And sayde, "For the love of Sent Marye,
  So leteth me with hym fyght!
For yesterday in the medes,
For hys falce wordys
1320  My treuthe Y dude hym plyght.        *troth; promise*

Y schall yow telle every word,
How it began, ende and ord,          *beginning to end*
  The stryf betwyn ous to.
He sayde that oure God vas nought worth a tord,  *worthless*
1325 And that he wold prove with dynt of swerd,
  To whom that it wolde do,         *attest*
And sayde that we were thourgh Hym ylore,    *lost*
That of a womman was ybore,
  And schent forevermore;         *ruined*
1330 For Hys lesyng and for Hys sawe,       *tale*
Uppon a cros He was ydrawe.
  Alle thus sayde he me to thare.       *there*

Y answered and sayde, 'Nay,
fol. 52v That He was bore of a may         *maiden*
1335   To save al menkynde,
And ros, and to helle toke the way,
That byfyl uppon the drydde day,       *third*
  And Satan brought in bonde;
And toke therout Eve and Adam,
1340 And all with Hym tho God nam;       *then; took*
  And sythe the Holy Gost sende,      *afterwards; sent*
And after Hys rysyng upsty         *ascended*
To Hys Fadyr up an hy.
  Thys we haven in mynde.'

1345 Of my wordys he ne helde no pryse,      *no worth*
And cleped me 'schrew unwys,'       *rascal*
  And low me to skorne and game."    *laughed*
Tho sayde Charles of Seynt-Denys,
"Otuel, as tou sayst it ys,
1350   Go fyght, in Godys name!"
The dussyperes weren alle prest
To arme Otuel of the best;
  Thay spedden al in same.
Duk Roulond an helm fette,
1355 And on hys heued he hyt sette,
  That was withowten blame.

The helm was worth muche thyng;
Hit aught sumtyme an hethen kyng,      *belonged once to*

|        | Of Babylone the sawdan. | |
|--------|-------------------------|-------------|
| 1360   | And Syr Olyver, over hying, | *hurrying* |
|        | A scharp spere gan hym bryngge, | |
|        | In Spayne hymself it wan. | |
| fol. 53r | Thenne henged thay aboute hys swyre | *neck* |
|        | A schyld that was ryche and dere, | |
| 1365   | That hym gaf hys lemman — | *sweetheart* |
|        | Thre swerdys of sylver bryght, | |
|        | And thre swerdys with gold ydyght, | *adorned* |
|        | With many a ryche ston. | |

Men broughten hym a stede broun,
1370 And two spores that were boun;                     *ready*
          On hys helys thay ham dyght.                  *heels*
He lep to hors and nought abode;
Over the water Otwel rod,
          With the grace of God Almyght.
1375 Thanne hym spak Kyng Clarel,
"Artou ycome, Syre Otwel,
          As thou me behyght?                           *promised*
Thou art welcome to batayle,
Thou myghte be fayn, sam fayle,
1380          Agens suche a kene knyght.

Thou schalt wete, er thou gon,                          *know*
That thou haddyst beter ben at hom,
          Thanne hedyr come to suche a thyng.           *come here*
For thou mayst wel wete, withoute fayle,
1385 That Y am ycome of heye parayle,                   *high nobility*
          And am a gret lordyng."
"Ye," quod Otwel, "Though thow be strong,
Alle it is in God long,                                 *It's all in God's power*
          That ys alle-weldyng.                         *all-wielding*
1390 Yut today schulle we that se,
That God ys bettyr in Trinité
fol. 53v          Thanne Mahon and all hys ospryng."    *descendants*

No lengyr they wolde abyde,
But togedyr thay gonne ryde,                            *against each other*
1395          As folke that weren fone.                 *foes*
With grete sperys and unryde,                           *menacing*
So that they bothe fyllen in that tyde,
          Ryght ther to grownd anon;
But up thay sprong, so yt ys wrete,                     *written*
1400 And aftyr sones togyder thay smyte,
          That men hyt seyon uchon,                     *That every man spoke of it*
The schaftys were stronge and gode,

The knyghtys scheuyn as they were wode,                    *thrust; insane*
   Ne was ther no bettyr wone.                              *course of action*

1405  Heyr peytrelys broston atwo,                          *horses' breastplates*
  And the gerthys also,                                      *saddle straps*
    Her scheldes fellen to grownde,
  The knyghtys weren ful wo,
  To grounde thay yede bothe two
1410    In that ilke stownde,                             *same moment*
  And eythers stete went forthe,                             *steed*
  That on sowthe, that othyr north,                          *one*
    That weren fayre and rownd.
  Thanne sayde Roulond to Belysent,
1415  That was the kynges doughtor gent,
    "Here ys a fayre fyght yfownde."

Sythe he sayd that he was bore,                             *He said that since the time he was born*
  "Ne sey Y never her byfore
    Suche two men of myghtys.
1420  Though a man sought syxti skore,                      *sixty score [i.e., 1200]*
  Ne schulde he fynde none doughtyer,                        *worthier*
    Ne suche othyr to knyghtys."                   *two*
  Tho sayd Oliver that dussyper,
fol. 54r  And the abbot of Seynt-Omer,
1425    That yt was a fayre fyghtys.
  Tho sayd Belysent that may,                               *maid*
  "God save Otuell today,
    For Hys moche myghtys!"

The knyghtys eft togedyr yede,                             *once more*
1430  To fyght on fote thay most nede;
    Here stedys weren schent.                      *gone*
  Of helmes, hauberk, in lenthe and brede,
  The fyr sprange oute as sparcle of glede,                  *burning coal*
    So stronge was others dynt.
1435  Clarel with hys swerd of stel,
  So harde strokys he smote to Otuel,
    To sle hym he hadde ment.
  Kyng Clarell was nygh wood,
  For that Otuel so longe agen hym stode,
1440    And for harme that he hent.                    *received*

He hytte hym on the helme an heye,                         *on top*
  That golde and stonys adown flye,
    Al off hys helme so rownde.
  Though Otuel were of werre sly,                           *crafty*
1445  He nas never hys deth so ny,                           *so near death*

He fylle in swowe on the grownd.					*swoon*
Kyng Charles to Jhesu gan speke,
"Lord," he sayd, "Thou me awreke					*avenge*
	Uppon thys hethen hounde!
1450 And schyld from schame thys Crystyn knyght,
That he be nought slayn in thys fyght,
	In the worchyp of Thy wownde."					*wound*


Syr Otuel that gode knyght
Stert up tho anoneryght,
1455	And was nothyng aferd.
And thought that hys body wolde brest aplyght					*burst*
fol. 54v But he myght be awreke anoneryght					*Unless*
	With Cursins hys swerde.
He smote hym on the helme anone,
1460 That a quarter of hym away gan gone,
	Bothe hys schelde and hys berde,
Forsothe, the boke wytnessed,
That men myght sen hys tethe,
	Bothe lewed and lered.					*unlearned and learned*


1465 Tho lowe Otuel, and sayd,					*laughed*
"Y sawe never, so God me rede,
	Sythe that Y was bore,
Never man in knyghtys wede,
Al so fer as Y have rede,
1470	A berd so clene yschore!					*shaved*
So God me save and sent savour,					*send salvation*
Now ys Cursins a good rasour!					*razor*
	Hyt were harm that it were lore,					*It would be a shame if it were lost*
Hyt ys scharp, and that ys sene!
1475 Hyt had yschave thy berd ful clene
	That ther nys laft no more!


Now be thou syker in alle thyng:
Nyl never Garcy the Kyng
	Byleve on thee after thys,
1480 Neyther Enfamé, that fayrer thyng,
Sche nyl namore of thy playyng,
	Ne for no love thee kysse.
Now thy behoveth to grenne,					*grin*
And to make thee to mowe on menne,					*grimace*
1485	For thy mouth syttyth alle onmys.					*amiss*
Now ne helpth ne nought thy god Mahound,
Jubiter, ne that breythen Platoun,					*worthless*
	That thou ne art syker of thys."					*be protected from this*

Kyng Clarel to hymself sayde,
1490 "Allas, that Y began thys dede
fol. 55r       Ageynes that Cristen knyght!
Though Y sle hym in thys mede,
Alle the world in lengthe and brede,
      Schal me skorne aplyght:
1495 'None fayrer knyght myght by founde,
And now he grenneth as an hounde,
      Both day and nyght.'
He schall abye, be Appolyn!"       *pay for this*
And with hys swerd Melyn
1500       To deth he wolde hym dyght.


............................................

Syr Otuel hys dynt wel sye,       *saw*
      And kept it on hys schylde;       *deflected it with*
Kyng Clarel tho fast fly,
1505 And Otuel clef hys targe atouey,       *cut Otuel's shield in two*
      That halfe fley in the felde,
And thorough Otuel had be born;       *would have struck through Otuel*
Ne hadde ben hys haberjon,       *Had it not been for his coat of armor*
      Syr Otuel hadde he queld.       *He would have killed Otuel*
1510 Of that strok Clarel was blythe,
And sayd "Yf Y thee hytte anothyr syde,       *again*
      Thy lyf hys adoun feld!"       *is*


Thanne sayd Otuel, "Y have ment       *intend*
That myn schal be that other dent,
1515       As Y am a trewe knyght!
To fyght fast wyl Y nought stent."
That feer flye out as sparkyl of flynt,       *fire*
      Out of helm and hauberk bryght.
With Cursins that byttyr bot       *bitterly cut*
1520 To Kyng Clarel he smote,
      Thoroweoute the helme aplyght.
Kyng Clarell fyl tho adown —
fol. 55v Tho men myght se that ys god Mahon       *his*
      Was but of lytyl myght!


1525 Syr Otuel namore ne gradde,       *cried out no more*
And the Sarisins were ful madde       *dismayed*
      For Clarel the Kyng.
The dussypers tho forthe Otuel ladde,
And thonkyth God that day hym hadde       *he had won that day*
1530       And had overcome that fytyng.
Kyng Garcy and hys knytys
To the temple yede anonryghtys,

|   |   |   |
|---|---|---|
| | And kneleden, elde and yong; | |
| | And cryed on Mahon and Appolyn, | |
| 1535 | Termagaunt and Jovyn, | |
| | "Why suffur ye all thys thyng, | *allow* |

| | | |
|---|---|---|
| | That Clarel had lore the swete, | *lost his lifeblood* |
| | So ofte as hym ye hadde hete | *So often did he pray to you* |
| | Whenne he wolde bygynne? | *Whenever he would begin [battle]* |
| 1540 | And Kyng Charles we schult mete, | |
| | And with grysly lawnces hym grete, | |
| | All Cristendom to wynne? | |
| | Allthough Y make to thee my mone, | |
| | Ye stondyn stylle as ony stone, | |
| 1545 | No word nyl ye mynne! | *speak* |
| | Y wene that ye ben doume and def; | *dumb and deaf* |
| | On yow was all my bylef | |
| | More thanne to alle my kynne! | |

| | | |
|---|---|---|
| | For longe ye have forhete, | *Too long; disregarded [me]* |
| 1550 | Y wene that ye most be bete, | *beaten* |
| | Howe so it ever byfalle." | |
| | Bothe hym was longe to threte, | *Both [i.e., Mahoun and other idols]; he was determined* |
| | He dud fette stonys grete, | |
| fol. 56r | Toforn hym in the halle, | *Before* |
| 1555 | All hys goddys he gaf a cloute, | *beating* |
| | He gaf hem strokys styf and stoute; | |
| | "Harawe!" they ganne to calle. | *they [the Saracens]* |
| | He brake bothe legges and swere, | *necks* |
| | And kest hem bothe into the fere, | *cast; fire* |
| 1560 | Mahon and hem all. | |

### Fitt 6

| | | |
|---|---|---|
| | *Here bygynneth a batayle, sykerly,* | |
| | *Of Charles and of Kyng Garcy,* | |
| | *That wondyr yt ys to here,* | |
| | *And howe Garcy ycristeneth was.* | |
| 1565 | *Herkeneth nowe a mery pas,* | *while* |
| | *I pray yowe nowe all in fere.* | |

| | | |
|---|---|---|
| | Anone bad Kyng Garcy, | |
| | "Lordynges, doth arme you redy, | |
| | And every man redy to fyght! | |
| 1570 | And thus we schulle bete oure mametrye. | *idolatry* |
| | For that thay nolde nought ous socurye, | *aid* |
| | Thus we schulle hem dyght." | *treat them* |
| | There were in the fyrst warde | *battalion* |

Syxty thousand stoute and harde,

1575          With helm and breny bryght,                                    *mail shirt*

With pencelys of sykelaton,                                              *banners; silk*

Of grene sendal and of broun —                                          *linen*

          Ther was a semely syght!

Syxty thousand in thys maner

1580   Come after with brod baner,

          Alle thretyng Charles the Kyng,                                 *threatening*

And both Otuel and Olyver,

And also eche dussyper,

          And Rouland, hys gode derlyng.

fol. 56v   Kyng Charles that was so fre,

1586   Hys ost hath partyd at thre                                        *divided into three parts*

          Ryght erlyche in the morownyng.

In eche warde there were tho

Syxty thousand and wel mo

1590          Of knyghtes eld and young.

Ac couthe no man telle the route                                         *But no man could count the number*

Of folk that were goyng abowte,

          Speremen and arblasteres,                                       *crossbowmen*

Wel yarmed and stoute;

1595   Of the hethen thay hadde no doute,                                 *fear*

          Thow they were cruel and fel and fers.

Charles to hys barones sayde,

"Lorthynges, ye mote do by rede,

          Bothe barones, knyghtes, and squyers,

1600   Bowmen, slyngers, withoute fayle,                                  *soldiers armed with slings*

Holdeth yow in youre batayle,                                            *Maintain your ranks*

          With youre gode wynteners.                                      *commanders of twenty soldiers*

Charlys the Duk Neymes hym bythought,                                    *chose*

In that nede, ne fayle hym nought

1605          To bere hys gode baner.

And he answerd with word and thought,

"By Hym that hath alle thys world ywrought,

          Y am ful redy now ryght here!"

The trompes bygonne fer to blow                                          *far*

1610   For that the Sarisins schulde knowe

          That the Cristen men were there.

The Sarisins wenten into the feld,

With helm and spere and ek with schyld,

          Of Kyng Garcyons power.

1615   A Torkeyes was pryketh out beforn,                                 *Turk*

..................................................                       *(see t-note)*

fol. 57r  And threw hem over the castyll wal,                    *them [Ogier's guards]*
          And brak hys cheynes to peces alle,
                 And outward faste hym drow,
          So he dude in that yle,                                 *came to; island*
1620      Thorugh hys queyntys and hys gyle,                      *cunning*
                 That hym thought game ynow.                      *enough*

          Hys good stede sone he fond,
          And in hys hond hys good brond,
                 And alle hys other gere;
1625      He armed hym, Y undyrstande,
          And into the sadyll anone he wond,                      *sat*
                 With good schyld and spere.
          Oger tho gan to crye,
          "Have good day, Dame Enfamye,
1630             Y wyll dwelle no lenger.
          And yf thou, fayre, prayest me,
          Tomorwe Y schall speke with thee,
                 By Jhesu Crist Y swere!"

          Into the ost rod Oger,
1635      And fond Roulond and Olyver,
                 With many a doughty knyght.
          Thay cleptyn and kyssedyn alle in fer,                  *embraced*
          And askedyn yf he hole were;
                 He sayde, "Ye, anoneryght!
1640      Never sythe that Y was bore,
          In alle my lyf here byfore,
                 Ne felt Y me so lyght!                           *well*
          Go we blyve into batayle,                               *quickly*
          The hethen houndes to assayle,
fol. 57v         And sle we hem doun ryght."

1646      To the Turkeyes thay gonne to ryde,                     *Turks*
          And leyde hem doun in yche syde,
                 Thay schedde here brayn an blode;
          There nas none that myght hym hyde,
1650      That thay ne lore in that tyde
                 The balles in here hod.                          *heads; helmets*
          Kyng Garcy thereof tok hede,
          And with hys spore he smot hys stede,
                 And fley as he were wood.
1655      Syr Otuel that gan aspye,
          And gan a country with Kyng Garcy,                      *battle*
                 With welle egre mood.                            *eager*

"Yelde, ye traytours!" Otuel gredde,                                    *cried*
"Thou lyest, by Hym that for ous bledde!
1660          Ne bost ne gynne to crake,              *For neither boast nor attempted trick*
Tofore Charles thou schalt be ladde,
And legge thy lyf there to wedde,                             *answer for; wager*
          But thou Mahoun forsake."                    *Unless you forsake Mahoun*
Garcy hys stede smot,                                                *spurred*
1665    And to Otuel he rod,
          Hys spere he gan to schake.
Hys hors stomblyd at a stone,
He felle and brast hys arme anone,
          And Olyver gan hym take.                                *overtake*

1670    Thenne bede he Olyver, pur charité,
That he ne schulde hym nought sle;
          Hys hondys began wryngge,
And he wolde cristen be.                                          *baptized*
And Olyver graunted, that was so fre,
fol. 58r          To court he gan hym bryng.
1676    And kneled tofore Charles and tolde            *[Garcy] kneeled*
That he hys londys of hym wolde holde     *hold his lands [as Charles' vassal]*
          Ryght into hys enthyng.                              *until death*
Charlys of hym tok goode hede,
1680    And to Parys he dude hym lede,
          With trumpes and daunsyng.

The Erchebyschop Syre Turpyn,
A swythe good clerk of dyvyn,                                  *divinity*
          Crystened hym that day;
1685    The soule of that Sarsin
Forto save fro helle pyn,
          He lered hym Goddys lawe.                            *taught*
Thus Charles and hys dussypers
Lyved in warre many yerys
1690          And faughten, the soth to say;
For every batayle that he began,
Thorugh the grace of God he it wan,
          As Y yow telle may.

**Fitt 7**

*Here bygynneth a batayle grym,*
1695    *Of Charles and of Ebrayn*                                *Ebrahim*
          *That was wonderlyche strong.*
*At Cordys how thay foughten same,*                      *Cordoba; together*
*Alle for the love of Cristendom,*
          *Herkeneth and thenketh nought long!*

fol. 58v  Afftyr Garcy, nought longe hyt nas
1701      To Kyng Charles told hyt was                              *Until*
                  That Ebrayn, the stronge kyng,
          Wyth strenthe was come to Cordys,
          With hym many a Sarisin, ywys,
1705              And many a grete lordyng.
          The Almayns, saum fayle,                                  *Germans*
          Tha aschapeden fro the batayle                            *escaped*
                  Of Angulaittes werryng.                           *[i.e., those from Anjou]*
          Tho Charlys thys herde                                    *When*
1710      Of that kyng, how hyt ferde,                              *About; fared*
                  He com thydyr anon hying.                         *hurrying*

          With hys knyghtys of pris,
          And tho he come to Cordys                                 *when; Cordoba*
                  And neghhode the cyté,                            *neared*
1715      The Sarisins com ageyns hym,
          Syxty thousand stout and grym,
                  Forsothe, in parties thre.
          Charlys syker nadde no mo
          But syxti thousand tho                                    *Only*
1720              Ageynes hem all to be!
          Tho Charlys made thre batayl:                             *battalions*
          The furst of knytys, saum fayl,
                  That ryght symly hyt was to se;                   *seemly*

          That other of fotemen tho;
1725      The trydde knyghtys also,
                  As the fyrst were.
          The kyng with grete rawndoun                              *[i.e., Ebrahim]; speed*
          Come agen Syr Charlemon,
                  As ye mowe here,
1730      With batayles stern ten.                                  *ten fierce battalions*
fol. 59r  The furst weren fotmen
                  That gryslyche were of chere.                     *gruesome; appearance*
          With her thay war behong,                                 *hair; covered*
          And berdys swyde long,                                    *so*
1735              And hornys on hond bere.

          And al so that on batayle                                 *in the event that*
          Schulde that othyr assayle,                        *Should the other side attack*
                  The bowmen weren byforn,                          *in front*
          And come ageyne the knyghtys.
1740      And tho ther, anonryghtys,                                *then; immediately*
                  Everyche blewe hys horn.
          Tho the stedys gonne here and se,                  *When; heard and saw*

Fast away thay gonne to fle,
    They ne spared thyk ne thorn;               *avoided; thicket*
1745  Forsothe, the knyghtys bolde
Myghten nought hem withholde,                 *Couldn't restrain them*
    Though thay hadde ysworn.

Whenne thay that weren on fote,
Ne say no bettyr bote,             *Didn't see any better remedy*
1750    Away that flowyn also;              *they fled*
For her knyghtes gode,             *safety*
Ageyn hem nought ne stode;      *Nothing protected against them*
    Thay seye wel thay myght nought don.    *saw; could do nothing*
Tho Charles that gan se,           *When*
1755  That hys fotemen gonne fle,
    In hert hym was ful wo.
Hys stede he turnyd agayn anon,
For he ne seye no bettyr wone,         *course of action*
    But faste went aftyr tho.

1760  Tho the Sarisins seyen that cas,
They swed aftyr wel gret pas          *pursued*
    Tylle they comyn to an hylle.
fol. 59v  Two myle uppon that playn,
The Cristened turnyd manlyche agayn,   *Christians; courageously*
1765    As hyt was Goddys wylle.
The Sarisins seyen hem come,        *saw*
And flewen away, all and somme,
    Hom to her cyté wel stylle.       *quietly*
Charlys with hys knyghtys
1770  Setten her pavylons upryghtys,      *Set up*
    And all nyght ther gonne dwelle.

Tho on morwe whan hyt was daylyght,
Charlys bad anonryght
    That all here horsys of the ost
1775  With wex to stoppe here ere,        *wax; their ears*
That they myght nought yhere
    Her noyse ne her bost.      *Their noises nor their boasts*
Forsothe, hys hest was sone ydone,      *command*
An her eyyen yhudde anon,    *[the horses'] eyes were blinkered*
1780    Bothe lest and mest
And Charles prayed to God Almyght
To helpe hym that day in fyght,
    So wyss hem the Holy Gost.   *As the Holy Ghost may guide them*

Alle they come togederes on morwe,
1785  The Sarisins to moche sorowe,

              Into the felde to fyght;
       And the Kyng Ebrayn
       Come ful evyn ageynes hym
              With hys ost aplyght.
1790   Togedyr thay gonne smyte;
       Eythyr spared other lyte —                    *very little*
              Ther was a symly syght!              *seemly*
       Of the hethen lawe,
       Many onothyr was yslawe,
1795            Well longe or hyt were nyght.         *before*

       The Sarisins seyen alle
fol. 60r  Howe her felawys down gonne falle;
              Ther rose a rufull crye.
       Togyder they gonne hem drawe,      *gathered themselves*
1800   That folk of hethen lawe;
              Forsothe, they were sory.
       Amyd hem was a char                 *chariot*
       That here banerer that tyme bar     *their banner then bore*
              Uppon a spere on hye.
1805   With twelf oxen yt was ydrawe;
       That tyme hyt was the lawe
              That none schulde fle away

       The whyle her syne stood.              *insignia*
       Charlys, by the rode,           *[swore] by the cross*
1810            That the baner schulde adown.
       Forsothe, he semyt wood outryght      *utterly crazed*
       So fast tho he gan to fyght,          *As soon as*
              As hyt were a wylde lyon.
       Ther nas neythyr spere ne schyld,
1815   That dury myght in the feld          *endure*
              A strok of hys faucon.        *falchion*
       Tho Rouland and Oliver,
       And everyche of the dussyper,
              To batayle were ful boun.        *eager*

1820   All tho that hey mette wyth,        *All those whom they*
       Forsothe, to grownd thay yede ryght,
              So fast they faught thare.
       Kyng Charles tho, anoneryght,
       Thorugh the grace of God Almyght,
1825            Evene come into the char,       *Skillfully*
       And with hys gode fawchon
       He smote the baner adown
              That with hymself were;       *All by himself*
       He smote the baner adownryght —

|  |  |  |
|---|---|---|
| fol. 60v | Tho that hyt sawe, they were aflyght | *When; took to flight* |
| 1831 |       And in sorowe and care. | |
| | He smote tho suche a dynt, | *When he struck* |
| | That fyre flye out as sparke of flynt, | |
| |       And tho the Sarisins were in hart sare, | *sorrowful* |
| 1835 | An gonne to fle in eche syde. | |
| | They ne durst no lengyr abyde — | |
| |       Of blysse they were alle bare! | |
| | | |
| | Tho Ebrayn the strong kyng | |
| | Come wyth spere kervyng | *slashing* |
| 1840 |       To the Kynge Charlemayn, | |
| | And yaf hym suche a wownde | |
| | That Charles fylle to growd | |
| |       Off hys stede adown. | |
| | Charles, forsothe, that hym yeld, | *returned that to him* |
| 1845 | That helm and heued fly in the feld, | |
| |       Tho ryght with hys fauchon; | |
| | And many anothyr paynym, | |
| | Forsothe, ther was yslawe with hym, | |
| |       ................................ | |
| | | |
| 1850 | That were yholde of grete renown. | |
| | To Charles they yeld the gode toun, | *yielded* |
| |       And cristened wolde he be. | *they* |
| | Gret othes they swore thare: | |
| | "Of hym wyl we holde evermore | |
| 1855 |       Cordys the good cyté." | |
| | Therof Charles was glad tho, | |
| | And all were cristened in a thro, | *quickly* |
| |       With grete joye and solempnité. | *ceremony* |
| | | |
| |    *       \*      \** | |
| | | |
| | Welle sone theraftyr come tythyng | |
| 1860 | To Charles the ryche kyng | |
| |       By a well trwe messanger, | |
| fol. 61r | That the kyng of Naverne | *Navarre* |
| | Gan to robbe and to berne | |
| |       In hys lond bothe fer and nere. | |
| 1865 | Tho Charles hyt wyst afyn, | *When Charles fully understood it* |
| | He com to Mount Gardyn, | |
| |       And ther they mette in fere. | |
| | Eythyr had othyr behyght | *promised* |
| | Togedyr on morowe forto fyght | |
| 1870 |       In the same stede ther. | *place* |

Tho Charles made an oryson                                        *prayer*
With ryght gode devocion
   To Jhesu and to Marye,
He sende hem grace, withoute fayle,                   *That they grant him*
1875 To wete who schulle in bataylle                                   *know*
   Wynne the maystrye;
And who schull be yslawe
Of knyghtys of Cristen lawe                             *Among the knights*
   In Kyng Charles partye,
1880 That everych that schuld be ded            *So that everyone destined to die*
Most bere a croys red                                               *May*
   On hys schuldyr on hye.               *High upon his shoulder*


On morwe wanne yt was day,
Charlys rose with gret noblay
1885   And to hys knyghtys cryed,
"To batayle forto fare!"
Thenne sey he moche care                                       *saw; grief*
   Of ten hundred that tyde.
Then was the kyng in grete dolour,
1890 And prayed to ten hundred, par amour,                   *fervently*
   At the chapel to abyde.               *To remain at the chapel*
And sayde yf thay with hem went,
fol. 61v They schuld be de, verrament,                           *dead*
   With the Sarisins ful of pride.          *On account of*


1895 Thay answerd and askeden, "Why?"
Then sayde Charles, "Sykerly,
   Y se on you the sygne of deth, withoute drede.       *for certain*
Loke nowe echon on othyrs schulder:
Amonge you alle nys none othyr
1900   But beryng the croys red;
For why Y wote, thorough my prayer,
That ye schulle be ded, all in fer,
   Yf Y yowe with me lede.
Ac dwellyth here vithouten stryf,                        *If you remain*
1905 Today Y schall save your lyfe;
   To spylle you yt ys no nede."


Tho to batayl the kyng gan ryde,
Hys good dussypers by hys syde,
   And faste the ganne to fyght.                     *they*
1910 Of the Sarisins thay slowyn so yern                    *eagerly*
That the kyng tho of Naverne
   Ageyns hem he had no myght.
Kyng Charles slowe that day,
He and hys ost, sothe to say,

1915          Syxty thousand tho ful ryght.
         And whenne he come to the mede,                                    *returned*
         He fonde hys knyghtys al dede
              Ther he hem left, aplyght,                                    *Where; truly*

         By the ensampyl who mowe se                                       *anyone*
1920     That no man schall hys deth fle                                   *escape*
              For nones kynnes nede.                                        *By any means*
         Tho all Naverne Charles toke
fol. 62r  Into hys honde, so saythe the boke,
              In trewthe, so Y nowe rede,                                   *as*
1925     And gaf hyt hys, saum fayle,                                       *[to] his [people]*
         That hadde hym holpe in batayle,
              That doughty were of dede;
         And was departyd amonge hem uchon,                                *[it] was divided*
         And were yfeffyd therwith anon                                    *enfeoffed*
1930          To lyve in joye and pryde.

         And whenne the Kyng Charlemayn
         Hadde ywonne Naverne and Spayne
              And yslawe the hethen knyghtys,
         Hys catel and hys townys                                          *property*
1935     He gaf to hys barownys,
              And made hem grete lordynges.
         Portyngale, Naverne,                                              *Portugal*
         To the Brytons he gaf hyt yerne,
              And thus parteth hys wynnyngys.                              *distributed his winnings*
1940     Tandylyf, a strong castel,
         To the Jercos he gave hyt yche a del,                            *(see note)*
              Ryght in grete hyynges,                                      *With great honor*

         And the londe of Galeys                                           *Galicia*
         He gaf the Frenchemen, ywys,
1945          But thay nolde dwelle nought thare.                          *declined*
         Thay forsokyn that ylke londe
         Forto have into her honde,
              For yt was so dere.                                          *expensive*
         In Spayne Charles tok,
1950     As Y fynde in my boke,
              All that hethen were,
         That lyved in false lawe;
         He dud hem honge and to drawe
fol. 62v      Wel fast by the swere.                                       *neck*

1955     Charles stabeleth forto be                                        *established*
         An erchebyschop in that cyté
              Ther that Sent James lys;                                    *lies*

And alle the bysschopys in Spayne,
By the hest of Charlemayn,
1960      And eke in Galys                                         *also; Galicia*
Schulde be undyr hym.
Ac the Byschop Syr Turpyn                                          *Then*
          Halowed that stede, ywys,                    *Hallowed (consecrated)*
For ther nas arst no cyté,                                    *never before*
1965  Charles hote, that ther schuld be                            *declared*
          Composterne of prys.                          *equal to Compostela*

And in the moneth of Yver,                                         *April*
Charlys comaund, fer and nere,
          In Galys and ek in Spayne,
1970  That eche hous of power                               *religious house*
Schulde gef twelf penyes a yer,                                   *coins*
          By the hest of Charlemayne,
To Seynt Jams of Galys,
And be quyt of other servys,                       *freed of other obligations*
1975          That hous to sustayne.              *In order to sustain that house*
And so thay dude withoute lete;                                 *hesitation*
For Charles hyt hade sette,                            *Because; decreed*
          Durst no man be ther agayn.                           *against*

**Fitt 8**

*Here bygynnyth a rewful tale:*
1980  *How Rowlond deyde at Rouncyvale.*                          *Roncevaux*

Now lete we be of thys,
And speke we of Charles,
          That muche was of myght.
Of hys lengthe and hys brede,
1985  As clerk ye doth in boke rede,
fol. 63r          Y schal yow telle aryght.
Twenty fot he was of lengthe,
And therto man of gret strength,
          And a man of sterne syght;                        *appearance*
1990  Blake of here, red of face,
Ther he come in many place,
          He was a doughty knyght.

Foure tymes in the yer,
Uppon hys heued he wolde ber
1995          The holy croune of thorne:
At Ester and at Whytsontyde,
At Seynt James Day with pride,
          And at the tyme that God was born,

At the mete in the halle,
2000  Among hys knyghtes alle,
      With drawe swerd hym byforn.
That ys in the maner ay           *As ever had been the manner*
And schal be tyl Domesday
      Of emperour that ys corne.      *divinely chosen*

2005  Whereso he slepe a nyght —
Wyse he was, as felle to hys ryght,      *was his right*
      And ever douted treson —      *suspected*
An hundred knyghtes schulde hym kepe      *guard*
Were that ever he schuld slepe,      *Wherever*
2010      Of knyghtes grete renoun:
And everych doughthy knyght,
Hold a torche brennyng bryght
      And a nakyd fachoun.
Thus the Kyng Charles lay
fol. 63v  With hys ost many a day
2016      In the cité of Pampulon.      *Pamplona*

Twey Sarsins tho of Spayne
Were ysent to Charlemayne,
      With hym forto be;
2020  The sawdan of Babylonye,      *sultan*
He sent hem to Paumpylayne
      Fram Perce, the ryche cité.      *Persia*
Mansour hyght that other,
And Beligans hys brother,
2025      That was of gret pusté.      *power*
Thay dwelleth there long whyle,
Kyng Charles to bygyle,
      Whenne thay myght here tyme se.      *see their chance*

Charlys bythought hym tho      *thought to himself*
2030  That thay ne scholde nought dwelle so
      But thay cristen were.      *Unless; baptized*
He sent to hem sone
A knyght into Aragone —      *from*
      Gwynes a dussyper —      *Ganelon*
2035  But Charles wyst nought      *didn't know about*
The treson of Gwynes thought,      *intent*
      The wykked fals messanger.

Forsoth, he hath hys way ynome;      *taken*
To Mansure that he ys come,      *He arrived before Mansour*
2040      And sayde that Charles hem grette.
He sayde that hys brother and he

Scholde, forsothe, ycristened be,

fol. 64r          Withouten any lette.

Mansure was full fel,                                   *treacherous*

2045    And made a ryche jeuel;                          *produced*

Forth he lete it fette,                     *He had it brought forth*

And gaf the messanger,

And sette hym to the soper —                            *supper*

Wel fayre, forsothe, thay hym grette,


2050    Mansure tok tho Gwynes,                          *then*

And sayde to hym thus,

"I pray thee, Gwynes, lysten to me.

Yf thou wylt Charles forsake

And to my consayle take,

2055          Full ryche schal tou be.

Thrytty somers and yut mo,                      *packhorse loads*

Bathe of sylver and gold also,

Forsothe, Y wyll geve thee."

Thorugh that ylke tresour,

2060    Gwynes bycome traytour —

Evyl mote he the!                           *Ill may he thrive*


Thenne dyvysed Gwynes                                   *plotted*

That he wolde sey thus

To the Kyng Charlemayn,

2065    That Mansour and Belyganns

Wolde come into Fraunce;

Thereto thay were they boun.                    *ready to go*

And Mansure therewhyle                          *at that time*

Trayeth hys ost with gyle,                  *Would betray; guile*

2070          To sle hym with treson.

Charlys was wel apayede,                *would be well satisfied*

And to Gwynes tho sayde,                        *would say*

"Thow art a good baroun."


fol. 64v   Tho was Mansoure glad

2075    That the treson was ymad,

And gaf that traytour

Thrytty somers and mo

Of gold and sylver also,

With swythe gret honour.

2080    And thrytté stedes with gold fyn

To Charles sent that Sarsin,

Alle they were whyt a flour;                    *as a flower*

And an houndred tonne of wyn,

That was bothe good and fyn.

2085          And swythe fayre colour.

Gwynes hys leve tok
And went hym hom, so sayth the bok,
　　　Wyth that presaunt so ryche.
And sayde Syre Charles tho,　　　　　　　　　　　*said [to]*
2090　"Mansure wylle come thee to,
　　　Ryght wel blythelyche.　　　　　　　　　　　*joyfully*
Forsothe, hys brother and ek he
Wyllyn bothe ycristened be,
　　　With here folk, lytell and muche."　　　　　*of low and high station*
2095　Forsothe, Gwynes tho was
A fals traytour, as was Judas,
　　　And many mo beyt suche!　　　　　　　　　　*shall be so*

Charlys grethed hym to wende　　　　　　　　　　*prepared*
To Fraunce with hys knyghtes hende,
2100　　　By the traytours rede.　　　　　　　　　　*counsel*
There he fond fomen fale　　　　　　　　　　　　*many foes*
In the forest of Runcyvale,
　　　That wolde hym do to dede.　　　　　　　　　*bring to death*
The kyng bad Roulond hys cosyn
fol. 65r　Twenty thousand to take with hym,
2106　　　Stouttelyche forto lede.　　　　　　　　　*Boldly*
Whenne Charles hadde yhote tho,　　　　　*commanded this be done*
The best bodyes that were tho
　　　With Roulond, forsothe, thay yede.　　　　　*went*

2110　Twenty thousand Charles ladde,　　　　　　　　*led*
And also fele Roulond hadde
　　　Into the rere batayle.　　　　　　　　　　　*rear guard*
Charlys ne tok no dussyper
But Gwynes and Turpyn yfer,　　　　　　　　　　*Except for*
2115　　　That weren of heyghe parayle.　　　　　　*high nobility*
Mansoure lete tho passe
Charlys folk, bothe more and lasse,　　　*of high and low station*
　　　Forsothe withouten fayle.
Tho com Roulond with hys ost,　　　　　　　　　　*Then*
2120　And Mansoure with muche bost
　　　Hard hym gan assayle.

Syxty thousand and ek mo
Mansoure with hym brought tho,
　　　Out of the wode aplyght.
2125　The Cristen thay gonne assayle;
Many deyde in that batayle
　　　Or it ever were nyght.　　　　　　　　　　　*Before*
Togyder thay gonne smyte;
Neyther ne spared other but lyte;

2130            There was a wel gryslych syght.
               Roulond was there yslawe,
               And good Olyver hys felawe,
                        And wel many a trewe knyght!

fol. 65v   Syre Constantyn of gret Rome
2135       Ageynes Belyngas, forsothe, come,
                        With a gret spere kervyng,
               And to hym he it bare;
               He brast it on peces thare,
                        Withouten any lesyng.
2140       With swerd and with mas,                                   *mace*
               Forsothe, in that plas
                        Togedyr thay hem thryng.                      *pressed*
               Jhesu Crist, Kyng of blys,
               Lord withouten mys,
2145                    Here soules to hevene bryng!

               Whenne Oger Denys seye thys,
               That hys good felaw yslawe ys,
                        In hert hym was full who.                     *sorrowful*
               He faught as he were wood,
2150           That alle ageyn hym stod,
                        To grounde he fylle hem tho.
               Raynold of Auby d'Espyne
               Com prikyng on a stede fyn,                            *galloping*
                        And faught ful hard also.
2155           Wel sone the Cristen were byset
               As der that beyth withinne the net,                   *deer*
                        With ten thousand and mo.

               Thay faughten wel by the lawe,                        *for the faith*
               But sone thay were alle yslawe,
2160                    Withinne a lytel stounde.
               Men seyeth in old sawe,
               That ten men in a lytel thrawe,                       *in a moment*
fol. 66r                Mowe be brought to grownd.
               Though Oger faught fast,
2165           Yut sone at the laste,
                        He hadde dethys wounde,
               And Raynold wyth also,
               And wel many a gode knyght mo,
                        In boke as hyt ys fownde.

2170       Tho Sir Bertram the baner,                                 *When; banner-bearer*
               Bothe Rouland and eke Olyver,
                        And Sir Gaumfres the kyng

|      | | |
|---|---|---|
| | Gonne tho to fyght ful fast, | |
| | And also ground tey caste | *they cast down* |
| 2175 | Wel many a gret lordyng. | |
| | Forsoth, Olyver and Rouland do | *then* |
| | Cleven men and hors atowo, | *Split* |
| | So thay faught in that thryng. | *throng* |
| | Syre Bertram the baner, | |
| 2180 | Bothe Roulond and Olyver | |
| | Ne spared elde ne yong. | |
| | | |
| | Ful sone after in a stounde, | |
| | Ganfres was brought to grounde | |
| | With the cursed Sarisins. | *By* |
| 2185 | Tho good Olyver was slawe tho, | |
| | And many a doughty knyght also, | |
| | With the develes lemes. | *By; followers* |
| | A Sarsyn that hyght Langelye, | |
| | He com with gret envye, | |
| 2190 | As Y yow say in rymes. | |
| | He com and smot Olyver on the croune, | |
| | That bode hys eyghen fyl adown, | *both; eyes* |
| fol. 66v | Fram hym in that tymes. | |
| | | |
| | Whenne that Olyver was blynth, | *blind* |
| 2195 | Bothe byfore and ek byhynde | |
| | He leythen faste aboute; | *struck* |
| | And evermore as he rod, | |
| | He made a way swythe brod | *very wide path* |
| | Of the Sarisins that were stoute. | |
| 2200 | And as he faught wondurlyche fast, | |
| | Roulond com ate last | |
| | To helpe hym, saun doute. | |
| | So hard Olyvere smot Roulond | |
| | That hys schyld from hym wond | *fell* |
| 2205 | Among the hethen route. | *company* |
| | | |
| | "Allas!" sayde Roulond tho, | |
| | "Olyver, why faryst thou so? | |
| | Artou paynym bycome?" | |
| | "Nay!" sayde Olyver, "God it wot, | |
| 2210 | Y ne wyst never whom Y smot! | *did not know* |
| | My syght ys me bynome!" | *taken* |
| | Tho thay bode layden on in fere, | *both fight together* |
| | Bothe Roulond and Olyver, | |
| | And slowyn there many a gom. | |
| 2215 | With that com l'angelye, | *an angel* |

The cours have he of Oure Ladye,												*from*
    That most hath myrthes mone.							*Who most has inspired mirth*


......................................................
And with a spere swythe feloun,												*dangerous*
2220     That dede he fyl to grounde.							*he [Oliver]*
Tho Roulond sey that fyght,													*When*
With sorow and care he smot a knyght,
fol. 67r     That same hethen hound,
That hors an man, bothe at onys,											*once*
2225 He evene cleved hys body and bonys,										*evenly*
    Ne myght no man hym hele that wounde.
Bothe Ganfer and Ganfres,
Ryght besyde Oger Denys,
    There lay yslaw that stounde.


2230 Anguler and Anastes ther,
And Syr Yvory, here gode fer,												*companion*
    Alle quyk thay were ynome,								*alive; captured*
And yhongeth heyghe on a tre,
That grete dele it was to se												*sorrow*
2235     Uppon many a Cristen gom.								*man*
Therfore Mansoure was ful fawe											*determined*
That thay were so alle yslawe,
    The Cristen, bothe alle and sum.
But Roulond skaped away													*escaped*
2240 In a busk of an hegge, forsoth to say,									*bush; hedge*
    With hys drydde gome.					*third companion [perhaps Baldwin]*


And as Rouland the gooth knyght											*good*
Com framward that strong fyght,											*away from*
    A Sarsin ther he fand,
2245 That resteth hym ther upryght											*rested*
Y say, forsothe aplyght,
    With foure of hys bond.									*vassals*
So upryght by a tre,
He yede forth and let hem be,												*them*
2250     Styll for to stonde,
fol. 67v And went uppon an heyghe hylle,
And hys horn he blew wel schylle,											*loudly*
    That he held in hys honde.


The Cristen gonne it knowe
2255 That weren away yslowe,

           And comyn to hys cry.[1]  
        Wel an hundred on a drowe                   *in a group*  
        Ageyneward gonne drawe  
           To the Sarsins, sykerly.  
2260  Roulond hys swerd gan drawe,  
        To the Sarsin he sayde in a thrawe,        *in a moment*  
           "Anone thow schalt deye,  
        But thow me telle, ywys,  
        Where Mansoure thy lord ys —  
2265        Sey me hastlye!  

        ...................................................  
        Thenne wyl Y save thee,  
           My treuth Y thee plyght."  
        The Sarsin was blythe                  *eager*  
2270  To askape with hys lyve,  
           And sayde, "Go we anoneryght!"  
        Forth thay went alle prist,             *swiftly*  
        Bothe togederes in that forest,  
           So faste as thay myght.  
2275  The Sarsin sayde, "He ys thys  
        That bereth the schylde of prys      *costly shield*  
           With a dragon of gold bryght."  

        Roulond mette an hathen hounde;  
        Suche a strok he hym founde  
2280        That ded he fyll in that plas.  
        Hard he layde on bothe syde;        *fought*  
fol. 68r  Whome Roulond mette in that tyde,  
           Hym byfyll a sory cas.  
        Mansure he mette, saun fayle,  
2285  In that same batayle,  
           As it was Goddys grace.  
        Roulond let tho the Sarsin gon,  
        And to the batayle he went anone,  
           There Mansure in was.  

2290  Strong fyght was hem bytwene,  
        They al tohewen the helmes schene,    *demolished*  
           And here schyldes dude also.  
        Thorugh the hauberk the blod was sene,  
        For the strokys weren ful kene,  
2295        That theleth were bytwene hem to.    *dealt*  

---

[1] Lines 2254–56: *The Christians then understood that those who were away were slain, and came to his call [i.e., Roland's blowing of his horn]*

Roulond smot a strok with yre
On the helm of Syre Mansure,
      And clef hys body tho.
Welle a thousand Sarsins,
2300   Alle of Godys wytherlyngges,          *enemies*
      Thay flowyn away hym fro.

Whenne Belyngans hys brother
Sey that hit was none other,
      He fleye with hys ost
2305   To Saragous, that ryche cyté,          *Zaragoza*
Bothe he and eke hys mayné,
      Wyth bobaunce and with bost.      *arrogance*
Roulond had so many a wounde,
Wondyr that he ne fyl to grounde,      *[It is a]*
fol. 68v      And that was sorw most.
2311   "God!" he cryed, "mercy, blyve!"      *quickly*
Lord, help hym in hys lyve,
      As Tou art the Holy Gost!

Roulond com doun anone,          *fell down*
2315   Of febelnesse he hadde gret wone;      *in full*
      With that come Syre Baudewyne,   *Baldwin*
And Terry also, withouten fayle,
That weren askaped from that batayle;
      That on was hys owyn cosyn.      *That one*
2320   He seye hys armur al totore,      *saw; broken*
Hys body with speres thorugh-bore,      *stabbed*
      Hys lyf in poynt to tyne.   *to lose (i.e., near death)*
Roulond throw out Dorundale,      *drew out*
And sayde there a rewfull tale,
2325      And wroth was in fyn.      *utterly upset*

Tho he bygan to make hys mone,
And faste loked there uppon,
      As he it held in hys hond:
"O, swerd of gret myght!
2330   Better bar never no knyght,
      To wynne with no lond!
Thow hast ybe in many batayle,
That never Sarsin, saum fayle,
      Ne myght thy strok withstonde!
2335   Go! Let never no paynym
Into batayle bere hym
      After the deth of Roulond.

          O, swerd of gret power!

          In thys world nys nought thy per,                    *equal*

fol. 69r           Of no metal ywrought.

2341      Alle Spayne and Gales,                          *Galicia*

          Thorugh grace of God and thee, ywys,

             To Cristendom ben brought.

          Thow ert good, withouten blame;

2345      In thee ys graveth the Holy Name,              *is engraved*

             That alle thyng made of nought."

          Roulond smot it on a stone,

          And he it karf ato anone,                    *it [the stone]*

             To breke it tho was hys thought.        *it [the sword]*

2350      Tho he hadde that ston yschorne,          *When; carved*

          Wel lowde he blew tho hys horne,

              To have yhad more socour.

          Thre note he blew so,

          That hys horn clef atwo,

2355            That was of good yvour,                 *ivory*

          That the temple and hys vayne,      *his temple and his vein*

          Brost bothe with gret mayne,          *Burst; powerfully*

              Of Roulond the conquerour.

          Syxty myle men herde the soun;         *Sixty thousand*

2360      Tho the Kyng Charles of renoun,

              Made gret dolour.                    *lament*

          "Gyne, Y can Roulond knowe,          *Ganelon*

          Ryght now, forsothe, Y herde hym blowe,

              Y drede lest he mysfare.        *suffer misfortune*

2365      As armes anone, gret and smale,         *To arms*

          To that forest of Rouncyvale,

              To loke yf he be dare."               *there*

          Gwynes, that wyst of thys dede,

          To the kyng anone he sayde,

fol. 69v           "Syre, have ye no care!

2371      Roulond ys so jolyf a man

          That he hys blewyng bygan

              For huntyng of an hare."

          Lo, thys falce traytour —

2375      God yeve hym myssauntour             *misfortune*

              For hys falce lesyng!

          *          *          *

          Rowlond now lyth on the gras,

          And Baudewyn with hym was,

              And schulde hym water bryng.

2380      To fecche hym water he gan gon,

But he ne myght fynde none,
     For nones kynnes thyng.                          *By any means*
Tho he tolde that there none was,               *When; reported*
Roulond sayde, "Allas, allas!"
2385       With swythe gret mornyng.

To fecche eft yede Baudewyn.           *fetch [water] again*
With that there come a Sarsin
     There that lay Roulond,                          *Where*
And tok that swerd Dorundale,
2390   And thus he sayde in hys tale,
     As he it held on hond:
"O, Dorundale, thou art wel founde!
Wyth thee hath Roulond ybrought to grounde
     Many a Sarsin of oure lond!
2395   Now schal may a Cristen berd        *many; beard [i.e., men]*
Wynne schame here afterward
     Thorugh help of Mahoundys honde!"

Whenne Roulond herd hym speke so,
In hys hert hym was ful wo,
fol. 70r     And hastylyche up he stert.
2401   He yede anon to that paynym,
And with hys horn he smot hym,
     That he felle overthwart.                    *sideways*
That blod and brayn start up byforn;   *spewed in front of him*
2405   Forsothe, hys lyf there was lorn,
     That he nas never after quart.          *healthy*
Deth he fel, so sayd my tale,
For he wolde have stolyn Dorundale;      *Because*
     He hadde a stroke ful smert.              *strong*

2410   With that com Baudewyn anone agayn,
And fond Roulond on the playn;
     He leyde hym on hys stede.
Swerd and horn he tok also,
As man that was in muche wo;
2415     Away he gan hym lede,
Out of that forest of Rouncyvale
Into another dep dale,
     And leyde hym a mede,               *in a meadow*
And sayde, "Roulond, pur charité!
2420   Thenk our God in Trinté            *Think upon*
     That for ous wolde blede!"

With that, Roulond Godys knyght
Loketh up to hene lyght,                   *heaven's*

And sayde on hys maner:

2425 "Jhesu, that syttyth in Trinté,
O God and Persones Thre!         *One*
    Now here my prayer!
Y com to thys contré,
fol. 70v  Lord, for the love of Thee,
2430     And Thy moder there,         *dear*
The hethen for to slo,
That wrought Thee so muche wo
    Whyle that Thou were here.

Lord, as Thou art Kyng ycorne,         *chosen*
2435  Let Thou me be nought forlorne,         *lost*
    But bryng me to blys,
There that ys Thy reynyng,         *reign*
Jhesu Criste, hene Kyng,         *heaven's*
    Therof that Y ne mys,
2440  And thylke that ben yslawe         *those who have been slain*
For the ryght lawe,         *faith*
    And for the stedfastnesse."

Ryght in thys same prayer,         *Directly after*
Roulond the very martyr         *true*
2445     Passed out of hys lyve.
Angelys comyn fro hevene,
By syxty and by sevene —
    Of hym thay were ful blythe —
And broughten hym into blys
2450  That never more schal mysse,         *be lacking*
    There joye ys ful ryve.         *Where; plentiful*
Now Jhesu, Mary Sone,
Graunt ous alle therre to wone         *dwell*
    For Thy woundys fyve.

2455  And as the angel Mychael,
Gabriel and Raphael
fol. 71r     Roulondys soule bare
Over Charles chapyll, ywys,
As Turpyn messed, ywys,         *gave mass*
2460     A gret crye he gan here,
Of fendys that weryn felle
That weren towarde helle         *were headed to*
    With the soule of Mansur.
Turpyn bad hym abyde,         *ordered them to*
2465  And axed hem in that tyde         *asked*
    What thyng that they beryn there.

   "On that ys ous ful sure,        *One is very certainly ours*

   Forsothe, the soule of Mansure;

      He hath yserved ous ay.

2470 He schall have to hys hure        *reward*

   The pyne of helle sure —

      None other be it ne may!

   And Roulondys soule ys

   Ybrought into paradys,

2475     With joye and with play,

   Thereinne for to be,

   And there hyt to se,

      Forsoth, Y thee say."


   Whenne the masse was don,

2480 The Byschop Turpyn anon

      To Charles went and sayde,

   "Charlys Syre, forsothe ywys,

   Ryght now none other there nys,

fol. 71v     Roulond ys do to deth.

2485 Forsothe, Y sey now ryght        *I just now saw*

   Angls of muche myght

      Hys soule to hevene lede."

   Wyth that com Baudewyn,

   Roulondys owyn cosyn,

2490     Rydyng on hys stede.


   The swerd and the horn

   He brought the kyng beforn,

      And tolde hym of that cas:

   How Roulond was yslawe,

2495 And Olyver hys gode felaw,

      And alle that that ever was;

   Thorugh Mansures rede,         *plot*

   Alle hys folk were dede

      And yspylt in that plas.

2500 Tho Charles wust thys,         *When; knew*

   He was ful sory, ywys,

      And sayde, "Allas, allas!"


   With dwele and muche crye,       *grief*

   Charles went in hye         *at once*

2505     Roulond for to se;

   And fond hym there ded,

   And thus to hym he sayde,

      As Y schal telle thee:

   "O, Roulond, the good conquerour

2510 And the noblyst warryour

That ever more schal be,
How Y have thee forlore?
Dey Y wylle thee before                                    *I wish to die in your presence*
    But God wyl save!"                                   *Unless God prevents it*

fol. 72r  On swowne he felle to grounde,
2516    Anone in that same stounde,
        As a man that was in care;
    And whenne he up stood,
    He cryed as he were wood,
2520        And wep and tor hys here.
    With a rewful rage,
    He cracched hys vysage,                                 *scratched; face*
        And sayde with sykyng sore,
    "Roulond, now for the love of thee,
2525    Dede now wyl Y be;
        Of blys Y am alle bare!

    Thow were strong as Sampson,
    And bolder thanne any lyon,
        In batayle and eke in fyght.
2530    I may wepe for thy partyng
    So dude David the kyng                                  *As*
        For Absolon the whyte!                               *mighty*
    Best me ys myself to sle,
    For glad ne worthe Y never mo                           *will I nevermore be*
2535        After thys ylke syght.
    Thow were in were good and wys,                         *war*
    As was Judas Machabeus,
        That was Godys knyght."

    The barouns beden hym let be,
2540    And sayde, "Syre, pur charyté,
        Lete away thys ylke mornyng.
    Wel ye seth how it geth —                               *goes*
    There nys no bote of mannys deth.                       *remedy*
        Take to thee confortyng."
fol. 72v  The kyng let that body dyght,                         *be prepared*
2346    With myrre and baume aryght                             *balm*
        For drede of rotyng;                                 *To avoid*
    And sythe went to Rowncyvale,
    Ther the bodyes lyen be tale,                           *one by one*
2550        Of many an heyghe lordyng.

    And also Oliver ther they fownde,
    With foure wythes harde ybownde,                        *willow ropes*
        And ded he lay undyr a tre.

On hys body was many a wownde.
2555 Charlys sayd tho in that stownde,
         "Allas, that yche schulde thys ever se."
Her pavylons ther they pyght,
And waketh the bodyes all that nyght,                              *kept vigil*
         With swythe grete solemptnité.
2560 The kyng swore by God Almyght,
That ys an heye in hevene lyght,
         Therof he wolde awreke be.                                *avenged*

Anonryght that trewe kyng
Made there ryght hys prayng                                *Prayed there directly*
2565          To Jhesu ful of myght,
That He wolde sende hym grace
Ryght ther in that same place,
         To have the dayes lyght
For to sle hys enemys,
2570 And also to wynne the peys                                          *peace*
         Or come the next nyght.                                        *Before*
An angel come ther sone,
And sayd, "Yherd ys thy bone.
         Ryse an wende to fyght,

fol. 73r  For tylle thou have thy wylle,
2576 The sonne schall stonde stylle                                       *sun*
         In the firmement."
The kyng was tho glad and blythe,
And thonked God fele sythe,
2580          Jhesu Lord Omnipotent.
Kyng Charles and Turpyn,
Terry and eke Bawdewyn,
         To batayl sone they went,
And sworyn by Goddys mounde,                           *mount [i.e., Calvary]*
2585 Thay schulde never stytnt stownde                          *pause for a moment*
         Tylle the Sarisins were schent.                               *defeated*

## Fitt 9

*Here bygynnyth a batayle stronge and fyn*
*Of Kyng Charles and of Turpyn*
         *That joye ys of to here;*
2590 *That faughten agens the Sarisins stoute*
*At Saragous, wythoute dowte,*
         *As gode men schulde and sure.*

Charlys hys ost gan oute lede,
And comyn to Sadrak, so Y rede,

2595          That ys a fayre watyr and clere,                    *river*
        Two myle from Saragon.
        Belyngas thay fownde sone,
              That was wel stoute and fere;
        Of Percy the ryche sowdan                                 *From Persia*
2600    That hyght Syre Perygan —
              Ne wust nower hys per;                              *nowhere*
        And also many a paynym
        That were bothe stoute and grym,
              And of swythe gret power.


fol. 73v   Too thowsand of Percyans
2606       And also fele Affricans
              Thay browten to the feld.
        Of Babyloyn the sowdan
        He brought with hym many a man
2610          With spere, swerde, and schylde.
        Syxty thowsand and mo
        He brought with hym do;                                   *there*
              Thus Turpyn had ous told.
        Two hundred of Percy,
2615    Charlys ne hadde but thyrty
              Of knyghtes that were bold.


        To batayle thay were boune,                               *headed*
        Bothe with spere and gomphanoune,                         *banner*
              And fast thay gonne to fyght.
2620    Syre Turpyn and Charlyon
        With here gode swerde broun                               *polished swords*
              Hewyn on the helmes bryght.
        Many a paynym there fyl adoun
        That weren of swythe gret renoun,
2625          Longe er it were nyght.
        Otuel tho with hys fauchoun,
        And the gode Duk Hugoun,
              A man of muche myght,


        In the fyrst batayle
2630    The saudan they gonne assayle,
              Of Percy that hyght Perigon.
        Syre Otuel smot hym tho,
        That evene he cleft hym ato,
              Syker bothe hors and man.
2635    Byschop Turpyn with hys spere
fol. 74r   To Belyngans he gan it bere,
              That thorugh hys body it ran.
        Therewhyle the Kyng Charlyoun

Slow with hys fauchoun
2640       Of Babylone the sawdan.

Tho Turpyn was byset
As a der in the net
      There among the paynemes,
And neygh yslawe that stounde,          *was almost slain*
2645 And hadde many a wounde
      Of the falce Sarsins.
Of strokes hard and sore
Turpyn suffred thare
      Of Godys wytherlynges.          *enemies*
2650 And Turpyn and Tybaut
Made a swythe noble saught          *assault*
      To slen the fyndes lemes.          *devil's followers*

Thay and here ost faughten so
That syxty thousand and mo
2655       Suffreth dere dedes wounde.          *their*
Grete peple thay gonne sle,
And wenten fele into the se,          *many jumped into*
      For drede of deth that stounde.
No Sarsin, syker aplyght,
2660 From that batayle skapyn myght
      That owher myght be founde.          *anywhere*
Alle thay were yslawe,
And ybrought of here lyve dawe,          *to the end of their life days*
      There uppon the grounde.

2665 And ever schon the sonne bryght
To yeve Kyng Charles lyght
      In that fayre fyrmement.
fol. 74v Thre dayes of mowntans ryght,          *Exactly the length of three days*
Tylle he hadde ywonne the fyght
2670       Thorugh grace that God hym sent.
And he slowe alle hys enemys,
And worschyplyche he wan the pris          *worshipfully (honorably)*
      Wyth swythe gode entent.
The kyng was do glad and blyde,          *then; blithe*
2675 And thonketh God many sythe
      For the grace that He hath hym sent.

Anon thereaftyr he toke the way
Ther that Rowlandys body lay,
      And with hym many a knyght.
2680 "Forsothe," sayd Turpyn and Turry,
"Gwynes had made thys, sekerly,          *caused*

   And thys fals treson had ryght."         *has arranged*
  Tho the Kyng Charlyon
  Commawndyth swythe anone
2685     To brynge hym forthe anonryght.
  Terry to hym anone forthe wonde,          *leapt forth*
  And of the deth of Rowlond
    He hym withclepyth aplyght,       *accuses him at once*

  And sayde, "Thorugh thy false treson,
2690   Many a gode lorde ys brought adown,
    And hathe suffryd dedes wownde."
  Gwynes sayd, "Nay!
  Thowe lyxt falsly, by thys day!            *lie*
    And that schall be well yfownde,
2695   Thy body anoneryght ys to myn.   *Your body immediately against mine*
  Arme thee anon wel afyn,          *completely*
    And Y wyth a spere ygrownde.      *sharpened*
  But Y me defende,             *Unless*
fol. 75r  Y grawnt, so God me amende,
2700     Byhonged and trawe thys stownde."    *drawn*

  Anone Turry the gode knyght
  Armed hym wel aplyght,
    And Gwynes dude also.
  Thay come bothe into the felde,
2705   Bothe with spere and with schelde,
    Togedyr thay reden tho.       *made ready then*
  Gwynes smote Turry
  That hys schylde sykerly
    Evene clef atoo
2710   Turpyn and Charles the kyng
  Bothe thay say that fyghtyng —         *saw*
    In hert hem was ful wo.

  But Turry with hys half-schylde,
  To Gwynes rod in the felde
2715     With a grete rawnan.           *roar*
  He gafe the traytour suche a wownde
  That down he fel to grownde
    Wyth Crystys malyson.          *curse*
  Ther the traytour was overcome,
2720   And swythe anone he was ynome        *seized*
    By the hest of Charlyon.
  And ther he was byknowe,        *exposed as guilty*
  Byfore heye and eke lowe
    Of that ylke false treson:

| | | |
|---|---|---|
| 2725 | The Crystyn howe he solde | *How he had sold the Christians* |
| | For thrytty somers of golde | |
| | To her enomys. | *enemies* |
| | "Forsothe," sayd Charles, "hyt ys the lawe | |
| fol. 75v | That thow be honged an drawe, | |
| 2730 | By Crst and Sent Denys." | *Christ* |
| | He tolde that Mansure and Belygans, | *He [Ganelon] confessed* |
| | How thay schulde have come into Fraunce | |
| | And have ywone the prys, | *gained the prize* |
| | And have yslaw Kyng Charles, | |
| 2735 | Turpyn, and alle hys barounes | |
| | Ryght at here Dynys. | *here at Saint-Denis* |
| | | |
| | Tho by the heste of Charles the kyng | *command* |
| | The traytour was don to hongyng, | *sentenced to* |
| | And was ydrawe thorugh the toun. | |
| 2740 | And after yhonged wel faste, | |
| | Forsothe, tho in haste, | *then* |
| | Alle quyk he was leten doun, | *Still living* |
| | And ybounde to a stake, | |
| | And hys bowels out ytake, | |
| 2745 | To brenne hym byforn. | |
| | To foure stedys he was yknyt | *horses; tied* |
| | By the hondys and by the fet, | |
| | At the heste of Charlyoun. | *command* |
| | | |
| | On eche stede sat a knyght, | |
| 2750 | And thus he was totwyt, | *dismembered* |
| | Gwynes the falce traytour. | |
| | Forsothe, hit were skele and ryght, | *wise* |
| | That everych traytour were so ydyght, | |
| | And hadde muche myssaunter! | *misadventure* |
| 2755 | Charlys tok hys knyghtes | |
| | And went to Roulond anoneryghtes | |
| | With swythe gret dolour. | |
| | Roulondys body he let dyght | *prepared* |
| | With murre and baune anoneryght, | *myrrh; balm* |
| fol. 76r | With swythe good othour. | *aroma* |
| | | |
| 2761 | Bothe Roulond and Olyver | |
| | And everych of the dussyper | |
| | With baune weren ydyght. | *balm; anointed* |
| | Of some, withoute fayle, | *From some [of the dead]* |
| 2765 | Men duden out the entrayle, | |
| | And in lede layde hem aryght. | *lead* |
| | And tho that weren nought so, | |
| | Ful wel in salt men dude hem do, | *preserved them* |

         To be swete bothe day and nyght.               *uncorrupted*

2770  Thus thay weren dyght anone,
       Wel ynoynted everychon,
           Withouten any unryght.               *impropriety*

       Thus Charles doth, that ys so hende,
       To bryng hys knyghtes to good ende,
2775          Forsothe, as hym thought best.
       Other lordys that weren there,
       Men layde hem on hors bere,         *horse-drawn biers*
           And were rychelyche brought in cheste.    *caskets*

       Charlys bysyde Runcyvale
2780  Lete rere a chyrche good withalle          *Built*
           For hem to rede and syng.
       Now Jhesu Crist in Trinté,
       O God and Persones Thre,              *One*
           To joye and blysse ous bryng.

2785  Here endeth Otuel, Roulond, Olyver,
       And of the twelf dussypers,
           That deyden in the batayle of Runcyvale.
       Jhesu Lord, hevene Kyng,
       To Hys blysse ous and hem bothe bryng
2790          To leven wythoute bale.             *suffering*

       *Amen quod J. Gage.*                *says*

# EXPLANATORY NOTES TO OTUEL AND ROLAND

**ABBREVIATIONS**: *DR*: *Duke Roland and Sir Otuel of Spain*; **MED**: *Middle English Dictionary*; **OED**: *Oxford English Dictionary*; **OK**: *Otuel a Knight*; **OR**: *Otuel and Roland*; **Otinel**: Anglo-Norman *Otinel*; **Pseudo-Turpin**: *The Chronicle of Pseudo-Turpin*, ed. and trans. Poole; **Song of Roland**: *The Song of Roland: An Analytical Edition*, ed. and trans. Brault; **RV**: *Roland and Vernagu*; **Whiting**: Whiting, *Proverbs, Sentences, and Proverbial Phrases*.

1–45     *Herkenyth lordynges . . . . tell you aryght.* The opening announces that the poem will tell of Charlemagne's conquest of Galicia in Spain, and then adds details about the various episodes. Curiously, one of the cited episodes — Roland's slaying of Vernagu (lines 16–18) — is not included in *OR*. Others are misleading: the combats against Ebryan and Emon take up only a few lines (lines 19–21; compare lines 1700–1858), and Roland does not overcome Otuel (lines 25–26).

16–18     *Vernagu . . . . in false lore.* The poet's reference is to Otuel's uncle Vernagu, slain by Roland in a duel, an action occurring prior to the events recounted in *OR*. Vernagu, a well-mannered giant Saracen, arrives at Charlemagne's court as a messenger. When given the opportunity, he will not convert to Christianity, and is therefore killed by Roland. The story is told in *RV* and *Pseudo-Turpin*. In *OR*, this mention of the back-story raises familial vengeance as a motive for Otuel's coming to Charlemagne's court. Compare the more expanded references to Vernagu in *DR*, lines 313–18, and in *Otinel*, lines 204–09.

31     *dussyperys.* "Twelve peers." According to legend, Charlemagne recognized twelve knights — his *dussepers* — as his greatest, noblest warriors.

40–41     *Ercheboschope Syr Turpyn . . . . wrote in Latyn.* Archbishop Turpin is a key militant and ecclesiastical character in the *Song of Roland* and the Middle English Charlemagne romances. In *Otinel*, *RV*, and the three Otuel romances, Turpin's role is limited to episcopal duties: performing Mass and baptizing converts. In the fifth Otuel-cycle romance, *The Siege of Milan*, Turpin plays a central role. Here, in *OR*, Turpin is named as an eyewitness chronicler of events, as in *Pseudo-Turpin*. On Turpin's role in the *Song of Roland*, see the note to line 2114 below.

48     *Chyldermasse Day.* Holy Innocents' Day (December 28). See *MED childermass-dai* (n.), "the feast day commemorating Herod's slaughter of the infants" (Matthew 2:16). This detail is borrowed from the source; see *Otinel*, line 17, and compare *OK*, line 55.

50      *Parys*. Here, Charlemagne appears to live in Paris and hold court in Saint-Denis. The other Otuel romances also set this scene in or near Paris. In *Otinel*, Charlemagne holds court in Paris, having come from Clermont Ferrand (line 18). In *DR*, Charlemagne dwells in Paris (line 39). In *OK*, Charlemagne appears to arrive from Saint-Denis to hold court in Paris (lines 57–58). Although the poet identifies Paris as a key location for Charlemagne, this is historically inaccurate. The Roman town of Lutetia Parisiorum did not develop into the administrative center of France until the eleventh and twelfth centuries. Hugh Capet, count of Paris and duke of the Franks, was elected king of the Franks in 987, and subsequent Capetian kings expanded the city's size and influence. During the Carolingian age, Aix-la-Chapelle, also called Aachen, was where Charlemagne lived and ruled.

51      *Seynd-Denys*. Saint-Denis, located near Paris, is the site of the Basilica of Saint-Denis, housing the relics of the martyred first bishop of Paris. It has long been connected to the royal line, and was the burial site for French kings from the tenth century until the French Revolution.

55–87   *Thenne came . . . . hope to spylle*. Compare *Otinel*, lines 33–58.

71      *hore berde*. The reference here is to Charlemagne's iconic white beardedness. In *Otinel*, lines 36–37, Charlemagne has a "fluri gernun" (white moustache) and "grant barbe" (great beard). See also *RV*, line 664 ("hore bard"); and *DR*, line 80 ("white berde large and lange").

88–93   *Roulond sayde . . . . none wynne*. Compare *Otinel*, lines 59–61.

106     *Cursins*. Corsouse is Otuel's named sword. It is later described as a "falchion," a long sword with a curved blade (lines 531, 1816, etc.). See *MED fauchoun* (n.). On other named swords, see the notes to lines 183, 900–04, 1240, and 2326–49 below.

121–22  *Mahon / Jubiter and Syre Platon*. Middle English romances often misrepresent Muslims as polytheists who worship idols, naming three or four gods as central to their fictionalized faith: Mahoun, Jubiter, Apollin, and Termagaunt. *Platon* is another, though less common, fictional god. See the discussion in the General Introduction, p. 16.

124     *So mote Y thee*. "so may I thrive," an common idiomatic phrase; see *MED thriven* (v.), sense 1c. See also lines 523 and 979. For a negative variation ("Evel mote he the"), see line 2061.

128     *mametrye*. "idolatry." Muslims, as Saracens, are inaccurately depicted as worshiping idols. On Western Christian beliefs about Muslim idolatry, see the discussion in Strickland, *Saracens, Demons, and Jews*, pp. 166–69.

151–56  *And yut hath . . . . none so ryche*. The location of Utaly as a major Lombard city situated between two rivers makes it likely that the poet is referencing Pavia, the capital of Lombardy in the seventh and eighth centuries, which is located on the Ticino River three miles upstream from its confluence with the Po River. The Ticino (which the poet names "Coyne" in line 693) rises in the Swiss Alps, descends into Italy through Lake Maggiore, and is the largest left-bank tributary of the Po. It is over the Coyne/Ticino that Charlemagne builds the bridge over which the French will pass to attack the city; see the notes to lines 695–701 below. In *DR*, Garcy's city in Lombardy is called Ataly (Atelie in *Otinel*, line 167).

154      *uyterly*. "completely, fully." See *MED*, *witterli* (adv.), sense 2.c, which cites this line.

164–74   *Come nought there . . . . And thynne arn al yong*. Otuel insults Charlemagne by calling him too old to engage in battle and saying he might match his strength only against birds. At the end of Otuel's taunt, he says that Charlemagne's knights are incapable of besieging Utaly because they are too young and inexperienced.

166      *ferhede*. "armed combat." *MED ferreden* (n.), sense 2b. Compare "ferede," meaning "army" (sense 2a), at line 1169.

183      *Dorundale*. Durendal is the name of Roland's famous sword. In Rocamadour, France, one may see a chapel with a sword embedded in its outside wall. By local legend, this sword is Durendal. De Veyrières notes the claim (found in l'abbé Cheval's 1862 guidebook, *Guide du Pélerin à Roc-Amadour*) that the real Durendal was stolen in 1183 when Henry II pillaged the chapel, and he includes a drawing of the current sword ("L'Épée de Roland," pp. 139–41). Compare the note to lines 2326–49 below.

239      *Seynt-Omeres*. Saint-Omer is a place in northern France named for Saint Audomarus (Omer), a seventh-century bishop and founder of the monastery alluded to here. This detail is borrowed from the French source. See *Otinel*, line 226, and compare *DR*, line 329.

245      *florens*. A florin was a gold coin minted in Florence and stamped with the figure of a lily. An English florin was worth 6 shillings and 8 pence. See *MED floren* (n.).

252–69   *. . . n to honouryng . . . . Sarsin Otuel*. Damage to folio 34v renders these lines only partially visible. The ritual is that Roland offers his sword as a pledge to Saint Denis, then retrieves the sword as he redeems the pledge through charitable alms (a cash payment). When Mass has ended, Otuel arrives and, apparently not seeing Roland, accuses him of cowardice for not showing up to fight as promised. Roland kneels in prayer before calling Otuel a liar. Compare *Otinel*, lines 223–51, *OK*, lines 395–422, and *DR*, lines 329–48.

272      *Dogge thou lyest by Seynt Mychel*. Roland responds to Otuel by calling him a dog and a liar. He swears by Saint Michael the archangel, patron saint of warriors and the leader of God's army (Jude 1:9; Apocalypse 12:7). On calling a Saracen a dog, compare the note to line 1449 below.

292      *grene as glas*. "Green" is not one of the usual adjectives linked with "glass" in Middle English. See *MED grene* (adj.), sense 1a (where this line is cited), and *glas* (n.), sense 1a. The original may have read "clene as glas" (a more common phrase), meaning "as shiny as glass."

331–32   *Leire . . . Some*. The Loire and the Somme are French rivers. The Loire, the longest river in France, stretches from the Massif Central in southern France to the Atlantic Ocean near Nantes in southern Brittany. The Somme runs westward through Picardy in northern France to its mouth in the English Channel.

349–50    *Sche toke . . . . Resonet de Rowenele.* Compare *Otinel*, lines 327–28.

364    *for the nonys.* The term *for the nonce* means approximately "for the moment" or "for the occasion," though it is primarily used as a meaningless metrical filler. See *MED nones* (n.1) and *none* (n.).

375    *With thre Sarisins heuedys of sabyl.* Medieval knights were identifiable by the images on their shields. Otuel carries a racialized emblem: three black Saracen heads. Roland carries a lion on his shield (line 301). Compare the note to lines 1366–68 below.

377    *Mygades.* Mygades is the name of Otuel's horse. Compare *DR*, line 434 ("Mekredose").

384    *Withouten ony fayle.* "Without doubt." The manuscript reads "fable," which is here emended to "fayle" because the corresponding b-rhymes make the substitution obvious. For this common tag, used frequently for rhyme, see *MED faile* (n.), sense 2.

456    *To wetyn and nought to wene.* "Of certainty and without doubt." On this tag, see *MED, witen* (v.1), sense 1h.

491    *was ther no chyldys game.* Proverbial. See Whiting C221.

511–31    *Roulond to Otuel . . . . Cursins my fauchon.* Compare *Otinel*, lines 454–69.

552    *felonye.* "violent temper, violent nature, ruthlessness." See *MED felonie* (n.), sense 4a.

568–73    *With that . . . . holy myght.* A white dove is a traditional sign for the presence of the Holy Spirit (one of the Three Persons of the Trinity), which is associated with God's grace (see Luke 3:22). Compare *Otinel*, lines 516–18; *OK*, line 585–88; and *DR*, lines 578–79.

658–63    *Lemosyns . . . . stoute and fere.* Compare *Otinel*, lines 636–42.

679–81    *Syre Otuel . . . . mule a prys.* The poet borrows the idea of Belesent riding on a mule from *Otinel*, line 656, but adds the detail that Otuel mounts her upon it. Compare *DR*, line 736.

686    *ferdales.* "furlongs." This word is a misrepresentation of the original French word, "Versels" (*Otinel*, line 664), referring to the city Vercelli. See the explanatory note to *DR*, lines 742–56.

689–90    *mount . . . . Poyne.* If this name is intended to denote a real mountain in Lombardy ("Mount Point"), its identity is unknown. Also mentioned at line 864 ("Mount Paynt"), it is said to overlook Utaly, a city situated on the banks of the Coyne River (another unknown name). The poet borrows the name from *Otinel*, line 667 ("Munpoun"). Pavia itself is situated on a small hill, but the plains surrounding Pavia are quite flat, with no significant heights between the Monferrat Hills and Pavia. The meadow where the French army encamps is across the Coyne/Ticino River from Pavia, around five miles from the city. See the explanatory note to *Otinel*, lines 664–68.

695–701    *Charles chese . . . . come and go.* The bridge that Charlemagne has built over the Coyne/Ticino River helps to locate Pavia as the site of Utaly. See the note to lines 151–56 above; and compare *OK*, lines 697–706; *DR*, lines 754–56; and *Otinel*, lines 674–80.

696    *telden on hys pavylon.* "pitch his tent." See *MED telden* (v.), sense a, and *paviloun* (n.), sense 1b, where this line is cited.

721–23    *Curables . . . . here fere.* Compare *Otinel*, lines 696–702.

740    *Agelond.* An unknown Saracen place, of which Roland has slain the lords. For this action, Clarel vows revenge.

781    *Oger Denys.* Ogier the Dane is one of Charlemagne's *dussepers* in the *chanson de geste* tradition. See the discussion in the General Introduction, p. 5n13.

794    *With that cours.* "Forcefully, vigorously"; literally "with that force of movement, impetus." See *MED cours* (n.), sense 3a, for the phrase *with cours.* Oliver is charging his opponent.

864    *Mount Paynt.* "Mount Point." On this unidentified mountain in Lombardy, see the note to line 689–90 above.

884–88    *Good hyt ys . . . . a grete lordyng.* Compare *Otinel*, lines 848–50.

900–04    *Cursable . . . . Haunchecler.* Ogier's sword is named Cursable, and Oliver's is Haunchecler. Like Roland's Durendal and Otuel's Corsouse, the mightiest warriors' swords of *chansons de geste* often acquire names that associate them with their owners. Oliver's sword is also named at *DR*, line 914 ("Haunkclere"), and at *Otinel*, line 873 ("Halteclere"). Ogier's sword is named "Curteine" at *Otinel*, line 877. On other named swords, see the notes to lines 106, 183, 1240, and 2326–49.

954    *yeve nought an hawe.* Proverbial. See Whiting H190 and note to *OK*, line 200.

980    *waraunt.* The Saracen lord is saying that he will not permit Clarel to be Ogier's protector from being killed or dismembered.

1039–47    *Otuel aspyede . . . . lordynges yare.* Compare *Otinel*, lines 1000–17.

1039    *Otuel.* The large red initial *O* of this word opens this line, indicating a secondary transition (not a fitt division). See the discussion in the General Introduction, p. 23.

1058–74    *And sayde . . . . a lytel thrawe.* Compare *Otinel*, lines 1043–47.

1071    *plawe.* "battle, fight, conflict." See *MED pleie* (n.), sense 4c.

1091    *he ne flycted.* Literally, "he did not flee." See *MED, flighten* (v.).

1099–110    *Olmadas . . . . grete renoun.* Olmadas of Aschomoyne, a Saracen, unhorses Duke Reyner (Charlemagne's chamberlain; see line 223) and takes the steed. The

Christian knight Emoleres then attacks Olmadas, striking off the Saracen's head with a mighty blow.

1146        *grenned as an hownde.* Proverbial. See Whiting H584; and compare line 1496. Otuel's strike at Empater's face anticipates his later strike at Clarel, which will also expose a Saracen's teeth (line 1463).

1165–203   *Anone Clarel . . . . Y thee plyght.* Compare *Otinel*, lines 1195–1234.

1240        *Melyn.* This is the name of Clarel's sword. Compare *DR*, line 847, where it is named "Melle," and *Otinel*, line 807, where it is named "Mellee." On other named swords, see the notes to lines 106, 183, 900–04, and 2326–49.

1267–350   *Thou olde Charlys . . . . in Godys name.* Compare *Otinel*, lines 1311–52.

1324        *nought worth a tord.* Proverbial. See Whiting T526. Compare Chaucer's Tale of Sir Thopas (*CT* VII[B² 2120]).

1366–68    *Thre swerdys . . . . a ryche ston.* Belesent has replaced Otuel's old shield, which bore an emblem of three black Saracen heads, with a new, bejeweled one bearing an emblem of three silver and three golden swords. Compare the note to line 375 above.

1388        *Alle it is in God long.* "It's all in God's power." See *MED bilong* (adj.), sense 1b.

1433        *sprange oute as sparcle of glede.* Proverbial. See Whiting S562. Although the phrase is used more often to describe the swiftness of knights' movements (i.e., springing out of a saddle or into battle), it is also conventional for knights' blows to be so violent that sparks fly from their weapons. See, for example, *Lybeaus Desconus* (Lambeth Palace, MS 306), ed. Salisbury and Weldon, lines 1176–78 and 1980–82. In *Sir Gawain and the Green Knight*, the Green Knight's horse famously strikes sparks with its hooves exiting King Arthur's court (ed. Winny, line 459).

1449        *hethen hounde.* The phrase commonly appears in Middle English romances as a term of abuse to describe Saracens. See *MED hound* (n.), sense 2b, which also notes the use of "cristen hound — said in disparagement by an infidel." The phrase reappears at lines 1644 and 2278. Otuel calls Roland "worse than ony hounde" at line 467, and Clarel imagines himself being called a "hounde" at line 1496. Compare, too, the notes to lines 272 and 1146 above.

1459–85    *He smote hym . . . . syttyth alle onmys.* Compare *Otinel*, lines 1445–56.

1463        *That men myght sen hys tethe.* Compare the note to line 1146 above.

1464        *lewed and lered.* This phrase literally means "the uneducated and the learned," but it can be used more generally to mean "people of all types."

1615        The Fillingham manuscript lacks several folios after this line at the base of fol. 57v. If seven leaves are missing, as O'Sullivan suggests (*Firumbras and Otuel and Roland*, p. xliv), that would constitute a gap of over 400 lines, but comparison to other versions of the story suggests that three to five leaves (approximately 186 to 310 lines) are missing (see also O'Sullivan, p. xiv). The corresponding passages in *Otinel* (approximately 302 lines), in *OK* (approximately 250 lines), and in *DR* (approximately 190 lines) suggest that, on the absent folios, the poet recounted some of the following episodes: one-on-one combats featuring Roland (killing a Turk), Oliver, and Otinel; more melees between Christians and Saracens; a conversation between Garcy and a Saracen about their losses; a moment when Otinel, Roland, and Oliver join together to rout the Saracens; Charlemagne's pleasure at watching the Saracens flee; and a few lines of transition to Ogier as he is about to escape from captivity.

1616–36   *And threw . . . . doughty knyght.* In the penultimate scene of the Otuel section of the romance, just before the capture of King Garcy, Ogier the Dane breaks out of prison and rejoins his comrades. In this version, which lacks the opening lines of the scene due to missing folios, Ogier throws guards over the castle wall, breaks his chains, finds his horse and armor, and shouts a gracious farewell to Enfamy. For alternate scenarios, see *Otinel*, lines 1836–69; *OK*, lines 1629–78; and *DR*, lines 1543–60.

1646–81   *To the Turkeyes . . . . trumpes and daunsyng.* Compare *Otinel*, lines 1873–1901.

1682–93   *The Erchebyschop . . . . Y yow telle may.* On the different endings among the French and Middle English accounts of Otuel/Otinel, see the explanatory note to *Otinel*, lines 1899–904.

1694–978   *Here bygynneth . . . . ther agayn.* Fitt 7 recounts two episodes that appear in neither *Otinel* nor the *Song of Roland*, one in which Charlemagne fights against Ebrayn, a strong Saracen king (lines 1700–1858), the second in which he fights against the king of Navarre (lines 1859–1921). A large red initial at line 1859 marks the beginning of the second episode. As a result of the two battles, Charlemagne takes control of Spain and Galicia.

1700–858   *Afftyr Garcy . . . . joye and solempnité.* King Ebrayn has brought a Saracen army to Cordoba, where they are joined by Germans escaped from the battle against Garcy. Charlemagne travels to Cordoba, kills Ebrayn in single combat, takes Cordoba, and converts the city's inhabitants.

1716–20   *Syxty thousand . . . . all to be.* Ebrayn's army is said to number sixty thousand Saracens, but since Charlemagne is said to have only sixty thousand men to fight against "hem all," the first number may reflect a scribal error.

1859   *Welle.* The large red initial *W* of this word opens this line, indicating a secondary transition (not a fitt division). See the note to lines 1694–1978 above, and the discussion in the General Introduction, p. 23.

1859–921   *Welle sone . . . . kynnes nede.* This passage presents a moral lesson that no man may escape his preordained death. On learning that the king of Navarre has begun a campaign of pillage and burning, Charlemagne comes to fight. Before the battle, he beseeches Jesus and Mary that each warrior who is fated to die be marked with a red cross on his shoulder. When, on the morning of the battle, he sees a thousand men so marked, he commands them to stay behind. After he has defeated the king of Navarre, Charlemagne returns to camp to find that the marked knights are dead.

1866         *Mount Gardyn.* A unidentified place-name.

1929         *yfeffyd.* Charlemagne has enfeoffed each man who helped him in battle; they are
             now his honored vassals, bound to fight for him when he requires it, and
             rewarded for their service.

1941         *Jercos.* It is unknown who the "Jercos" are. Based on the passage, they are
             inhabitants of a place in Spain to whom Charlemagne rewards the castle
             Tandylyf.

1979–2790    *Here bygynnyth . . . . wythoute bale.* The retelling of the *Song of Roland* in Fitts
             8 and 9 is unique to the Fillingham manuscript. Fitt 8 (lines 1979–2586)
             recounts the Battle at Roncevaux in which Roland dies while leading
             Charlemagne's rearguard against a vastly larger Saracen army. For another
             retelling in English, see the Middle English *Song of Roland* (*Fragment of the
             Song of Roland,* ed. Herrtage) and the discussion in the General Introduction,
             pp. 12–13.

1981–2016    *Now lete . . . . cité of Pampulon.* These lines are also found (with slight
             variations in wording) in *RV,* lines 425–60. The overlap contributed to the
             now-discarded "Charlemagne and Roland" theory of a lost romance. See the
             discussion in the General Introduction, pp. 7–8.

1982–90      *speke we of Charles . . . . red of face.* On the description of Charlemagne, borrowed
             in part from Einhard's *Life of Charlemagne,* p. 34, see the discussion in the
             General Introduction, p. 9. On his gigantic size, compare the explanatory note
             to *RV,* lines 474–83.

2017–28      *Twey Sarsins . . . . here tyme se.* In this section of *OR,* Charlemagne and Roland's
             opponents are two Saracen rulers from Persia — Mansour and his brother
             Beligans — who have been sent to Pamplona by the sultan of Babylon to harass
             Charlemagne. In the first part of the *Song of Roland* (lines 1–2608), Charlemagne
             and Roland's foe is Marsile, Saracen king of Spain. His overlord Baligant, the
             aged emir of Babylon, is not mentioned until line 2614 of the *Song of Roland,*
             after Marsile's armies have been defeated.

2023         *Mansour.* The name *Mansour* means "the one who is victorious." Al-Mansur (Abu
             Ja'far Abdallah ibn Muhammad al-Mansur) ruled from 754 to 775 over the
             Abbasid Caliphate (750–1258, the second of the two great Muslim caliphates).
             Al-Mansur moved the Abbasid capital city from Syria to Iraq, where he found the
             city of Baghdad in 762–63. The Abbasid dynasty fell to the Mongol Hulagu
             Khan (a grandson of Ghengis Khan) who conquered Baghdad in 1258.
             Regardless of whether the *OR* poet knew any of this, he clearly associated the
             name Mansour with a Muslim military leader.

2029–97      *Charlys bythought . . . . beyt suche.* In the *Song of Roland,* Gwynes (Ganelon) was
             Charlemagne's brother-in-law and Roland's uncle. He is also, famously, one of
             the great traitors of Western European literary history. Dante places Ganelon
             among the traitors to country, who lie eternally in Cocytus, the frozen lake at the
             very bottom of Hell (*Inferno,* ed. Sinclair, 32.122). For the classic account of
             Ganelon's treason, see the *Song of Roland,* lines 10–702. The lines in *OR* offer an

abbreviated rendition of how Ganelon joins with the Saracens to plot Roland's death.

2082      *whyt a flour*. Proverbial. See Whiting F308.

2096      *Judas*. Judas is the disciple who betrays Jesus, hence a common model for traitors. See, for example, Matthew 26:14–25.

2098–106  *Charlys grethed . . . . forto lede*. On the assignment of Roland, Oliver, and the other *dussepers* to lead the rearguard during Charlemagne's passage through the Pyrenees Mountains, see the *Song of Roland*, lines 737–825.

2114      *Turpyn*. Here, Turpin stays with Charlemagne, whereas in the *Song of Roland* the warrior-archbishop accompanies Roland in the rearguard and plays a major role: when Marsile's army attacks the rearguard at Roncevaux, Turpin blesses the French warriors, explains why they must fight to martyrdom, comforts the dying Roland, and is himself one of the last three French warriors to die. The *OR* poet names Turpin as a surviving eyewitness; see the note to lines 40–41 above.

2122–478  *Syxty thousand . . . . Y thee say*. This 357-line account of the battle at Roncevaux summarizes 1549 lines in the *Song of Roland* (lines 848–2396). The *OR* poet's concern is to convey the general story and a few highlights, not to provide a thorough account of the battle and its political ramifications.

2122–23  *Syxty thousand . . . . brought tho*. While Mansour here leads a force of 60,000 fighters, Marsile's army in the *Song of Roland* numbers 400,000 Saracens. In each text, Roland leads a rearguard of 20,000.

2156      *As der that beyth withinne the net*. Proverbial. See Whiting D148. See also line 2642.

2164–66  *Though Oger . . . . dethys wounde*. This account of Ogier the Dane's death as he fights under Roland's leadership does not occur in the *Song of Roland*, where Ogier remains with Charlemagne and eventually leads one of the emperor's three columns in the battle against Baligant.

2187      *develes lemes*. In its literal sense, "lemes" usually means "limbs"; here, the Saracens are characterized as limbs of the devil, much as Christians were often characterized as parts of the body of the Christ. See *MED lim* (n.1), sense 4a; and compare line 2652.

2188–211  *A Sarsyn . . . . ys me bynome*. This scene in which a blinded and dying Oliver unintentionally strikes his companion Roland is conveyed with great drama in the *Song of Roland*, lines 1989–2009.

2252–53  *hys horn . . . . in hys honde*. These two lines show Roland blowing his horn. In the *Song of Roland*, the act of Roland blowing his horn fills three of the poem's most poignant *laisses* (lines 1753–95), and follows two lengthy scenes in which brave Roland and wise Oliver debate whether it is proper for Roland to blow his horn to call back Charlemagne, first when the enemy has been spotted but the battle has not yet begun (lines 1049–1109), later when all but a handful of the French have been killed (lines 1691–1736). See the discussion in the General Introduction, p. 14.

2300      *wytherlyngges.* "enemies." See *MED witherling* (n.), a word derived from Old English *wiþer*, meaning "hostile, adverse, fierce; contrary, opposite, wrong" (*OED wither* (adj.), senses A1, A2). Compare *MED wither-wine* (n.), often used as an epithet for Satan, and *wither-iwinne* (n.), "adversary." The word in this form is rare, but it appears twice in *OR*, here and at line 2649.

2326–49  *Tho he bygan . . . . hys thought.* On Roland's address to Durendal and his unsuccessful attempt to break it so as to keep the sword out of Saracen hands, see the *Song of Roland*, lines 2297–2354. On a local legend that Durendal survives, and is now embedded in a wall in a chapel in Rocamadour, France, see the note to line 183 above.

2356      *the temple and hys vayne.* Roland blows his horn so loudly that his temples burst. This scene is one of the most famous moments in the *Song of Roland* (lines 1753–95, especially 1761–64). See the note to lines 2252–53 above.

2377      *Rowlond.* The large red initial *R* of this word opens this mid-stanza line. It marks a major moment in *OR*: Roland's death scene. See the discussion of the initials in the General Introduction, p. 23.

2425–42  *Jhesu that syttyth . . . . for the stedfastnesse.* For an alternate account of Roland's final prayer, see the *Song of Roland*, lines 2369–72 and 2384–88.

2446–57  *Ayngelys . . . . Roulondys soule bare.* Here Roland's soul is carried to paradise by sixty-seven angels, under the leadership of the angels Saints Michael, Gabriel, and Raphael. In the *Song of Roland*, Roland's soul is borne to paradise by just three angels: his "angel Cherubin," Saint Michael of the Peril, and Saint Gabriel (lines 2390–96).

2503–38  *With dwele . . . . Godys knyght.* On Charlemagne's grief at seeing the bodies of Roland and the dead French soldiers, see the *Song of Roland*, lines 2398–2414 and 2855–2944.

2527–38  *Sampson . . . . Godys knyght.* In praising Roland, Charlemagne makes comparison to three biblical figures. Samson was renowned for his strength (Judges 13–16); David (to whom Charlemagne compares himself) was famous for his grief upon the death of his son Absalom (2 Kings 18:33); Judas Maccabeus fought successfully against the Seleucid empire that had been occupying Israel (1 Maccabees 3–9). Medieval thought imagined Nine Worthies who represented the most valiant men of the Pagan, Judaic, and Christian eras. David and Judas Maccabeus were two of the Three Jewish Worthies, and Charlemagne one of the Three Christian Worthies.

2543      *There nys no bote of mannys deth.* Proverbial. See Whiting D78.

2584      *Goddys mounde.* The reference is to Calvary, the hill upon which Jesus was crucified. See Matthew 27:33; Mark 15:22; Luke 23:33; and John 19:17.

2587–664  *Here bygynnyth . . . . uppon the grounde.* Fitt 9 tells of Charlemagne's battle against Belyngas (the sultan of Persia) and Perigon (the sultan of Babylon). Otinel slays Perigon, while Turpin and Charlemagne join to kill Belyngas. The brief encounter bears little resemblance to the second battle in the *Song of Roland* (lines 2974–3647), wherein Charlemagne's forces defeat a mighty multinational army brought to Spain by Baligant (the emir of Babylon). When Charlemagne and Baligant meet in single combat, the emir staggers Charlemagne with a weighty blow. The emperor recovers and kills Baligant after the angel Saint Gabriel asks Charlemagne, very simply, what he is doing (line 3611).

2594      *Sadrak*. An unidentified river-name, said to be two miles from Zaragoza. The river that flows through Zaragoza is the Ebro.

2605      *Too thowsand of Percyans*. Here, the *OR* poet counts two thousand Persians, while line 2614 reads "Two hundred of Percy." One line would seem to be in error.

2606      *Affricans*. The references to Africans and Persians reflect the inclusion among the Saracen armies of people of color from distant lands, further emphasizing the Otherness of the enemies of Christendom.

2649      *wytherlynges*. See the note to line 2300 above.

2652      *fyndes lemes*. See the note to line 2187 above.

2668      *mowntans*. Not to be confused with "mountain," *MED mountaunce* (n.), sense 1b means a "length of time."

2680–754      *Forsothe . . . . muche myssaunter*. After Turpin and Turry accuse Ganelon of treason and Ganelon denies the allegation, Turry defeats him in a brief single combat on the battlefield in which Roland lies dead. Ganelon is then hung and drawn, in a gruesome scene. In the *Song of Roland*, the judicial combat takes place not at Roncevaux but at Charlemagne's court in Aix-la-Chapelle, and the episode is long and complicated. Ganelon insists that he is not a traitor against Charlemagne, but has simply avenged himself against Roland, who had shamed him in public. When Ganelon's mighty kinsmen Pinabel steps forward on his behalf, Charlemagne's barons are cowed, and the only man willing to stand against him is an inexperienced knight, Thierry. Thierry's victory over the much stronger Pinabel carries political significance: not only is Ganelon drawn and quartered as befits a traitor, but thirty kinsmen who had supported him are hung. On the trial and punishment of Ganelon, see the *Song of Roland*, lines 3735–3974.

2688      *withclepyth*. "accuses." See *MED withclepen* (v.), sense c, which cites this line.

2693      *Thowe lixt*. "You lie." *Lixt* ("liest") is the second-person present tense of *MED lien* (v.2), sense 2a.

2759      *murre and baune*. The fragrant ointments with which Roland's body is anointed are reminiscent of the exotic "spices, and balm, and myrrh" carried by the Ismaelite merchants to whom Joseph is sold by his brothers (Genesis 37:25); and also of the "gold, frankincense, and myrrh" brought by the Magi as gifts to the newborn Jesus (Matthew 2:11).

2785–90      *Here endeth . . . . wythoute bale*. The closing stanza unites the two parts of *OR* by naming Otuel, Roland, Oliver, and the twelve peers, and praying that Jesus may bring them and ourselves (the readers) to bliss.

Explicit     *Amen quod J. Gage.* The explicit has been interpreted as the scribe's (not the poet's) signature. The final word is smudged, but in the British Library Catalogue "Explore Archives and Manuscripts" description of the Fillingham manuscript it is read as "Gage" ("Additional MS 37492"), viewable at searcharchives.bl.uk (search term "Additional MS 37492"). See also O'Sullivan, *Firumbras and Otuel and Roland*, p. 146.

# TEXTUAL NOTES TO OTUEL AND ROLAND

**ABBREVIATIONS: MS**: London, British Library MS Additional 37492 (Fillingham), fols. 30v–76r; **O**: *Otuel and Roland*, ed. O'Sullivan, in *Firumbras and Otuel and Roland*, pp. 59–146.

| | |
|---|---|
| 2 | *worchyp.* So MS. O: *worchype.* |
| 8 | Ellipses have been added because the rhyme scheme indicates that a line is missing. There is no break in the MS. |
| 11 | *do.* So MS. O: *tho.* |
| 16 | *Rowlond.* So MS. O: *Rowland.* |
| 19 | *Emon.* So MS. O: *Emoun.* |
| 24 | *Albene.* So MS. O: *awbane.* |
| 28 | O inserts a blank line here though no line is missing in the manuscript. |
| 30 | *dere.* So MS. O: *der.* |
| 42 | *syght.* So MS. O: *fyȝt.* |
| 66 | *Charlyon.* So MS. O: *Charlyoun.* |
| 69 | *renon.* So MS. O: *renoun.* |
| 81 | *tylle.* So O. MS: *stylle.* |
| 92 | *Ere.* So MS. O: *Or.* |
| 116 | *grylle.* So MS. O: *yvylle.* |
| 121 | *Mahon.* So MS. O: *Mahoun.* |
| 122 | *Platon.* So MS. O: *Platoun.* |
| 123 | *fayn.* So MS. O: *fayne.* |
| 125 | *thay.* So MS. O: *day.* |
| 129 | *lastyd.* So MS. O: *lastyth.* |
| 139 | *Charlyon.* So MS. O: *Charlyoun.* |
| 140 | *Mahon.* So MS. O: *Mahoun.* |
| 152 | *Has don.* So MS. O: *Don.* |
| 172 | *wordy.* So MS. O: *worthy.* |
| 176 | *thede.* So MS. O: *dede.* |
| 195 | O inserts a blank line here though no line is missing in the manuscript. |
| 207 | *Mahon.* So MS. O: *Mahoun.* |
| 213 | *Mahon.* So MS. O: *Mahoun.* |
| 215 | *deme.* MS: *dene.* O: *thone.* |
| 222 | *comaunded.* So MS. O: *commaunded.* |
| 228 | *syght.* MS, O: *fyȝt.* |
| 252–69 | Folio in MS is torn, which has corrupted the text. |
| 293 | *Tha.* So MS. O: *That.* |
| 311 | *schon.* So MS. O: *schone.* |
| 333 | *sayth sure the bok.* MS, O: *sayth the bok sure.* |

367    *The*. So MS. O: *tho*.
370    *The*. So MS. O: *tho*.
383    *fettyn*. So MS. O: *settyn*.
384    *fayle*. MS, O: *fable*. Emended for rhyme.
400    *heued*. So O. MS: *houed*.
419    *foo*. So MS. O: *foe*.
455    *foeld*. So MS. O: *feeld*.
465    *sede*. So MS. O: *dede*.
486    *thonkyth*. So MS. O: *thonkyd*.
497    *Dronke*. So MS. O: *Drouke*.
506    *do*. So MS. O: *tho*.
507    *lyght*. So MS. O: *hyʒt*.
509    *cristen*. So MS. O: *cristene*.
532    *Efte*. So MS. O: *Erste*.
553    *holme*. So MS. O: *helme*.
559    *Rouland*. So MS. O: *Roulond*.
560    *Sarisin*. So MS. O: *sarsin*.
576    *fyght*. So O. MS: *syʒt*.
580    *drewe*. So MS. O: *threwe*.
610    *an answere*. So MS. O: *andswere*.
615    *woman*. So MS. O: *womman*.
624    *yslowe*. So MS. O: *y-slawe*.
640    *Charles*. So MS. O: *Charlys*.
646    *the*₁. So MS. O: *tho*.
676    *thay*. So MS. O: *day*.
686    *Two ferdales*. So MS. O: *To Vergels*.
697    *sojourned*. MS: *sorourned*. O: *soiourned*.
706    *goode wede*. So O. MS: *wys*, struck through, is placed between *goode* and *wede*.
714    *hedynesse*. So MS. O: *hethynesse*.
763    *Askeward*. So O. MS: *Asterward*.
781    *Denys*. So MS. O: *danys*.
794    *cours to*. So MS. O: *cours he to*.
796    *The schaft was strong and the heued brod*. In MS and O, this line is broken into two lines between *strong* and *and*. Metrically, it should be a single line, so I have combined it.
801    *Non*. So MS. O: *No*.
803    *yet*. MS, O: *ʒyt*.
822    *overdrew*. So MS. O: *over threw*.
843    *Smertilyche*. So MS. O: *Smertelyche*.
856    *do*. So MS. O: *tho*.
871    *yendyrward*. So MS. O: *ʒenderware*.
875    *ower*. So MS. O: *ewer*.
880    *tabeures*. So MS. O: *taboures*.
881    *chynoures*. So MS. O: *chymours*.
882    *afryght*. MS, O: *aflyght*.
891    *Assaylethen*. So MS. O: *Assayleden*.
       *elthe*. So MS. O: *elde*.

| 913 | *de.* So O. MS: *and.* |
|---|---|

913     *de.* So O. MS: *and.*
928     *do.* So MS. O: *tho.*
976     *de.* So MS. O: *the.*
980     *hys.* So MS. O: *his.*
982     *wroth.* MS, O: *vroth.*
1001    *had.* So MS. O: *hath.*
1015    *do.* So MS. O: *tho.*
1033    *do.* So MS. O: *tho.*
1052    *hys*₁,₂. So MS. O: *ys*₁,₂.
1060    *Olyver.* So MS. O: *Olyuere.*
1061    *everchon.* So MS. O: *euerchone.*
1065    *hedyn.* So MS. O: *hethyn.*
1068    *Yet.* MS, O: *ȝyt.*
1070    *fone.* So MS. O: *sone.*
1073    *enthyng.* So MS. O: *endyng.*
1084    *overdrew.* So MS. *over threw.*
1087    *Langares.* So MS. O: *langars.*
1130    *rwed.* So MS. O: *rived.*
1164    *thynketh.* So MS. O: *thynkyth.*
1176    *God.* So MS. O: *good.*
1177    *Otul.* So MS. O: *Otuel.*
1219    *hem.* So MS. O: *hym.*
1232    *warlok.* MS, O: *garlok.*
1237    *fettan.* So MS. O: *fetton.*
1246    *Twe hethe.* So MS. O: *Two of þe.*
1252    *That.* So MS. O: *Than.*
1266    *launce.* So O. MS: *saunce.*
1272    *of myschaunce.* So MS. O: *of my myschaunce.*
1283    *dretest.* So MS. O: *thretest.*
1290    *hedynesse.* So MS. O: *hethynesse.*
1294    *dare.* So MS. O: *þare.*
1311    *to.* So MS. O: *he.*
1337    *drydde.* So MS. O: *þrydde.*
1339    *Eve.* So MS. O: *ous.*
1347    *low.* MS, O: *lew.*
1360    *Syr.* So MS. O: *Syre.*
        *over.* So MS. O: *on.*
1411    *stete.* So MS. O: *stede.*
1420    *sought.* So MS. O: *fouȝt.*
1432    *helmes hauberk.* So MS. O: *helmes and hauberk.*
1462    *wytnessed.* So MS. O: *wytnesseth.*
1475    *had.* So MS. O: *hath.*
        *yschave.* MS: extra minim struck out.
1486    *ne*₂. So MS. O: *the.*
1501    Ellipses have been added because the rhyme scheme indicates that a line is missing. There is no break in the MS.
1508    *haberjon.* So MS. O: *haberioun.*

| 1511 | *thee*. So O. MS: *tho*. |
| | *syde*. So MS. O: *sythe*. |
| 1529 | *thonkyth*. So MS. O: *thonkyd*. |
| | *day*. So MS. O: *thay*. |
| 1537 | *had*. So MS. O: *hath*. |
| 1546 | *doume*. So MS. O: *domne*. |
| 1564 | *ycristeneth*. So MS. O: *ycristened*. |
| 1590 | *eld*. So MS. O: *old*. |
| 1597 | *barones*. So MS. O: *borones*. |
| 1598 | *Lorthynges*. So MS. O: *lordynges*. |
| 1609 | *fer*. So MS. O: *for*. |
| 1615 | *pryketh*. So MS. O: *prykyng*. |
| | *beforn*. So MS. O: *before*. |
| 1615–16 | An unknown number of folios are missing. |
| 1648 | *blode*. So O. MS: *blede*. |
| 1678 | *enthyng*. So MS. O: *endyng*. |
| 1798 | *Alle*. So MS. O: *All*. |
| 1702 | *the*. So O. MS: *the the*. |
| 1714 | *neghhode*. So MS. O: *neʒhede*. |
| 1734 | *swyde*. So MS. O: *swythe*. |
| 1750 | *that*. So MS. O: *thay*. |
| 1783 | *wyss*. So MS. O: *wysser*. |
| 1803 | *banerer*. So MS. O: *banere*. |
| 1809 | *Charlys by*. So MS. O: *Charlys swore by*. |
| 1823 | *tho*. So MS. O: *thon*. |
| 1849 | Ellipses have been added because the rhyme scheme indicates that a line is missing. There is no break in the MS. |
| 1868 | *othyr*. So MS. O: *othyyr*. |
| 1874 | *He sende*. So MS. O inserts *that* at the start of the line. |
| 1893 | *de*. So MS. O: *ded*. |
| 1925 | *hys saum fayle*. So MS. O: *hys barownes saumfayle*. |
| 1928 | *And was*. So MS. O: *And hyt was*. |
| 1939 | *parteth*. So MS. O: *parted*. |
| 1955 | *stabeleth*. So MS. O: *stabeled*. |
| 1967 | *Yver*. So MS. O: *yuner*. |
| 1968 | *comaund*. So MS. O: *comaunded*. |
| 2010 | *Of knyghtes grete*. So MS. O: *knyʒtes off grete*. |
| 2026 | *dwelleth*. So MS. O: *dwelled*. |
| 2057 | *Bathe*. So MS. O: *Bothe*. |
| 2082 | *a*. So MS. O: *as*. |
| 2108 | *bodyes*. So O. MS: *bedyes*. |
| 2138 | *peces*. So MS. O: *peses*. |
| 2153 | *fyn*. So MS. O: *fyne*. |
| 2174 | *also*. So MS. O: *al to*. |
| 2176 | *do*. So MS. O: *tho*. |
| 2192 | *bode*. So MS. O: *bothe*. |
| 2194 | *blynth*. So MS. O: *blynd*. |

| | |
|---|---|
| 2196 | *leythen.* So MS. O: *leyde.* |
| 2197 | *evermore.* So O. MS: *neuer more.* |
| 2198 | *brod.* So O. MS: *bred.* |
| 2210 | *whom.* So MS. O: *when.* |
| 2212 | *bode.* So MS. O: *bothe.* |
| 2218 | Ellipses have been added because the rhyme scheme indicates that a line is missing. There is no break in the MS. |
| 2231 | *fer.* So MS. O: *ser.* |
| 2233 | *yhongeth.* So MS. O: *y-honged.* |
| 2241 | *drydde.* So MS. O: *thrydde.* |
| 2242 | *gooth.* So MS. O: *good.* |
| 2245 | *resteth.* So MS. O: *rested.* |
| 2247 | *of hys.* So MS. O: *wythys.* |
| 2249 | *hem.* So MS. O: *hym.* |
| 2252 | *schylle.* So MS. O: *schrylle.* |
| 2255 | *yslowe.* So MS. O: *yflowe.* |
| 2265 | *Sey.* So MS. O: *bey.* |
| 2295 | *theleth.* So MS. O: *deled.* |
| 2310 | *that.* So MS. O: *than.* |
| 2345 | *graveth.* So MS. O: *graued.* |
| 2367 | *dare.* So MS. O: *thare.* |
| 2407 | *Deth.* So MS. O: *Ded.* |
| | *sayd.* So MS. O: *sayth.* |
| 2410 | *com.* So MS. O: *cam.* |
| 2423 | *Loketh.* So MS. O: *loked.* |
| | *hene.* So MS. O: *heuene.* |
| 2430 | *there.* So MS. O: *dere.* |
| 2464 | *hym.* So MS. O: *hem.* |
| 2486 | *Angls.* So MS. O: *Angels.* |
| 2557 | *ther.* So O. MS: word obscured by a blot of ink. |
| 2558 | *waketh.* So MS. O: *waked.* |
| 2561 | *lyght.* MS: *lyʒt.* O: *hyʒt.* |
| 2596 | *Saragon.* So MS. O: *Saragone.* |
| 2612 | *do.* So MS. O: *tho.* |
| 2613 | *had.* So MS. O: *hath.* |
| 2647 | *Of.* So MS. O: *Off.* |
| 2649 | *Of.* So MS. O: *Off.* |
| 2655 | *Suffreth dere.* So MS. O: *Suffred there.* |
| 2662 | *thay.* So MS. O: *they.* |
| 2674 | *do.* So MS. O: *tho.* |
| | *blyde.* So MS. O: *blythe.* |
| 2675 | *thonketh.* So MS. O: *thonked.* |
| 2676 | *hath.* So MS. O: *had.* |
| 2681 | *had.* So MS. O: *hath.* |
| 2682 | *had ryght.* So MS. O: *hath dyʒt.* |
| 2688 | *withclepyth.* So MS. O: *with-clepyd.* |

| 2700 | *Byhonged*. So MS. O: *Be honged*. |
| | *trawe*. So MS. O: *drawe*. |
| 2713 | *schylde*. So O. MS: *chylde*. |
| 2760 | *othour*. So MS. O: *odour*. |
| 2771 | *everychon*. So MS. O: *everychone*. |
| 2778 | *were*. So MS. O: *they were*. |

# DUKE ROLAND AND SIR OTUEL OF SPAIN INTRODUCTION

The last of the Middle English Otuel romances, *Duke Roland and Sir Otuel of Spain* tells the same basic story of Otuel's coming to Charlemagne's court, his duel with Roland, and his conversion to Christianity, which then leads to his heroic part in the defeat of Emperor Garcy. As another of the English *Otinel* translations, *Duke Roland* offers a slightly different rendering of some main characters; the romance deepens the relationship between Belesent and Otuel and heightens Belesent's active role. In this version, Otuel stands out for his sharp tongue and quick wit, qualities that are maintained after conversion. The poet blames French knights for their missteps, using Otuel's insults to voice criticism of French shortcomings.

*Duke Roland* has a single manuscript witness, the London Thornton manuscript (London, British Library MS Additional 31042), fols. 82r–94r, copied in the mid-fifteenth century.[1] The London Thornton is one of two manuscripts compiled by Yorkshire gentryman Robert Thornton, each containing a variety of devotional and popular texts, including many romances.[2] The London Thornton also contains the only copy of a second romance from the Otuel cycle, *The Siege of Milan*, fols. 66v–79v. Thornton is also the copyist of the unique text of the alliterative *Morte Arthure* in the Lincoln Thornton manuscript (Lincoln, Lincoln Cathedral MS 91), fols. 53r–98v. Sidney J. H. Herrtage, the nineteenth-century editor of *Duke Roland*, dates the composition of both it and *Siege* to the end of the fourteenth century. To judge by its dialect, *Duke Roland* was originally composed in northern England.[3]

An examination of the four touchstone scenes quickly unveils *Duke Roland*'s distinct character as the newest poem in the group.[4] To start with, the women in *Duke Roland* are the

---

[1] For *Duke Roland*, see *DIMEV* 3254; *NIMEV* 1996; and Smyser, "Charlemagne Legends," pp. 94, 264–65. The poem consists of 1596 lines composed in twelve-line tail-rhyme stanzas.

[2] On Robert Thornton and the Thornton manuscripts, see the essays in *Robert Thornton and His Books*, ed. Fein and Johnston. On the Thornton Charlemagne romances as being part of an aspirational vision for Christian world dominance (as displayed by manuscript context), see Hardman, "The *Sege of Melayne*"; and Warm, "Identity, Narrative and Participation." Seen in this light, Thornton sets Charlemagne among other celebrated "world conquerors" that include Arthur (the alliterative *Morte Arthure*) and Richard (*Richard Coer de Lyon*). On how iconic echoes of Charlemagne influenced English depictions of King Richard in romance, see, e.g., Hardman, "The *Sege of Melayne*," pp. 75, 85–86; Libbon, "The Invention of King Richard," pp. 133–38; and Taylor, "The *Chanson d'Aspremont*," pp. 111–12.

[3] *English Charlemagne Romances. Part II*, ed. Herrtage, pp. xii–xiii.

[4] On these scenes which involve women and Otuel's penchant for insult, see the introduction to *Otuel a Knight*, pp. 65–66.

most vocal of all females found in the Otuel romances. As in *Otuel and Roland*, Belesent is permitted to arm Otuel and then to watch the duel beside her father, but in *Duke Roland* she is also allowed to decide whether or not she will marry Otuel. When Charlemagne offers Belesent to Otuel, Otuel kneels and asks Belesent if she is pleased with the match (lines 637–41). The *Duke Roland* poet also hints at an instance of premarital lovemaking between Belesent and Otuel. When Otuel accepts her as his intended bride, he asks that the wedding be delayed until after Garcy has been defeated. This scene is the same in all versions, but it is especially meaningful in *Duke Roland* because it confirms that for most of the romance the two are not yet married. It is therefore curious that, when Charlemagne and his forces arrive in Ataly, and Roland, Oliver, and Ogier secretly go off to pursue adventure, Otuel is alone with Belesent in her chamber:

> Otuell that was so wighte
> Duelles with Belesent the brighte,          *Dwells*
>     Was comely one to calle.
> Oute of hir chambire he wendis righte,
> Als faste als ever that he myghte,
>     Into the kynges haulle
> To seche Olyver and Rowlande,
> Bot never nother he ther fande
>     Amonge the lordes alle.
> (lines 1009–17)

The *Duke Roland* poet's explanation for Otuel's absence from the group of adventurers is unique.

In *Duke Roland*, when Otuel first arrives in Charlemagne's court, he thoroughly berates Charlemagne and his knights, hurling insults, threats, and challenges for fifty lines before even beginning to deliver his message from Garcy. Otuel's insults are so outrageous that Estut, a knight of Charlemagne's court, tries to attack the Saracen. Roland reminds Estut that Otuel is protected from harm because he is a messenger, but Estut attacks him anyway and is then quickly killed by Otuel (lines 151–68). In the French *Otinel*, Roland is not bothered by Otinel's threats, but simply laughs at his insults, and it is not Estut who attacks Otinel but an unnamed knight who was "reared badly" (*Otinel*, line 91). In adapting this scene, the *Duke Roland* poet heightens the emotional reaction of the French court. It is not just a single, badly behaved knight who loses control and attacks Otuel; all of the knights, including Roland, are outraged by Otuel's insults and threats. Siobhain Bly Calkin discusses how this outrage reflects on the French court:

> The inefficacy of the prohibition points to traditional problems within Charlemagne's court, namely the king's inability to maintain discipline and the willingness of some of his knights to behave reprehensibly. The incident suggests that, as honourable and courteous as Charlemagne and Roland are, the larger court to which they belong does not share their sense of honour, and instead actively invalidates their assurances of safe conduct.[5]

As in the source, Charlemagne guarantees Otuel's safety while he stays at court, but the Saracen's shocking taunts push the *dussepers* past the point of maintaining their courtly decorum.

---

[5] Calkin, "Saracens," p. 187.

Otuel continues to make rude, sarcastic comments as the romance progresses. When he encounters Roland and Oliver fleeing the Saracen battle, his short speech reproves the knights, both for fleeing and for undertaking the foolish errand:

| | |
|---|---|
| He hailsede tham with steryn chere, | *greeted* |
| And sayde, "Sirres, whate make ye here? | |
|     Come ye fro fischeynge?" | |
| | |
| He reproved tham there full velanslye, | *mockingly* |
| And yit theire bodies were alle blodye | |
|     With wondes many one. | |
| "Wene ye, for youre chevalrye, | |
| For youre boste and youre folye, | |
|     That the Sarazenes will late yow one? | *grant you [victory]* |
| Charlles with his stronge powere | |
| Schall thynke this a grete gramaungere, | *foolish enterprise* |
|     This dede to undertone. | |
| Bot this chase schall thay by full dere!" | *cost them dearly* |
| (lines 1042–54) | |

Otuel devotes relatively few words to galvanizing his overcome comrades and encouraging them to return to battle. Instead, he aims his sharp comments at the shamefulness of their actions. The *Duke Roland* poet also changes the dialogue in which Otinel asks the knights whether they have gone fishing and then boasts that he can "fish" for Saracens as well as they (*Otinel*, lines 1041–47).[6] The English poet omits the wordplay, and the comment becomes a sarcastic critique of the bloodied knights, who are obviously running from a battle.[7]

In *Duke Roland*, the scene in which Alphany cares for Ogier the Dane's wounds closely follows the *Otinel* source while enhancing a sense of intimacy and attraction between the two characters. In the Anglo-Norman *Otinel*, Alfamie, aided by three maidens, disarms Ogier and tends his wounds outside in a courtyard (lines 978–90). In *Duke Roland*, Alphany assures Ogier that none of her men will harm him while he is under her care, and she tends to Ogier herself without any help from other maidens (lines 985–94). As she treats him, she asks who he is and says she has heard of him before when he reveals his identity. After Ogier's wounds have been attended to, he is "lyghte als lefe one tree" (line 996) despite the fact that he is being held as a prisoner of war. Ogier does not address Alphany when he escapes in *Duke Roland*, but her care of him is as suggestive of desire as it is in *Otuel and Roland*. Later, when Otuel taunts Clarel during their duel, the *Duke Roland* poet continues to focus on matters of sexual attraction. When Otuel slices Clarel's cheek off, he does not

---

[6] On this passage in *Otinel*, see Hardman and Ailes, *Legend of Charlemagne*, p. 355.

[7] According to Berlings, several romances in Robert Thornton's manuscripts — e.g., *The Siege of Milan*, *Sir Perceval of Galles*, and *Richard Coer de Lyon* — contain unflattering or derogatory depictions of the French ("The *Sege of Melayne*," p. 58). Otuel's accusation of cowardice among the preeminent knights of France follows this pattern; it is also notable that Otuel is superior to the French knights in combat, even before he has converted to Christianity. For *The Siege of Milan* (ed. Lupack, pp. 105–60), see *DIMEV* 408; *NIMEV* 234. For *Sir Perceval* (ed. Braswell, pp. 1–76), see *DIMEV* 3074; *NIMEV* 1853. For *Richard Coer de Lyon* (ed. Larkin), see *DIMEV* 3231; *NIMEV* 1979.

make a joke about shaving or tooth-pulling (as in the other Middle English versions), but instead asks why Clarel is grinning at him. Here, Otuel insults Clarel for his loss of sex appeal, telling him that Alphany will never again want to kiss him (lines 1321–26). This version closely mirrors the French source (*Otinel*, lines 1452–56).

## A NOTE ON GRAPHIC TAIL-RHYME IN THORNTON'S COPY OF *DUKE ROLAND*

*Duke Roland* differs from the Auchinleck and Fillingham Otuel romances in how its text is arranged on the manuscript page. Like *Roland and Vernagu* and *Otuel and Roland* (but not *Otuel a Knight*), *Duke Roland* is composed in twelve-line tail-rhyme stanzas. There are thirty-six extant Middle English romances written in tail-rhyme, comprising roughly a third of all surviving Middle English romances.[8] Tail-rhyme verse employs a twelve-line stanza with the rhyme scheme *aabccbddbeeb*; in other words, a stanza contains four rhymed couplets with four tail-rhyme lines placed in between the couplets. The couplet lines typically have four stressed syllables while the tail-rhyme lines have three, and it is the tail-rhyme lines' matching end rhyme that unifies the stanza.[9] The *Duke Roland* stanza is a more difficult three-rhyme variant: *aabaabccbccb*. As Rhiannon Purdie explains, although the tail-rhyme stanza appears in poetry in other languages, it was used for romance, and more rarely drama, only in English. By the fourteenth century, most English readers would have recognized that tail-rhyme stanza probably meant that an English poem was a romance.[10] A subset of the thirty-six tail-rhyme romances consists of six poems classified by Purdie as "graphic tail-rhyme romances" because of the way they are visually laid out by scribes.[11] Thornton employed the graphic layout for *Duke Roland*.

A graphic layout uses a system of brackets to link tail-rhyme lines to the corresponding couplet. The employment of brackets to highlight rhymes was a fairly common practice for medieval scribes, but the graphic tail-rhyme arrangement was much more difficult for both scribes and readers than was the basic bracketing that highlighted rhymes. In order to execute the graphic arrangement, scribes had to try to fit the marginal brackets on pages typically set up for two columns of equal width. In most cases, the scribe would scrub out the ruled lines, or simply write the graphic tail-rhyme lines on top of the ruled columns. Upon realizing that the graphic arrangement was unmanageable, half of the scribes who attempted the layout abandoned the endeavor and switched to single columns for the remainder of the romance. In the Lincoln Thornton manuscript, Thornton tried to fit the tail-rhyme lines of *Sir Degrevant* into the margins on a two-columned page (fols. 130r–39v). Although his copy of *Sir Degrevant* is cramped and messy, Thornton's dedication to the graphic tail-rhyme layout is noteworthy. In all, he persevered in copying three romances in the graphic tail-rhyme arrangement: *Sir Degrevant*, *The Siege of Milan*, and *Duke Roland*.[12]

---

[8] Purdie, *Anglicising Romance*, p. 1. For a comparison of tail-rhyme to other twelve-line stanza forms, see Fein, "Twelve-Line Stanza Forms."

[9] Purdie, *Anglicising Romance*, p. 4.

[10] Purdie, *Anglicising Romance*, p. 3.

[11] Purdie, *Anglicising Romance*, p. 7.

[12] For a reproduction that shows Thornton's graphic tail-rhyme layout for *Duke Roland*, see Thompson, *Robert Thornton and the London Thornton Manuscript*, plate 16 (fol. 94r); for *The Siege of Milan*, see plate 13a (fol. 79v).

The graphic tail-rhyme romance garnering the most critical attention is Geoffrey Chaucer's Tale of Sir Thopas, which almost certainly uses the form to parody the trite figures and tropes of the tail-rhyme romance genre. As Purdie explains,

> It is possible, of course, that the layout of *Sir Thopas* in these early manuscripts was the scribes' idea, but given the dates, number, importance and variety of these manuscripts, it is far more likely to have been Chaucer's own. It relies upon the reader's recognition that *Sir Thopas* is arranged in a layout traditional for Middle English tail-rhyme romances, thus adding another layer to Chaucer's parody of Middle English romance conventions.[13]

Like Thornton's choice to use the graphic display of tail-rhyme in some romances but not others, the choice of many scribes to replicate the graphic arrangement of Sir Thopas indicates that this layout was significant to the romance and a definitive mark of the genre for English audiences. Still, Thornton's use of the graphic arrangement for three romances is somewhat perplexing because there are other tail-rhyme romances in his books that he does not arrange in graphic form. Thornton's persistence in using the graphic arrangement for some romances and his choice not to use it for others suggests that his decisions to arrange graphically, when he did so, were purposeful. It may be that he was faithfully following the layouts he found in his exemplars, or it could be that he saw layout as a key component of poetic presentation.

MANUSCRIPT:

London, British Library MS Additional 31042 (London Thornton MS), fols. 82r–94r.

PREVIOUS EDITION:

*The Romance of Duke Rowlande and of Sir Ottuell of Spayne*. In *The English Charlemagne Romances. Part II*. Ed. Sidney J. H. Herrtage. EETS e.s. 35. London: N. Trübner & Co., 1880. Rpt. 2002. Pp. 55–104.

---

[13] Purdie, *Anglicising Romance*, p. 76.

# Duke Roland and Sir Otuel of Spain

*The Romance of Duke Rowland and Sir Ottuell of Spayne*
*Of Cherlles of Fraunce*

## Fitt 1

| | | |
|---|---|---|
| fol. 82r | Lordynges that bene hende and free, | *noble* |
| | Herkyns alle hedirwardes to mee, | *toward* |
| |     Gif that it be your will. | |
| | Now lates alle your noyse be, | *be quiet* |
| 5 | And herkyns nowe of gamen and glee | *merriment* |
| |     That I schall tell yow till. | |
| | Of doghety men I schall yow telle | *brave* |
| | That were full fayre of flesche and fell | *flesh and skin [i.e., body]* |
| |     And semely appon sille, | *handsome in the hall* |
| 10 | And with thaire wapyns wele couthe melle | *fight* |
| | And boldly durste in batell duelle | *endure* |
| |     And doghety proved one hill. | *on* |
| | | |
| | The sone of le Roy Pepyn | |
| | That was Sir Cherlles gud and fyne, | |
| 15 |     Als the cronykills us gan say, | *chronicles* |
| | With his dusperes doghety and dyin | *twelve peers; dignified* |
| | That wele couthe feghte with a Sarazene | |
| |     For to felle tham fey; | *slay them* |
| | Till Genyone with his traytorye | *Ganelon* |
| 20 | Solde tham ille and wikkedly | |
| |     Unto the false ley — | *faith* |
| | Fourty thowsande and fyfty | |
| | Of the flour of chevalrye | *flower* |
| |     There dyede apon a daye! | *in one day* |
| | | |
| 25 | Mynstrells in that lande gan duelle, | |
| | Bot alle the sothe thay couthe noghte tell | *truth* |
| |     Of this noble chevalrye: | |
| | How that Cherlles with his swerde gan melle, | *fought* |
| | Bot suche a menske hym befell | *Until; honor* |
| 30 |     That come hym sodeynly. | |

| | | |
|---|---|---|
| | They tentede to thaire daunsynge, | *attended* |
| | And also to thaire othir thynge, | |
| | To make gamen and glee; | |
| | Burdours into the haulle thay brynge | *Minstrels* |
| 35 | That gayly with thaire gle gan synge | |
| | With wowynges of lady. | *courting* |
| | | |
| | And forthir in romance als ye mon here, | *may hear* |
| | This noble kynge of grete powere | |
| | Duellede in Pariche, | *Paris* |
| 40 | With his lordes and his duspers | *twelve peers* |
| | That were holden felle and fers | *considered strong and fierce* |
| | And in batelle full wyse. | *skilled* |
| | All thay buskede tham for to bere | *prepared* |
| | Helme and hawberke, schelde and spere, | *coat of mail* |
| 45 | And rapede tham for to ryse | *hastened* |
| | Agaynes Kynge Merthill, forto were | *make war* |
| | And forto kepe the heythyn here, | *engage with* |
| | And struye there Goddes enymys. | *destroy* |
| | | |
| | Bot now come tham newe note one hande, | *trouble* |
| 50 | And wondirfull hasty tythande | *tidings* |
| | That grevede tham righte sore; | |
| | For of the chevallrye of the lande, | |
| | Ther hade dyede thritty thousande, | |
| | Gif Goddes helpe ne wore! | *Were it not for God's help* |
| fol. 82v | And owte of Spayne there come in hy | *in haste* |
| 56 | A Sarazene that was full doghety | |
| | With grymly grownden gare, | *sternly wrought armor* |
| | Fro the Emperour Sir Garcy | |
| | To Kyng Charlles full hastilye, | |
| 60 | That kyndilde alle thaire care. | *caused; worrying* |
| | | |
| | The messangere was mekill of pride. | *much* |
| | Thorowte Pareche gan he ryde | *Paris* |
| | And at the kynges sale he lighttis, | *hall; alights* |
| | And there he metys in that tyde | |
| 65 | That were faire of hewe and hide, | *[Those]; complexion* |
| | Thre full noble knyghtis: | |
| | Sir Otes and Sir Raynere, | |
| | Duke Naymes was theire fere, | *companion* |
| | That ofte thaire resouns rightes. | *Who often provided sound judgment* |
| 70 | He haylsede tham with steryn chere, | *greeted; stern expression* |
| | Sayd, "Fro the kynge am I sent a messangere, | *[as] a* |
| | That moste es provede of myghtis." | |
| | | |
| | Duke Naymes sayde full curtaysly, | |

"Sir, whate may thi name bee?"

75 He sayde, "I highte Otuell. *am called*

Kyng Cherlles, where es he?

Righte to hym byhovede mee *Directly; it is required of*

Mi message forto telle."

Duke Naymes saide, "He sittes his duspers imange, *among*

80 With white berde large and lange,

Faire of flesche and fell, *of body*

With a floreschede thonwange, *bearded cheek*

Oure noble kynge that es so strange, *strong*

His doghety men imelle. *among*

85 He sittes in riche meneuere; *manner*

The Duke Rowlande sittys hym nere

In rede siclaton, *silk*

And the gentill erle Sir Olyvere,

That es full noble and felle and fere *strong and fierce*

90 And in batelle ay full bowun." *eager*

Forthe passede than the messangere

Bifore the kynge with steryn chere, *stern*

It was hym grete renoun. *He was held in great renown*

He saide, "Ane evyll flawmande fyre *flaming*

95 Bryne thi berde, thi breste, and thi swyre, *Burn; throat*

Even to thi fote alle doun!

A messangere ame I sent in hy *in haste*

Fro my lorde the emperor Sir Garcy

That settis yow alle at noghte. *deems you worthless*

100 In paynym ne es none so doghety; *pagandom*

He hathe the flour of chevallrye

Allredy with hym broghte.

Charlles, I ne maye noghte honour thee,

For thou hase grevede Mahoun and me,

105 That alle this worlde hase wroghte.

And Rowlande, if ever I may thee see

At batayle or at any semblé, *combat*

Thi dedis schall dere be boghte! *sorely paid for*

And Rowlande, gif ever I maye thee mete,

110 With my swerde I schall thee hete *strike*

To hewe thi body in two,

And fulle thee under my horse fete, *knock you down*

Sarazenes myrthe with thee to bete, *Gladden Saracens by beating you*

For thou hase wroghte tham woo!"

115 And Rowlande at those wordes loughe, *laughed*

And said, "Sir, thou arte doghety ynoghe

Siche dedis to undirtoo! *undertake*

|  | Thou may jangill and make it toughe, | *mock; boast* |
|  | For here schall no man do thee woghe | *harm* |
| 120 | Till aughte dayes ben agoo." | *eight; have passed* |

| fol. 83r | The kyng spekes than the Sarazene till, |  |
|  | "Say one, felawe, whatte thou will. |  |
|  | Distroube thee schall righte none, | *No one shall disturb you* |
|  | Ne none of my men, lowde nor still, | *loud or quiet* |
| 125 | Touche thee with nonekyns ille | *May harm you; nothing* |
|  | Till heghte dayes ben gone." | *eight* |
|  | The Sarazene at those wordes hadde skorne. |  |
|  | "I dowte no man," he says, "that ever was borne, | *fear* |
|  | And I my stede hafe tone, | *If; have mounted* |
| 130 | Corsu my swerde me biforne, | *Corsouse* |
|  | That myche Cristen blode hathe schorne | *spilled* |
|  | And many a body slone." | *slain* |

|  | "Where?" sayde the kynge in hy. |  |
|  | "Sir, in the playnes of Lubardy — | *[Otuel speaks]; Lombardy* |
| 135 | Thou claymes it for thi lande, |  |
|  | The powere there of Sir Garcy. | *[Despite]* |
|  | Appon a daye we garte tham dy, | *caused* |
|  | Fully fifty thousande. |  |
|  | Nyne monethes es gone arighte | *months* |
| 140 | Sen I with Cursu was dobbide knyghte, | *dubbed* |
|  | My golde brayden brande. | *ornate sword* |
|  | A thosande there to the dede I dighte, | *sent to death* |
|  | Of Cristen men mekill of myghte, |  |
|  | Righte with myn awenn hande. | *own* |

| 145 | And thus hathe Lubades harmes laughte | *Lombards; received* |
|  | Bothe by dayes and by naghte, | *night* |
|  | Ne gladdes tham no glee. |  |
|  | Myselfe was then in batelle and faughte; |  |
|  | Myn neffes were bolnede dayes aughte | *fists; swollen; eight* |
| 150 | That selly was to see." | *remarkable* |
|  | Up than stirte ane hardy knyghte, |  |
|  | Sir Estut of Logres, forsothe, he highte, |  |
|  | A lorde of grete bountee. |  |
|  | With the Sarazene wolde he fighte; |  |
| 155 | A staffe in hande he takes hym righte |  |
|  | Was of sqwarede tree. | *squared wood* |

## Fitt 2

|  | Than Rowlande sayde full sobirly, | *earnestly* |
|  | "Now, gud Sir Estut, let it be. |  |

He es a messangere.

160 He es ensurede to myn eme and mee.                *in surety; uncle*

For thi gud, Sir, par charyté,

Thyn hert that thou wolde stere."                *You should control your anger*

Bot yit the knyghte ne wolde noghte spare,

Bot hent the Sarazene by the hare                *seized; hair*

165 And bakwarde doun hym bere.

The Sarazene stirte up breme as bare,                *angry as a boar*

Cursu his swerde he drewe reghte thare —

The knyghte hede off he schere.                *sheared*


Than saide the baronage with hole sowun,                *in unison*

170 "Lay hande one the traytoure feloun!

He hase done velanye!"

Bot he rollede his eghne both up and dowun                *eyes*

And ferde als a wilde lyoun,                *behaved*

Brayde up his browes one hye.                *Raised his brows quickly*

175 He braundescht hir swerde bare,                *his*

That trenchande was and wele schare,                *keen; sharp*

And sayde full sobirly

fol. 83v (And by his grete Mahown he sware),

"And any of yow duspers stirre thare,                *If*

180 The beste party schall dy!"                *better part of you*


The kyng his men sone sessed he,                *ordered to cease*

Sayd, "Sarazene, yelde thi suerde to mee,

And late be alle this bere."                *commotion*

And he sayde, "Naye, als mot I thee!"                *as I may thrive*

185 Up than rose Sir Rowlande full sobirly,

And with a lagheande chere                *laughing expression*

Said, "Yelde to me thi brande brighte.                *sword*

I schall thee save, als I ame knyghte,                *protect*

Whills that thou arte here.

190 And when thi message es doun and dighte,                *done and delivered*

I schall delyver thee thi brande so brighte,                *return*

Als I ame trewe duspere."


"In that covande I yelde it thee.                *By that promise*

I nolde gif it for twelve cité,

195 So bittirly will it bite!

And, Rowlande, yif ever I may thee see

At batayle or at any semblé,

Thi hede off therwith to smyte!"

Rowlande sayde, "Sir, thou art to outrage!                *too discourteous*

200 Fayrere myghte thou batayll wage

Than al daye thus to chide."

The Sarazene spake with stowte vesage,                *fierce expression*

     "Herkenys now to my message,
         And I schall tell yow tyte.                *quickly*

205     Kyng Cherlls, als thou may here,
     I am sent a messangere
         Fro hym that es doghty.
     He weldes paynym ferre and nere:         *rules pagan lands*
     Alysaundere of grete powere,             *Alexandria*
210         And the londis of Boty,
     Toures, Sedoyne, ferre and fre,     *Sidonia; far away and noble*
     Perse, semely one to see,         *Persia, pleasing to look at*
         And therto Fermorye.               *Also*
     This noble kynge of grete pousté,           *power*
215     He distruyes bothe londe and see         *destroys*
         Reghte into Fermorye.

     Forthi hathe he sent thee worde by mee:     *For this reason*
     That thou schall uncristen bee,
         And leve appon oure ley.        *believe in our faith*
220     For we will prove in oure degré          *victory*
     That the lawes of Cristyanté
         Ne are noghte worthe ane aye!        *an egg*
     Giffe thi hert unto Mahoun,
     That weldis bothe toure and towun        *rules; tower*
225         And alle myghtis maye;      *has almighty power*
     Hafe done belyfe that thou be bowne   *Give up the religion that holds you*
     Forto come to oure somoun —          *summoning*
         Thus am I sent to saye.

     Hafe done, sir! Buske thee to oure kynge,     *Go quickly*
230     For he hath ordeynede thi wonnynge,     *dwelling place*
         For alle thi chevalrye;          *Despite*
     House and londe, wodde and thynge,        *forests*
     He grauntes thee over all othir thynge
         The londes of Normaundy.
235     Inglonde also hathe giffen to thee;
     And to Rowlande thi nevieu fre        *noble nephew*
         To be sesede in Russy.      *in possession of Russia*
fol. 84r  Olyver, that es faire and free,
     The knyghte es provede of grete bounté,
240         The landes of Scamonye.

     To Sir Florance of Surry,
     He hathe giffen France in hye,          *already*
         That wele cane prike a stede —      *spur a horse*
     The kyng sone of Barbarye,           *[He is]*
245     To hafe it to his bayly              *rule*

Therone his life to lede."
Than the kynge sayde, "Nay!
Duspers, whate will ye say
Of this wonder dede?
250 Schall never Sarazene of heythyn ley    *law*
Welde France, by nyghte ne daye.
Now Jhesu it forbede!"

Then thay ansuerde sone in hye,
"Nay, Sir, we will oure batells guy,   *prepare our battalions*
255   And rape us for to ryde     *hasten*
Agayne the Emperor Sir Garcy.
Thurgh the myghte of mylde Marye,
  Hy schall schome betyde."    *experience shame*
The Sarazyn laughes full smothirly,   *menacingly*
260 "What, threte ye now Sir Garcy
  With your boste and your pryde?
Ther es none of yow so hardy,
And ye hade sene his chevalrye,   *That were you to see*
  Your hedis that ye nolde hyde!"  *Who wouldn't hide your heads*

265 The Duke Naymes talkes wordes one highte, *loudly*
Says, "Sir, if that the emperor will fighte,
  We schall to hy full even!"   *leave right away*
The Sarazene ansuerde with mekill myghte,
"He hath a hondreth thousande helmys brighte *helmets [i.e., men]*
270  And therto hundrethes seven!
Ther es no kyng in Cristyanté
Dare warne hym huntynge and fischynge fre, *prevent him from; freely*
  Ne discrye hym ther with steven!  *rebuke; voice*
Bitwix two watirs fayre and fre,    *lovely*
275 He hath bigged a cité hight Attaylé —  *erected; Ataly*
  Es none siche under the heven!

Cherlles, with thi longe berde,
That empoure schall make thee full ferde  *afraid*
  With his stronge powere!
280 For he hathe men in batell lerede   *skilled in warfare*
That wele kon feghte with floresched swerde *brandished*
  And hafe lemans full clere.   *beautiful paramours*
Lete Duke Naymes lenge at hame   *rest at home*
To kepe Pareche walles fro schame,   *Paris'*
285  That no gledes neghe tham nere,  *sparks come near*
Coo ne pye that there come none,   *Jackdaw; magpie*
For chevalrye es fro hym gone —
  An olde nappere als he were!"   *nap-taker*

The Duke Naymes asschamede was;
290 The blode stert up in his face —
      Agreved he was full sore.            *Incensed*
Than Sir Rowlande full rathely up he rase;            *quickly*
"Unconnande Sarazene!" he said, "In this place            *Foolish*
      Thi wykkednes es yare.            *excessive*
295 By Hym that dyede appon a tree,
Thou scholde have a velany of me,            *disgrace*
      Ensurede nyfe that I ware!            *If I had not given my oath*
Bot in batelle if ever I may thee see,
Schall never no kyng of Cristyanté
300       Be encombirde with thee mare!"            *troubled by; again*

fol. 84v   The Sarazene ansueres full stoutly,
"Be Mahownn, Rowlande, I ame redy
      For to fighte with thee!
Into yone medowe I rede we hye            *urge; go*
305 And luke that no man bee us by —
      Grete gamen than schall men see!
Whethir so werse es of us twoo,            *Whichever*
Lett hewe bothe his spourres hy froo;            *Let both his spurs be cut off from him*
      He never more honorede bee."
310 Rowlande was of hert full throo            *eager*
Siche dedys to undertoo;            *deeds*
      His hande upholdes hee.

"Sir Vernague of Barabas,            *[Otuel speaks]*
Sertys, myn eme I wote he was,            *Truly; uncle*
315       That Rowlande here hath slayne.
I chalange his dethe now in this place.
I schalle thee lede a wikkede pase,            *give you a grievous blow*
      Bothe with myghte and mayne."
The kynge at those wordes loughe,
320 And said, "Sir, thou arte doghty ynoghe!
      Garte calle a chambirlayne.            *call forth*
Garte delyvere hym innes withowtten woghe.            *Have him taken care of without harm*
To sue hym, lokes that thee bene toughe            *aid; diligent*
      Of alle that scholde hym gayne."            *assist*

325 The kynge garte calle Sir Grauntere,
Sir Raynere, and Sir Oggere,
      Bade take kepe of the knyghte.            *Ordered [them]; care*
One the morne thay rose alle in fere.            *together*
The abbott of Saynte-Thomers            *Saint-Omer*
330       Songe tham a messe full righte.
Elleven coupes fayre to fonde            *caskets*
Was offrede at the abbottes honde,

Full of golde so brighte.

Rowlande offrede Droundale his brande,                                *Durendal*

335   Boghte it agayne with golde at hande.               *Redeemed it with an offering of gold*

Alle honoured thay God Allemyghte.

### A Fitt                                                                   *Fitt 3*

And unnethes was the messe alle done,                                 *barely*

When that the Sarazene come full sone,

And cryed appon highte                                                *haughtily*

340   To Kyng Cherlles with steryn tone,

Sayd, "Send owte Rowlande withowtten hone!                            *delay*

I calle hym recreyande knyghte.                                       *cowardly*

I appelle hym for trouthe broken                                      *accuse; of*

For the wordes that were spoken

345   Yistreven within the nyghte.                                    *Yesterday evening*

In his armes that he be loken;                                        *armor; fastened*

Myn emes dethe I will hafe wroken —                                   *be avenged*

He was a kynge of myghte!"

Elleven duspers stode hym by

350   To arme Sir Rowlande full hastyly,

That provede was in batayle.

Ane actone they threwe appon hym hye,                                 *padded jacket*

And ane hawberke, sekerly,                                            *coat of mail*

That sekire was of mayle,                                             *sturdy*

355   Hose of hawberke, gesseraunte;                 *Chain mail leggings, jacket of scale armor*

Broghte hym ane helme of bettant,                                     *beaten metal*

And lacede his aventale.                                              *neck covering*

Iche a knyghte gane tham avante                                       *come forward*

For to sue hym to his avenaunte,                                      *help; advantage*

360   That no thynge scholde hym fayle.

Thay spende hym with his gilte sporres,                               *girded; gilded spurs*

And dressede hym in his armours,

Alle redy to the felde.

fol. 85r   Broghte hym a schelde of faire coloure;

365   He was a lofely creatoure,

Whoso hym than bihelde.                                               *[To] those who*

Girde hym with Drondale to the were;                                  *Armed; battle*

Appone a stede he leppes there,

That doghety under schelde.

370   And in his hande a noble spere,

A faire course he rydes there                              *Adeptly [i.e., in a fair manner]*

Hys wapyns for to welde.                                              *weapons*

Then sayde Cherlles the kynge,
"Loke rekreyande thou hym brynge        *to defeat*
375        That hathe made this derraye!        *disturbance*
Late hym noghte skape for nonkynsthynge."        *escape; anything*
He gaffe hym Goddes blyssynge
        And bade hym wende his waye.
Thay broghte tham bytwene two watirs brighte —
380        Sayne and Meryn le Graunte thay highte,        *Seine; Marne*
        Als the bukes gan us saye —
Into a medowe semely to sighte,
There als thies doghety men solde fighte
        Withowtten more delaye.

385        This while hovede the Sarazene still,        *awaited*
And called to the kynge with voyce full schrylle,        *loud*
        "Ane hawberke aske I thee!        *coat of mail*
Spere and schelde garre brynge me till,        *let be brought to me*
For I hafe horssynge at my will,        *an equipped horse*
390        None siche in Cristyanté."
The kyng than lokes hym besyde
And saughe his dogheter mekill of pryde,
        Belesent brighte of blee.
Than he comandide hir that tyde,
395        "Goo take hym fayre be thi syde,        *courteously*
        Wele armede that he bee."

And scho calles Flores of Maundelle,
Mayden Roselet of Barelle,
        And bade tham wende to the knyghte,
400        And haste tham that within awhile,        *hurry*
And til a chambire gan thay syle,        *to; proceed*
        And gayly gan hym dighte.        *colorfully*
To arme hym wele thay were full snelle:        *eager*
Out his aktone ane hawberke felle        *Above; strong*
405        Of colours that were brighte,
That aughte gud Kynge Ragnell,        *once belonged to*
That was bothe ferse and felle,
        And in felde full faire couthe fighte.

Thay armede hym wele withowtten fayle;
410        With golde thay lacede his aventaile
        For that it solde be trewe;        *should*
Broghte hym ane helme of riche entayle        *design*
Of precyouse stones, the appayrayle        *armor*
        That brighteste was of hewe.
415        His helme was bothe harde and holde;        *dependable*
Therone was sett a sercle of golde

That bett was wonder newe.                          *freshly and beautifully crafted*
Then sayde thies damesels fre one folde,                      *noble on earth*
A meryere armede knyghte one molde                              *on earth*
420        Never yitt thay ne knewe.

Thay broghte hym a schelde when he was bowun;                   *attired*
Thies maydens two thay broghte hym dowun.                    *led him forth*
He cried aftir his stede.                                      *called for*
He rollede his eghne up and dowun,
425   And sware by his grete Mahoun —
His enemy sore myghte drede!
Than spake those two maydens smale,                             *young*
"Sir, kepe thee wele fro Drondale,
For it will garre thee blede!
fol. 85v  Entyre thou ones into yone vale,              *Once you've entered; valley*
431    Comes thou never aftyr into this sale,                   *chamber*
And Sir Rowlande righte may rede!"           *If; is able to deal rightly*

He toke his leve and forthe he gose,
Lepe one a stede highte Mekredose,                          *Leapt onto*
435        In his hande a spere.
A faire course he rydes close,                        *Adeptly; sturdily*
Full egerly amonges his fose,
And dressede hym in his gere.                              *dressed up*
When the Sarazene comen was,
440   The kyng garte sone avoyde the place     *ordered that the place be cleared*
Of Cristen that there were.
To the castelle he wendes a pase,                        *takes a path*
And appone the kirnells gase                  *to the tower window goes*
To wayte appon that were.                                    *battle*

445   The kynge to Rowlande lowde gan crye,
"Feghte one, dere sone, hardely,
In the name of Marie of heven!"
The Sarazene saide, "I ame redy!"
Appon Sir Rowlande he gan defy                            *to taunt*
450        With a full hawtayne steven.                    *haughty voice*
Thies kene knyghtis togedir gan glide,                      *charged*
The medowe tremlyde one aythir syde,             *trembling; either*
In scheldes thay cowped full even.                          *fought*
Theyre joynynge was so harde that tyde
455   That theyre tymbir in sondire gan ryde       *lances; broke asunder*
In mo than sex or seven.

Thurghowte thaire scheldis than thay schare                *slashed*
And all the lethirs that thare ware —                  *leather parts*
Thay assembled soryly.                                *fought fiercely*

| | | |
|---|---|---|
| 460 | The poyntes appon the hawberke bare, | *bore down upon* |
| | Bot the mayles so sekir ware | *sturdy* |
| |     The spere hedis bigan to plye. | *bend* |
| | Rawlande owte his swerde wanne | *drew* |
| | And hittes hym on the helme thanne | |
| 465 |     That the nasell floghe full hye. | *nose guard flew* |
| | Thurgh the horse schuldirs the swerde rane — | *flanks* |
| | That was a styffe stroke of a man! | |
| |     His noble stede gan dy. | |
| | | |
| | The Sarazene off his horse tublys doun | *tumbles* |
| 470 | And stert up fers als any lyoun, | |
| |     And Cursu his swerde he drewe. | |
| | He brasede his schelde and made hym bowun; | *seized* |
| | He hitt Sir Rowlande one the crowun, | |
| |     That fore egirnes he loughe. | *Who eagerly he brought low* |
| 475 | The nasell of his helme off glade | *fell* |
| | Dowun bifore hym in the strade — | *path* |
| |     Hade almoste wroghte hym woghe! | |
| | Thurgh the horse schuldirs the swerde gan wade, | |
| | His stede even in sondere he hade — | |
| 480 |     The stroke was stythe ynoghe! | *fierce* |
| | | |
| | Rowlande one the grownde es lighte, | *has alighted* |
| | Uppon his fete he sterte uprighte; | |
| |     His swerde in his hande he helde. | |
| | The Sarazene cryed with mekill myghte, | |
| 485 | "This was a stythe stroke of a knyghte, | |
| |     And no thynge of a childe!" | |
| | Charlles herde those wordes wele; | |
| | Appon his knees dowun gan he knele, | |
| |     And bothe his handes uphelde. | |
| 490 | "God," he said, "that alle schall dighte and dele, | |
| | His modir mylde and Saynt Michael, | |
| |     Fro schame Ye Rowlande schelde!" | |
| | | |
| | Rowlande raysede up Drondale; | |
| | Abown his hede he gane it hale, | *Above; draw* |
| 495 |     His enemy forto dere. | *injure* |
| fol. 86r | He hade almoste wroghte hym bale; | *harm* |
| | A quartere of his helme awaye gane vale | *fall* |
| |     And halfendele his one ere, | *half of his own earpiece* |
| | That the Sarazene bygane to helde, | *fall* |
| 500 | And up he caste his noble schelde; | |
| |     In the bokells gane he schere. | *boss of a shield; he [Roland]* |
| | So thikke thaire dynttys togedir pelyde, | *struck* |

Thaire armours hewenn laye in the felde          *hewn pieces of armor*
  Als floures that strewede were.          *scattered*

505 Belesent sayde full curtaysly,
  "Mi lorde, thay feghten full gentilly;          *nobly*
   A grete travayle thay hafe!"          *hard labor*
  Up to God he caste a crye,          *she*
  And to His moder Saynt Marie:
510   "Fro schame Ye Rowlande save!
  And coverte us yone gentill knyghte          *convert [for] us*
  That es so hardy and so wighte,          *powerful*
   For elles it were grete wathe!          *pity*
  He es so ferse in armes to fyghte,
515 And a man of mekill myghte.
   Full doghety are thay bathe!"          *both*

Than Rowlande sayde full curtaysly,
  "Sarazene, will thou cristenyde be
   And leve appon oure laye?          *believe; faith*
520 A noble gifte I schall giffe thee:
  Belesent that es brighte of ble —          *complexion*
   In the worlde ne es siche a maye!          *maid*
  And thou and I and Olyver,
  We schall be felawes all in fere,          *together*
525   And travell nyghte and daye.
  We schall ryde bothe ferre and nere,
  Wyn citees and towunes dere,          *fine*
   And gode horses at assaye!"          *test*

The Sarazene ansuers full stoutly,
530  "Thou kan to littill of clergy          *know; learning*
   To leryn me siche a lare!          *teach; lesson*
  The wordes that thou hase spoken in hy,          *in haste*
  Thou schall tham full dere aby          *dearly pay for*
   With sadde dynttes and sare!          *hard blows; painful*
535 I swere thee, by my grete Mahoun,
  I schall thee lere a newe lessoun
   Or I fro thee fare,          *Before; go*
  With a bofete appon thi croun          *blow*
  That thou schall laye thi wapen doun,
540   Rekreyande als thou were!"          *Defeated*

Than was Sir Rowlande gretly grevede,          *aggrieved*
  And in his hert full sore amevede;          *enraged*
   At the Sarazene lete he flye.
  He hitt hym a bown appon the heuede          *blow*
545 That to the scholdire the swerde wefede;          *went*

|  | The fyre floghe owte full hye! | *sparks; at once* |
|  | Thurgh duble hawberke it hym schare, | *sheared* |
|  | To the girdilstede it made hym bare. | *waist* |
|  | Then bigane he forto plye. | *bend down* |
| 550 | Drondale felle so sadde and sare |  |
|  | That the Sarazene bigane to stare | *was stunned* |
|  | And fallen he was full nye. | *nearly* |

|  | The Sarazene than a lepe he made; |  |
|  | A stroke to Rowlande forsothe he glade, |  |
| 555 | And hit hym on the hede |  |
|  | That almoste top over tayle he rade, |  |
|  | And nere the swerde twynede hade, | *had not; broken in two* |
|  | His life ther hade he lefede. | *ended* |
| fol. 86v | Ane other stroke he to hym bere, |  |
| 560 | And doun byfore hym it strypes there; | *thrusts* |
|  | His schelde awaye revede, | *was shorn away* |
|  | And alle the skirtys of Rowlandes gere. |  |
|  | Otuell says, "My suerde kan schere!" | *cut* |
|  | And into the erthe it wevede. |  |

| 565 | Rowlande claghte up his noble schelde, | *clutched* |
|  | His wapyns wightly for to welde | *powerfully* |
|  | And helde it one his nefe. | *fist* |
|  | Thaire dynttis so thikke gan samen helde, | *so thickly began to come* |
|  | Thaire harnays hewen was in the felde — | *armor* |
| 570 | Full littill was tham levede! | *very little was left to them* |
|  | Thaire dynttis felle so sadde and sare |  |
|  | That bothe thaire bodies wexen bare, | *became* |
|  | Thaire armours all todreves. | *scattered* |
|  | Tharefore Sir Charlles hade mekill care; |  |
| 575 | Appon his knees he knelys thare |  |
|  | And bothe his handes upheves. | *casts up* |

|  | And als the kynge thus prayed faste, |  |
|  | A dofe come fro the Holy Gaste | *dove* |
|  | And one the Sarazene lightes. | *alights* |
| 580 | And than was he full sore agaste, |  |
|  | And unto Sir Rowlande saide he in haste, |  |
|  | "Sesse, Sir, of thi fighttes! |  |
|  | For I ame broghte in siche a will |  |
|  | That I youre lawes will fulfill, |  |
| 585 | And become a Cristyn knyghte." |  |
|  | Than doun thay layde thaire wapyns still, | *peaceably* |
|  | And aythere wente othire untill; | *toward* |
|  | A saughtillynge was ther dighte. | *accord; made* |

|       | Than wolde the kynge no lengere duelle, | *delay* |
| 590   | Bot hyed hym dowun of the castelle, | *hurried* |
|       | And grete lordes hym by. | |
|       | He askede Sir Rowlande how it bifelle, | |
|       | And he ansuerde with wordes snelle, | *noble* |
|       | "Mi lorde, full gentilly | |
| 595   | I hafe foghten with the beste knyghte | |
|       | In alle this werlde — es none so wighte | *valiant* |
|       | That ever yit provede I! | *tested* |
|       | And he hase yolden hym to the righte; | |
|       | Belesent I hafe hym highte. | *promised* |
| 600   | Gare cristen hym in hy." | *Let him be christened at once* |

Unto the grounde than knelide the kynge;
He loved God of alle this thynge                              *above*
    And His modir fre.
Two gude stedis thay garte forthe brynge,
605    And one thay lepe withowte lettynge                    *on they leapt; delay*
    And went home to the cité.
Bischope Turpyn was redy
With bukes and with stoles in hy.                              *vestments*
    A fownte sone halowes he                        *baptismal font; blesses*
610    To cristen hym that was doghety.
Many grete lorde stode thaym by                                 *lords*
    With myche solempnyté.

And when the Sarazene cristenned was,
The kynge tuke his doghetir faire of face,
615    And gyffes hir to that noble knyghte.
The lovelyeste inwith lace,                                   *dressed in*
And swetteste in armes for to enbrace —
    In the worlde was siche a wighte.            *was [never] such a creature*
Als lely-like was hir coloure,                                 *lily-like*
620    Hir rode rede als rose floure,                          *complexion*
    In lere that rynnes righte.                      *In an honest face*
The kyng toke that brighte in boure                       *lovely one in bower*
With menske and with myche honoure,                             *courtesy*
    And gaffe hym that birde so brighte.                      *lady*

625  He said, "Hafe here my doghetir fre,                        *noble*
And Rowlande felawe schall thou bee,
    And gentill Sir Olyver.
fol. 87r  Powunce and plesaunce I schalle gife thee,            *Power; delight*
With two full noble cités
630    With towrres heghe and dere.
I make thee lorde of Lubardye,
To hafe it alle to thi bayllye,                               *governance*

|  |  |  |
|---|---|---|
|  | That contreth ferre and nere. | *country* |
|  | For thi noble chevallrye, |  |
| 635 | Welcome to this companye, |  |
|  | Duelle and be a pere." | *Stay* |

|  |  |  |
|---|---|---|
|  | The Sarazene knelyde appon his knee, |  |
|  | And thankkes the kynge full gentilly |  |
|  | Of thies giftes so gude. |  |
| 640 | He sayde, "Damesell, arte thou payed of me?" | *pleased with* |
|  | And scho sayde, "Yee, als mot I thee." | *might I thrive* |
|  | Full frely was that fude. | *noble; young woman* |
|  | Than he said, "I make a vowe to mylde Marie: |  |
|  | Now that I hafe chosen to my lady |  |
| 645 | That es so mylde of mode, | *temperament* |
|  | That I schall wende to Attalé, | *go* |
|  | And for thi lufe do chevalrye, | *love* |
|  | And distruye the heythyn blode. |  |

|  |  |  |
|---|---|---|
|  | Sir Kyng, I giff agayne to thee |  |
| 650 | This mayden that es faire and fre, |  |
|  | And in clethynge comly clede. | *beautifully attired* |
|  | And lokes alle that we redy be |  |
|  | Into the landes of Lubardye, |  |
|  | Righte als we firste redde, | *Just as we first planned* |
| 655 | Forto distruye there Goddes enemy |  |
|  | That hathe to yowe ther grete envy, | *malice* |
|  | With folkes one fote wele fedde. | *With well-nourished foot soldiers* |
|  | When I hafe tane myn eme Garcy |  |
|  | And the cité of Attaly, |  |
| 660 | This mayden schall I wedde." |  |

## Fitt 4

|  |  |  |
|---|---|---|
|  | The king said than to his duspers, |  |
|  | "Now hafe herde the messangeres. |  |
|  | Your consell? What es beste? |  |
|  | Sir Garcy with his stronge powere |  |
| 665 | Distruyes my landes, both ferre and nere, |  |
|  | Mi cités brekes and bristes. | *breaks and crushes* |
|  | He confoundes so myche of Cristen blode | *harasses* |
|  | That I for sorowe goo nere wode, |  |
|  | And I may hafe no riste." | *rest* |
| 670 | And thay than ansuerde with steryn mode, |  |
|  | "To fende off, lorde, us thynke it gude; | *make a defense* |
|  | To batayle are we priste." | *ready* |

The kynge saide, "We will habyde     *wait*
Till it be nerre the somertyde,     *summertime*
675        The colde of Marche be gone.
We schalle sende letteres on ilke a syde,     *in all directions*
In dyverse contres, brode and wyde,
       To grete lordes ichone,     *every one*
Sqwyers doghety undir schelde
680   That wele kan thaire wapyns welde —
       Byhynde us leve we none!     *We won't leave anyone behind*
And alle that are within elde,     *of age*
Loke that thay to batayle helde,     *enlist in battle*
       Goddes enemys forto slone."     *slay*

685   Thus the kynge duellys there     *dwells*
Till the tyme comen were,
       The daye neghede neghe.     *came near*
With hym Rowlande and Olyvere,
And the gentill Grauntere,
690        In batayle that was so sleghe.     *skilled*
Sir Oggere and Sir Raynere,
Duke Naymes was thaire fere,
       And Gayryn of kynredyn heghe,     *noble lineage*
fol. 87v   Sir Estut and Sir Inglere,
695   Sir Otuell the werryeure,
       His dynttys were full dreghe.     *destructive*

Appon a mornynge thay lokede owte,
And saughe there powere stythe and stowtte     *strong and sturdy*
       Comynge ferre and nere.
700   Thay rode in many a ryalle rowte,     *company*
By thowsande tale, withowtten dowte,     *count (tally)*
       Under the Mount Marteres.     *Montmartre*
The Almaynes and the Tuskaynes,     *Germans; Tuscans*
The Flemynges full fele for the nanes     *numerous for the occasion*
705        With the banereres;     *banner-bearers*
The Provynce worthily inwith wone,     *Those who nobly dwell in Provence*
The Normandes gude of blode and bone —
       There semlyde faire powere!     *assembled*

There semled owte of Lubardye
710   A full noble chevalrye,
       And sekir at ilke a nede.     *trustworthy*
The Gayscoynes comen sone in hy,     *Gascons; in haste*
And the Burgoynes faste tham by,     *Burgundians*
       That worthily were in wede.     *splendidly; armor*
715   The Bretons come withowtten faile;
There semblede a full faire batayle     *battalion*

One many a stalworthe stede.
With helmys one hedis that walde avayle,                                    *protect*
Full riche was thaire appayraille,
720     And worthily was thaire wede.

One the forthirmaste daye of Averille,                                      *first*
The kyng assemblede appon ane hille
        Alle his mery menye.                                                *company*
Full faire he offres Saynt Denys till,                                      *Saint Denis*
725     And appon his knees he knelys still                                 *reverently*
        To God and Oure Lady;
Sayde to Olyvere, gud at ilke a nede,
"My sone, thou schall the vawarde lede,                                     *vanguard*
        For thou arte swythe doghety!"
730     The oste remowede and forthe thay yode.                             *advanced*
Thay stirrede one many a stalworthe stede;                                  *rode*
        To thaire journaye thay hye.

Olyvere his stede hathe hent,
With hym yode mayden Belesent,
735             That lady of grete renoun.
One a muyle then rode that gentyll maid,
And in hir company ther were arrayed
        A thousande bolde barouns.
Thay passed forthe than Bretayne by,                                        *Brittany*
740     Thurgh the landes of the Mandely,
        By many a ryalle toun.
Thay schipped over at Vertely                                               *Vercelli*
Into the landes of Lubardy,
        Thay passede bothe dales and dowun.                                 *hills and valleys*

745     Under a mountayne thay herberde than                                *took shelter*
Besyde a rever that highte Soltane,
        And in a medowe thay lighte.
Ther was many a worthy man,
Ryalle howssynges thay bygan                                                *lodgings*
750         Of pavylyons proudly pighte.                                    *erected*
So fortravellede were thay sare,                                            *fatigued; sorely*
That aughte dayes thay duelled thare,                                       *eight*
        Thaire harnays forto righte.                                        *armor and weapons; adjust*
Therefore Kyng Cherlles wolde noghte spare,                                 *Because; was diligent*
755     A noble brigge he garte make thare                                  *bridge he ordered to be made*
        Over the watir of Soltane dighte.

And a wonder poynte now schall ye here:                                     *wondrous event*
To the mete thay wente alle in fere                                         *meal; together*
        Iche lorde in thaire lyveré,                                        *heraldic clothes*

fol. 88r  Bot Duke Rowlande and Olyvere

761      And the Daynnes Oggere,                                    *Ogier the Dane*
                Stode armede undir a tree;
         And over the brigge than gan thay ryde
         Full prevaly that ilke a tyde                              *secretly*
765            That no mo wiste bot they three.                     *no one knew except*
         Awnters thoghte thay forto byde;                          *Adventures*
         Thay stale awaye by a wodde syde
                Righte towarde Attalé.

         And a mile withowtten Attalé                              *outside of*
770      There hovede foure kynges fre                             *rode*
                With speris in theire hande;
         And ichone sware in theire degree
         That thay wolde reghte gladly see
                Olyver and Rowlande.
775      Thay sware alle by thaire grete Mahowun,
         "We wolde that thay were nowe here bowun,                 *wish; headed*
                To loke how thay couthe stande!                    *find out; stand [in fight]*
         And so we scholde forjuste tham doun,                     *might; unhorse (defeat)*
         That thay solde never see Charllyoun,                     *might never [again]*
780            The chefe of Cristen lande!"

         Now, lordynges, forto rede yow righte,                    *tell*
         Thies kynges names, what thay highte,
                The sothe I will yow tell.
         Kynge Balsame, a mane of myghte;
785      Kynge Corsabell, another knyghte
                That bothe was ferse and felle.
         Kyng Askuardyne, that teraunt,                            *tyrant*
         Of wikkednes he myghte hym avaunte,                       *boast*
                Was lyke a fende of helle.
790      The ferthe was faire and avenante                         *honorable*
         With a full manly semblande;                              *appearance*
                Men callede hym Kyng Claryell.

         Kynge Clariell sayde, "Als mot I thee,
         Rowlande es holden full doghety —
795            Es none siche undir sone!
         Be Mahoun, I wolde he were here me by.
         I scholde assaye his body,
                My dynttes scholde he con!"                        *know*
         Thies knyghttes herde how thay therett were;              *were threatened*
800      With sporres thay brochede thaire stedis there,          *spurred on*
                Oute of the wodde thay rynn.                       *hastened*
         Than sayd Kynge Clariell, breme als bare,                *fierce as a boar*

"We hafe tham that we spake fare!                                                   *here of whom we spoke*
          Be Mahoun, alle es wonn!

805    Bot wendes now forthe, ye kynges three,
       And slees yone knyghtis of Cristyantee,
               And I schall hove here styll.
       Alle als ye done I schall see;
       There es no mache unto mee,                                                  *no match [i.e., no fourth knight]*
810            And that me lykes ille!"
       Kyng Askuardyn in his gere
       Rydes owte a course of were                                                  *charge*
               Full egerly and with ill will.
       And Rowlande thurgh his scholdir gan schere;                                 *stab*
815    His armours ne vaylede noghte a pere;                                        *was not worth a pear*
               His hert blode he gan ther spill.

       Kyng Corsabolyn in armes full clere
       Rydis owte to Sir Oggere,
               And hittes hym in the schelde.
820    The Cristen knyghte neghede hym so nere,
       Thurgh double hawberke he hym bere,
               Of horse he garte hym helde.                                         *He caused him to fall from his horse*
       Kyng Balsamy rode till Sir Olyvere.
       Thies thre kynges dyede in fere,
825            And lyen gronande in the felde.                                      *lay groaning*
       Thaire thretynge boghte thay there full dere;                               *paid for*
       Thaire saules went alle to Lucyfere
               That hade tham alle towelde.                                         *possessed*

fol. 88v  Then was Kyng Clariell full sory,
830    And flynges owte full fersely                                                *advances*
               With hert egire and throo.                                          *bold*
       He smyttys Rowlande that was doghety
       That his noble stede gan dy —
               His bakke braste even in two.
835    And up he keste ane heghe cry,                                              *loud cry*
       "This was a poynte of chevalry!"
               And busked hym for to goo.                                          *prepared to ride away*
       Oggere Dauynes gan aftir hym hye                                            *hastened after him*
       And stroke the kynge his sadill bye;
840            His stede he tuke hym fro.

       Olyvere anone hath hent the stede,                                          *taken*
       And righte to Rowlande he gan hym lede,
               And sayde, "Hafe this for thyne!"
       And he stert up bettir spede                                                *[Roland]; more quickly*
845    And drissede hym in his worthy wede                                         *got ready*

That lofesome under lyne.                    *was handsome under linen*
Kyng Clariell drawes Melle
And faghte agaynes tham all thre;
His swerde was gude and fyne.
850   He said, "Gud lordes, slees noghte me!
A noble cheke here wonn hafe yee,          *victory*
My lyfe wolde I noghte tyne."               *lose*

And when his vesage was alle bare,          *face*
A fayrere knyghte sawe thay never are,      *before*
855         And sett hym one a stede.
Thay wende awaye with hym to fare;     *expected to go away with him*
A thousande Sarazenes come one tham thare;    *came upon*
There bale bygan to brede.             *Their anxiety began to grow*
Than saide Rolande to Olyvere,
860   "Yondere I see full brighte banere
And worthily undir wede.
Tham semys bothe felle and ferse;          *They seem to be*
I wolde no worde come to oure peres    *don't want any; peers*
That we fledde tham for drede."

865   Ogger Daynes was moste wysse,
Sayd, "Sen we hafe getyn this kyng of price,
I rede we late tham goo.                    *him [Clarel]*
For bi God and Saynt Denys,
We may noghte skape in nonekynswyse,         *any way*
870         Ne hym will we noghte slo."
Than said Kyng Clariell there he stode,
"This was a worde of gentill blode,
To speke thus for thi foo!"
He tuke his leve and forthe he yode,
875   Thankede tham with mylde mode,
And agaynes a thousande was no moo.    *no more [i.e., only three]*

Rowlande and Olyvere
Dressede tham in armes clere,
Alle redy to the fyghte.
880   And the Daynes Oggere                    *And with*
Cryed "Mountjoy!" all in fere,              *together*
Bothe with mayne and myghte.
For the Sarazenes thay haden dowte,      *[Because] of; fear*
To Jhesus Criste thay crye and lowte,        *kneel*
885         That moste es man of myghte.
Thies paynyms put tham owte,            *troubled them*
That were halden full steryn and stoute,
And under thaire horses thay lighte.         *upon*

|     | Those thre to the thousande gan ryde, |     |
| --- | --- | --- |
| 890 | And hewed one faste one iche a syde, | *every side* |
|     | And brittenede blode and bone. | *destroyed* |
|     | Thay made thaire wayes wondere wyde; |     |
|     | Ther durste no Sarazene thair dynttis byde; |     |
|     | To gronde thay garte tham gone. | *made them fall* |
| fol. 89r | Then comes girdande Sir Carpé, | *charging* |
| 896 | The kynges sone of Aubré, |     |
|     | Was halden a noble man. |     |
|     | Upone highte he castis a krye: |     |
|     | "What schall saye to Sir Garcye? |     |
| 900 | Thre schendis us everichone?" | *overcome* |

|     | Sir Carpy come girdande suythe: | *swiftly* |
| --- | --- | --- |
|     | To Oggere Daynes gan he dryfe | *attacked* |
|     | That he swounede als he were wode. | *swooned; senseless* |
|     | Sir Rowlande gan doghety dedis kythe, | *perform* |
| 905 | With Drondale he gan hym ryfe | *cut* |
|     | Reghte to the girdillstede. | *waist* |
|     | Ogger Daynes wakkened than, | *recovered* |
|     | Pulled owte a swerde highte Curtane, |     |
|     | Was gude at ilke a nede; |     |
| 910 | Than to fighte Oggere bygane |     |
|     | To hewe doun many ane heythyn man — |     |
|     | Grete travayle ther thay hade! | *labor* |

|     | And the gentill Erle Sir Olyvere |     |
| --- | --- | --- |
|     | Hewes one with Haunkclere — |     |
| 915 | Mighte none his dynttis withstande! |     |
|     | He daunge tham doun bothe ferre and nere; | *beat* |
|     | It was a wonder thynge to here, |     |
|     | Thies thre men wroghte with hande. | *[What]* |
|     | Than comes a Sarazene sone in hye; | *soon in haste* |
| 920 | His name was Kyng Alphamanye, |     |
|     | Was fayre and wele farande. | *handsome* |
|     | He smyttes Olyvere that was doghety, |     |
|     | That toppe over tayle he garte hym lye |     |
|     | Appon a ley lande. | *meadow* |

| 925 | Bot than was Sir Rowlande never so woo; |     |
| --- | --- | --- |
|     | Full swythe that Sarazene gan he sloo, |     |
|     | That to the grounde he yede. |     |
|     | Olyvere rose with herte full throo; | *bold* |
|     | Belyfe his stede gan he too | *Quickly he regained his horse* |
| 930 | And sterte up in his nede. |     |
|     | He sayd, "Rowlande, drede thee noghte! |     |
|     | Now I am one horse broghte, |     |

I fayle thee at no nede!”
With Hankclere many wondirs he wroghte;
935    Fele Sarazenes to the grounde he broghte,
            And ferde als he wolde wede.                          *fought as if he were a madman*

This while was Ogger Daynes one fete;                       *During this time; on foot*
The Sarazenes that he myghte with mete,
            He wroghte thaire bodyes wo.
940    He gaffe tham woundes wyde and wete,                    *wet*
Full many one there lefte the swete                         *lifeblood*
            (The boke us telles soo)
Till almoste scomfet was he.                                *defeated*
Than comes Kyng Clariell with hert fre,
945            Als faste als he myghte go,
And bade the Sarazenes thay scholde late be:
“Oggere, yelde thi suerde to me!”
            Belyve he sayde hym yoo.                             *Quickly; then*

A Sarazene come with steryn ble,                           *stern countenance*
950    Sayd, “This Cristen doge sall not saved be,
            Bot sle we hym reghte here!”
“Yee,” sais Kyng Clariell, “as avenche thee                 *may you be avenged*
He schall be savede nowe, pardee!”
            He heued of sone he schere.                          *He [Clarel] cut off his head quickly*
955    He called seven paynyms of mekill myghte,
Said, “Gose, ledis hym to my leman brighte                  *Go, lead him; paramour*
            Of colours that es clere.                            *Of beautiful coloring*
Loke his wondes ben wele dighte,                            *tended*
And kepe me wele this Cristen knyghte,                      *protect for me*
960            For this es gentill of chere.”

fol. 89v    The Sarazenes toke hym that was hende,
And to that lady gan thay wende,
            Of coloures that was brighte,
Tolde hir the tale unto the ende,
965    Sayd, “Madame, this Duke Claryell yow sende            *this [man, i.e., Ogier]*
            To hele hym at your myghte.”
“What?” saide that lady, white als fame,                    *white as foam*
“Es this Kynge Charlles that here es tane,
            His men to dethe alle dighte?”
970    “Nay, by grete Mahoun!” thay sware, “Madame,
Thre knyghtes of his hath a thousande slane,
            That we helde hardy and wighte.

And Kyng Clariell under schelde
Hymselfe was taken in the felde,
975            Thre kynges by hym slayne.                        *near to*

Ther was nother bute nere belde,                                        *neither aid nor support*
Ne Mahoun that alle schall welde,
  For hym thay moghte nott gone.                              *succeed*
And there was none bot glotons three,                                   *villains*
980 And one of tham here may thou see
  That Kyng Clariell hathe tane."                             *captured*
"What, devyll?" scho said, "How may this be?                           *she*
Who durste neghe my leman free,                                         *attack*
  Es beste of blode and bone?"                               *[Who] is*

985 Scho said, "Comforthe thee, sir. Be noghte abayste.           *abashed*
Schall none of my men thee brayste.                                     *harm*
  What es the name of thee?"
"Madame," he sayde, "Oggere Daunays."
Than sayde the lady that was curtayse,
990  "I have herde speke of thee."
Belyfe scho garte unarme hym there,                                    *Quickly; had him disarmed*
And to hym comes that lady clere,
  And greses broghte that fre,                                *potions; noble one*
That Godd sett in His awenn herbere.
995 Als sone als ever thay dronken were,
  He was lyghte als lefe one tree.

Thus Oggere Daynas duelled there,
And heled es of his hurtes sare
  In the ladise presoun.
1000 And of his felawes speke we mare,
How that thay full harde handilde ware,                                *handled*
  Thies two knyghtes of renoun.
Ten thousande Sarazenes come girdande                                  *charging*
That hardy were of hert and hande,
1005  With helme and haberjoun.                               *coat of scale armor*
Bot than myghte thay no lengere stande,
Olyver and gud Rowlande —
  To flye now are thay boun.                                  *flee*

Otuell that was so wighte
1010 Duelles with Belesent the brighte,                             *Dwells*
  Was comely one to calle.
Oute of hir chambire he wendis righte,
Als faste als ever that he myghte,
  Into the kynges haulle
1015 To seche Olyver and Rowlande,
Bot never nother he ther fande
  Amonge the lordes alle.
Therefore Kynge Charlles his handes wrange,

And ever "allas!" was his sange,
1020          "What may of this byfalle?"

Ottuell sayde, "Where it be soo?                                    *Why has this happened*
Oggere Daynes and tho twoo
          Are went to Attalee.                                      *have gone*
Now buske we aftir thaym to goo,                                    *prepare*
1025   Or ells the Sarazenes will tham sloo —
          Forsothe, thay mon alle dy."
Thay busked tham in armes full clere,
Seven hundrethe bolde bacheleres
          With hym to wende in hy.
fol. 90r  Belesent sayde to Sir Grauntere,
1031   "Gude Sir, ryde my lemmane nere;
          The knyghte es full thethey."                            *headstrong*

Thies seven hundrethe knyghtis
Duellede with Belesante the brightes
1035          At hir awenn fyndynge.                                *By her [Belesent's] own maintenance*
Sir Otuell that was so wighte
Strykes Florence his stede brighte;
          Byfore tham forthe gan he flynge.                        *rush*
He metys Rowlande and Olyvere
1040   Faste rydande by a revere
          And fresche folke aftir tham dynge.                      *charging after them*
He hailsede tham with steryn chere,                                *greeted*
And sayde, "Sirres, whate make ye here?
          Come ye fro fischeynge?"

1045   He reproved tham there full velanslye,                      *mockingly*
And yit theire bodies were alle blodye
          With wondes many one.
"Wene ye, for youre chevalrye,
For youre boste and youre folye,
1050          That the Sarazenes will late yow one?                *grant you [victory]*
Charlles with his stronge powere
Schall thynke this a grete gramaungere,                            *foolish enterprise*
          This dede to undertone.
Bot this chase schall thay by full dere!"                          *cost them dearly*
1055   He smote to a knyghte highte Sir Glantere
          And belyfe he hathe hym slone.                           *quickly*

## Fitt 5

Syr Otuell there righte in that gere,
Full faste he dange tham doun there
          And garte tham go to grounde.

| 1060 | And his felawe Sir Ynglere | |
| | In a Sarazene breke a spere | |
| | Within a littill stounde, | *short time* |
| | And in his hande lefte a littill troncheoun, | *remained; cudgel* |
| | Therwith full faste he dange tham doun, | |
| 1065 | Full many ane heythyn hounde. | |
| | He crakkede full many a carefull croun, | |
| | And criede "Mountjoye!" with heghe sowun. | *loud voice* |
| | Fele folke thay there confounde. | |

| | Then come a knyghte that highte Sir Galias, | |
| 1070 | A noble Sarazene men saide he was, | |
| | And in his hande a spere. | |
| | For the lufe of his leman fayre of face, | |
| | A glofe to his pensalle he hase | *glove on; pennant* |
| | In sygnance of his were. | *As a sign of his pledge* |
| 1075 | He rydes to Sir Inglere, | |
| | And thurghe the schelde he gan hym schere | |
| | And unhorssede hym there. | |
| | Thurghe double hawberke he hym bere, | |
| | Bot, als Goddes will it were, | |
| 1080 | His flesche hade nonekyns dere. | *no injury at all* |

| | Appon hym also relevede a Sarazene wighte | *arose* |
| | That hardy was, and Ancole highte, | |
| | Sir Inglere for to sloo. | |
| | Bot Sir Ysope come with mekill myghte, | |
| 1085 | And Sir Estut a noble knyghte, | |
| | And Sir Davide also; | |
| | Sir Estut de ronoun, | *of renown* |
| | Sir Grauntere de Lyoun, | |
| | One bakke thay garte tham goo; | *horseback* |
| 1090 | And broghte hym upe that are was doun, | *before* |
| | And horsede hym one a stede browun | |
| | With hert egere and throo. | *brave* |

| | Than come rydande Sir Galyadose, | |
| | Of Sarazenes alle he bare the lose, | *was the most distinguished* |
| 1095 | Was halden a noble knyghte. | |
| fol. 90v | Faste he felled dowun of his fose! | *knocked down his foes* |
| | Sir Inglere righte to hym gose, | |
| | And cleves his hede full righte. | |
| | Forthe rydes than Sir Grauntere, | |
| 1100 | A Sarazene thurgh the body he bere, | |
| | Sir Megradyn he highte; | |
| | He dange tham doun, bothe ferre and nere, | *He [Megradyn] had struck* |

|  | Bot appon hym come a stronge powere | *strong power [i.e., the Christians]* |
|  | With baners brode and brighte. | |

| 1105 | Then was there no nother crye | |
|  | When grete batells togedir gan hye, | *rushed together* |
|  | With mouthe als I yow mene. | |
|  | Full thikke-folde gan Sarazenes dy | |
|  | And thaire horses thaym by, | |
| 1110 | To wete withowtten wene. | *know and not to guess* |
|  | Be thousandes thay tumblede doun dede, | |
|  | Thaire saules wente unto the quede | *to join the wicked* |
|  | That myghte not nombrede be. | |
|  | For braynes and blode in that stede, | |
| 1115 | The brode medowe was waxen rede | |
|  | That ere was growen grene. | |

|  | Than come a Turke appon a stede | |
|  | To Kynge Clariell better spede, | *at rapid speed* |
|  | And sayde, "Allas, how do wee! | |
| 1120 | For Cristen men we hafe grete drede, | |
|  | And bot thou helpe us in this nede, | *And unless* |
|  | Grete sorowe here may thou see!" | |
|  | Kynge Claryell come with his powere, | |
|  | Oure batells ferre one bakke he bere, | *He pushed our battalions further back* |
| 1125 | Ane Almayne sone sloghe he. | *German* |
|  | Also he dide the gude Gauntere, | |
|  | Sir Otes and Sir Raynere, | |
|  | And other grete plentee. | |

|  | By that it was so nere nyghte | *Because* |
| 1130 | Thay moghte no lengere see to fighte, | |
|  | Bot stynt one ayther syde. | *ceased* |
|  | Sir Otuell that was so wighte | |
|  | Stroke Florence his stede full righte, | *Spurred* |
|  | And byfore tham forthe gan ryde. | |
| 1135 | Then comes girdande Kynge Clariell, | *charging* |
|  | And cried to hym with wordes fell, | |
|  | "To speke thou schalt abyde, | *You will stop to speak [to me]* |
|  | Thi righte name that thou me tell!" | |
|  | He sayde, "I highte Otuell, | |
| 1140 | For no man will I hyde! | |

|  | And fro youre Mahoun ame I went, | *departed* |
|  | And Cristyndome hafe I hent, | *accepted* |
|  | And baptiste ame I full righte. | *baptized* |
|  | My leman es bothe faire and gent, | |
| 1145 | Hir reghte name es Belesent, | *proper* |

        Charlles dogheter the brighte."
     Bot than the Sarazene said, "Allas!
     Now is this a wikkede case,
        And thou so noble a knyghte!
1150  Whi duelles thou there amonges thi fase?           *foes*
     Foully there thou wichede was.             *bewitched*
        And whi es this dede thus dighte?

     I rede that thou coverte thee in hye,      *advise that you convert at once*
     And then sall saughtyll with thyn eme Sir Garcy,     *next; reconcile*
1155      And forsake not thy lawe."             *faith*
     Unto the Sarazene gon he defye,
     "Your lawes are noghte worthe a pye,          *magpie*
        That dare I savely saye!            *safely*
fol. 91r  And if thou wilt for Mahoun fighte,
1160  Loo, me here, a Cristyn knyghte,         *Lo, see me here*
        With Hym that myghtes maye
     Stalworthely to stande for oure righte!"
     Kyng Clariell his trouthe hafe plighte
        At morne to holde his daye.    *keep his appointment [i.e., challenged him to duel]*

1165  Kyng Clariell wendis to the cité
     That men callede Attalé,
        Ther into duelle al nyghte;
     Sir Otuell to his companye,          *[returned] to*
     To Kyng Charlles that was fre,
1170      And Belesent so brighte.
     That faire mayden of hewe and hide,
     Hirselfe unarmed hym that tide
        And thris scho kissede that knyghte,       *thrice*
     And groped hym wele, body and syde,       *(see note)*
1175  That he ne hade no woundes wyde,
        And esede hym at hir myghte.

     Knyghtis wache was there sett,          *look-out*
     Faire fyres was there bett            *made*
        To ese tham that there ware.         *comfort*
1180  Of dede folkes thay hepes fett         *gathered in heaps*
     To berye tham withowtten lett,        *bury; continuously*
        Those that Cristen ware.
     Leches come that couthe one booke      *Physicians; knew by book*
     Woundede men for to loke,         *how to look after*
1185      To salve tham of thaire sare.       *wounds*
     And grete lordes riste toke,         *rest*
     And nyghte wache full worthily wooke,    *watchmen; stayed awake*
        Blewe and made grete fare.      *Blew [horn]; fanfare*

Kyng Clariell rose at morne,
1190 Wiste whate othes that he hade sworne     *Remembered; oaths*
    And to his chambir went,
Garte kaste armoures hym byforne,     *Ordered his armor be laid out*
That riche was and comly korne.     *handsomely selected*
    Ane actone one he hent,     *padded jacket*
1195 One he dide ane hawberke schene,
Of the mayster handwerke of Galyene     *Made by*
    That never no wapyn rent.     *had never been torn by*
When that was armed clene,     *that one; thoroughly*
A fayrere knyghte was never sene,
1200     For joly ne for gent.     *jolity; gentility*

His creste was of an eddire hede     *adder's*
With golde abowte it was bywevede     *interwoven*
    And sett one hym Mahoun     *beset [with images of]*
And Appolyne that he one levede.     *in whom he believed*
1205 Alle his armours was overdrevede     *studded*
    With stones of grete renoun.     *[i.e., jewels]*
He girde hym with a suerde that hate Modlee,     *They*
Broghte hym a schelde of faire blee.     *appearance*
    He buskede and made hym boun,     *went forth; ready*
1210 Lepe on a stede semely to see,
With mekill myrthe and solempnytee
    He rydes thurghowte the toun.

An hundrethe knyghtes of Turkeye
Bare his mawmettis hym by,     *idols*
1215     And paste over that strande;     *passed; river*
And doun thay lighten all in hye.
Thay were halden full doghetye
    Alle in thaire awenn lande.
Thay sett thaire goddes appon a stone
1220 And dowun thay knelyde everichonee,
    And made tham thare offerande.     *offering*
Kyng Clariell his leve hase tone,     *took his leave*
Lepe one a stede that highte Browan —
    That horse was noble at hande.

1225 Charlles come rydande by a revere,
With hym Rowlande and Olyvere
    Appon the ferrere syde.     *further*
fol. 91v Duke Naymes was thaire fere,
And Sir Otuell the gude werryere,
1230     Full faire of hewe and hyde.
Than comes girdande Kynge Clariell,
And cried to tham with wordis felle:

"To speke ye schall abyde!

I beteche yow to the devell of helle!      *consign*

1235   How longe schall I aftir batelle duelle?"      *do I have to wait for battle*

Thus bygynnes he forto chide.


"And yitt," he cried, breme als bore,      *as savage as a boar*

"Wiche of yow foure es mayster thore?"

Kyng Charlles calles on, "Mee!"

1240   "Now cursede worthe thou ever mare,

For thou hase wroghte us myche care

In many dyverse contree."

The kyng sayde, "Be Saynt Marie,

And hir dere Sone Almyghtye

1245      That derely dyede one tree,      *cross*

With dyntt of swerde thou schalte aby,      *pay*

And take your Emperoure Sir Garcy,      *[I shall] capture*

And distruye alle youre citee."


The Sarazene ansuerde with wordes full bolde,

1250   "Charlles, methynke that thou scholdeste folde,      *give up*

And thou were streken sore.      *Before you are*

Thi vesage es crounkilde and waxen olde;      *crinkled*

A nobill suerde thee burde not wolde      *might not; wield*

Now for thi mellyde hare.      *gray*

1255   Bot, by righte, methynke thou scholde be founde      *treated*

Als those it were an olde grewhounde      *Like an old greyhound*

That myghte rynn no mare."

The kynge wex grevede in that stounde      *became aggrieved*

And keste his clothes appon the grounde      *cast clothes*

1260      "As armes!" he cried thare.      *To arms*


Bot Sir Otuell saide full curtasely,

"Gude Lorde, graunte this batell to me,

For trowthes hafe we plighte.

He sett the lawes of Cristyantee

1265   Nott at a pillynge of a tree      *At less than the worth of a tree bark*

Yistereven within the nyghte."      *Yesterday evening*

Charlles thankkes hym ther he stode,

Taughte hym to Godde that diede one rode,      *Commended*

That alle schall deme and dighte.

1270   Elleven duspers with hym yode,

To dresse hym in his armours gude,      *To get him attired*

Alle redy for to fighte.


When he was armede in his gere

That was bothe faire white and clere,

1275      Thay girde hym with a brande;      *sword*

Broghte hym ane helme was riche and dere
That aughte gud Kynge Galliere —                    *belonged to*
   Was none siche in that lande!
The lady lufsome under lyne                         *linen clothes*
1280 Garte the Bischope Sir Turpyne
   Assoyle hym with his hande.                  *Bless (absolve)*
Scho kiste hym thryse with herte full fyne,
Bytaughte hym unto dere Dryghtyne,                  *Commended; Lord*
   That mayden faire to fande.                  *behold*

1285 Lordes that weren of mekill pride
Overe the brigge than gan thay ryde,
   With mouthe als I yowe mene.                  *as I tell you*
Bot then the Sarazene begynnes to chide:
"Now schalte thou, fole, lose thi pryde,
1290    Bothe with traye and tene!            *pain and torment*
To oure goddes I rede thou gone
And knele bifore tham everichone,
   Of colours that are clene."                  *[Appearing] in bright colors*
"Nay!" he sayde, "There es no God bot one
1295 That ever made ne blode ne bone.
   Nowe sone it schall be sene!"

Than bothe thies kene knyghttes there,
fol. 92r Togedir thay reden a course of werre          *commenced a battle*
   With stronge speres in theire hande,
1300 That alle in sondre floughe thaire gere;          *pieces*
Tayle over tope bothe doun gon bere —               *Head over heels*
   The stroke was wele sittande!                *well aimed*
Belysent keste up a crye
Unto God and milde Marie;
1305    Scho wepede and handis wrange.
Bot up thay stert full hastily,
And ayther gan to other defye
   With swerdis large and lange.

This noble kyng this Clariell,
1310 Smyttes to Sir Otuell
   A dynt that he myghte fele;
Bot one his helme it myghte nott duelle,
So sadly one his scholdire it felle;                *grievously*
   The knyghte bygane to knele.
1315 Bot up he stirte full hastilye,
"I vowe to God thou schall abye,                     *pay for it*
   That alle schalle deme and dele!"
Cursu thurghe his helme gan hye                      *carve*

|  | That alle his one cheke hyngede bye — | *hung sideways* |
| 1320 | His tethe were schaven wele! | *well shaven* |

|  | He said than, "Clariell, als mote thou thee, | *thrive* |
|  | Whi grynnes thou nowe so one mee, | |
|  | As thofe thou wolde me byte? | *though* |
|  | Alphayné, thi leman white and fre, | *fair and noble (generous)* |
| 1325 | Thare never yerne to kysse thee; | |
|  | Therfore I may nott hir wyte!" | *I would not blame her* |
|  | The kynge ferde than als he wolde wede; | *as if he were mad* |
|  | To the knyghte he hyed hym bettir spede, | *at great speed* |
|  | Full egerly to smyte, | |
| 1330 | And thurgh his schelde he gan hym schrede, | |
|  | That schulde hafe savede hym at his nede — | |
|  | Almoste he was scomfite! | *defeated* |

|  | The kynge woundede Otuell so sore, | |
|  | Hade he nott schounte his stroke thore, | *dodged* |
| 1335 | Forsothe, he hade bene slayne. | |
|  | Bot than Cursu that the knyghte bare | |
|  | Thorowowte the kynges herte it schare, | *sheared* |
|  | Bothe with myghte and mayne. | |
|  | And to the grounde he tumbills doun; | |
| 1340 | His saule went unto Mahoun, | |
|  | Than by those gates gayne. | *Then; quickly* |
|  | And a full blythe man was Charllyoun, | |
|  | And lovede God with full heghe sowun, | *praised; loud outcry* |
|  | And Belesent was full fayne. | *elated* |

**Fitt 6**

| 1345 | For sorowe Sir Garcy went nere wode | |
|  | For Clariell dede, was stronge of mode, | *death* |
|  | And sware by Appolyne | |
|  | That mete ne drynke scholde done hym gude | *That he would neither eat nor drink* |
|  | Are he struyed hade Cristen blode | *Until he had ruined Christendom* |
| 1350 | And broghte tham alle to pyne. | *pain* |
|  | His grete bataylls he garte arayee | *battalions; gathered* |
|  | And his baners brode dispieye | |
|  | With coloures noble and fyne. | |
|  | And Charlles wele thynkes that he maye | |
| 1355 | Forto kepe the heythyn laye | *Restrain the heathen law* |
|  | With the helpe of dere Drightyn. | *[his] dear Lord* |

|  | Sir Barlott of Perse come girdande swythe | *Persia; charging* |
|  | Also faste als he myghte dryfe — | |
|  | Was holden a noble knyghte — | |

| | | |
|---|---|---|
| 1360 | And doghety dedis gun he kythe; | *perform* |
| | Ther myghte no wapen his wedys ryfe, | *tear* |
| | So savely was he dighte. | *securely; armored* |
| | He rydes owte a course of were | |
| | And in his hande a noble spere, | |
| 1365 | His armours glyssenede full brighte. | *glistened* |
| fol. 92v | He askede leve at Sir Garcy there | *permission of* |
| | To juste with Rowlande and Olyvere, | |
| | Theire bothere dede to dyghte. | *dead brother to avenge* |

| | | |
|---|---|---|
| | And one his horse he come rynnande | |
| 1370 | With his spere faste in his hande; | |
| | His armour glessened clere. | |
| | He called firste one Rowlande, | |
| | One Otuell stalworthe forto stande, | |
| | And sythen one Olyvere. | |
| 1375 | "Hafe done," he saide. "Brynge mee forthe your kynge, | |
| | Or ells to dethe I schall yow dynge, | |
| | Forsothe, alle foure ifere." | |
| | Rowlande askede the kynges blyssynge; | |
| | He stroke his stede and forthe gan flynge — | *spurred* |
| 1380 | His thretynge boghte he dere! | *paid for* |

| | | |
|---|---|---|
| | When that thay togedir mett, | |
| | A sekere stroke was there sett | |
| | That bothe thay tynte thaire stedys. | *fell off* |
| | And up thay rose withowtten lett, | *delay* |
| 1385 | And ayther harde one othir bett | *either beat hard against the other* |
| | And persed some of thaire wedys. | *pierced; garments (i.e., armor)* |
| | Rowlande doghty dedis gan kythe; | *display* |
| | With Drondale he gan hym ryve | |
| | That reghte to the girdill it yede. | *waist* |
| 1390 | And Sir Barlot loste his lyfe; | |
| | He faughte nothir with foure ne fyve; | |
| | His lyfe was hym full gnede. | *lacking [i.e., he is dead]* |

| | | |
|---|---|---|
| | Then comes a Sarazene girdande there; | |
| | His name was called Sir Lamagere, | |
| 1395 | Was holden a noble knyghte. | |
| | He come als breme als any bore, | *fierce as any boar* |
| | And woundede Sir Rowlande wonder sore | |
| | Thurgh his brenyes brighte. | *mail shirt* |
| | And Olyvere saughe his felawe blede, | |
| 1400 | With sporres he touches his noble stede; | |
| | The Sarazene garte he lighte. | *struck down* |
| | The grete batells by than togedir yede; | *battalions; clashed together* |

Thay hewede one faste and full gude spede,
    And now bygynnes thaire fyghte.

1405  Bot other noyse was ther none
When the grete togedir gun gone          *the great encounter had begun*
    Bot stronge strokes and steryn!
Thay hewede one faste and full gud wone,    *furiously and a long while*
Brusten bothe bak, blode, and bone —
1410      Of wandrethe myghte men leryn!       *misery; learn*
Be thousandes thay doun gan dryfe,
For bothe helme and haberjeone thay ryfe —   *jacket of scale armor*
    Ther myghte no man tham werun!        *ward off*
Kyng and duke there loste thaire lyfe;
1415  With dynt of swerde, spere, and knyfe,
    Thay brittenede many a beryn.          *man*

Doun thay dange thaire baners brade
Bothe in slakkes and in slade,          *in valley and on hill*
    One bukes as we rede.
1420  Full fele Sarazenes feble thay fade,      *feebly they weakened*
And many one to the grounde thay hade —
    Thaire lyfe was tham full gnede.
Full grisely thay grone and grenne;        *grimace*
Maisterles thaire horse thay rynne —       *Riderless*
1425      Of tham toke no man hede.
The Cristen men gan the maystry wynn,    *won the upperhand*
Bot yitt thaire barett ne wolde not blyn.    *conflict; cease*
    On nowe bygynnes thaire dede.   *And now their [heroic] deeds begin*

Sir Elys come with mekill myghte,
1430  With seven hundrethe newe-made knyghtes
    Oute of Bretayne.               *Brittany*
Thise fresche men so freschely fyghte
That it was joye to see that sighte,
    Bothe with myghte and mayne.
fol. 93r  A Sarazene come with felawes fyve,
1436  Thorowte Sir Briane gane he dryfe;
    That nobill knyghte was slayne.
And yitt that paynym loste his lyfe;
With a spere thay gan hym ryfe;
1440      His saule went unto payne.

Sir Otuell that noble man,
To his awenn cosyn he ran
    Full grymly in his gere.
He strikes the Duke Balamé,
1445  The kynges sone of Alphané,

        Even thurghowte with a spere.
        Than Kynge Alphané come in hye
        With twenty thowsande of Barbarye
           That wele couthe wapyns bere,
1450    And the Kynge Cursabolee
        With thritty thousande of Turkee,
           And alle one fote thay were.             *on foot*

        Thies futemen so stalworthe were        *[heathen] footmen*
        That oure batells full ferre one bakke thay bare,[1]
1455        Ther myghte none stirre thaire schelde.   *disturb; shield-wall*
        Thaire dynttes felle so sadde and sare       *truly and sorely*
        That wele ané alblastire schott and mare,  *however well a crossbowman could shoot*
           Thay myghte no wapyns welde.      *He couldn't wield a weapon*
        Thay were so mekill and so unryde,       *numerous; savage*
1460    And so foulle of hewe and hyde,
           That thay hade almoste wonn the felde.
        Thay gafe thaym wondes wete and wyde,
        And brittenede tham bothe bake and syde;     *battered*
           Oure batell garte thay helde.    *They held back our battalion*

1465    Than come girdande a gude sqwyere,
        Sir Grym sone, the gude duchere,         *duke*
           That was borne in Pareyche —       *Paris*
        With hym an hundrethe that hardy ware —
        His name was hatten Naymere,
1470        A man of mekill pryce.           *much worth*
        To arme thaym grete hye thay hade,        *haste*
        Dispoyle the bodyes that laye one brade,  *By despoiling the bodies that lay broadly*
           Ichone one thaire beste wyse.         *way*
        Of thaire clothes pensalles thay made;      *pennants*
1475    To Kyng Cherlles belyfe thay rade:     *quickly; rode*
           "Mountjoye!" was thaire discrye.     *shout*

        The grete batell than relyed agayne,      *rallied*
        Both with myghte and with mayne,
           And brittenede blode and bone.
1480    Kyng Charlles than was full fayne,
        And lovede God, es noghte to layne,      *it is no lie*
           And His Modir allone.
        Kynge Corsable hoved by Apparoun  *waited; [the statue of] Apollin*
        And seese hys men alle doungen doun,       *sees*
1485        And sone gane he to tham goo.
        Bot Aymere hitt hym one the crowun,

---

[1] *That they pushed back our battalions very far*

That that lorde hathe loste alle his renoun,
    In the felde he hathe hym tone.                              *captured*

Aymere hathe the kynge hent,
1490  And to Kynge Charlles he hathe hym sent
        By foure of his sqwyeres.
    Bot when that he made hym that ther sent,        *[Aymere] had sent [Corsable] there*
    He loves Gode that luffe hade lent                *[Charles] praises; peace*
        And His mylde Modere dere.
1495  Thies fresche men so fersely fighte,
    It was grete joye to see that syghte,
        And a wondere thynge to here!
    This noble man Sir Ottuell,
    Thilke-folde he gane tham felle                              *Thickly*
1500        With strengthe and noblitee.

fol. 93v  And certis, als the bookes gane telle,
    Thaire saulles wente unto helle,
        Those fele that there gun blede.             *Those many who bled there*
    Thus kynges and dukes to the dede thay dighte;       *they struck to death*
1505  A hundrethe dubbide thamselfe to knyghte,           *were dubbed as knights*
        That worthy were and welde.                            *powerful*
    And to the banere belyfe thay wanne,            *banner [i.e., the battle]*
    And foure gude kynges thay sloughe ther thane —
        Thaire lyfes was tham full gnede.                    *completely lost*
1510  Thurgheowte the oste are that he blane                 *without delay*
    Unto Kynge Charlles als a mane.                        *large group*
        He thankede hym of that dede.           *He [Charles] thanked him [Otuel]*

    Than for sorowe Sir Garcy said, "Allas!"
    To a kynge that highte Sir Abars,
1515        That was armede full clere.
    "Yone renayede thefe my cosyn was;                 *That recreant thief*
    He ledis us here a wikkide pase,                *gave us a wicked turn*
        Bothe with traye and tene!"                    *treason and trouble*
    The kyng ansuerde to Sir Garcy,
1520  "Loo, where Sir Cherlles commes thee by
        And dynges alle doune bydene,                         *completely*
    Now, for Mahomis lufe, that thou thee hye
    With twenty thousande of Turkye
        Till that we redy bene!"

1525  The kyng dide als the emperour bad:
    With those Turkes that he hade
        He stroke into the stourre.                         *struck; battle*
    There were oure folkes full styffely stadde;      *thoroughly challenged*
    Thay hewede one faste als thay were madde,

1530        And brittenede brighte armour.
            The Duke Naymes stede was slayne,
            And hymselfe in the felde tan —
                    That boughte thay sythen full sourre.          *They paid for that later quite bitterly*
            Rowlande, gude of blode and bone,
1535    And Sir Otuell hase thre kynges slone,
                    And reschewsede hym with honoour.                              *rescued*

            Than was there no nother crye,
            Bot thik-folde gane the Sarazenes dy,
                    And grysely gane thay grone.
1540    A sory man was Sir Garcy,
            And alle the Sarazenes that hoved hym by —
                    Thaire herttis was fro tham tone!
            Oggere Daunays laye in presoun,
            And of that noyse he herde the soun;
1545            A heghte men kepede hym one.                    *haughty; guarded him*
            Bot prevaly he made hym boun;                              *readied himself*
            With an astell schide he slewe tham doun;              *piece of firewood*
                    Hys wardens thus hath he slayne.

            He armede hymselfe iche a thwnge,                          *at each point*
1550    And to a stabill gan he gange                                       *went*
                    And hent a noble stede.
            The horse was styffe, thuoghe, and strange,       *sturdy, tough; strong*
            He caughte a spere, was large and lange,                       *took*
                    And leppe up better spede.                            *at great speed*
1555    He kayres forthe owte of the cité,                                    *goes*
            "Nowe hafes alle gude daye!" says he,
                    And to his felawes thus he yede.                          *went*
            And gladdere men there myghte none bee
            Ne thay were when thay Sir Oggere Daynnes see,       *As they were*
1560            That doghety was of dede.

            Now Oggere Daynas bygynnes to fighte,
            And to hew doun many ane heythen knyghte,
                    And brittyne blode and bone.
            Kynge and duke to the dede he dighte;
1565    The emperour tooke hym to the flighte —                        *[Garcy]*
                    To the toun he wolde hafe gone.
fol. 94r  Sir Otuell stroke his stede Floryne
            With two sporres of golde full fyne,
                    And belyfe he to hym come.
1570    "Nay, Sir!" he sayde, "Be Sayne Drightyne,                   *Holy Lord*
            Thou schall noghte to the toun to dyne,                          *dine*
                    Bot here thee moste be tone!"                               *taken*

Sir Otuell hase there tane the emperour;
That lorde hath loste there his honour;
1575       To Charlles he hathe hym sent.
Knyghtis streghte in ilke a stourre            *at once in every battle*
Token up cité, toun, and toure;                *Captured*
      The Sarazenes are alle schent.             *overcome*
When thay had wroghte one swilken wyse,     *conquered in such a way*
1580  Home thay wente than to Pariche,              *Paris*
      Full wightly one thaire waye;            *boldly*
And Charlles lovede God of this enpryce,     *praised; achievement*
And Sir Otuell that worthy es,
      Now weddede he Belesent.

1585  And than thay helde a mangery              *feast*
With alle the noble chevalry
      That semely was to see.
Thay made hym lorde of Lubardy            *Lombardy*
To hafe it alle in his bayly,               *governance*
1590       That contré faire and free.
And thus he duellys and es a pere,
Rowlande felawe and Olyvere,
      A gud Cristyn man was hee.
And Jhesus Criste that boghte us dere,
1595  Brynge us to Thi blisses sere.            *many*
      Amen, par charité.

*Charlles*      ⎡ *Here endes the romance*
           ⎣ *Of Duk Rowland and Sir Otuell of Spayne.*
              *Explycit Sir Otuell*

# EXPLANATORY NOTES TO
 DUKE ROLAND AND SIR OTUEL OF SPAIN

**ABBREVIATIONS**: ***DR***: *Duke Roland and Sir Otuel of Spain*; ***MED***: *Middle English Dictionary*; ***OED***: *Oxford English Dictionary*; ***OK***: *Otuel a Knight*; ***OR***: *Otuel and Roland*; ***Otinel***: Anglo-Norman *Otinel*; ***RV***: *Roland and Vernagu*; **Whiting**: Whiting, *Proverbs, Sentences, and Proverbial Phrases*.

| | |
|---|---|
| Incipit | *The Romance . . . . Of Cherlles of Fraunce.* The incipit, which can be attributed to the scribe Robert Thornton, takes care to specify the genre: *DR* is a romance of Charlemagne, that is, it belongs to the Matter of France. |
| 13 | *le Roy Pepyn.* Son of Charles Martel and father of Charlemagne, Pepin le Bref (Pepin the Short; c. 714–68), was the first of the Carolingian kings, ruling from 751 to 768. Like Charlemagne, he spent much of his life in military campaigns to consolidate, expand, and defend his realm. |
| 16 | *dusperes.* "Twelve peers." According to legend, Charlemagne recognized twelve knights — his *dussepers* — as his greatest, noblest warriors. |
| 39 | *Pariche.* The poet identifies Paris as the location of Charlemagne's court. The other Otuel romances also set this scene in or near Paris. In *Otinel*, Charlemagne holds court in Paris, having come from Clermont-Ferrand (line 18). In *OK*, Charlemagne appears to arrive from Saint-Denis to hold court in Paris (lines 57–58). In *OR*, Charlemagne appears to dwell in Paris and hold court in Saint-Denis (lines 50–51). These settings are historically inaccurate. The Roman town of Lutetia Parisiorum did not develop into the administrative center of France until the eleventh and twelfth centuries. Hugh Capet, count of Paris and duke of the Franks, was elected king of the Franks in 987, and subsequent Capetian kings expanded the city's size and influence. During the Carolingian age, Aix-la-Chapelle, also called Aachen, was where Charlemagne lived and ruled. |
| 49–54 | *Bot now . . . . helpe ne wore.* Compare *Otinel*, lines 24–26. |
| 71–90 | *Sayd . . . . ay full bowun.* Compare *Otinel*, lines 33–44. |
| 80 | *white berde large and lange.* The reference here is to Charlemagne's iconic white beardedness. In *Otinel*, lines 36–37, Charlemagne has a "fluri gernun" (white moustache) and "grant barbe" (great beard). See also *RV*, line 664 ("hore bard"); and *OR*, line 71 ("hore berde"). |
| 82 | *floreschede thonwange.* "profusely bearded cheeks." See *MED florishen* (v.), sense 2, and *thun-wonge* (n.), sense b. The primary meaning of *thun-wonge* is "temple" |

249

(sense a, where this line is cited), but the secondary meaning, "cheeks," is more likely because the reference here is to Charlemagne's beard.

94–168     *He saide . . . . he schere*. Compare the *Otinel*, lines 59–99.

130        *Corsu*. Corsouse is Otuel's named sword. In *Otinel*, it is called Curçuse; in *OR*, it is Cursins; and in *OK*, it is Corsouse. See the explanatory note to *OR*, line 106.

134        *the playnes of Lubardy*. Lombardy, as region in north Italy, figures prominently in many of the Otuel-cycle romances. Medieval Lombardy bordered on France. In *The Siege of Milan*, the central conflict between Saracens and Christians is over the city of Milan and the surrounding Lombard region. In *Otinel*, *OK*, *OR*, and *DR*, the Saracen Emperor Garcy has conquered many key Christian cities and made Lombardy his command center.

149        *neffes*. "fists." This word, of Old Norse origin, is a mark of *DR*'s Northern dialect. See *MED neve* (n.2), "the clenched hand, fist." Robert Thornton, the scribe of *DR*, was from Yorkshire. On Northern words, see also the notes to lines 967, 1032, and 1418 below.

166        *breme as bare*. "as fierce as a boar." Proverbial. See *MED breme* (adj.), sense 3b(a), which notes the ambiguity of "bare": does it designate a boar or a bear? To judge by Thornton's Northern dialect and his later spellings of the word ("bore"), the named animal is a boar. See also lines 802, 1237, and 1396.

172–74     *rollede his eghne . . . . browes one hye*. In Middle English romances, eye-rolling and dramatic facial expressions are behaviors that distinguish Saracens from Christians. On this detail, Phillipa Hardman comments, "The comparison with a wild lion is of course a commonplace figure for fierce martial prowess, but the details of Otuell's facial gestures are interesting. He seems to be contorting his face into an image of terrifying hostility, and by exaggeratedly raising his brows, gives even greater prominence to the strange motion of his eyes, rolling up and down in his head . . . . Roland does nothing comparable, nor do any of the other French knights, nor does Otuell himself once he is converted . . . . This detail, then, may express something of Otuell's bloodthirsty fierceness as champion of Mahoun, overlaid with the disturbing appearance of real madness. Rolling eyes are clearly cause for alarm and may signal specifically alien hostility" ("Dear Enemies," pp. 69–70). Emily Lavin Leverett adds that Otuel's emotive response is used to distinguish between the Saracen and the French Christians of Charlemagne's court: "the bestial nature displayed by Otuel is a mark of his excess; in this case, his inability to control his emotions. Though he professes to know and understand chivalry, his excess emotion spills out after he is forced to defend himself and contained violence rapidly shifts to uncontained savagery" ("Holy Bloodshed," p. 154). To "ferd als a . . . lyoung" is proverbial. See Whiting L344. On Otuel's eye-rolling, see also line 424.

184        *als mot I thee*. Proverbial. See *MED thriven* (v.), sense 1c. See also lines 641, 793, and the second-person variant at 1321 ("als mote thou thee").

210        *Boty*. An unidentifiable place in Emperor Garcy's Saracen empire. Perhaps the name is intended to evoke Buthrotum (modern day Butrint, Albania), a

Mediterranean site known to readers of Virgil's *Aeneid*, 3.375–79 (trans. Mandelbaum).

213–16    *Fermorye . . . . Fermorye*. There is no identifiable location to which this place-name refers, but the other cities listed in this passage suggest that it is likely an actual city-name that the audience might recognize. For the second reference (line 216), the manuscript reads "Fermonye" (here emended).

222    *noghte worthe ane aye*. Proverbial. See Whiting A25.

232–46    *House and londe . . . . life to lede*. Compare *Otinel*, lines 130–36.

240    *landes of Scamonye*. There is no known place named "Scamonye."

259    *smothirly*. "menacingly." This unusual word is not attested elsewhere; see *MED smotherli* (adv.).

274–75    *Bitwix two watirs . . . . cité hight Attaylé*. Garcy's city in Lombardy is called Atelie in *Otinel*, and Utaly in *OR*. As discussed in the notes to lines 659 and 742–43 below, the city being referenced is most likely Pavia. Compare *Otinel*, lines 165–67.

283–88    *Lete Duke Naymes . . . . als he were*. In his taunt, Otuel asserts that Naimes should be left behind to protect Paris, implying that *dussepere* is too old and feeble to engage in combat. In regards to the idea that no scavenger birds of war will come to Paris, compare Otinel's taunt in *Otinel*, lines 173–76.

313–18    *Sir Vernague . . . . myghte and mayne*. Compare *Otinel*, lines 204–09.

329    *Saynte-Thomers*. Saint-Omer is a place in northern France named for Saint Audomarus (Omer), a seventh-century bishop and founder of the monastery alluded to here. This detail is borrowed from the French source. See *Otinel*, line 226, and compare *OR*, line 239.

334    *Droundale*. Durendal is the name of Roland's famous sword. In Rocamadour, France, one may see a chapel with a sword embedded in its outside wall. By local legend, this sword is Durendal. De Veyrières notes the claim (found in l'abbé Cheval's 1862 guidebook, *Guide du Pèlerin à Roc-Amadour*) that the real Durendal was stolen in 1183 when Henry II pillaged the chapel, and he includes a drawing of the current sword ("L'Épée de Roland," pp. 139–41). On other named swords, see the notes to lines 130, 847, 914, and 1196.

361    *spende*. "girded." See *MED spennen*, sense b, where this line is cited.

374    *rekreyande thou hym brynge*. "cause him to admit defeat or surrender." See *MED recreaunt* (adj.), senses a and b.

397–98    *And scho calles . . . . Roselet of Barelle*. Compare *Otinel*, lines 327–28.

424    *rollede his eghne up and dowun*. See the note to lines 172–74 above.

447    *In the name of Marie of heven*. According to Hardman, the characters of *DR* exhibit a heightened reliance on Mary, a feature also seen in the other Thornton Otuel-cycle romance *Siege of Milan* ("The *Sege of Melayne*," p. 85).

456        *sex and seven.* Proverbial. See Whiting S359, and *MED six* (num.), sense 2d: "bix six or seven" meaning "in large quantities in great numbers."

470        *fers als any lyoun.* Proverbial. See Whiting L311.

474        *loughe.* "humbled, brought low, made to bow." The phrase is appositional to "made hym bowen" in line 472. See *MED louen* (v.1), senses 3a and 4a. Otuel is eagerly (and prematurely) feeling victorious because he has cowed Roland.

476        *strade.* The *MED* defines this word as either "? a skirmish" or "? a pathway in a battlefield"; see *MED, strade* (n.), where this instance is cited as the only appearance of the word.

518–40   *Sarazene . . . . als thou were.* Compare *Otinel,* lines 454–69.

578–79   *A dofe . . . . lightes.* A white dove is a traditional sign for the presence of the Holy Spirit (one of the Three Persons of the Trinity), which is associated with God's grace (see Luke 3:22). Compare *Otinel,* lines 516–18; *OK,* lines 585–88; and *OR,* lines 568–73.

607        *Bischope Turpyn.* Archbishop Turpin is an important military and ecclesiastical character in the *Song of Roland* and the Middle English Charlemagne romances. In *Otinel, RV,* and the three Otuel romances, Turpin's role is limited to episcopal duties: performing Mass and baptizing converts. In the fifth Otuel-cycle romance, *The Siege of Milan,* Turpin plays a central role.

620        *rede als rose.* Proverbial. See Whiting R199.

659        *the cité of Attaly.* Ataly is most likely Pavia, the capital of Lombardy in the seventh and eighth centuries, which is located on the Ticino River three miles upstream from its confluence with the Po River. The Ticino, which the *DR* poet names the Soltane (lines 746 and 756), rises in the Swiss Alps, descends into Italy through Lake Maggiore, and is the largest left-bank tributary of the Po. It is over the Soltane/Ticino that Charlemagne builds the bridge over which the French will pass to attack the city (see the note to lines 754–56 below).

702        *Mount Marteres.* Montmartre is a hill in what is now the northern part of Paris, and the location where Saint Denis was purportedly beheaded by Romans. According to legend, after he was decapitated, he picked up his head and carried it some distance away before he died on the site thereafter known as Saint-Denis. For more, see "St. Denis" in the *Catholic Encyclopedia.*

703–17   *The Almaynes . . . . a stalworthe stede.* Compare *Otinel,* lines 636–42.

704        *for the nanes.* The term *for the nonce* means approximately "for the moment" or "for the occasion," though it is primarily used as a meaningless metrical filler. See *MED nones* (n.1) and *none* (n.).

724        *Saynt Denys.* See the note to line 702 above.

733–38   *Olyvere his stede . . . . thousande bolde barouns.* The detail of Oliver accompanying Belesent is unique to *DR.* It is possible that "Olyvere" at lines 727 and 733, are errors for "Otuel." The poet borrows the idea of Belesent riding on a mule from *Otinel*. See *Otinel*, lines 655–60, and compare *OR*, lines 679–81.

739    *Bretayne*. "Brittany." In the source *Otinel*, line 661, the French army passes through Burgundy ("Burgonie"); *OR*, line 685, follows *Otinel*: "Burgoyne." The *DR* substitution of Brittany for Burgundy indicates an English poet's (or scribe's) confused geography. Another reference to Brittany appears at line 1431.

740    *Mandely*. An unidentified region corresponding to the place-names Mungiu and Morie in *Otinel*, lines 662–63.

742–56    *Thay schipped . . . . Soltane dighte*. These lines describe the final stages of Charlemagne's journey to his encampment outside Ataly. "Vertely" refers to Vercelli, a city on the Po River around forty-five miles west-northwest of Pavia, in Piedmont on the border with Lombardy. An ancient site, settled around 600 BCE, Vercelli became an independent commune in 1120, and in the years that followed was a member of the first and second Lombard leagues. The city housed the University of Pavia from 1228 to 1372. In *DR*, the name given to the river near Ataly is the Soltane (in *OR*, it is the Coyne; in *Otinel*, it is the Ton). This river is most likely the Ticino, on the left bank of which lies Pavia (Ataly). The historical Charlemagne laid siege to Pavia, then the Lombard capital, in the winter and spring of 773–74, after which he had himself crowned king of Pavia and its surrounding territories. The "mountayne" (line 745) is likely borrowed from *Otinel*, lines 664–68 (see explanatory note). Pavia itself is situated on a small hill, but the plains surrounding Pavia are quite flat, with no significant heights between the Monferrat Hills and Pavia. The "medowe" (line 747) where the French army encamps is across the Soltane/Ticino from Pavia. See the note to line 659 above.

754–56    *Therefore . . . . Soltane dighte*. The bridge that Charlemagne has built over the Soltane/Ticino helps to locate Pavia as the site of Ataly. When Roland, Oliver, and Ogier cross the bridge to seek Saracens, they meet Clarel and his companions "a mile" from Ataly. See the note to line 659 above, and compare *OK*, lines 697–706; *OR*, lines 695–701; and *Otinel*, lines 674–80.

784–92    *Kynge Balsame . . . . Kyng Claryell*. Compare *Otinel*, lines 696–703.

802    *breme als bare*. See the note to line 166 above.

815    *ne vaylede noghte a pere*. Proverbial. See Whiting P79.

846    *lofesome under lyne*. Proverbial. See *MED lofsom* (adj.), sense 1a.

847    *Melle*. Melle is the name of Clarel's sword; elsewhere it is called "Modlee" (line 1207). Compare *OR*, line 1240, where it is named "Melyn"; and *Otinel*, line 807, where it is named "Mellee."

851    *A noble cheke here wonn*. "a noble victory here won." See *MED chek* (interj. and n.), sense 3, "feat, enterprise," where this line is cited.

866–70    *Sayd . . . . we noghte slo*. Compare *Otinel*, lines 848–50.

881    *Mountjoy!* The war cry of the French. See *MED mon-joie* (n.), and compare *Otinel*, line 860.

914    *Haunkclere*. This is the name of Oliver's sword. Like Roland's Durendal and Otuel's Corsouse, the mightiest warriors' swords of *chansons de geste* often acquire names that associate them with their owners. Oliver's sword is also named at *OR*, line 904 ("Haunchecler"), and in *Otinel*, line 873 ("Halteclere"). On other named swords, see the notes to lines 130, 847, and 1196.

920    *Kyng Alphamanye*. King Alphamanye, who dies in this scene, is a different person from the King Alphané who leads "twenty thowsande of Barbarye / That wele couthe wapyns bere" (lines 1448–49).

967    *white als fame*. Proverbial. See Whiting F361. The phrase is a compliment of beauty, like "white as snow." See *MED whit* (adj.), sense 6a(b), and *fom* (n.), sense 4. The spelling of "foam" with an *a* is Northern, and the phrase "a dogheter, white als fame" appears in another Thornton romance: *Sir Eglamour*, line 26 (ed. Cook and Schleich, p. 14).

996    *lyghte als lefe one tree*. Proverbial. See Whiting L140.

1009–35    *Otuell . . . . hir awenn fyndynge*. Compare *Otinel*, lines 1000–17.

1032    *thethey*. "Headstrong, irritable." The *OED* specifies that this word is chiefly Scottish and Northern. The only instances of it cited in the *MED* are this line and one in a Townley play (c. 1500); see *MED tethi* (adj.). On Northern words and spellings in *DR*, see also the notes to lines 149, 967, and 1418.

1043–54    *And sayde . . . . by full dere*. Compare *Otinel*, lines 1043–47.

1052    *grete gramaungere*. "foolish enterprise." This line contains the only attestation of the French-derived word (from *grant mangier*). See *MED gramaunger* (n.), "a great meal; *fig.* an overambitious enterprise." Otuel is calling Roland and Oliver foolish for fighting a Saracen army by themselves. The poet's word "gramaungere" may reflect the joke about eating the pagans found in the source-text *Otinel*, line 1044, which reads: "Quidez vus sul les paiens tuz mangier?" ("Do you think that you alone can eat all the pagans?").

1135–64    *Then comes . . . . holde his daye*. Compare *Otinel*, lines 1195–1233.

1157    *noghte worthe a pye*. Proverbial. See Whiting P177.

1174    *groped hym wele*. "examined him well," i.e., probed and tended his wounds, like a physician. See *MED gropen* (v.), sense 5c. The scene of Belesent touching Otuel has an amorous suggestion as well (*gropen*, sense 1d). See the discussion in the *OR* Introduction, p. 118.

1196    *Galyene*. Though this master swordsmith cannot be identified, some medieval armorers were renowned. Dirk H. Breiding of the Department of Arms and Armor, The Metropolitan Museum of Art, New York, writes: "The earliest references to both armorers and famous regions of manufacture occur in myths and legend, such as the famed Hephaistos, armorer to the Greek gods, or Wieland, the smith from Germanic mythology. During the eighth century,

Ingelri and Ulfberht, two blade smiths (or their workshops) from the Rhine region, apparently produced such high-quality sword blades that their names are found inscribed on swords produced over the following two centuries. Indeed, makers of arms and armor appear to have been among the first craftsmen to 'sign' their works, and some of the later court armorers were as highly esteemed as any of the celebrated court painters" ("Famous Makers of Arms and Armor").

1207      *Modlee*. See the note to line 847 above.

1214      *mawmettis*. "idols." Muslims, as Saracens, are inaccurately depicted as worshiping idols. On Western Christian beliefs about Muslim idolatry, see Strickland, *Saracens, Demons, and Jews*, pp. 166–69; and the discussion in the General Introduction, p. 16.

1231–69      *Than comes . . . . deme and dighte*. Compare *Otinel*, lines 1311–52.

1237      *breme als bore*. See the note to line 166 above.

1254      *mellyde hare*. "gray hair." See *MED medlen* (v.), sense 1b(c), which cites this line.

1318–26      *Cursu thurghe . . . . nott hir wyte*. Compare *Otinel*, lines 1445–56.

1341      *gayne*. "quickly." See *MED gein* (adv.), sense a.

1396      *breme als any bore*. See the note to line 166 above.

1418      *slakkes*. "valleys." For this word of Scandinavian origin, see *MED slak* (n.2.). Here the word is conjoined with an Anglo-Saxon-derived word — *MED slade* (n.), "slope" — to form a Northern-flavored alliterative phrase ("on valley and on hill"). On Northern words or spellings, see also the notes to lines 149, 967, and 1032 above.

1445      *Alphané*. King Alphané of Barbarye, father of Duke Balamé, is a different person from the King Alphamanye who knocks Oliver from his horse before Roland kills him (lines 919–27).

1510      *are that he blane*. Taken literally, this phrase means "before one might stop." See *MED blinnen* (v.), sense 1f, "without stopping or delay, right away," where this line is cited.

1543–60      *Oggere Daunays . . . . of dede*. Ogier the Dane is one of Charlemagne's *dussepers* in the *chanson de geste* tradition; see the discussion in the General Introduction, p. 5n13. In the penultimate scene of the romance, just before the capture of King Garcy, Ogier the Dane breaks out of prison and rejoins his comrades. In this version, Ogier slays his guards with a piece of firewood, puts on his armor, finds his horse and a spear, and gallops off. For alternate scenarios, see *Otinel*, lines 1836–69; *OK*, lines 1629–78; and *OR*, lines 1616–36.

1565–75      *The emperour . . . . hathe hym sent*. Compare *Otinel*, lines 1873–1901.

1580–96      *Home thay wente . . . . par charité*. On the different endings among the French and Middle English accounts of Otuel/Otinel, see the explanatory note to *Otinel*, lines 1899–1904.

Explicit  *Here endes . . . . Sir Otuell*. The first two lines of the explicit are inclusively bracketed on the left, with the word "Charlles" written outside the bracket. In both the explicit and the incipit, therefore, Thornton signals that *DR* is a Charlemagne romance. It is notable that Thornton elsewhere copies more legends of the Nine Worthies: the prose *Life of Alexander*, the alliterative *Morte Arthure*, and the *Parlement of the Thre Ages*. See Fein, "The Contents of Robert Thornton's Manuscripts," pp. 16–19. A reproduction of fol. 94r, showing the explicit, may be viewed in Thompson, *Robert Thornton and the London Thornton Manuscript*, plate 16.

#  TEXTUAL NOTES TO DUKE ROLAND AND SIR OTUEL OF SPAIN

**ABBREVIATIONS: H**: *The Romance of Duke Rowlande and of Sir Ottuell of Spayne*, ed. Herrtage, in *The English Charlemagne Romances. Part II*, pp. 55–104; **MS**: London, British Library Additional MS 31042 (London Thornton), fols. 82r–94r.

| | |
|---|---|
| 88 | *gentill*. So MS. H: *gentille*. |
| 94 | *flawmande*. So MS. H: *flawmandre*. |
| 121 | *spekes*. So MS. H: *spekis*. |
| 165 | *bakwarde*. So MS. H: *backwarde*. |
| 175 | *hir*. So MS. H: *his*. |
| 201 | *al*. So MS. H: *all*. |
| 211 | *fre*. MS: *nere* was initially written and then canceled. |
| 216 | *Fermorye*. MS, H: *Fermonye*. |
| 234 | *Normaundy*. So MS. H: *Normandy*. |
| 244 | *kyng*. So MS. H: *kynges*. |
| 263 | *chevalrye*. So MS. H: *cheualry*. |
| 281 | *kon*. So H. MS: *couthe* was initially written and then canceled. |
| 307 | *so*. So MS. H: *oo*. |
| 314 | *myn eme I*. So H. MS: *myn I*. |
| 349 | *Elleven*. So MS. H: *Eleuen*. |
| 361 | *sporres*. So MS. H: *sperres*. |
| 372 | *Hys*. So H. MS: Scribe initially copied *hes*, then canceled the *e* and wrote a *y* on top of the canceled character. |
| 383 | *thies*. So MS. H: *these*. |
| 463 | *Rawlande*. So MS. H: *Rowlande*. |
| 502 | *dynttys*. So MS. H: *dynttis*. |
| 523 | *thou*. So MS. H: *thow*. |
| 559 | *Ane*. So MS. H: *And*. |
| 597 | *yit*. So MS.  H: *ʒitt*. |
| 618 | *was*. So MS. H: *nas*. |
| 632 | *bayllye*. So MS. H: *Bayllyee*; Herrtage mistook the curl of the bracket for an additional *e*. |
| 633 | *contreth*. So MS. H: *contrey*. |
| 641 | *scho*. So MS. H: *sche*. |
| 644 | *Now that I hafe chosen*. MS: *now* inserted in the left margin. H: *that I hafe now chosen*. |
| 657 | *one*. So MS. H: *on*. |
| 661 | *The king said*. So H. MS: *The said*. |
| 662 | *Now hafe*. So MS. H: *Now ʒe hafe*. |

730      *yode*. So MS. H: *ȝede*.

731      *one*. So MS. H: *on*.

736      *maid*. MS: word is obscured. H: *mayd*.

737      *were arrayed*. MS: end of word *were* and following word are obscured. H: *were arrayd*.

756      *Soltane*. MS, H: *Roltane*.

796      *me by*. MS: Scribe initially copied by *me* and canceled it, then copied *me by*.

798      *dynttes*. So MS. H: *dynttis*.

800      *sporres*. So MS. H: *spores*.

803      *fare*. MS: word obscured. H: *faire*.

813      *egerly*. So MS. H: *werly*.

832      *smyttys*. So MS. H: *Smyttis*.

862      *semys*. So MS. H: *semes*.

866      *getyn*. So MS. H: *gettyn*.

899      *What schall saye*. So MS. H: *what we schall*.

903      *wode*. So MS. H: *wede*.

925      *than*. So MS. H: *þan*.

948      *yoo*. So MS. H: *þoo*.

954      *He₁*. So MS. H: *his*.

967      *saide*. So MS. H: *sayde*.

982      *said*. So MS. H: *sayd*.

1008     *now*. So MS. H: *nowe*.

1043     *ye*. So H. MS: Scribe initially copies, then cancels, *he*, then replaces canceled word with *ȝe*.

1091     *one*. So MS. H: *on*.

1113     *be*. So MS. H: *bene*.

1114     *blode*. So H. MS: *bolde*.

1126     *Gauntere*. So MS. H: *Grauntere*.

1163     *hafe*. So MS. H: *hase*.

1168     *to his*. So H. MS: *to his to his*.

1179     *ware*. So MS. H: *were*.

1218     *Alle*. So MS. H: *All*.

1220     *everichonee*. So MS. H: *euerichone*.

1230     *faire*. So MS. H: *fayre*.

1231     *Kynge*. So MS. H: *kyng*.

1237     *yitt*. So MS. H: *ȝit*.

1239     *on*. MS, H: *men*.

1256     *those*. So MS. H: *þofe*.

1268     *one*. So MS. H: *on*.

1287     *yowe*. So MS. H: *ȝow*.

1297     *Than bothe thies kene knyghttis there*. So H. MS: line is copied twice — once at the bottom of fol. 91v and once at the top of 92r, with spelling *knyghttes* on 91v and *knyghtis* on 92r.

1305     *handis*. So MS. H: *handes*.

1326     *may*. So MS. H: *maye*.

1385     *one*. So MS. H: *on*.

1413     *werun*. So MS. H: *werynn*.

| | |
|---|---|
| 1428 | *nowe*. So MS. H: *Newe*. |
| 1429 | *Elys*. So H. MS: *Elys Elye*. |
| 1453 | *stalworthe were*. So MS. H: *staleworthe ware*. |
| 1481 | *And lovede God*. So H. MS: *god* inserted in left margin. |
| 1483 | *hoved by*. So H. MS: three characters obscured: the *ed* in *hoved* and the *b* in *by*. |
| 1491 | *squyeres*. So MS. H: *Sqwyere*. |
| 1502 | *saulles*. So MS. H: *Saules*. |
| 1507 | *to the banere*. So H. MS: *þe* inserted in margin to left of line. |
| 1522 | *Mahomis*. So MS. H: *Mahonns*. |
| 1539 | *thay*. So MS. H: *þey*. |
| 1549 | *thwnge*. So MS. H: *thynge*. |
| Explicit | *Charlles*. MS: *Charles* is written in the margin to the left of the first two lines of the explicit and linked to them with a bracket. |

# THE ANGLO-NORMAN *OTINEL* INTRODUCTION

*Otinel*, a late-twelfth- or early-thirteenth-century *chanson de geste*, recounts the deeds of its titular hero, a young Saracen knight who converts to Christianity, fights nobly against the pagans (including some relatives), and marries Charlemagne's daughter. It is the main source for the three Middle English romances of Otuel edited in this volume, its plot supplying in basic outline the narratives they convey. The *chanson* begins as Otinel arrives at Charlemagne's court in Paris as a messenger from the pagan king Garsie, who has just conquered Rome and now demands Charles' fealty. Otinel himself is eager to encounter Roland, who has killed his uncle. After much boasting and exchange of insults, the two agree to engage in a single combat, in preparation for which Otinel is armed by Charles' beautiful daughter, Belisant. The two young fighters exchange a succession of ferocious blows, punctuated by sarcastic conversation, which leave their horses dead, their armor shredded, their heads dazed, and their flesh somehow unpierced. As the battle progresses, Roland appears to be in danger, but, in response to Charles' worried prayer, the Holy Spirit descends upon Otinel in the form of a dove. The astonished knight immediately decides to abandon paganism, accept Mary as his protector, and undergo baptism. He also accepts the promise of marriage to Belisant once he has defeated Garsie. Following the baptismal ceremony, Charles consults with his barons and makes plans to travel to the city of Atelie (Pavia) to confront Garsie once the winter has passed and he can gather his troops.

Spring having arrived, Charles assembles his army and leads it to Atelie. While the troops are resting up from their journey, Roland and his companions Oliver and Ogier sneak off in search of the enemy. They defeat four kings in quick jousts, killing three and capturing the handsome Clarel, the Saracens' foremost combatant and a cousin of Otinel. As they move to lead Clarel to Charles, the three Frenchmen find that a force of fifteen hundred Saracens blocks their return. They release Clarel, so as not to be distracted, and then kill numerous Saracens. Ogier is separated and grievously wounded, but he is saved when Clarel intervenes, accepts his surrender, and sends the captive back to town to be watched over by Alfamie, Clarel's sweetheart. Roland and Oliver manage to fight their way through the army, and they meet up with Otinel as they flee toward Charles' encampment. A battle ensues between the two armies, in which each of the many French barons has a shining moment. As night falls, the beleaguered Saracens flee back to their city. The next morning begins with Otinel fighting in single combat against Clarel, who cannot convince him to return to belief in Mahomet. Otinel kills Clarel, and the pagans then make a short-lived last stand. At about the same time, Ogier escapes and rejoins his fellow barons. His army destroyed, Garsie seeks to slip away, but Otinel and Roland quickly capture him. The *chanson* ends as they present Garsie to Charles, who has the captive led to Paris.

The base text for this edition and translation is Cologny, Fondation Martin Bodmer Cod. Bodmer 168, fols. 211ra–22rb, which supplies the best and most complete extant version of *Otinel*.[1] Dated to the late thirteenth century, this previously unedited Anglo-Norman text contains 1907 irregular decasyllabic lines in assonanced *laisses* of varying length. A 2133-line fourteenth-century continental French version of the poem survives in a less authoritative manuscript: Vatican City, Biblioteca Apostolica Vaticana Reg. lat. 1616. The Vatican City text was edited in 1859 by François Guessard and Henri Michelant, who incorporated sections from Cologny to fill gaps in the manuscript's narrative.[2] Two fragments are also available in Paris, BnF nouv. acq. fr. 5094 and Paris, BnF MS. f. fr. 25408. Remnants of frescoes in Treviso and Sesto al Reghena provide evidence that some version of the Otinel story was popular in northern Italy in the fourteenth century. The Treviso fresco is of particular importance as it "seems to be the only fresco representing Roland still surviving in Europe."[3] It represents Otinel as a Saracen giant who is black, with scenes displaying his fight with Roland and his subsequent baptism. The Sesto al Reghena remnant does not depict Otinel, but is identifiable by a scene displaying "BELIXANT" and Charlemagne sitting together on a throne.[4]

The popularity of the story of Roland's death at Roncevaux recounted in the *Song of Roland* was such that later French poets, whether simply appreciating the Roland characters or recognizing a public demand, devised pre-histories for Roland, Oliver, and other popular heroes. Among the best of these poems are *Le Voyage de Charlemagne a Jérusalem et a Constantinople*, an early-twelfth-century parodic narrative in assonanced *laisses* that expands humorously on Roland's pride, Oliver's love life (along with his wisdom), and William of Orange's prodigious strength; and the *Chanson de Aspremont*, which recounts how a youthful Roland acquired his horn, horse, and shield.[5] *Otinel* falls into this category, as do, by extension, the poem's various English adaptations: the poets present *Roland* characters warring happily in Italy at a time prior to their heroic deaths in Spain, and they direct much of their attention to a new character, Otinel/Otuel, a Saracen convert to Christianity who rivals Roland in his ferocity.[6] There is no evidence that authors of the Otinel poems knew the assonanced text of the *Song of Roland* that is found in Oxford, Bodleian Library MS Digby 23 (many versions of the Roncevaux story may be presumed to have been in circulation), but it hardly matters: the poets knew enough of the basic story to draw upon the protagonists' surface characteristics without worrying about the subtleties of Roland's bravery, Oliver's good sense, or Charlemagne's age and anxieties. And, of course, they all

---

[1] The Bodmer manuscript may be viewed by digital facsimile at https://www.e-codices.unifr.ch/en/fmb/cb-0168. Its other contents are *Waldef* and *Gui de Warewic*, two Anglo-Norman romances of lineage. For background on *Otinel* (including information about the incomplete OF version edited by Guessard and Michelant in 1859), see Dean and Boulton, *Anglo-Norman Literature: A Guide*, pp. 53–54 (no. 78).

[2] Problems in the texts of the French-language manuscripts are discussed by Hardman and Ailes, *Legend of Charlemagne*, pp. 353–66.

[3] Boscolo, "Two Otinel Frescoes," p. 202.

[4] Boscolo, "Two Otinel Frescoes," p. 209.

[5] *Le Voyage de Charlemagne*, ed. Aebischer. The poem was first edited by Michel (*Charlemagne: An Anglo-Norman Poem*) in 1836, and has been edited and translated by Picherit (*Journey of Charlemagne to Jerusalem*) in 1984.

[6] The only monograph on the *Otinel* story is Aebischer, *Études sur Otinel*.

knew, with complacent satisfaction (less so from the perspective of modern readers), that pagans are bad, Christians are good, and violence is admirable.[7]

Among the qualities that distinguish the *Otinel* poet's voice is mordant humor, especially common when a French warrior derides an opponent. Otinel's taunting of Clarel after returning a powerful blow is typical of the poet's scenes of witty repartee:

> La jowe enprent od trestut le jower,
> Si que les denz en vit blanchoier.
> "Par Deu," dit Otes, "issi deit l'um chanchier
> Colp pur colee, maille pur dener!
> Bien semblez humme qui voillie eschiner.
> Ne t'avera mes Alfamie mester —
> James pucele ne te voldra baiser!" (lines 1450–56)

> [He slices off the cheek with the whole jawbone,
> So that one might see his white teeth.
> "By God," says Otinel, "thus may one exchange
> A blow for a tap, a farthing for a denier!
> You resemble a man who'd want to grin;
> Alfamie won't have any more business with you —
> Never will a girl want to kiss you!"]

In a similar vein, when Roland's warhorse has been killed, Oliver wastes no time regretting the dead steed but gleefully supplies Roland with a handsome horse that Ogier has just taken from Clarel: "De part Ogier le vus doins e present — / Meildre est del vostre. Jo qui qu'il valt les cent!" ("On Ogier's behalf, I give and present it to you — / It's better than yours. I think it's worth a hundred!"; lines 803–04). A live horse is surely at least a hundred times better than a dead one!

Also of interest is the bold confidence the poet assigns to noblewomen, both Christian and pagan. When, for example, Charles is impressed by Otinel's endurance while fighting Roland, Belisant grants herself partial credit for his success: "Bon sunt mi garnement" ("My armor is good"; line 397). When an aged emir brings the captured Ogier to Alfamie and tells her that a hundred pagans have just had their heads cut off by three Frenchmen, she blithely commands that he and his companions return to battle and fetch Roland and Oliver. All the disconsolate pagans can reply is "Einz passera estez!" ("It will happen as before!"; line 971). When the Saracen fighters leave, Alfamie quickly turns her attention to Ogier, whom she somehow knows by reputation.

Overall, the general sense one has on reading *Otinel* is of a typical *chanson de geste* that recounts a series of violent jousts and battles, the latter largely presented as single combats. As is normal in *chansons*, the duration of any given clash is a function of the importance of the defeated or winning warrior. Other traditional elements are dialogue comprised mostly of boasts and taunts, extended accounts of mustering troops, brief evocations of the landscape, assertions of the ugliness and wickedness of Saracen warriors (with the occasional

---

[7] On various ways in which the author of the French *Otinel* departs from the *Roland* tradition, see Ailes, "*Otinel*: An Epic in Dialogue." For other treatments of *Otinel*, see also Ailes, "Chivalry and Conversion" and "What's in a Name?"

handsome or noble Saracen noted as a figure of contrast), and setpieces that describe the arming of individual warriors.

We are glad to bring this seven-hundred-year-old song of adventure finally to light, both in its original Anglo-Norman language and in modern English translation. It fittingly accompanies the Middle English romances centered on the Saracen hero Otuel, a warrior who is first a rival and then a comrade-in-arms to the famous Roland. In his own culture, Otinel possesses status (like Roland) as an illustrious nephew (of Emperor Garsie), but he eventually shifts his allegiance to become a French peer and Charlemagne's own son-in-law. The historical valences — both optimistic and deeply prejudiced — to be found in the tale of Otinel/Otuel's confrontational Otherness, and yet final and full assimilation into the community of Western Christendom, should be of no small interest to audiences today.

MANUSCRIPTS:

Cologny, Fondation Martin Bodmer Cod. Bodmer 168, fols. 211r–22r. [1907 lines; Anglo-Norman; dated last third of thirteenth century. The most complete witness, this manuscript contains *Waldef*, *Gui de Warewic*, and *Otinel*. Base text for this edition.]

Paris, Bibliothèque nationale de France MS f. fr. 25408. [A fragment of 4 lines; Anglo-Norman. dated c. 1267.]

Paris, Bibliothèque nationale de France MS nouv. acq. fr. 5094, fols. 7r–8r. [A fragment of 292 lines; Anglo-Norman; dated late twelfth to early thirteenth century.]

Vatican City, Biblioteca Apostolica Vaticana Reg. lat. 1616, fols. 93r–102v, 109r–24v [2133 lines; northeast France; of poor quality. Old French. Copied at Saint-Brieuc in 1317, this manuscript also contains *Fierabras*.]

FACSIMILE:

"Cologny, Fondation Martin Bodmer, Cod. Bodmer 168." e-codices — Virtual Manuscript Library of Switzerland, 2005. Online at https://www.e-codices.unifr.ch/en/fmb/cb-0168/ 211r/0/Sequence-887.

PREVIOUS EDITION:

*Otinel, Chanson de Geste*. Ed. M. M. F. Guessard and H. Michelant. Paris: Maison A. Franck, 1859. Rpt. Nendeln: Kraus Reprint Ltd, 1966. [Based on the Vatican City MS, supplemented with passages from the Cologny MS.]

fol. 211ra Ki volt oir chançun de beau semblant
    Dunt bien sunt fait les vers per consonant,
    Ore laist la noise si se treie avant!
    Dirum la flur de la geste vallant
5   Del fiz Pepin, le noble combatant,
    Des duze pers qui s'entramerent tant
    K'unc ne severent, tresk'a un jor pesant
    Ke Guenes les trai od la salvage gent.
    Un jor mururent vint millier e set cent
10   De cel barnage, dunt Charles ot doel grant.
    Cil jugleor n'en dient tant ne quant;
    Tuit l'ont leissé k'il ne sevent nient
    Li plusur danger e de l'autri chantant —
    Les paroles menues qu'il vont controvant!
15   Mes il ne sevent une le grant desturbement
    K'avint a Charlemaine si subitement.

    Seingnurs, ço fu le jor dunt li innocent sunt
    A Paris en France: Charles de Clermunt
    U tint sa curt plenere; Li duze per i sunt.
20   Mult par est la joie grant que li baruns i funt.
    Un plai ont establi k'en Espanie irunt,
    Sur le rei Marsilie le serement i funt.
    Ço ert aprés averil, quant herbe fresche averunt.
    Einz que finent lur parole, teles noveles orunt
25   Dunt vint mil chevaler de noz franceis murunt,
    Si Dampnedeu n'en pense, qui sustent tut le mund!

    Un Sarazin d'Espanie, qui Otuel a nun —
    Messager Garsie, bien resemble barun —
    Parmi Paris chevalche a corte d'espurun.
30   Quant vient al paleis, si descent al perun,
    Les desgrez monte, si demande Charlun.
    Ogier encontre e Galter e Naimun.
    "Seignur," fait li paen, "kar me mustrez Charlun.
    Messager sui un rei qui nel aime un butun."
35   Premer ja parle Galter, cil de Valun:

All who'd like to hear a beautiful song
With verses well-made and fine-sounding,
Be quiet now and come forward!
We'll tell of the flower of noble deeds
5     By Pepin's son, the noble warrior,
And the twelve peers who loved each other so dearly
That they never parted till the weighty day
When Ganelon betrayed them to the savage people.
In one day there died twenty thousand seven hundred
10    Of the baronage, for which Charles had profound sorrow.
These jongleurs never speak of this story at all;
They all ignore it because they know nothing
Of the hardship, and sing of other things —
Trivial words that they go on composing!
15    But none of them understands the great distress
That came upon Charlemagne so suddenly.

Lords, it occurred on Holy Innocents' Day
At Paris in France. Charles of Clermunt
Held his full court there with the twelve peers.
20    Very great was the barons' rejoicing.
They devised a plan that they'd go to Spain,
Vowing an oath against King Marsile.
It was after April, when the grass is fresh.
Before their talk's done, they shall hear news
25    For which twenty thousand of our French will die,
Unless God attends to it, He who sustains all.

A Saracen from Spain named Otinel —
A messenger from Garsie, noble in bearing —
Rides through Paris at a full gallop.
30    When he arrives at the palace, he dismounts at the stone,
Climbs up the steps, and calls out for Charles.
He encounters Ogier, Gautier, and Naimes.
"Lords," says the pagan, "show Charles to me.
I'm a messenger from a king who doesn't like him."
35    Gautier of Valois speaks first:

"Vei le tu la, u set, a cel fluri gernun,
Celui o la grant barbe a cel veir peliçun.
Ço est Rolland, si nies el vermeil ciclatun,
De l'altre part, veez u siet son compaignun,
40      Le gentil conte qui Oliver a nun.
Ço sunt li duze pier qui lur sunt envirun."
"Mahun," fait li paen, "ore conus jo Charlun.
fol. 211rb Mal feue male flambe li arde le mentun
Ke li fende le piz desk'al talun!"

45      Li Sarazin en vient devant le rei.
"Charles," feit il, "ore entent vers mei.
Messager sui, ço quid, al meillur rei
K'unques feust en la paiene lei.
Ne te salu — k'a dreit faire nel dei —
50      Forfait en es vers Mahumet e vers mei.
Cil te confunde, en la ki lei jo crei,
E tuz ces altres qui sunt envirun tei.
E ton nevu Rollant, que jo ci vei,
Si uncore un jor le truis en turnei,
55      Ke mun destrer puisse acurser vers sei,
De m'espee la quid faire un espei
Parmi le cors — mult ert fort si nel plei!"
Rollant se rit si reguarde le rei.

"Sarazin frere," fet Rollant la losez,
60      "Tu poez bien dire tutes tes volentez —
Ja pur Franceis ne serras atuchez."
"Nun," ço dit Charles, "puiske vus le volez,
De meie part, est il bien afiez
De hui en cest jor desk'a uit jurs passez."
65      Dist Otuel, "De folie parlez!
Ne redut humme qui de mere seit nez
Tant cum averai cest espee a mun leez —
Ço est Curçuse, dunt jo sui adubez.
Nen at mie uncore nef meis passez
70      K'a mil Franceis en ai les chefs colpez."
"U fu ço, frere?" fet Charles li remembrez.
Dit Otinel, "Jo vus dirra assez.
Ore at uit meis, el nefme sui entrez;
Destruite iert Romme, ta vaillante citez,
75      De laquele estes emperere clamez.
Li reis Garsie la prist e sis barnez,
Vint mil hummes tut acunte numbrez;
Hummes que femmes uncore plus assez
I avium mort — n'est un eschapez!
80      E jo i feri tant de m'espee delez

"See him there, where he sits, with the white moustache,
With the great beard and the ermine robe.
That one's his nephew Roland with the crimson silk,
And on the other side look where his companion sits,
40    The noble count named Oliver.
Those around them are the twelve peers."
"By Mahomet," the pagan says, "now I see Charles.
May flames and hellfire burn his chin
So that his chest splits open down to his heels!"

45    The Saracen comes before the King.
"Charles," he says, "now listen to me.
Understand that I'm a messenger from the best king
Who's ever existed under pagan law.
I do not greet you — in truth, I must not —
50    For you're offensive to Mahomet and me.
He whose law I believe in will destroy you
And all who surround you.
And as for your nephew Roland, whom I see here,
Should I ever encounter him in combat,
55    With my steed able to gallop toward him,
I intend to strike a sword stroke
Through his body — he'd be tough not to yield!"
Roland laughs and looks at the King.

"Brother Saracen," says illustrious Roland,
60    "You can say anything you like —
You'll not be touched by a Frenchman."
"No," says Charles, "because you request it,
As far as I'm concerned, he's fully vouchsafed
From now until eight days have passed."
65    Says Otinel, "Nonsense!
I fear no one born of a mother
So long as I have this sword by my side —
It's Corçuse with which I was dubbed.
It's been scarcely nine months since
70    I used it to behead a thousand Frenchmen."
"Where was that, brother?" asks famous Charles.
Says Otinel, "I'll tell you everything.
It was eight months ago, nine when I entered;
Destroyed was Rome, your mighty city,
75    Where you were proclaimed Emperor.
King Garsie captured it with his army,
Twenty thousand men by count;
So many men and then women
Did we kill there — no one escaped!
80    I killed so many with this sword by my side

Ke uit jurs pleners or les poinz enflez."
Dient Franceis, "Mar fustes unques nez!"
Estult de Lengres est en piez levez,
Tint un bastun que devant fu quarrez.

fol. 211va Ja le ferist, ço savum nus assez,
86 Meis li nies Charles en encontre alez,
Se li a dit, "Sire Estult, reposez.
Pur meie amur, si de rien m'amez,
Kar li paen est de mei afiez,
90 Laissez lui dire tutes ses volentez."
Un chevaler i sist que fu mal senez —
Provencel iert de Seint-Gile fu nez.
Al messager est derere alez,
Amdui ses puinz li at el chief mellez,
95 Trait le a terre, kar cil ne s'est gardez.
Meis Otinel est mult tost relevez,
Trait Curçuse, dunt le punz fu dorrez.
Ferir le veit, ne s'est pas ubliez:
K'as piez le rei en est le chef colpez.
100 Franceis s'escrient, "Barun, kar le pernez!"
Otinel s'est a une part turnez,
Les oilz roille, les gernuns a levez,
Liun resemble qui seit enchaenez.
En halt s'escrie, "Baruns, ne vus remuez!
105 Kar par icel Dex a qui me sui donez,
Ja murent set cenz, si vus croulez!"
L'emperere s'en est en piez levez,
Si lui a dit, "L'espee me donez."
Dit li paien, "De folie parlez!"
110 Dunc dist Rodlant, "A mei la rendez.
Assez l'averez quant vus departirez."
Dit Otinel, "Beal sire, ore la tenez,
Mes mult vus pri ke bien la me guardez.
Ne la doreie pur set de vos citez —
115 Uncore, en ert de celui vostre chief colpez!"
Dist Rodlant, "Par fei, trop vus avancez!
Vostre message dites, puis vus en alez!"
"Jo volenters," dist il. "Ore escutez."

Charles," feit il, "jo ne te celerai mie.
120 Messager sui l'emperur Garsie,
Ki tient Espanie, Alixandre, e Rucie,
Tyre e Sydonie, Perse e Barbarie.
Par mei, te mande: leisse cristienie —
Cristienté ne valt une alie!
125 Mes serf Mahun qui tut le munde guie;
fol. 211vb Ki si ne creit il feit grant folie.

That for eight entire days I had swollen fists."
The French say, "Evil were you born!"
Estult of Lengres has risen to his feet,
Holding before him a squared-off staff.
85     He would've struck him, we know this well,
But Charles' nephew moved to stop him,
And said to him, "Lord Estult, relax.
For my love, if you love me at all,
Since the pagan has gained surety from me,
90     Let him say whatever he wants."
A knight who'd been reared badly sat there —
He was a Provençal born in Saint-Giles.
He went behind the messenger,
Grabbed him by the head with both fists,
95     Dragged him to the ground, for he hadn't noticed him.
But Otinel quickly got back up
And drew out Corçuse with its gilded pommel.
Urged to strike him, he didn't hold back:
His head lay severed near the King's feet.
100     The French cry out, "Barons, seize him!"
Otinel darted to one side,
Rolling his eyes, raising his whiskers,
And resembling a chained-up lion.
He cries out loudly, "Barons, don't move!
105     By the god to whom I've pledged myself,
Seven hundred will die if you make a move!"
The Emperor stood up on his feet,
And said to him, "Give me the sword."
The pagan responds, "Nonsense!"
110     Then says Roland, "Give it to me;
You'll have it back when you go."
Says Otinel, "Good lord, then take it,
But I pray that you guard it well for me.
I'd never give it up for seven of your cities —
115     Moreover, it's by it that your head shall be severed!"
Says Roland, "In faith, you go too far!
State your message, and then get going!"
"Gladly," he says. "Now pay attention."

"Charles," he says, "I'll hide nothing from you.
120     I'm a messenger from Emperor Garsie,
Who holds Spain, Alexandria, and Russia,
Tyre and Sidon, Persia and Barbary.
Through me he orders you to renounce Christianity —
Christianity's not worth a bitter sorb-apple!
125     Instead serve Mahomet who guides the world;
Whoever fails to believe in him commits folly.

Deviene sis, tu e ta compaignie,
Puis si t'en vien al riche rei Garsie.
Il te dorra aver et manantie,
130      Ensurketut, te larra Normendie,
E d'Engleterre les porz e la navie.
A tun nevu Rodlant durra Russie,
E Oliver prenge Esclavunie.
Mes duce France ne vus larra il mie —
135      Il at doné Florian de Sulie,
Fiz a cel rei Russet de Barbarie.
N'at plus prodom en tute paienie,
Ne que tant ert los de chevalerie,
Ne qui meuz ferge od espee furbie.
140      Cil tendra France qui ce en sa baillie."
Dist l'emperere, "Issi n'ert il mie!
K'en dite vus, ma meisne nurie?"
Tut le barnage a une voiz escrie:
"Dreiz emperere, nus nel suffrum mie
145      Que ja paien eient France en baillie.
Mes, fai venir ta grant chevalerie,
Puis, se tu vols, deske la nus guie
Tant que verrum la pute gent haie!
S'en bataille trovum le rei Garsie,
150      Ja de la teste n'en portera il mie!"
Dist Otinel, "Ore oi grant briconie —
Tel manace ore l'emperur Garsie,
K'il matera e toldra la vie!
Quant il verra sa grant chevalerie,
155      Li plus hardi n'avera talent qu'il rie;
Meuz voldrent estre de la Normendie!"
Ço dist duc Naimes a la barbe florie:
"Si Charles mande sa grant chevalerie,
U trovera il cel riche rei Garsie?
160      Combaterent sei a sa grant compaingnie."
Dist Otinel, "Ore oi grant briconie!
Ja sunt il par set feiz set cenz mile,
As blancs halbercs as enseingnes de sire,
K'unques ne furrent pur pour de lur vie.
165      Une cité ont fete en Lumbardie,
Entre dous ewes l'ont fermé e bastie.
Paiene gent l'apelent Atelie,
fol. 212ra   Deu ne fist humme qui lur tolsist essie,
Ne lur pescher ne lur gaanerie.
170      Si Charles i venist od la barbe flurie,
La conuistrum ki avera amie,
Ki meuz fer, ni d'espee furbie.
Meis, dan vilein, ni venez vus mie —

Become his men, you and your people,
And then proceed to rich King Garsie.
He'll give you possessions and wealth,
130    Above all, he'll leave you Normandy
And the ports and ships of England.
To your nephew Roland he'll give Russia,
And Oliver will get Slovenia.
But he'll grant you nothing of sweet France —
135    He's given it to Florian of Syria,
Son of King Russet of Barbary.
There's no worthier man in all heathendom,
Nor anyone more renowned for chivalry,
Nor better equipped to wield a sword.
140    He will hold France as his domain."
Says the Emperor, "That will he never!
What say you, my household retainers?"
All the assembly cries out with one voice:
"Rightful Emperor, we will never allow
145    A pagan to have France as his domain.
Instead, gather your mighty army,
And then, as you like, lead us there
Till we find those rotten, loathsome men!
If we find King Garsie in battle,
150    He won't be carrying his head any longer!"
Says Otinel, "Now I hear big boasting —
Such threats directed at Emperor Garsie,
That he'll defeat him and rob him of life!
As soon as you see his magnificent army,
155    The bravest will have no urge to laugh;
They'll wish instead to be in Normandy!"
Then speaks white-bearded Duke Naimes:
"If Charles assembles his mighty army,
Where might he find this rich King Garsie?
160    They will battle his large host there."
Says Otinel, "Now I hear big boasting!
Seven times seven hundred thousand are already there,
With white hauberks of the lord's insignia,
Who'll never flee in fear for their lives.
165    They've established a city in Lombardy,
Constructed and built between two rivers.
The pagan army calls it Atelie.
God's not created the man who can capture it
Or take their rivers and fields.
170    If white-bearded Charles comes there,
Then we will see who can win a sweetheart,
Who can do the best, furnished with a sword.
But you, unworthy sir, don't ever come —

Par mun conseil, garderez Paris la vile,
175      K'escufle n'i entre ne corneile ne pie,
Kar par vus n'ert mes faite chevalerie!"
Tel vergoine at li duc ne set qu'il die.

Li duc Rodlant s'est en piez levez,
Mal talent at, a poi n'est forsenez.
180      Vers le paen s'en est treis pas alez,
Si li a dit, "Culvert desmesurez,
Mult par casur e prisez e vantez,
De ta parole devant Franceis loez.
Mes, par celui k'en croiz fu penez,
185      Ja murriez ne fuissez afiez.
Mes s'en bataille puissez ester encontrez,
Tel ce dorrai de m'espee delez
Ja puis de tei n'ert franc humme encombrez!"
Dit Otinel, "Ja le savum assez,
190      Bataille averas si ferre l'osez —
Demain matin vus sumuns en ces prez!"
E dit Rodlunt, "Kar le m'aseurez."
Fet le paen, "La meie fei tenez,
E ma creance, e tutes mes lealtez,
195      Par ki remaine seit cuard pruvez,
L'espurun lur seit des piez colpez;
James en curt ne seit mes honurez."
Lur feiz en donent ore sunt asseurez.

Ço dist li reis Charle de Seint-Denis:
200      "Sarazin, frere, par la lei dunc tu vis,
De quel parage es tu en tun pais?
Cum as a nun? Par ta lei, kar me dis."
"Otinel, sire," ço dist li Sarazins,
"Fiz sui al rei Galien al fier vis —
205      Plus a mort hummes, e de ses mains occis,
K'um ne trouvereit en trestut cest pais.
Li reis Garsie est mis germeins cusins;
Mis uncle fu Fernagu li hardis,
Icil de Nazre que Rodlant m'at occis.
fol. 212rb   Demain en ert en fier calenge mis."
211      E dit li reis, "Tu es assez gentilz!
Mar, fu tis cors, que baptesme n'at pris."

Li reis apele sun chamberlene Renier:
"Venez avant. Pernez cest messager,
215      S'il me menez a la maisun Garner.
Dunez al hoste cenz souz pur son manger,
E altre tant donez pur son destrier."

By my advice, stay in the city of Paris,
175    Where crows and magpies never come,
Because you'll never succeed at chivalry!"
The Duke's so insulted he can't think what to say.

Count Roland rises to his feet,
Angry, nearly maddened with rage.
180    He takes three steps toward the pagan,
And says to him, "Unbridled villain,
You've taunted and boasted too much today,
By your arrogant words said to Frenchmen.
Indeed, by He who suffered on the Cross,
185    You'd already be dead if you weren't vouchsafed.
But should we ever meet in battle,
I'll give you such a blow with my sword
That no Frenchman will ever be bothered by you!"
Says Otinel, "Obviously,
190    A battle should be set, if you dare —
I call you to the field tomorrow morning!"
And Roland says, "Pledge this to me."
Says the pagan, "Take my pledge,
My promise, and all my loyal honor,
195    That whoever defaults be named a coward
And have the spurs removed from his boots;
Never again should he be honored in court."
They pledge their oaths and are sworn to each other.

King Charles of Saint-Denis says this:
200    "Saracen, brother, by the faith you live under,
Of what lineage are you in your country?
What's your name? Tell me, by your faith."
"Otinel, lord," the Saracen says,
"I'm the son of fierce-eyed King Galien —
205    More men are dead, killed by his hands,
Than a man might find in all these lands.
King Garsie's my first cousin;
My uncle was the noble Fernagu,
The one from Nazareth killed by Roland.
210    He'll be brought to account for that tomorrow."
And the King says, "Indeed, you are noble!
Alas, for your body, that you've not been baptized."

The King calls for his chamberlain Renier:
"Come forth. Take this messenger,
215    And bring him to Garnier's inn.
Give the host a hundred sous for his food,
And give him some more for his horse."

Puis si apele le vielz chanu Richer,
Galter de Liuns, et li Deneis Oger.
220    "Pernez," feit il, "garde del chevaler,
S'il servez bien de ço qu'il at mester."
Cele nuit l'unt leissé issi ester
Jesk'al demein. Que li vir parut cler,
Charles se lieve si fait Rodlant mander.
225    En la chapele sunt alé pur urer.
La messe chante l'abés de Seint-Omer.
Un hanap d'or fait li reis aporter,
De paresins si l'at bien fet cumbler.
Offrende sunt il e li duze pier.
230    Rodlant offri Durendal al brant cler;
Pur rancum i feit set mari doner.
Apris la messe funt les ures chanter.
Del mustier eissent, puis si vont esgarder
Le Sarazin qui vient al rei parler.

235    Li Sarazin vient orguillusement.
Le rei apele, si li dit fierment.
"Charles," fait il, "u est ore Rodlant,
Li vostre nies que vus paramez tant,
Par ki Franceis se vont asseurant?
240    De fei menti l'apel cum recreant
Se il ne tient vers mei mun covenant,
Ke et feimes tute la curt veant!"
A ces paroles se treit li quons avant,
Trestut irré e plein de maltalant:
245    "Par cel apostle ki que rent penant,
Jo ne larreie pur nul humme vivant
Ke jo en cui ne te rende teisant,
Mat u vencu, mort u recreant."
Dist Otinel, "Feites dunc itant!
250    Pernez vos armes par itel covenant;
Si jo vus fail, pendez moi! Jo'l vus grant."

fol. 212va  Fait Oliver, "Mult parlez haltement,
Ne vos paroles n'abeissent nient —
Grant merveil est si bien vus avient!"
255    L'unze per en ont amené Rodlant.
El dos li vestent un halberc jacerant;
Grosse est la maille, derere e devant.
El chief li lacent un vert healme luisant.
Ço fu le healme Golias le jehant;
260    Charles le prist quant il occist Brachant.
Puis li aportent Durendal le trenchant.
Ja del espee, n'estoet dire neant;

Then he calls for the old white-haired Riquier,
Gautier of Lyons, and Ogier the Dane.
220 "Look after this knight," he says,
"And supply him fully with whatever he needs."
That night they leave him there
Until morning. When daylight appears,
Charles arises and has Roland summoned.
225 They've gone to the chapel to pray.
The Abbot of Saint-Omer sings Mass.
Charles has a golden goblet brought in,
Filled entirely with Parisian coins.
He and the twelve peers make their offerings.
230 Roland offers Durendal his bright sword;
He gives seven marks to redeem it.
After Mass the hours are sung.
They leave the church and then go to observe
The Saracen who's come to speak to the King.

235 The Saracen approaches with haughty pride.
He calls to the King, speaking fiercely to him.
"Lord King," he says, "where's Roland,
Your nephew whom you love so much,
In whom the French are so very confident?
240 I call him an oathbreaker and a forswearer
If he does not hold to my pact,
Made by us before the whole court!"
At these words the count advances,
Thoroughly angry and wholly irritated:
245 "By the apostle tortured with pain,
I won't hesitate for anyone alive
To reduce you to silence,
Defeated or vanquished, dead or forsworn!"
Responds Otinel, "Then do it!
250 Take up your arms by our agreement;
If I fail you, then hang me! I grant you this."

Says Oliver, "You talk too proudly,
And you don't mince words —
It'd be amazing if any good comes your way!"
255 The eleven peers take Roland aside.
On his back they place a mail hauberk;
The chain is thick, both before and behind.
On his head they lace a bright green helmet.
It was the helmet of the giant Goliath;
260 Charles took it when he killed Brachant.
Then they bring him keen-edged Durendal.
About that sword enough's already been said;

Bien le conuissent, li petit e li grant —
Ke n'a si bone, jesk'en Orient.
265     Li quons la ceint, qui l'a paraimé tant.
El col li pendent un fort escu pesant,
Peint a azur, a jalne, a orpiment.
Envirum l'urle current li quatre vent,
Li duze signe, e li meis ensement,
270     Sicum chascun vers altre se contient.
E del abisme i est le fundement,
E ciel e terre fait par compassement,
E le soleil mis par grant estudiement.
La guige fu d'un paile Escarimant,
275     E la fuille est feite d'un Almant.
Puis li aportent un fort espé trenchant,
Sa lance redde, e sun gunfanun gent
Vermaile e inde tresk'a poinz li tent.
Li quons Gerins li chalce ignelement.
280     Enmi la place li meine l'um Bruiant,
Ki plus tost vait que quarel ne destent;
Deus ne fist beste ki tant voist esmuvant
K'a lui se tenist a dreit curs un arpent!
La sele fu de cristal e d'argent,
285     E la suzcele d'un paile d'Orient,
Li estriu d'or overé menuement.
Li quons i munte tant ascemeement
K'il n'astriu ne arçun ne se prent.
Fist un esleis veant tute la gent,
290     Si s'en returne vers Charle, riant.
"Sire," fait il, "le congé vus demant.
Si li paen viene, par mien escient
Ja de mort vers moi n'avera garant!"
fol. 212vb "Nies," dit li reis, "a celui te comant
295     Ki le ciel fist e tut le mund si grant."
Leve sa main si a seinié Rollant.
Li quons s'en vait as espuruns fichant.
Aprés lui vunt puceles e enfant,
Ki tuit li dient: "A Jhesu te comant.
300     Seinte Marie te seit de mort garant!"
Li unze per muntent de meintenant;
Entre dous ewes ont mené Rodlant:
L'une est Seine, l'altre Marne la grant.
Devant le rei vint le messager estant.
305     L'emperere apele fierement:
"Charle," fait il, "un halberc te demant,
Escu e healme, e une espee trenchant;
Meis un destrer ai jo, bon e currant,
N'en a meillur desk'en Oriant,

All know it well, commoners and aristocrats —
There's none so good from here to the Orient.
265 Valuing it greatly, the count girds it on.
Around his neck they hang a heavy shield,
Painted with blue, gold, and yellow hues.
Around the rim race the four winds,
The twelve signs, and also the months,
270 As if each contains all the others.
And there are the depths of the oceans,
The earth and the sky encompassed,
And the sun positioned very carefully.
The strap was made of Persian cloth,
275 And the board was made by a German.
They bring him then a strong, sharp sword,
His stiff lance, and his noble pennon
Tinted red and blue up to the grip.
Count Gerins efficiently straps on his shoes.
280 Into the courtyard they lead in Bruiant,
Who races faster than an arrow flies;
 God never made any beast as swift
And as able to go straight an arpent's length!
The saddle was made of crystal and silver,
285 The undersaddle of an Oriental cloth,
And the stirrups of finely worked gold.
The count mounts there so gracefully
That he grips neither stirrup nor saddlebow.
He sprints forward in front of everyone,
290 Then returns laughing toward Charles.
"Lord," he says, "I ask your leave.
Should the pagan approach, I think
He'll not be spared from death by my hand!"
"Nephew," says the King, "I commend you to Him
295 Who made the sky and all this world."
He raises his hand and blesses Roland.
The count rides off at a full gallop.
After him go maidens and children
Who all say to him: "I commend you to Jesus.
300 May holy Mary protect you from death!"
The eleven peers quickly mount;
They lead Roland between two rivers:
One is the Seine, the other the great Marne.
The messenger comes to stand before the King.
305 He calls fiercely to the Emperor:
"Charles," he says, "I request a hauberk,
Shield and helmet, and a keen sword;
But I have a warhorse, strong and swift;
There's none better from here to the Orient,

310    E de m'espee taille bien le trenchant.
       De sur ma fei, te promet lealment
       A me ure de prime cunterai Rollant!"
       Charles l'oi, a poi dire ne fent.
       "Paien," dit il, "Deu del ciel t'acravent,
315    Kar mult m'as feit curecé e dolent."
       Le reis reguarde vers sa fille Belisent,
       Que de la chambre eisseit el pavement.
       Tut le paleis de sa bealté resplent.
       Li reis l'apele, si la ceine de sun guant.
320    "Fille," fait il, "cest paien te comant.
       Armez le bien, tost e ignelement.
       Bataille a prise a mun nevu Rodlant.
       Ke pur les armes n'en eit decheement."
       "Sire," dit ele, "tut a vostre talent,
325    Li Sarazin iert armé gentement;
       Ja par les armes n'i perdera nient."

       Belisent apele Flandrine de Muntbel,
       E la pucele Rosette de Runel.
       Ces treis danceles ameinent Otinel.
330    Al dos li vestent le halberc le rei Samuel,
       E la ventaille a un gentil fresel —
       Celui li ferme Flandrine de Muntbel.
       El chief li lacent le healme Galatiel,
       Feit a quarters a flurs e aanael,
335    E li nasel enfurmé d'un oisel.
fol. 213ra  La fille Charle, qui out le cors danzel,
       Li ceint l'espee al fort rei Akael.
       Ço est Curçuse, taillant cum cutel;
       Ceste muverat encui a Rollant le cervel —
340    Dunt al rei Charle n'en ert guerel bel!
       El col li pendent un fort escu novel,
       Blanc cum neif desuz a un listel,
       La bucle est d'or, e d'argent li clavel.
       Fer i out bon e gunfanun novel
345    Blanc cum flur, peint i out un oisel;
       Entre ses piez portout un draguncel,
       Tresk'as poinz li penecel.
       Uns esperuns qui valent un chastel
       Li at chalce Rosette de Rinel.
350    La seele est mise en Migrados l'ignel,
       Qui plus tost curt ke ne destent quarel.
       Li bon destrier a veu le danzel;
       Henist e grate — bien conuist Otinel.
       Cil li salt sure, ki plus set de cenbel
355    E de bataille que fevere de martel!

310      And my sword's blade cuts well.
        By my faith, I promise you truly
        That by prime I'll have settled accounts with Roland!"
        Hearing him, Charles can barely speak.
        "Pagan," he says, "May heaven's God confound you,
315      For you've made me furious and vexed."
        The King looks toward his daughter Belisant,
        Who issues from her chamber into the courtyard.
        The entire palace shines with her beauty.
        The King calls her, then signals with his glove.
320      "Daughter," he says, "I commend this pagan to you.
        Arm him well, quickly and straightaway.
        He's taken up battle with my nephew Roland.
        See that he not be impeded by his arms."
        "Lord," she says, "just as you please,
325      The Saracen will be nobly armed;
        He'll lose nothing there on account of his arms."

        Belisant calls to Flandrine of Muntbel,
        And the maiden Rosette of Runel.
        These three damsels lead Otinel away.
330      On his back they fastened King Samuel's hauberk
        And the aventail with a beautiful clasp —
        With this Flandrine of Muntbel attaches it.
        On his head they lace Galatiel's helmet,
        Quartered with flowers and enamel,
335      And a nosepiece fastened with a bird.
        Charles' daughter, with a maiden's heart,
        Attaches the sword of great King Akael.
        It is Corçuse, which cuts like a knife;
        It will swing today toward Roland's brain —
340      King Charles has nobody else as noble!
        On his neck they hang a strong new shield,
        White as snow below the rim.
        The boss is gold, the studs are silver.
        There's good iron, and a new pennon
345      That sports a painted bird, white as a flower;
        Between its feet it carries a young dragon,
        With a small emblem on its wristbands.
        A set of spurs fully worth a castle
        Were placed on his feet by Rosette of Runel.
350      The saddle is placed on the speedy Migrados,
        Who races more swiftly than an arrow flies.
        The good warhorse sees the young man;
        He whinnies and paws — he knows Otinel well.
        He leaps up on him, who knows more about jousting
355      And battles than a smith knows a hammer!

Li Sarazin est el destrer muntez,
Fait un eslais si s'en est returnez.
Vers Belisent s'en est tut dreit alez.
"Pucele gente, mult sui bien adubez.
360    Se truis Rollant, morz est u afolez."
Dist la pucele, "De Durendal vus gardez!
Si de Curçuse bien ne vus defendez,
Ja par vus meis n'en ert tenu citez."
A icel mot, li messager est turnez.
365    Ogier l'ameine, li Daneis alosez,
E li duc Naimes est ovec eus alé.
Entre dous ewes l'ont mené es prez.
A haltes fenestres est li reis alez,
Les duze pers at a sei apelez.
370    "Seingnurs," fait il, "od mei vus venez;
Faites Franceis tuz eissir des prez."
Il si funt a eus dous les ont abandunez.
Charle escrie, "Des ore vus combatez!"
Dist Otinel, "Jo sui tut aprestez!"

375    Rodlant a dit al paen mescreant:
"Jo te defi des ci en avant."
Dist li paen, "E jo tei ensement.
fol. 213rb    Bien vus guardez, kar jo ne t'aim nient:
La mort mun uncle Fernagu vus demant!"
380    Rollant lait curré le bon destrer Bruiant,
Otinel Migrados le bien curant:
Des esperuns les destre mult forment.
Entre le bruit e lesort ele vent,
Li prez encroule e la terre ensement.
385    Les hantes brandient e beissent forment,
Li gunfanun ventelent vers le vent.
Granz colps se donent en lur escuz devant;
Trenchent les fuz e les quirs ensement,
Meis li halberc sunt serré e tenant.
390    Maille ni false, ne clavel ni destent.
Sur les peitrines plient li fer trenchant.
Les hanstes brisent amdus continuiement.
Ultre s'en passent li chevaler vallant,
Que l'un ne l'altre ni pert nient.
395    "Deu," dist li reis, "or vei merveille grant
Quant cist paien s'est tenu vers Rodlant."
Dit Belisent, "Bon sunt mi garnement,
E cil ki les porte n'est pas cuard ne lent."
Rodlant a treit Durendal le trenchant,
400    Fiert Otinel sur le healme luisant

The Saracen mounts his warhorse,
Sprints forward and then returns.
He goes straight toward Belisant.
"Noble maiden, I'm equipped well.
360    If I find Roland, he'll be dead or wounded."
The maiden says, "Watch out for Durendal!
If you don't defend yourself well with Corçuse,
Never again will you capture a city."
At these words the messenger turns away.
365    Ogier the renowned Dane leads him,
And Dukes Naimes goes with them.
They lead him to a meadow between two rivers.
The King has gone to the high windows,
And calls the twelve peers to him.
370    "Lords," he says, "come with me;
Make all the French leave the meadow."
Two of them do this and clear the meadow.
Charles cries out, "Start your fight now!"
Says Otinel, "I am ready!"

375    Roland said to the false-believing pagan,
"From this time forward I challenge you."
The pagan said, "And I challenge you too.
Protect yourself, for I bear you no love:
I impugn you for the death of my uncle Fernagu!"
380    Roland lets the good warhorse Bruiant charge,
Otinel the swift Migrados:
They spur the horses fiercely.
Between the noise and the tumult,
Both meadow and ground tremble.
385    They brandish their lances and meet fiercely,
Their banners blowing in the wind.
They deliver great blows upon shield-fronts;
They split both shafts and leather,
But the hauberks are tight and firm.
390    The mail doesn't fail, the links don't slacken.
The keen iron pushes against their chests.
They both smash their lances repeatedly.
The valiant knights exchange blows,
And neither one loses a thing.
395    "God," says the King, "I'm wholly amazed
How this pagan endures against Roland!"
Belisant says, "My armor is good,
And its bearer is neither cowardly nor slow."
Roland grasps the keen-edged Durendal,
400    Striking Otinel on the shiny helmet

Que flurs e pieres cheent avalant,
E sun nasel lui a toleit devant.
A l'altre colp fiert le destrer currant,
Le chief li trenche del col tut rundement.
405 Li paen, quant sun cheval li ment,
Dis dous moz: "Par Mahumet, Rollant,
Vus avez feit vilainie mult grant
Que mun destrier m'avez mort pur nient!
Que demandiez a mun bon auferant,
410 Mes ja le vostre ne s'en irra gabant!"
Del fuerre sacke Cureçuse la grant,
L'escu enbrace e feit un salt avant;
Si fiert Rollant sur le healme luisant
Ke li nasel se vait tut avalant.
415 Li colp glaceie sur l'arçun devant,
Trenche le fust e le feutre ensement;
Par les espaules a trenché le Bruiant,
Desk'en la terre feit culer le brant.
En halt s'escrie, "Ço n'est pas colp de nisant!"
fol. 213va "Deu," dist li reis, "cum ço culp fu pesant!
421 Sainte Marie, guardez mei Rollant!"
Se li quons chiet, ne mes merveil nient.
Il tient l'espee si estreint durement,
Fiert le paen sur le healme que resplent
425 K'un quartier en contreval descent;
Trenche les mailles del halberc jacerant,
E del oreille une partie en prent,
Sun bon escu desk'en la bucle fent.
La l'éust mort, vencu, u recreant,
430 Mes Otinel at hardement mult grant.
De Cureçuse l'acuilt durement,
E Rodlant lui, od l'espee trenchant.
De Durendal, le fiert menuement.
Granz colps s'entredonent e derere e devant.
435 Vers les espees, ne valt le halberc nient —
Des mailles luist tut li pre e resplent!
Dist Belisent, "Ore fierent gentement.
Ceste bataille ne dura mie lungement
Ke li vassal sunt de grant hardement.
440 Mult trenche bien Durendal la Rodlant,
Meis Cureçuse ne li deit nient!"
"Deus," dist li reis, "cum le cuer me ment!"
En cruiz se jette a Deu vers orient,
Une preiere at feit mult gentement:
445 "Deus, ki es sire e rei sur tute gent,
Tu me garis mun chier nevu Rodlant,
E convertissez Otinel le tirant,

So that ornaments and gems fall to the ground,
And he's cut away the front of his nosepiece.
With another blow he strikes the racing warhorse,
Completely severing its head from its neck.
405 As his horse fails him, the pagan
Declares outright: "By Mahomet, Roland,
You've committed a terrible disgrace
In killing my warhorse for no cause!
For what you've asked of my fine steed,
410 Now yours must nevermore amuse itself!"
From his scabbard he draws mighty Corçuse,
Grasps his shield and leaps forward;
He strikes Roland on his shiny helmet
So that his nosepiece falls to the ground.
415 The blow falls in front of his saddlebow,
Splitting both wood and saddlecloth;
He slashed through Bruiant's shoulders,
And sliced the blade down to the ground.
Loudly he cries, "This is not a useless blow!"
420 "God," says the King, "That blow was weighty!
Blessed Mary, protect Roland for me!"
Were the count to fall, it wouldn't be surprising.
He holds his sword and grips it mightily,
Strikes the pagan on his burnished helm
425 So that a quarter of it falls off;
He slices the links of his mail hauberk,
And takes off a good part of the shield's edge,
Splitting the strong shield down to the boss.
He almost killed, conquered, or maimed him,
430 But Otinel has tremendous courage.
He attacks mightily with Corçuse,
And Roland attacks back with his sharp blade.
With Durendal he deals him quick strokes.
They hit each other with blows behind and before.
435 Against the swords, hauberks aren't worth anything —
Links glitter and shine on the ground!
Belisant says, "Now they fight nobly.
This battle won't last a long time at all
Because the vassals are so very brave.
440 Durendal slashes extremely well for Roland,
But Corçuse is every bit as good!"
"God," says the King, "how my heart fails me!"
With a sign of the Cross, he turns to God in the east,
And very nobly utters a prayer:
445 "God, Lord and King over all people,
May You protect my dear nephew Roland for me,
And convert the young soldier Otinel,

Que sur son chief prenge baptizement."
Baise la terre, si se leve a tant,
450  A la fenestre at mis sun chief avant
Veit les baruns cumbatre gentement.
Des lur escus n'ourent mie tant
Dunt il cuverir peussent lur puinz devant.

Rollant dit al paen, "Kar guerpissez Mahun
455  E trei en Deu ki suffri passiun.
Ber, kar le fai, si recevez gent dun:
Ço est Belisent, la fille al rei Charlun.
Ma cusine est, e jo te faz le dun,
E jo e tu serrum tut dismes compaingnun,
460  E Oliver a nus avisterun.
Si conquerrum chastel e dunchun;
fol. 213vb  Cité ne marche ne bon chastel gascun
Ja plus de tei ne quier un esperun."
Dist Otinel, "Ore oi parler bricun —
465  Mal dehez eit ki te fist cleriun!
Meis jo sui maistre, si te lirrai lesçun,
M'en escient, ainz que departirun:
Tel ce durrai sur le healme brun
Ke ne purras dire 'oec' ne 'nun.'"

470  El nevu Charle n'out que curecer.
Mal talent a merveillus e fier;
Tint Durendal, u le punt fu d'ormier,
Sur le healme fiert Otinel le guerreer,
Ke fu en salt del fer e del ascier.
475  Cil lui guenchist, qui bien sout del mester;
Deliez l'espaule en fait le colp beisser,
Trenche les maelles del jacerant dubler,
Tut le desço vere tresk'al nu del braier,
Meis a la char ne poeit mie tucher.
480  Li colp fu grant, le vassal fet pleer;
Pur un petit nel fait agenuisser.
Franceis s'escrient, "Quel colp de chevaler!"
Li plusur dient del curteis messagier
Ke vencuz est ne se pot meis aider,
485  Meis poi conuissent Otinel le guerreer,
Le fiz le rei Galien al vis fier!
Il fait un salt si volt le colp venger;
S'ore ne se sace li nies le rei guarter,
Ja ne ferra meis colp sur chevaler.

490  Li Sarazin a la culur muee,
Les oilz ruille cum beste devee.

So that he may be baptized upon his head."
He kisses the ground, then rises,
450    And leans his head forward out the window
To watch the barons battle nobly.
They don't have enough of their shields left
To cover the front of their chests.

Roland says to the pagan, "Now give up Mahomet
455    And believe in God who suffered the Passion.
Baron, if you do it, you'll receive a fine gift:
Belisant, King Charles' daughter.
She's my cousin; I give her to you as a gift,
And you and I can be comrades forever,
460    And Oliver will join with us.
Then we'll conquer castles and strongholds;
No borderland, city, or good Gascon castle
Will ever be worth a spur more than you."
Says Otinel, "Now I hear a fool speak —
465    He who made you a clerk must be ashamed!
But I'll be a master to teach you a lesson,
It seems, before we separate:
I'll give it to you on your burnished helm
Till you're unable to say 'yes' or 'no.'"

470    Charles' nephew feels nothing but anger.
His power is marvelous and strong;
He grips Durendal with the gilded hilt,
And strikes warrior Otinel on his helmet,
Attacking it with iron and steel.
475    Otinel deflected the stroke, knowing well the art;
The blow landed near his shoulder,
Cutting through links of his shiny doublet,
Crushing everything down to the neck,
But it wasn't able to touch the flesh.
480    The powerful blow made the pagan double up;
It almost knocked him to his knees.
The French cry out, "That's a knightly blow!"
Most of them say about the courtly messenger
That he's been beaten and can't help himself,
485    But little do they know the warrior Otinel,
The son of fierce-eyed King Galien!
He leaps up and goes to repay the blow;
Should the King's nephew not guard himself,
He'll never again strike a knight.

490    The Saracen has changed color,
Rolling his eyes like a deranged beast.

Tient Cureçuse, s'il at amunt levee,
Al nevu Charle le fra ja privee
Sur le healme d'or, li at ja presentee.

495     Un colp li done par si grant randunee
Ja fust la teste Rollant del cors severé.
Quant Cureçuse li est el puin turnee,
Un altre colp li jete a celee.
Entre le cors e l'escu vint l'espee,

500     Sur les en armes a la targe colpee
K'as ses piez l'abat enmi la pree.
Del bon halberc consiut la gerunee,
Desk'en la terre fet culer l'espee.

fol. 214ra     Al resacher, Otinel s'est escrié,

505     "Par Mahumet, mult trenche bien m'espee!"


Li chevaler reguardent fierement,
Forment redutent les colps qui sunt pesant;
Les halbercs detrenchent e derere e devant,
E desmaile sunt mult menuement;

510     De lur escuz n'en ovrent mie tant
Dunt il pussent coverir lur puinz devant.
Franceis se jetent tuit contre orient,
Grant pour ont de lur seingnur Rodlant.
Il prient Deu ke bon conseil lur mant,

515     U peis u trives, u bon desevrement.
A ices paroles vient un columb volant,
Si ke Charles le vit e tute sa gent.
Sainz Espiriz sur Otinel descent,
Dous moz a dit: "Trei tei en sus, Rollant.

520     Ne sai quel chose me vait devant volant
Ki m'at changé le sens e le talent.
Ceste bataille remainie a itant.
Pur tue amur, prendrai baptizement.
Sainte Marie trai jo mes a garant."

525     Rollant l'entent, si li dit en riant,
"Gentil hoem sire, as le tu en talant?"
Fait Otinel, "Jo'l vus di veirement,
Jo guerp ici Mahun e Tervagant
E Apolin e Jovin le puant."

530     Les branz i jetent sur l'erbe verdiant,
Amdui s'enbracent li chevaler vaillant.
"Deus," dit li reis, "cum ci vertuz est grant!
Ja m'est avis k'il funt covenant.
Kar i alez, franc chevaler vaillant."

535     E il si sunt qui plus tost poet currant —
Maismes li reis i vait espurunant.
"Beals nies," fait, "cum vus est covenant?"

He grips Corçuse, raises his hand,
And suddenly strikes Charles' nephew
On his golden helmet, set right before him.
495 He deals him a blow with so much force
That Roland's head was nearly split from his body.
As soon as he turns Corçuse in his fist,
He quickly deals him another blow.
The sword strikes between body and shield,
500 Cutting the shield above his arms
So that it falls to his feet in the field.
He hits the apron of Roland's fine hauberk,
Gliding his sword down to the ground.
Pulling it back, Otinel cries out,
505 "By Mahomet, my blade slices well!"

The knights look fiercely at each other,
Preparing themselves for heavy blows;
They slash hauberks behind and before,
And the links of mail are in little bits;
510 Little remains of their shields
By which to cover their chests.
The French all turn toward the east,
Fearing greatly for their lord Roland.
They pray to God that He send them aid,
515 Either peace or truce or a good breaking-off.
With these words a dove comes flying,
Where Charles and all his people see it.
The Holy Spirit descends upon Otinel,
Who declares outright: "Draw near, Roland.
520 I don't know what thing's come flying before me
That's transformed my mind and my will.
I call an immediate end to this battle.
Out of love for you I shall accept baptism.
I now call on blessed Mary to protect me."
525 Roland hears him, then laughingly says to him,
"Noble lord, is this your desire?"
Says Otinel, "I tell you truly,
I here abandon Mahomet and Tervagant
And Apolin and loathsome Jove."
530 Throwing their swords on the green grass,
The two knights embrace.
"God," says the King, "great is Your power!
It appears that they've reached an accord.
Let us go over there, brave French knights."
535 And they hurry there as fast as they can —
The King gallops there himself.
"Good nephew," he says, "what's your agreement?"

"Sire," fait il, "mult m'esta gentement,
Kar tut sui sein n'en ai de malment,
540     Mes combatu sui al meillur combatant
K'unques feust en la paene gent.
Meis, merci, nus avum fait itant
Ke cristienté volt e baptizement.
Recevez le, beals sire, alez avant
545     Si li donez honur a sun talant,
fol. 214rb     En surketut, ta filie Belesent."
"Deus," dit li reis, "ore avez fait mun talent:
C'est la preere ke j'aloue deperant!"
Si se desarment li chevaler vaillant.
550     Rollant munte sur un destrier currant,
E Otinel sur un mul amblant,
Vers la cité se vont esperunant.
Ore s'en irrunt al baptizement.

Al muster l'ont mené Sainte Marie.
555     Turpin de Reins a l'estole seisie,
Le salter overe si dist la letanie.
Puis vient al funz. S'il seinie e sentefie.
Grant est la presse de la chevalerie
Pur Otinel le pruz, ki se baptie.
560     Charle le tient od la barbe flurie,
E ote li pruz Girard de Normendie.
Le nun li leissent, nel remuent mie.
Baptizé est si at sa lei guerpie.
A tant es vus Belesent l'eschevie,
565     Ke plus est bele que la rose flurie.
Danz bele barbe vers Charles la guie.
Li reis la prent par la mance enermie.
"Fillie," fait il, "mult estes cislurie!
Ki une nuit vus avera en baillie
570     Ne li deit puis remembrer de cuardie;
Pruz humme deit estre de sa chevalerie.
Si serra il, si Deu li done vie,
De quei Franceis ont li plusur envie.
Fillol," fait il, "oras ta lei complie:
575     Baptizé es si as ta lei guerpie.
Pernez ma fillie Belesent a amie.
Pur lui, te donis Vercels e Morie,
Aulte e Plesence, Melan e Pavie:
Sire serras de tute Lumbardie."
580     Otinel l'ot, vers la terre se plie;
Les piez li baise forment sumilie.
"Sire," fait il, "ço ne refuis jo mie
Si la pucele le comant e otrie."

"Lord," he says, "he's treated me quite nobly,
For I'm all sound and haven't been injured,
540     Even though I've fought with the finest fighter
Who's ever been among pagan people.
But thankfully we've so managed it
That he wants Christianity and baptism.
Receive him, good lord, by moving forward
545     And giving him the honor he deserves
And, above all, your daughter Belisant."
"God," says the King, "now I've got what I hoped for:
It's the prayer I was praying!"
Then the brave knights disarm themselves.
550     Roland mounts a swift warhorse,
And Otinel an ambling mule,
And they gallop toward the city.
Now they hasten to the baptism.

They led him to the Monastery of St. Mary.
555     Turpin of Reims has donned the stole,
Opens the psalter and says the litany.
They approach the font. He blesses and sanctifies him.
Great is the gathering of knights
On behalf of worthy Otinel, who accepts baptism.
560     White-bearded Charles leads him,
And also the worthy Girard of Normandy.
They leave him his name, don't change it at all.
He is baptized and has abandoned his faith.
The lovely Belisant appears quickly,
565     More beautiful than the flowering rose.
Bearded men guide her to Charles.
The King takes her by the low-hanging sleeve.
"Daughter," he says, "you're blushing!
He who'll possess you in one night
570     Must never have thoughts of cowardice;
He must to be a man worthy of knighthood.
And he'll be the one, should God preserve his life,
Of whom the French are the most envious.
Godson," he says, "Your faith's now complete:
575     You're baptized and you've renounced your old faith.
Take my daughter Belisant as your betrothed.
For her, I give you Vercelli and Morie,
Ault and Plesence, Milan and Pavia:
You shall be lord of all Lombardy."
580     Otinel hears him and bows to the ground;
He kisses his feet with great humility.
"Lord," he says, "I'll not at all refuse
If the maiden so commands and assents."

Dit Belisent, "Jo me tiens pur garrie;
585     De bon mari ne me deit peser mie.
La meie amur ni ert ja vers vus guenchie."
Dist Otinel, "Quant vus estes m'amie,
fol. 214va   Pur vostre amur frai chevalerie
Devant Atille, de m'espee furbie.
590     Mort sunt paien, quant ai pris baptisterie!
Dreiz emperere, a vus comant m'amie
Treske vendruns al pleins de Lumbardie.
Les noeces erent es prez desur Hatilie
Quant averai mort l'emperur Garsie."

595     En sun paleis est li reis montez.
Si grant barnage est aprés lui alé.
Li mangier est ja prest e conreez;
Cil le mangerent a ki il fu donez.
Aprés supers, est li vins aportez
600     Enz en la chambre u li reis est entrez.
Dormir s'en vont, si ont les vis fermez
Desk'al demain que li soleil est levez.
Li reis se leve ses baruns at mandé,
Sur une table de savine est muntez.
605     Tient un bastun tut a or neelez.
"Seingnurs," dit Charle, "un petit m'entendez.
Conseilez mei, kar faire le devez,
Del rei Garsie, dunt vus oi avez,
Ki par sa force est en ma terre entrez,
610     Mes chastels art e brisé mes citez.
Ja ert destruite sainte Cristientez.
Irrum nus i ainz que vienge estez
U atendrum treske yver seit passez?"
Dient Franceis, "De merveille parlez —
615     Celui ni a ne seit tut aprestez;
Mar i avera altre terme nomez."
"Si ert," fait Charle, "puis que tuit le volez,
Al entre d'averil quant marz iert passez.
Pur meie amur, lores vus aprestez."
620     Dient Franceis, "Si cum vus comandez."

Nostre emperere fait escrivere ses brefs —
Par sun empire tramet ses messagers —
Ke ne remanie neis uns chevalers,
N'ume a pié, ne sergant, n'arblaster
625     Que dunt ni vienge; e qui ne poet aler
A Seint-Denise rende quatre deners.
Or va decembre si est passé jenevers,
Feverier, e marz, e vient li tens legers.

Says Belisant, "I consider myself well cared for;
585      With a good husband nothing will burden me.
My love will never be withdrawn from you."
Says Otinel, "When you are my betrothed,
I will wage war for your love
Before Atelie, with my steel sword.
590      Now that I've been baptized, pagans are dead!
Rightful Emperor, I entrust my betrothed to you
Until we come to the plains of Lombardy.
Our nuptials shall take place in the fields around Atelie
After I've killed Emperor Garsie."

595      The King ascended to his hall.
His grand baronage followed after him.
The food was prepared and soon served;
Those being served ate it heartily.
After dinner, wine was brought
600      Into the room the King had entered.
They've gone to sleep, closing their eyes
Till morning when the sun has risen.
The King arises and calls for his barons,
Mounting a dais of juniper wood.
605      He holds a gold-gilded sceptre.
"Lords," Charles says, "listen a moment.
Advise me as you ought,
About King Garsie, of whom you've heard,
Who has entered my land by force,
610      Burned my castles and invaded my cities.
He's now destroying holy Christianity.
Should we go there as soon as possible,
Or wait until winter has passed?"
Say the French, "What you propose isn't possible —
615      We're not prepared now nor can we quickly go;
It will have to be the later time."
"Thus will it be," says Charles, "as you please,
In the beginning of April when March is over.
Now, for my love, prepare yourselves."
620      Say the French, "As you command."

Our Emperor has his summons written —
Sending messengers throughout the empire —
That none of his knights should hold back,
Or footman or fighter or bowman
625      Not come; and anyone who cannot come
Must remit four deniers to Saint-Denis.
Now December passes and January is over,
February, March, and soft weather arrives.

A Paris est nostre emperere fiers.
fol. 214vb Li duze pier — Rollant e Olivers,
631    E Ansels, Girard, e Engeliers,
Estult de Lengres e Turpins e Giriers,
Bertoloi li bier e Otinel li guerreers,
Naimles li duc e li Daneis Ogiers —
635    As granz fenestres en ont mis hors les chies.
Virent venir Alemans e Beivers;
E Loerenes ceus as corages fiers;
E Peitevins, Provencels le guerriers;
E Burguiuns, Flamenes, e Puiers;
640    De Normendie la flur des chevalers.
Bretuns i vienent as escuz de quartiers,
En destre meinent les auferanz destriers.
Celui ni a n'ait quatre esquiers —
Se mestiers ont, dunt il frunt chevalers.
645    Desuz Munmartre s'amient a milliers.

Prim jor d'averil quant l'aube est esclarzie,
Munte li reis Charle ove sa chevalerie.
De Paris eissent si vont a Saint-Denise,
Le congé prennent, lur veie ont acullie.
650    Plurent ces dames si maldient Garsie;
Sonent ces corns, e cil destriers henissent.
Ore s'en irra li reis desk'en Lumbardie,
Li duc Rollant al primer chief les guie;
Deriere est Naimes od la barbe florie.
655    Mais Otinel ne volt leisser s'amie.
Belisent munte sur un mul de Hungrie
Que plus tost veit l'ambleure serrie
Ke par la mer ne veit nef ne galie.
Set cent baruns at en sa mainburnie,
660    Tuit joefne gent de grant chevalerie.
Eissent de France, Burgonie ont guerpie,
Passent Mungiu la fiere compaingnie,
Eissent des munz, vienent a Morie.
Desuz Versels passerent a navie,
665    Muntferant muntent, si veient Hatelie —
La forte cité u est la gent haie.
Suz Munpoun prennet herbergerie,
Lez l'eue del Ton en la praerie.

Nostre emperere fait Franceis arestier;
670    Sur l'eve del Ton les a feit osteilier;
Vint jors plenier les i feit demurer.
fol. 215ra Lur chevals funt seiner e reposer,
E lur malades guarir e mesciner.

Our fierce Emperor is in Paris.
630 The twelve peers — Roland and Oliver,
And Ansels, Girard, and Engeler,
Estult of Lengres and Turpin and Girier,
Baron Bertoloi and the warrior Otinel,
Duke Naimes and Ogier the Dane —
635 Lean their heads out the large windows.
They see Germans and Bavarians arrive;
Lorrainers with courageous ferocity;
And Poitevins and Provençal warriors;
Burgundians, Flemings, and men of Puy;
640 From Normandy comes the flower of knighthood.
Bretons arrive with wooden shields,
And lead mighty warhorses on the right.
Among all of them only four are squires —
If they show their skill, they'll be made knights.
645 They gather by the thousands below Montmartre.

On the first day of April at the rising of dawn,
King Charles and his horsemen mount.
They leave Paris and go to Saint-Denis,
Where they take leave, going on their way.
650 Their ladies weep and curse Garsie;
Horns sound; warhorses whinny.
Now the King travels as far as Lombardy,
With Duke Roland guiding the vanguard;
At the rear is white-bearded Naimes.
655 But Otinel doesn't want to leave his betrothed.
Belisant mounts a Hungarian mule
That can travel at a trot more quickly
Than a galley or ship moves on the sea.
She has seven hundred under her command,
660 All young men of great skill.
They exit France, leaving behind Burgundy;
The brave company passes through Mungiu,
Leaving the mountains, coming to Morie
They pass below Vercelli by ship
665 And, climbing Muntferant, they see Atelie —
The strong city where the hated people are.
They set up camp below Munpoun,
On the plain beside the Ton River.

Our Emperor orders the French to halt;
670 At the Ton River he orders encampment;
For a full twenty days he orders them to rest.
They give their horses care and repose,
And treat and tend to their own ailments.

Le fiz Pepin ne se volt ublier,
675        Tant dementiers a feit un punt lever
Par unt Franceis deivent ultre passer.
Sur le punt est nostre emperere ber,
U fet ses haies a sulives fermer
A mailz de fer cum fire e soldeer.
680        Fait est li punz, bien i pot hum passer.
Franceis se vont as herberges manger,
Mes Rollant s'est curu dunc aduber
Ke nul nel sorent ne nis li duze pier
Ne mes Oliver e li Daneis Ogier.
685        Tut treis s'adubent suz l'umbre d'un lorer,
As destres muntent, si vont le punt passer,
Vers la cité comencent a aler.
Meis ainz que viengent cil trei al returner,
Li plus hardi avera tant a penser —
690        Ni voldreit estre venuz pur un mui d'or cler!

Defors Hatillie, a une liue grant,
Ont quatre reis de la lei mescreant.
Issu se sunt, si se vont deportant,
Bien sunt armé, chascun a sun talent.
695        Ces sont lur nuns, si la chançun ne ment:
L'un Balsami, li reis de Ninivent;
L'altre Curable, un rei de pute gent,
Unques n'out fei vers nul hume vivant;
Li tierz a nun Askanart li tirant,
700        Forz est e fiers, e hardement a grant —
Mort a mil hummes de s'espee trenchant;
Li quart, Clarel a la chiere riant —
N'a tant bel humme; tant cun soleil resplent!
Ne treve nul qui juste li demant,
705        Ni ert si hardi, si a colp li atent,
Que nel occie u abate sanglent.
Par le champ vont destriers aleissant,
Forment manacent Oliver e Rollant,
E iurent deu s'il poent vivere tant
710        K'en duce France peussent mener lur gent!
Ja Charlemaine n'avera vers eus guarant;
Des duze piers, frunt trestut lur talent!
Ço dit Clarel a la chiere riant,
fol. 215rb   En manacer ne guanie l'um nient:
715        "J'ai oi grantment preiser Rollant,
N'at plus produmme de ci k'en Oriant,
Envers s'espee n'at humme guarant,
Meis mes deus pri, Mahun e Tervagant,
K'uncore eie de li assaiement,

Pepin's son wishes to neglect nothing,
675 So in the meantime he orders a bridge built
Over which the French will be able to pass.
Our noble Emperor stands on the bridge,
And orders the supports be strengthened
With steel bands of iron and solder.
680 Men can now safely cross the finished bridge.
The French head to their lodgings to eat,
But Roland hurries to arm himself
In such a way that no peer knows of it
Other than Oliver and Ogier the Dane.
685 The three arm themselves in the shade of a laurel,
Mount their warhorses, pass over the bridge,
And start to ride off toward the city.
But before it happens that these three return,
The bravest will have lots to ponder —
690 He'd not be there for a bushel of pure gold!

Outside of Atelie, a good league away,
Are four kings of the pagan host.
They've set out alone, taking a break,
Each one armed as he chooses.
695 Here are their names, if the song doesn't lie:
The first is Balsami, king of Ninivent;
The next is Corsable, a king of dissolute people,
Who's never given allegiance to anyone living;
The third one's name is Askanart the tyrant,
700 Who's strong and hardy, ferocious and huge —
He's killed a thousand with his sharp-edged sword;
The fourth is Clarel with the laughing face —
There's none more handsome; he shines like the sun!
There's none anywhere who'd challenge him to joust,
705 None so sturdy that, were Clarel to deal him a blow,
He'd not be killed or cut down bleeding.
They travel across the fields, letting their horses run,
And fiercely threatening Oliver and Roland,
While swearing to god to let them live long enough
710 To lead their army into sweet France!
Never would Charlemagne be protected from them;
Against the twelve peers, they'll do as they please!
Then says Clarel with the laughing face,
From whose menace none may escape:
715 "I've heard much praise given to Roland,
That none is as worthy from here to the Orient,
And that no one can be safe against his sword,
But I pray to my gods, Mahomet and Tervagant,
That, should I ever get to try him out,

720 K'un colp li duinse de m'espee trenchant
  Amunt le chief, sur le healme luisant.
  Mult par iert dur si desk'al denz nel fent!
  Kar jo ai grant dreit, si ne l'aim devient,
  Kar il m'occist Samsoinie de Muntbrant,
725 Sire Panpelume, a un turneiment.
  Il fu mis freres, si ai le quor dolant —
  Murrai de doel si mun frere ne vent!"
  Franceis chevacent tut celeement
  Delez un bois qui ad a nun Forestent.
730 La noise entendet si arestunt a itant.
  Li duc Rollant les veit premierement.
  "Seingnurs," fait il, "ore esteit gentement!
  Veez paens sur la roche qui pent.
  Ne sunt ke quatre, par men escient;
735 Bien i poum juster séurement,
  La merci Deu Omnipotent."
  E cil respunent, "Tut a vostre talent."
  Les hanstes mettent sur les feutres devant,
  Vers les paiens se vont esperunant.
740 Clarel reguarde vers levant
  E veit les contes brochier mut fierement;
  Ses compaingnuns apele ignelement:
  "Seingnurs," fait il, "aiez grant hardement!
  Treis chevalers vei de deça puinant;
745 Alez encontre! Sachez qu'il vont querrant!"
  E il leissent curre sanz nul retenement;
  N'i ont plus dit ne demandé nient
  Qu'il sunt, d'unt vienent, ne qu'il vont querrant,
  Meis de lur lances fierent durement.
750 Ascanard fiert sur l'escu Rollant,
  Desuz la bucle le depiece e fent;
  Fort est la bruine, ne depiece nient.
  Frusse la lance en sum le fer devant.
  Li quons le fiert tant ascemeement
755 Ke sen ne halberc ne li valt nient;
fol. 215va Le piz li frenche, le curaillie li fent,
  Mort l'a bati del bon destrier curant.
  Puis a dit Rollant, en riant,
  "Fiz a putain, trové avez Rollant,
760 K'aliez ore si forment manaçant!"

  Cursable juste a Ogier le curteis,
  Gent colp li done sur sun escu de peis,
  Ultre l'enpasse l'enseinie de cicleis,
  Del halberc trenche mailles trente treis,
765 Lez le costé li met le fer galeis;

720    I may deal him a blow with my sharp sword
        Right on his head, upon his shiny helmet.
        It would slice mightily down to his teeth!
        I have a righteous cause and no reason to love him,
        For he killed Samson of Muntbrant,
725    Lord of Pamplona, in a tournament.
        He was my brother, which breaks my heart —
        I'll die of sorrow if I don't avenge my brother!"
        The Frenchmen ride stealthily
        Below a woods called Forestent.
730    They hear noise and halt at once.
        Count Roland sees them first.
        "Lords," he says, "now things go nobly!
        Look at the pagans near that leaning rock.
        There are only four by my count;
735    Here we can joust quite comfortably,
        Thanks be to Almighty God."
        And they answer, "Just as you please."
        They set lances in sockets, aimed forward,
        And gallop toward the pagans.
740    Clarel looks to the east
        And sees the counts charge ferociously;
        He calls at once to his companions:
        "Lords," he says, "muster your courage!
        I see three knights approaching over there;
745    Let's meet them! You know what they want!"
        And they let loose without restraint;
        They said nothing and asked nothing
        Of who they are, where they're from, what they want,
        But with their lances they strike forcefully.
750    Askanart strikes Roland's shield,
        Shattering and splitting it above the boss;
        The mailshirt is strong, doesn't break at all.
        He breaks his lance high on the iron in front.
        The count strikes him so sharply
755    That his hauberk's worth nothing to him;
        He cracks the breastplate and splits his heart,
        Knocking him dead off his racing warhorse.
        Then said Roland, laughing,
        "Son of a whore, you've met Roland!
760    You who now charged so hardily!"

        Corsable jousts with Ogier the courteous,
        Dealing him a huge blow on his wood shield,
        Which passes through his silk standard,
        Cutting thirty-three links from his hauberk,
765    And thrusting the Galician iron along his side;

Enpeint bien, mes ne li valt un peis.
Ogier le fiert en l'escu clemaneis,
Parmi les armes li met le fer galeis;
Ne li valt mie le bon halberc un peis.
770 El cors li met le penun a orfreis,
Mort le tresturne del destrier espaneis.
El repairer li dit dous moz curteis:
"Fiz a putain, ço est Ogier le Daneis.
Pur tels colps feire, m'aime Charle li reis!"

775 Oliver juste al rei de Ninivent —
A Balsami qui at grant hardement
Sur sun escu u ont un liun peint.
Mes Oliver le fiert si dreitement
Sur la ruele que parmi le fent —
780 La melle bruinie ni li valt nient.
L'ensenie met tut dreit el cors devant,
Mort l'abati del destrier, sanglent.
Puis li a dit, "Al malfé te comant!"
Al turn k'il feit, si vint Clarel puinant —
785 Cil enprendra del paien vengement.
Si Oliver a icest colp l'atent,
Meis li niés Charle li traverse devant.
Clarel le fiert sur l'escu devant —
La bone bruinie li fu de mort garant!
790 Li bon destrier lieve les piez avant
Le destrer recule, sil veit consivant
K'en un munt chiet le destrer Rollent.
En halt s'escrie s'enseine, "Naimant!"
Vers la cité s'en volt aler fuiant,
795 Mes li Daneis li est alé devant,
Grant colp li dune del espee trenchant
En mi le piz, sur cel halberc luisant —
fol. 215vb La bone bruinie ne false ne n'estent.
Delez un munt l'abat del auferant.
800 Oliver prent le bon destrier curant,
Vient a Rollant, par le frein li rent.
"Sire," fait il, "muntez ignelement!
De part Ogier, le vus doins e present —
Meildre est del vostre. Jo qui qu'il valt les cent!"
805 Li quons salt sure k'a arçun ne se prent.
E li paen est lievé en estant,
Treit at s'espee, Mellee la trenchant,
L'escu enbrace, forment se defent.
Rollant sake Durendal le vaillant.
810 Un colp li veit doner de maintenant,
Meis li paen jette l'escu devant,

It prods well, but to him it's not worth a pea.
Ogier immediately strikes him on his shield,
Placing the Galician iron mid-armor;
To his good hauberk's not worth a pea.
770 He thrusts the gold-adorned standard into his body,
Twists him down dead from the Spanish warhorse.
He returns to speak some courteous words:
"Son of a whore, this is Ogier the Dane.
King Charles loves me for striking blows like this!"

775 Oliver jousts with the king of Ninivent —
Balsami who's so very bold
That a lion is displayed on his shield.
But Oliver strikes him so directly
On the round shield that it splits down the middle —
780 His mailshirt's now worthless to him.
He stabs with his banner straight through his body,
Knocking him from his horse, dead and bloody.
Then Oliver says, "I consign you to the devil!"
As he turns to go back, Clarel arrives at a gallop —
785 He plans to take vengeance for the pagan.
Oliver awaits the blow,
But Charles' nephew crosses in front.
Clarel strikes him on the front of his shield —
His good mailshirt has saved him from death!
790 Then his good warhorse lifts its front hooves
And recoils, and Clarel pursues it
Till Roland's warhorse falls dead in a heap.
Clarel loudly shouts his war cry, "Naimant!"
And intends to flee toward the city,
795 But the Dane has ridden in front of him,
Dealing him a huge blow with his keen sword
Amid the breastplate of his shiny hauberk —
His good mailshirt doesn't fail or stretch.
Close to a hill Ogier knocks him off his steed.
800 Oliver grabs the good warhorse as it's running
And, coming to Roland, hands him its reins.
"Lord," he says, "mount quickly!
On Ogier's behalf, I give and present it to you —
It's better than yours. I think it's worth a hundred!"
805 The count leaps on without grabbing the bow.
Meanwhile the pagan has stood up,
Drawing his sword, the keen-edged Mellee,
And grasping his shield to defend himself well.
Roland draws the magnificent Durendal.
810 He intends to give him a sudden blow,
But the pagan thrusts forward his shield,

Trestut li trenche quanke l'espee enprent.
Fort se combat mes ne li valt nient:
"Seingnurs, ma veie vus demant;
815        Pernez mei vif — eschec avez fait grant.
Quels est li sires, par m'espee me rent?"
S'espee rent; li quons Rollant la prent.
Puis li ameinent un neir destrier muvant
Dunt fu occis li rei de Ninivent.

820        Li compaingnun repairent de juster,
Clarel ont pris, s'il quident mener
A Charlemaine le volent presenter.
Meis einz qu'il puissent une liwe aler,
D'altre matire lur estuvera parler,
825        Kar Sarazin repairent de preer —
Mil e cinc cenz, tant i pot hum aismer.
Oient les corns, les busines suner,
Veient les healmes menu estenceler,
E les enseines par amunt venteler.
830        Rollant les veit si comence a sifler,
A ses estrius s'afiche li ber.
Envers Ogier prist li quons a jurer:
"Par cel Seingnur qui Deu se fait clamer,
S'a Durendal me peusse a eus meller,
835        Tant me verrez occire e decolper
Ke les noveles irreient ultre mer."
"Seignurs baruns," ço li dit Oliver,
"A sages hummes l'ai oi reconter
Hum ne se pot de tut ses mals garder,
fol. 216ra   Ne um ne pot tuz jurs senz juste ester,
841        E quant hum quide grant leesce encontrer,
Idunc est il plus pres del desturber."
"Veirs," dit Ogier, "ci a mal a penser,
Ne ci n'avera mester d'esponter.
845        Veez paens! Nes poez eschiver!
Parmi lur lances nus estuvera passer.
Ore deit chascun sa pruesce mustrer.
Puis k'um est pris, nel deit hum afoler;
Kar bien al rei nel pouns amener,
850        Bien le nus pot encui reguerdoner."
E dist Clarel, "Franc quor te fist parler."

"Sire Rollant," ço dit Ogier le ber,
"Fort estes e fiers, hardiz e redutez,
E de bataille bien enluminez,
855        E Oliver est chevaler pruvez,
E jo méisme de maint pas eschapez.

And the sword cleaves it as it strikes.
Clarel fights hard, but it's of no use:
"Lords, I ask you to grant me my life;
815     Take me alive — you've won a great prize.
Which of you is in charge, to receive my sword?"
He yields his sword; Count Roland takes it.
Then they convey him on the black warhorse
Upon which the king of Ninivent was killed.

820     The companions withdraw from the joust;
Having captured Clarel, they plan to return
And present him to Charlemagne.
But before they can travel a league,
They'll have to handle another matter,
825     For Saracens are returning from prayer —
Fifteen hundred, as well as one can guess.
They hear horns and trumpets,
And see helmets sparkle in succession,
And banners fluttering on high.
830     Roland sees them and begins to whistle,
Standing upright in his stirrups.
The count starts to make a vow to Ogier:
"By that Lord who has Himself called God,
If I'm able to engage them with Durendal,
835     You'll see me kill and cut up so many
That the news will spread beyond the sea."
"Lord barons," Oliver says to them,
"I've heard wise men say that
A man cannot protect himself from all evils,
840     Nor can a man live always without battle,
And just when a man believes he's found happiness,
Then is he the nearest to distress."
"Truly," says Ogier, "that man has trouble ahead,
And he'll have cause to be frightened.
845     Look at the pagans! We cannot avoid them!
We'll need to pass among their lances.
Each of us must now show his prowess.
Because this man's been captured, he mustn't be killed;
Since we can't very well lead him to the King,
850     He might still yet be able to reward us today."
And Clarel says, "A noble heart makes you speak."

"Lord Roland," says the noble Ogier,
"You're strong and brave, hardy and fearsome,
And illustrious in battle,
855     And Oliver is a proven knight,
And I myself have escaped from many ordeals.

Veez paens! Refuser nes poez,
N'altre sucurs d'umme n'atendez.
Ki ore n'i fierge, il seit cuard pruvez."
860        "Munjoie," escrient, eis les vus a justez
Ja i avera des morz e des naverez.

Rollant feri un paien, Berruier,
Qui plus est neir que mure de murer;
Mort le tresturne en miliu d'un sentier.
865        E Oliver fiert Balsan de Muntpellier;
E li Danais juste al Sarazin Motier.
Mort les abatent; cil furent li primer.
Treis ont occis des hanstes de pummer,
Puis ont treit les espees d'ascer.
870        Rollant les veit od Durendal trenchier,
Par un e un les feit trebuchier.
Oliver trovent li paien mult fier —
A Halteclere i fait tel sentier
Bien i purreient quatre chars encontrer.
875        Li bons Daneis i fet mult a preiser;
De bien ferir ne se volt targier:
Estreint Curteine si broche le destrier,
A trente paens a fait les chiefs voler.

Atant est venu Carmel de Tabarie,
880        Un Sarazin qui tus les altres guie.
Bien est armé, si set sur Pennepie.
fol. 216rb    En sun language a halte voiz escrie:
"Ke faites vus? Mahumet deu vus maldie!
Que dirrum nus a l'emperur Garsie —
885        Ke par treis hummes est si grant gent hunie?
Jo toldrai a un des treis ja la vie."
Puint le destrier, la lance a brandie,
E fiert Oger sur la targe flurie,
Desuz la bucle l'a freint e percie.
890        La bone bruine ne li valt une fie.
El cors li met l'enseinie d'Orcanie,
Naveré l'abat, ki ke peist u rie.
Veit le Rollant, ki ke peist u ki rie,
Ferir le vet sur le healme de Buzie,
895        Tut le purfent sanz nule garantie.
"Culvert," fet il, "Deu del ciel te maldie!
De quel vassal m'as tolu la compaingnie!"
Par le champ broche l'Alfage de Nubie,
Un Sarazin que Dampnedeu maldie,
900        Cusins fu a la bele Alfamie —
Hui matin li promist druerie,

Look at the pagans! We cannot avoid them,
And we can't expect help from anyone else.
Whoever doesn't fight now is a proven coward."
860    They cry out "Mountjoy!" and make battle vows
That soon there will be many dead and wounded.

Roland strikes a pagan named Berruier,
Blacker than a mulberry on a mulberry tree;
He drops him dead in the middle of a path.
865    And Oliver strikes Balsan of Montpellier;
And the Dane jousts with the Saracen Motier.
They strike them dead; they were the first.
They killed three with their applewood lances,
And then they drew their steel swords.
870    Roland proceeds to slice them with Durendal,
Overthrowing them one by one.
The pagans find Oliver very ferocious —
He made such a path with Halteclere
That they could easily drive four carts through it.
875    The good Dane does much that's praiseworthy;
He doesn't want to stop striking hard:
Drawing Curteine and spurring his warhorse,
He made the heads of thirty pagans fly.

Then there arrived Carmel of Tabarie,
880    A Saracen who led all the others.
He's well armed and seated on Pennepie.
He cries out loudly in his language:
"What are you doing? Mahomet curse you!
What shall we tell Emperor Garsie —
885    That so great an army was shamed by three men?
I'll take the life of one of the three now."
He spurs his warhorse, brandishes his lance,
And strikes Ogier on his decorated shield,
Crushing and piercing it above the boss.
890    His good mailshirt's not worth a fig.
Carmel thrusts the Orcanie standard into his body,
Knocking him down wounded, despite everything.
Roland sees it, despite everything,
Strikes him on his Buzie helmet,
895    Splitting straight through its protection.
"Villain," he says, "God of heaven curse you!
You've robbed me of a good warrior's company!"
Across the field spurs Alfage of Nubia,
A Saracen whom the Lord God curses,
900    And a kinsman of the beautiful Alfamie —
This very morning she'd promised him love service,

E il promist colp de chevalierie.
Si Deu n'en pense, le fiz seinte Marie,
Il lur fra mult grant estultie.
905    Fiert Oliver sur la bruine sarzie;
Fort est l'auberc qui li garda la vie.
Jus l'abiti, mes il nel n'aila mie.
Le quens relieve, si salt sur Pennepie,
Li bon destrier Carmel de Tabarie.
910    A halte voiz sun compaingnun escrie,
"Sire Rollant, ne vus esmaez mie!
Jo vus en ai la meie fei plevie
Ne vus faldrai tant cum averai la vie."
Ore comence le bruit e la folie
915    De nos Franceis e de la paienie.

Li bon Deneis haste de relever;
Grant est la presse, ne pot el bai monter.
Lores comence l'espee a reguarder:
"Oi Curteine, tant vus poi amer;
920    En la curt Charle vus feissez a loer.
Hui estuvera mei e vus deseverer,
Mes, einz que muire, vus voil esprover."
Fiert un paen sur sun healme cler,
fol. 216va  Desk'al denz li fait le brant culer.
925    Rollant recleime, mes il ne l'ot, li ber,
Kar il a tant endreit sei a penser
Qu'il ne set quel part il deit aler.
Oger assaillent Sarazin e Escler,
Il se defent cum gentil e ber.
930    Li reis Clarel le veit mult pener
E del espee ruistes colps doner.
En halt escrie, "Paien, laissez ester!
"Rent tei, Ogier. Ne t'estuet pas duter —
Tu te poz bien sur mei a fier.
935    N'averas mal dunt te peusse aider."
Dist l'almoafle, "Vus nel poez tenser;
Ja li verrez tuz les membres colper!"
Clarel l'entent, vif quide forsener;
Treit a s'espee, un colp li veit doner
940    K'en mi le champ li fet le chief voler.
Puis li a dit, "Leissez Ogier ester."
Vient al destrier, si fait le duc monter;
Uit Sarazins a fet demander,
De sa meinee, u plus se deit afier.
945    "Seingnurs," fet il, "ore pensez del errer.
Dites m'amie que face Ogier guarder."
Il lur livera, sis a laissé aler.

And he promised knightly blows.
Should God, holy Mary's son, not pay attention,
He'll soon inflict great harm upon them.
905 He strikes Oliver on his Saracen-made mailshirt;
It's a strong hauberk that saves his life.
He strikes him down but doesn't pierce him at all.
The count gets back up and leaps upon Pennepie,
The good warhorse of Carmel of Tabarie.
910 He calls out loudly to his companion,
"Lord Roland, don't be dismayed!
To you I've pledged my vow
Not to fail you as long as I live."
Now begins the noise and disturbance
915 Between our French and the pagans.

The worthy Dane hastens to get back up;
The crush is so thick he can't mount his bay horse.
Then he starts to look upon his sword:
"O Curteine, much do I love you;
920 You're praiseworthy in Charles' court.
Today you and I be must parted,
But, before I die, I want to test you."
He strikes a pagan on his bright helmet,
Causing the blade to slice to his teeth.
925 He calls upon Roland, but the baron doesn't hear
Because he has so much on his mind
That he doesn't know which way to turn.
Saracens and Slavs attack Ogier,
Who defends himself nobly and bravely.
930 King Clarel sees him greatly distressed
By savage sword blows raining upon him.
He shouts out, "Pagans, leave him alone!
Yield yourself, Ogier. Don't be afraid —
You can rely on me with confidence.
935 You'll come to no harm so long as I can help."
Says the emir, "You can't protect him;
Soon you'll see his limbs all hacked up!"
Clarel hears him and at once feels enraged;
He draws his sword, moving to deal him a blow
940 So that amid the field his head goes flying.
Then he says to him, "Leave Ogier alone."
He brings the warhorse and lets the duke mount;
He orders that eight Saracens be summoned,
Very loyal members of his own household.
945 "Lords," he says, "prepare now to travel.
Tell my betrothed to have Ogier watched over."
He delivers him and then has them depart.

Sovent li funt ses plaies pasmer.
La fille al rei, Alfamie al vis cler,
950      En un vergier entra pur deporter,
Ensembl'od lui Guaite e Belamer.
Virent paiens a la barre passer,
Dit l'une a l'altre, "Alum a eus parler
De lur corage saver e demander."

955      Dist Alfamie, "Baruns qu'iluec estez,
De vos noveles kar nus recontez.
Cil chevaler u fu il encontrez?
Fu il pris en juste u en estur naverez?"
"Pucele gente," fait li velz almafez,
960      "Par Mahumet, purquei nus engabez?
Ja avum nus les quors itant enflez
Ke nus nen prent de rire volentez."
"Ki a ço fait? Guarde nel me celez."
E dient cil, "Cist fol buinard pruvez.
965      Il e dui altre ont si les noz menez
fol. 216vb  K'a cent paens ont les testes colpez.
Clarel vus mande, vostre ami le senez,
Pur sue amur, que cestui bien guardez."
Dist la pucele, "Ore vus returnez
970      Pernez mei les altres, sis mi amenez."
Dient paiens, "Einz passera estez!"
Puis dit al cunte, "Ore vus en venez,
Jo vus promet que bon ostel averez.
Cum avez nun? De quele gent estes nez?"
975      "Ogier ai nun le Daneis alosez.
En la curt Charle en est mi parentez."
Dist la pucele, "Ore vus conuis assez."

Ces treis puceles ont amené Ogier
En une place desuz un oliver.
980      Primerement areinent le destrer,
Puis desarment le curteis chevaler.
L'une prent le halme, l'altre le brant d'ascer,
Del dos li treient le bon halberc dublier.
Ses plaies levent, sil mettent culchier.
985      D'une herbe duce li donent a mangier
Ke Deu meisme planta en sun vergier.
"Tost-seine" at a nun, tel pot hum preiser.
Cil s'endormi, qui at grant mester.
Quant il s'esveille, si se senz tut legier
990      E plus fu sein que pume de pumer.
Ore leissum ici del curteis Ogier,
Qui assez at de quank'il at mestier.

His wounds cause him to swoon frequently.
The king's daughter, Alfamie with the fair face,
950 Has entered a garden to amuse herself,
Bringing with her Guaite and Belamer.
They see the pagans pass through the gate,
And say to each other, "Let's go speak with them
To ask and learn about their courage."

955 Alfamie says, "You barons standing here,
Tell us now your news.
Where did you encounter this knight?
Was he taken by joust or wounded in battle?"
"Noble maid," says an old emir,
960 "Why do you mock us, by Mahomet?
Our hearts are already so deflated
That we don't need to be laughed at."
"What did he do? Don't hide it from me."
And they say, "He's a proven madman.
965 He and two others have so handled us
That a hundred pagans have been beheaded.
Clarel, your wise sweetheart, requests
That, for his love, you guard this one well."
The maiden says, "Return now
970 To capture the others and bring them to me."
The pagans respond, "It will happen as before!"
Then she says to the count, "Now that you've come,
I promise you'll have good lodging.
What's your name? Among whom were you born?"
975 "My name's Ogier the renowned Dane.
My kinsmen are in Charles' court."
The maiden says, "Now I know who you are."

These three maidens have led Ogier
Into a courtyard beneath an olive tree.
980 They first take care of the warhorse,
And then disarm the courteous knight.
One takes his helmet, the other his steel sword,
From his back they remove his fine double-ring hauberk.
They wash his wounds, then have him lie down.
985 They give him food spiced with a sweet herb
That God himself planted in His garden.
Its name is "heal-all," so much do men value it.
He falls asleep quickly, having great need of rest.
When he wakes up, he feels entirely refreshed
990 And healthier than a plum on a plum tree.
Let us now leave here the courteous Ogier,
Who has plenty of whatever he needs.

Del duc Rollant dirum e d'Oliver,
Qui se combatent as espees d'ascer.
995     Uncore i a des paens un millier.
Ne poent mes les granz colps enhacier —
Sil s'enfuient n'est pas a merveiller.
Fuiant, s'en vont tut un chemin plener,
Paens les siwent pur les testes colper.
1000    Otinel fait les contes demander,
Lors s'aveit bien quant nes poeit trover
Ke vers Atille sunt alé pur juster.
Ignelement se curut aduber,
E ovec lui tel set cenz chevalier,
1005    Trestut li pire purreit un rei mater.
El destrier munte si veit al rei parler:
"Sire, faites Franceis vistement armer!
fol. 217ra  Alum le siege mettre e ordener,
Kar vostre nies m'at pur cuard prover —
1010    K'ui matin est alé pur juster.
Si mal li vient, qui en deit blasmer?
Trop se volt faire sur tuz hummes loer!
Meis, par celui qui Deu se fait clamer,
Si jo puis hui Sarazins encontrer,
1015    Bien m'i orrez "Munjoie!" escrier,
E de m'espee si ruiste colp doner
Ja de Rollant n'estuvera parler."


Nostre emperere a fait un corn soner.
Franceis s'adubent, si vunt le punt passer.
1020    Al duc Samsun fist l'enseine porter.
La veissiez tant gunfanuns lever,
Tanz hanstes dreites, tant pennuns venteler,
Deu ne fist humme kis peust anunbrer.
Forment s'afichent cil legier bacheler;
1025    Les uns vers les altres comencent avanter,
De ruistes colps sur Sarazins doner.
De l'ost s'en partent cil set cent bacheler,
Ke Belesent a tuz a sun manjer.
Otinel broche Fluri sun destrier,
1030    Devant les altres, al treit d'un archer.
Bien est armé a lei de chevaler.
Ses cunuissances d'un paile cursier
Ne peisent une quatre fuilz d'un saltier —
N'est une nez qu'is peust alegier.
1035    Kar feu ne flamme nes poet damager,
E cil qui at le pesant d'un dener,
Tant nes peusse naverer ne blescier,
Ke ne sente tut sein e legier.

Let's speak of Duke Roland and of Oliver,
Who are battling with steel swords.
995   There are still a thousand pagans there.
They can no longer fight off the great blows —
It's not surprising that they'd run away.
Fleeing, they take an open path,
While pagans chase them to sever their heads.
1000   Meanwhile Otinel asks about the counts,
And figures out when they can't be found
That they've gone off to Atelie to joust.
He hurries at once to arm himself,
And to bring seven hundred with him,
1005   Of whom even the worst could defeat a king.
He mounts his horse and informs the King:
"Lord, order the French to arm quickly!
We're going to prepare and set up the siege,
For your nephew's taken me for a coward —
1010   This morning he went out to joust.
If trouble comes to him, who'd be responsible?
He desires too eagerly to be praised above all!
But, by He who has Himself called God,
If I can meet with Saracens today,
1015   You'll surely hear me cry "Mountjoy!"
And I'll give such savage blows with my sword
That we'll never again have to speak of Roland."

Our Emperor ordered a trumpet sounded.
The French arm themselves and then cross the bridge.
1020   It's given to Duke Samson to carry the standard.
You could see so many flags raised,
So many upright lances, so many flowing pennons,
That God never created a man who could count them.
The skilled young knights stand strong;
1025   Some begin to boast in support of others,
To strike savage blows upon the Saracens.
Seven hundred youths depart from the army,
All kept by Belisant at her table.
Otinel spurs Flori, his warhorse,
1030   Riding an arrow-flight's length in front of others.
He's thoroughly armed according to chivalric law.
His fine coverings of Turkish cloth
Weigh barely as much as four psalter leaves —
One mightn't lighten them by even a whit.
1035   Neither fire nor flame might do them harm,
And whoever has just a penny's weight of them,
No matter how he might be injured or wounded,
Would feel totally healthy and sound.

La fille Charle, ki mult fait a preiser,
1040          Les li dona, e l'enseignie Galtier.
Rollant encontre a l'eissir d'un viver,
De sa parole le volt contralier:
"Sire," fait il, "venez vus de peschier?
Quidez vus sul les paiens tuz mangier?
1045          E jo e vus i averum assez a rungier.
Turnez ariere ja vus poez vengier;
Mort sunt paens m'arivrent l'enchascier."
Guarde sur destre, si at veu encombrier
Ki s'en veneit consiwint Oliver.
fol. 217rb     Ja li aveit si naveré sun destrier
1051          Ke de set parz i vit le sanc raier;
Mult li aveit sucurs grant mester!
Otinel broche Fluri sun destrer,
Brandit sa lance, veit ferir encumbrier.
1055          Desuz la bucle en fait l'escu percer —
Ne li valt mie li clavels un denier.
L'enseinie blanche li fet el cors banier;
Mort le tresturne en un liu d'un sentier.
Estult de Lengres ala ferir Claver;
1060          Escu ne halber nel pot de mort aider —
Mort l'abati delez un genester.
"Munjoie!" escrient. "Ferez i, chevaler!"
E il si funt qui meuz se pot aider.
La out grant bruit as enseingnes beisser
1065          Dunc veissez fier estur comencer:
Tanz hanstes freindre, tanz escuz percier,
E tanz halbers rumpre e desmaeiler;
E Sarazins verser e trebuchier —
Suz ciel n'at humme kis peust aconter!

1070          Engelers en veit les reues cerchant,
Sa hanste a freinte, en sum poin sum brant.
Veit Clariados qui tient Numilliant,
K'a justé a Reiner de Melant —
A batu la . . . . . . . . . . . . . .
1075          Mais Engeler li contredit itant,
"Nel amerras ainz te frai dulant!"
Ferir le vet sur sun healme devant
Par tel vertu que desk'as denz le fent;
Le cors chiet, vis l'alme vet a turment.
1080          Un Sarazin i veit espurunant:
Ço est Galatas qui tient Tyrie la Grant.
Desur ses pers, a pris grant hardement;
Beise sa lance, l'enseinie vole al vent.
Envers le conte met sum çoes en present,

Charles' daughter, worthy of much praise,
1040    Gave them to him with King Gautier's standard.
He meets Roland at the outlet of a fish pond,
And begins by greeting him contrarily:
"Lord," he says, "have you come from fishing?
Do you think that you alone can eat all the pagans?
1045    Both of us will have enough to gnaw on there.
Turn around now and take vengeance;
The pagans are dead if they choose to chase me."
He looks to the right and sees trouble
Coming from one who pursued Oliver.
1050    He'd already injured his warhorse
So that blood flowed from seven wounds;
He was direly in need of help!
Otinel spurs Flori his warhorse,
Brandishes his lance and proceeds to strike.
1055    He pierces his shield below the boss —
The chain mail's not worth a penny to him.
The white banner plunges through his body;
He throws him down dead amidst a path.
Estult of Lengres moves to strike Claver;
1060    Neither shield nor hauberk can protect him from death —
He knocks him dead beneath a thicket of broom.
"Mountjoy!" they cry. "Strike them, knights!"
And they all do the best they can to assist.
There was loud noise around lowered banners
1065    As we saw the fierce battle begin:
So many lances shattered, so many shields pierced,
And so many hauberks torn and broken;
So many Saracens upset and overthrown —
No man under sky is able to count them!

1070    Engeler goes searching along the paths,
His lance shattered, his sword in his fist.
He sees Clariados, the lord of Numilliant,
Who had jousted with Renier of Melant —
He'd knocked him . . . . . . . . . . . .
1075    But Engeler responds to him,
"For love of him, I'll make you grieve!"
He goes to strike him on his helmet-front
With such power that he splits him to the teeth;
The body falls, then the soul goes to torment.
1080    A Saracen arrives, spurring his horse:
Galatas who governs Tyrie the Great.
He has great strength, surpassing his peers;
He lowers his lance, his standard blowing in the wind.
He presents himself before the count,

1085 As espuruns tant cum cheval li rent.
   Fiert Engeler sur sun escu devant,
   Ultre li met l'enseinie aliant,
   Bien pleine palme le descire e estent.
   Desuz l'essele li met le fet trenchant,
1090 Deu le guarist k'en la char nel prent.
   Nel pot tenir sele n'estriu d'argent,
fol. 217va Voilie une voile a terre le descent.
   "Gaite," escrie, "k'il ne porte le guant!"

   Engeler est en la presse entrez.
1095 Sil bons escuz li est del col volez!
   Mien escient, il fust bien remuntez,
   Quant Talot broche, un Turc de fine Surez,
   Mort at mil hummes puisqu'il fu adubez;
   Od seisante altres est sur li arestez.
1100 Lancent les lances, les gros darz enpennez,
   E gavelocs, e fausarz quarrez.
   Mult malement fu le jur debutez!
   Sil haubercs fu en trente lius nafrez;
   N'est pas merveille s'il est mult blescez,
1105 Mais il n'a plaie dunt il se sent encombrez.
   Si a cheval puisse estre muntez!
   Sil branz d'ascer iert as Turcs privez;
   Tels sunt seins k'il trenchera les chiefiez.
   A recusse nient puingnant Ysorez,
1110 Galtier de Huns e Dain li membrez,
   Girard d'Orliens, e Hertald li barbez —
   De bien ferir s'est chascun aprestez.
   "Munjoie," escrient, si les ont reculez
   Si k'Engelers est el bai muntez.
1115 Granz colps se donent en ces escuz listez,
   Ensemble justent Talot e Ysorez;
   Les eis depiecent si ont les quirs percez,
   Les fers se plient sur ces halbers safrez.
   Nes pot tenir sele n'estriu dorrez,
1120 Peitrel, ne cengle, ne frein d'argentez —
   Tut li plus fort est a terre versez.
   Talot relieve si salt sus Ysorez.
   Mettent lur mains as espees delez,
   L'ascer luist des branz qu'il unt levez.
1125 Forment se fierent sur ces healmes gemmez.
   Ja feust le champ de quei que fust finez
   Ne fust la presse que lur a desturbez.
   Galtier de Huns a Armagot s'est comitez,
   Mort l'abati — l'alme en portent malsfez!
1130 Franceis i fierent as bons branz acerez,

| | |
|---|---|
| 1085 | Galloping as fast as his horse can manage. |
| | He strikes Engeler directly on his shield |
| | So that the standard goes right through it, |
| | Tearing and extending it an entire palm's width. |
| | He sets the sharp iron under the armpit, |
| 1090 | But God protects him, so it doesn't pierce his flesh. |
| | He can't retain his saddle or silver stirrups, |
| | But glides down to earth like a sail. |
| | "Watch out," he shouts, "lest he win the day!" |
| | |
| | Engeler has thus entered the melee. |
| 1095 | His sturdy shield about his neck was needed! |
| | It seems to me he's gotten back up, |
| | When in rides Talot, a Turk from distant Surez, |
| | Who's killed a thousand since he was dubbed; |
| | He attacks him along with sixty others. |
| 1100 | They throw spears and large feathered arrows, |
| | Short javelins, and squared-headed falchions. |
| | This day has begun inauspiciously! |
| | His hauberk was cut in thirty places; |
| | It'd be no surprise if Engeler were badly wounded, |
| 1105 | But he has no injury that bothers him. |
| | If only he could be mounted on a horse! |
| | His steel sword was seized by the Turks; |
| | Their intentions are to cut off his head. |
| | Spurring to the rescue comes Ysorez, |
| 1110 | Gautier the Hun, and the renowned Dane, |
| | Girard of Orléans, and the bearded Hertald — |
| | Each one prepared to strike well. |
| | "Mountjoy," they shout, and push them back |
| | So that Engeler is mounted on the bay horse. |
| 1115 | They exchange strong blows on edged shields, |
| | Talot and Yzorez fighting each other; |
| | They've cut up the shields and pierced the leathers, |
| | With iron rings bending on adorned hauberks. |
| | Neither can hold onto saddle or gilded stirrups, |
| 1120 | Onto breastpiece, saddle girth, or silver harness — |
| | Despite their strength, both are thrown down. |
| | Talot rises up and jumps toward Ysorez. |
| | They place their hands on ready swords, |
| | The steel shining from blades they've raised. |
| 1125 | They strike powerfully on gemmed helmets. |
| | It would have been the field upon which they died |
| | Were it not that the press separated them. |
| | Gautier the Hun has jousted with Armagot, |
| | Striking him dead — may devils take his soul! |
| 1130 | The French have struck with good steel blades, |

Trenchent espalles, eschines, e costez.
D'ambes parz i trebuchent assez
Li plus delivre en est trestut encombrez.
fol. 217vb De sanc vermail en est tuschie li prez.


1135 Arepater broche — un Turc de Florient,
D'une cité de la Inde la Grant.
Vint a Clarel par la reidne le prent.
"Sire," fait il, "par vus ne faisum nient.
Ço dist, ja aurez mun talent:
1140 Selunc les eues, nel eissent nient;
Envers les noz vont espurunant."
Clarel s'escrie s'enseinie, "Naimant!"
Arapater la sue, "Floriant!"
A ces enseinies vienent Mor e Persent
1145 E Arabiz — tuit bien tresk'a cent,
Celui n'i a nen art gunfanun gent,
U arc turkeis u gaveloc trenchant.
Franceis reculent bien demi arpent.
Li reis justa a Droun l'Alemant,
1150 L'escu li brise suz la bucle d'argent,
L'escu li false li clavel en estent,
El il cors li met sun espé trenchant,
Entre les francs l'abiti mort sancglent.
Arapater tient l'espee trenchant,
1155 Girard d'Orliens en fiert tant egrement
Ke la cervele e les oilz li espant.
Quant il l'at mort, si s'en veit gualopant,
Mes Otinel li est venuz devant,
S'espee treite, sun escu portant.
1160 Arapater curt vers li auferant,
Ferir le veit par mut grant hardement
Si ke l'escu e le healme li fent;
Dur sunt li quir, ne pot ester nient;
Mes la grant targe tresk'as armes prent,
1165 Ço m'est avis ja feist tut sun talent,
Quant li brise s'espee en estraant.
Otinel le fiert abandunement
Par tel vertu ke desk'as quor li fent.
Li cors iet jus, a diables le comant,
1170 Puis si a dit, "Nus esteium parent.
Pur tel servise tel guerdun te rent!"
Li reis Clarel est al turneiement,
De tutes parz veit tresbucher sa gent,
Murir e brave e occire a turment.
1175 Entre Franceis ses leisse irrément.
fol. 218ra A ceste puinte occist Ricard d'Eiglent,

Slitting shoulders, chests, and sides.
On both sides they overthrow so many
That even the most powerful are involved.
The meadow is covered with vermilion blood.

1135    Arapater rushes in — a Turk from Floriant,
A city in India the Greater.
He takes hold of Clarel by the reins.
"Lord," he says, "we've not brought you success,
But, even so, listen now to my news:
1140    Beside the rivers it's not going well;
They are galloping toward us."
Clarel cries out his battle-cry, "Naimant!"
Arapater his, "Floriant!"
Toward their standards come Moors, Persians,
1145    And Arabs — all told nearly a hundred,
Every one of them bearing a noble pennant,
Or Turkish bow, or sharp-pointed javelin.
The French withdraw a half-arpent's length.
The king jousts with Droun the German,
1150    Piercing his shield on the silver boss,
And so much damaging the links on his shield
That he stabs the sharp blade in his body,
Striking him dead and bloody among the French.
Arapater holds his keen-edged sword,
1155    And strikes Girard of Orléans so fiercely
That his brains and eyes burst out.
After killing him, he gallops away,
But Otinel cuts in front of him,
And, holding his shield, draws his sword.
1160    Arapater races his warhorse toward him,
Moving to strike him with tremendous ferocity
So that he pierces shield and helmet;
The leathers are tough, but they're useless;
If the great shield hadn't covered Otinel's arms,
1165    I think he'd have accomplished all his intent,
But fortunately the blade broke.
Otinel strikes him with such skill
And power that the blow cuts right to the heart.
He throws down the body, consigns it to the devil,
1170    And then says to him, "We were kinsmen.
I render you reward for your service!"
King Clarel in the midst of battle
Sees his men fleeing in all directions,
Dying, bereft, and painfully killed.
1175    He strikes angrily in the midst of the French.
He kills with his blade Richard of Eiglent,

Garnier d'Angiers, e Hugun de Clarvent;
Nelis le pruz jeta mort sanglent.
Fors de la presse eissi si gentement
1180   K'il ni perdi un espurun vaillant.
Sune sun gresse pur ralier sa gent,
Meis il ne pot aver od sei que cent.
Cil s'en vont vers la cité fuiant.
Franceis le siwent qui les tresbuchent sovent.

1185   Paiens s'enfuient e cil de barbarie
Desk'as destreiz sur la roche navie,
Iloquis encontrent la riche compaingnie
De la meisnee l'emperur Garsie —
Vint mile sunt la pute gent haie!
1190   Ja feust bataille ne remansist mie.
Meis li jur vait, si passe complie.
Clarel met jus la grant targe flurie,
Trait la ventaille de la bruinie sarzie,
A halte voiz, vers Otinel s'escrie:
1195   "Va, ki es tu? Mahumet te maldie!
Di mei tun nun, s'il nuncirai Garsie."
Dist li convers, "N'el te celerai mie.
Ço est Otinel a la chire hardie,
Fiz Galien. Ma mere at nun Clye.
1200   Baptizé sui. Laissé ai la folie.
Charles de France m'at doné Lumbardie
E Belesent sa fillie a amie.
Jameis paien n'amerai en ma vie."
Ço dit Clarel, "Merveille ai oie!
1205   As tu dunc issi ta fei mentie?
Enchanté es, si as ben l'ester lie,
De quei cil mirie des t'en prent l'esturdie.
Ber, kar ce viene si te reconcilie.
Fai dreit Mahun de si grant felonie
1210   Cum tu as fait de ta lei k'as guerpie.
Jo metrai peis entre tei e Garsie,
Si te durrai la metrai d'Almarie."
Dist Otinel, "Ço ne frai jo mie,
Mal dehez ait la vostre compaingnie,
1215   Mes, par la fei que dei Sainte Marie,
Si te puis prendre u l'emperur Garsie,
Jo vus pendrai as puis de Satanie!"
fol. 218rb   Fait li paien, "Or as dit grant estultie.
Des meillurs hummes de tute paienie,
1220   Mult avez le quor plein de felonie.
Prest sui ke face vers tei un aatie,
Tut sul a sul, de m'espee furbie,

Garnier of Angers, and Hugh of Clarvent;
He throws down worthy Nelis, dead and bloody.
He emerges from the melee so worthily
1180　That the brave one loses not even a spur.
To rally his men, he sounds his horn,
But can't summon more than a hundred to him.
They gallop fleeing toward the city.
The French pursue and frequently kill them.

1185　The pagans and barbarians escape
As far as the edge of the rocky shore,
Where they meet the powerful army
Of Emperor Garsie's household —
Twenty thousand rotten, loathsome men!
1190　Very few were left from the battle.
But daylight fails, and compline has passed.
Clarel lays down his large decorated shield,
Pulls off the aventail of his Saracen mailshirt,
And shouts loudly toward Otinel:
1195　"Say, who are you? May Mahomet curse you!
Tell me your name. I'll announce you to Garsie."
The convert responds, "I'll hide nothing at all.
I'm Otinel of courageous bearing,
Son of Galien. My mother's named Clie.
1200　I am baptized. I have abandoned error.
Charles of France has given me Lombardy
And his daughter Belisant as my betrothed.
I will never in my life love a pagan."
Answers Clarel, "That's incredible!
1205　Have you then abandoned your faith?
You've been bewitched, your spirit coerced,
By doctors who've rendered you senseless.
Baron, come now and be reconciled.
Make amends with Mahomet for the evil
1210　You've committed against the faith you've given up.
I'll bring peace between you and Garsie,
And grant you lordship over Almary."
Says Otinel, "No, I won't do that,
For I despise your company,
1215　But, by the faith I owe blessed Mary,
If I'm able to capture you or Emperor Garsie,
I'll hang you over the hell pits of Satan!"
The pagan responds, "Now you talk like a fool!
Despite being one of the best of all heathendom,
1220　Your heart's the most full of treachery.
I'm ready to meet you in an ordeal by combat,
One to one, with my polished sword,

Ke tis baptesmes ne la cristienie
Ne cele messe ke prestre sacrefie
1225    Vers nostre lei ne valt un alie.
Melz valt Mahun ke fait le fiz Marie!"

Dist li convers, "Diable sunt en tei!
Si vols Mahun defendre envers mei,
Fai mei seur ke ne remanie en tei,
1230    E jo defendrai Dampnedeu e sa lei."
Li Sarazin en a lievé le dei,
E Otinel li a promis sa fei
Ke la bataille ne remaindra en sei.

En la cité en est Clarel entrez,
1235    E Otinel en a les suens amenez.
Herbergié sunt nos Franceis es prez;
Tendent lur loges si ont feu alumez.
Cil mirie portent uniement as naffiez;
Les morz en ont en fosses enterrez.
1240    Al trief le rei est Otinel alez;
Nostre emperere est encontre alez,
E Belisent e Naimes li barbez.
L'estrui li tenent liber est desmuntez.
La fille Charles li cerche les costez
1245    K'il ne seit entamé ne nafrez;
Treis feiz la beise quant il fu desarmez.
"Filiol," dist Charle, "curteise amie avez."
"Sire," fait il," Deus en seit loez,
Ço comparunt li paen malsenez."

1250    L'ost le rei guaitent Burguinun e Alemant.
La nuit dormi Charle seuremant,
E li paien guaitent fierement;
Cornent e crient desk'al soleil levant.
Clarel se lieve al jur aparissant,
1255    Ist de la chambre, si s'arme ignelement.
A l'adubier fu Canor de Muntbrant,
E Meliens, e Apolin le grant,
Quatre feiz est majur d'un giant.
En dos li vestent un halberc jacerant —
fol. 218va    Ki l'at vestu ne crient arme trenchant,
1261    Ke maele en oste tant sunt li clou tenant,
Meis si Otinel pusse apresmer tant,
K'a Cureçuse k'il fierge del trenchant,
Ja vers l'espee n'avera hauber guarant!
1265    El chief li lacent un healme al rei priant —
N'est pas de fer ne de fust ne d'argent,

To prove that neither your baptism nor Christianity
Nor the Mass consecrated by priests
1225   Is worth a bitter sorb-apple next to our law.
Mahomet is worth more than Mary's son!"

The convert says, "There are devils in you!
If you choose to uphold Mahomet against me,
Swear to me that he dwells in you,
1230   And I'll stand for Lord God and His faith."
The Saracen raised his finger at this word,
And Otinel pledged his faith to him
That the battle would be theirs alone.

Clarel goes into the city,
1235   And Otinel leads away his people.
Our French are camped in the fields;
They pitch their tents and light fires.
Doctors carry ointment to the wounded;
They've interred the dead in graves.
1240   Otinel has gone to the King's tent;
Our Emperor goes to meet him,
Along with Belisant and bearded Naimes.
Freed from his stirrups, he dismounts.
Charles' daughter examines his sides
1245   Lest he be injured or wounded;
When he's disarmed, she kisses him three times.
"Godson," Charles says, "you have a noble sweetheart."
"Lord," he says, "May God be worshiped,
And so may the evil pagans be punished."

1250   Burgundians and Germans guard the King's army.
That night Charles sleeps safely,
And the pagans boldly keep watch;
They sound trumpets and shout till sunrise.
Clarel awakens at the break of day,
1255   Leaves his chamber, and quickly is armed.
At his arming were Canor of Muntbrant,
Meliens, and the great Apolin,
Who's four times larger than a giant.
On his back they place a mail hauberk —
1260   The one wearing it fears no sharp weapon,
For its battle-ready links are made of nails,
But if Otinel can get close enough to it,
With Corçuse, which he wields so keenly,
Never will the hauberk protect against that sword!
1265   On the devout king's head, they lace a helmet
Not made of iron, wood, or silver,

Ainz est dost de la teste d'un serpent.
Escrit i sunt Jovin e Tervagant,
E Mahumet en la guise d'un enfant:
1270 Cil sunt li deu k'il recleime sovent,
Par ces quide il aler seurement.
Al col li pendent un fort escu peisant,
Tut est de quir, ni a de fust nient;
Dis e uiit bucles en ja d'or luisant.
1275 Puis li aportent un enseinie pendant
D'un vermail paile percie menuement.
Puis ceint Mellee, s'espee trenchant,
K'il ne dureit pur mil mars d'or luisant.
Enmi la place li meint l'um Turnevent,
1280 Qui tant va tost, quant il espurun sent,
Que l'arundele post prendre en volant.
Salt en la sele k'a arçun ne se prent,
Sunt sun gredle pur esturmir sa gent.
Par la cité sarment li mescreant;
1285 Li reis s'en trane, as esperuns brochant.
Dist Alphamie, "A Mahun te comant.
Apolin, sue victorie li consent:
De mil mars d'or te frai acressement!"
Fors de la porte se vet espurunant;
1290 Aprés lui vunt Sarazin e Persant,
E Arabis e Turcs bien desk'a cent.
Mahumet levent en un char vertant,
Ultre li passent la fort eue bruiant.
Sur un halt pui, le leissant en estant,
1295 Forment l'atachent a chaenes d'argent,
K'il ne chere n'ariere n'avant.
Trestuit l'aurent e prient humlement
Que vertu i face; chascun i fet present.
Tut li plus povre i offri un besant.
1300 Clarel s'en veit, sun destrier aleissant,
Arestez est sur un eue curant.
fol. 218vb Veit l'ost de France e derire e devant.
Suavet le dit, que nul nel entent,
"Mahumet, sire," fet il, cum faite gent,
1305 "Icil frunt Garsie al quor dolent."

Nostre emperere est par matin levez.
Sur l'eue del col depoeter est alez,
E ovec lui de ses meillurs privez.
Rollant i est, e Naimes li barbez,
1310 E Oliver e Ote li menbrez.
Clarel s'est a la rive arestez,
A haute voiz escrie, "Vus, ki la estez!

But instead designed from a snake's head.
Etched upon it are Jove and Tervagant,
And Mahomet in the form of a child:
1270 To these gods he frequently appeals,
By whom he believes he'll be protected.
Around his neck they hang a tough, heavy shield,
Made entirely of leather without any wood;
They attach it with eighteen bright gold buckles.
1275 Then they bring him a standard from which hangs
A fine-woven vermilion Persian cloth.
Next they gird on Mellee, his keen-edged blade,
Which he'd not give up for a thousand bright gold marks.
In the middle of the square they lead out Turnevent,
1280 Who, when it feels the spur, races as fast
As a swallow can speed when it flies.
He jumps in the saddle without gripping its bow,
And sounds his horn to awaken his army.
Throughout the city he summons nonbelievers;
1285 Spurring his horse, the king draws them together.
Alfamie says, "I commend you to Mahomet.
Apolin, may you grant him victory:
I'll give you a gift of a thousand gold marks!"
He rides swiftly out of the gate;
1290 After him go Saracens and Persians,
And as many as a hundred Arabs and Turks.
They mount Mahomet on a moving cart,
Passing beyond the strong, roaring river.
On a high mound they leave it standing,
1295 Attaching it securely with silver chains,
So that it couldn't fall backward or forward.
All of them worship it and pray humbly
That it work a miracle; each gives it a gift.
Even the poorest offers a bezant.
1300 Clarel rides forth, racing his warhorse,
And stops by a flowing stream.
He sees the French army behind and before.
Speaking softly, so that no one may hear,
"Mahomet, lord," he says, like a nobleman,
1305 "These warriors will sadden Garsie's heart."

Our Emperor arose in the morning.
He went to the fork of the river to relax,
Having with him his closest companions.
There are Roland and bearded Naimes,
1310 Oliver and the renowned Otinel.
Pausing at the bank, Clarel
Shouts out loudly, "You, over there!

Est iloec Charle li chanu li membrez?"
E dit l'emperere, "Frere, que me volez?"
1315    "Jo te durrai, que mar fussez vus nez!
Trop as vesçu! Chanu es e barbez —
Presca ke dussez estre a un pel tuez!
Travellez estes, e destruiz e deseritez.
Ja est ta corune e cis empires donez
1320    Al meillur humme k'unques mes fust nez —
Florien de Sulie — ki tant est alosez.
Cil estera reis de France clamez!"
Ço dit li reis, "Mut par es enparlez,
E de mençunge dire bien endoctrinez.
1325    Uncore s'ail al destrier tut armez,
Qui de seez reis ai par force matez.
Ore ce promet ma fei, si ert veritez,
James n'en ert cest siege deseverez
Si ert prise Garsie e destruite sa citez."
1330    E dit Clarel, "Dire ce fist malfez!
Ne fais a creire; trop as tes jurs usez;
Chief as chanu; si sunt ci peis mellez!
Par tei ni ert mes faite nule buntez —
N'estur comencé ne tur enfermez!"
1335    Vergunie a Charle si a Francs esgardez;
Al curuz, ka si est desafublez,
Dit a Galdin, "Mes armes m'aporter."
"Sire," dit Otes, "vostre ire atemprez.
Pur meie amur, ne vus desmesurez,
1340    Kar j'ai ma fei vers Clarel afiez.
D'un grant afeire ore voil ke m'entendez:
Jo di Mahumet ne deit ester honurez —
N'en ot ne veit d'enfer est malfiez;
fol. 219ra    Tute sa force ne valt treis oefs pelez!
1345    A diables seit la suen cors comandez!
Il dit n'est pruz seinte Cristientez,
Ne li baptesme dunt sui regenerez.
Mes par le funz u fui baptizez,
Si la bataille de lui ne me dunez,
1350    Jameis de mei ne serrez bien amez."
"Filiol," fait Charle, "par cest guant, la tenez;
Cil vus aie qui en croiz fu penez."

Li reis Clarel entendi la reisun,
Irreement en apele Otun:
1355    "Culvert," feit il, "purquei guerpis Mahun —
La lei seintisme que nus aver devum,
Parquei les suens vendrunt a rançun
Al grant juise u nus tuz en irrum?

Are you the famous white-haired Charles?"
And the Emperor says, "Brother, what do you want?"

1315 "I'll tell you! I curse the hour you were born!
You've lived too long! You're white-haired and bearded —
Long ago you ought to have become dead flesh!
You're worn out, ruined, and disinherited;
Your crown and your empire have already been given

1320 To the best man who's ever been born —
Florian of Syria — so highly renowned.
He'll be proclaimed king of France!"
The King answers, "You've spoken a lot,
And you're well schooled in telling lies.

1325 I can still ride fully armed on my warhorse,
And I have forcibly conquered six kings.
Now I promise you, in faith and truly,
That this siege will not ever be lifted
Before Garsie is captured and his city destroyed."

1330 And Clarel says, "That's how a devil talks!
You don't increase; you've used up too many days;
Your head is bald; and your skin is spotted!
Nothing will ever be accomplished by you —
No battle begun, no tower built!"

1335 Charles felt insulted and looked at the French;
He takes off his cloak in anger,
Saying to Galdin, "Bring me my arms."
"Lord," says Otinel, "moderate your anger.
For my love, don't lose control,

1340 For I've given my pledge to Clarel.
Please listen to me now about an important affair:
I swore that Mahomet should not be honored —
That wicked one can't ever escape hell;
His power's not worth three peeled eggs!

1345 May Clarel's soul be sent to the devil!
He says that holy Christianity is worthless,
And so is the baptism by which I'm reborn.
But by the font in which I was baptized,
If you don't grant me this duel against him,

1350 Never will you be dearly loved by me."
"Godson," says Charles, "have it, by this glove;
May He who suffered on the Cross help you."

King Clarel hears the conversation,
And calls out angrily to Otinel:

1355 "Wretch," he says, "why did you leave Mahomet —
The holy faith that we ought to uphold,
By which your people will be redeemed
At that great judgment to which we'll proceed?

Ki iloc ert avera tel guerdun
1360 K'en parais irra senz contenciun.
Meis icil deu qui Jhesu at nun
Estera pris e iert en prisun
Cum traitre e fel de Tartarun,
E tun meisme el puz de baratrun,
1365 El grant enfern u gisent li larun.
James nul jur n'averas rançun!
Va, prent tes armes, jo t'apel felun!"
Dit Otinel, "Ja ne vus en defendrun."

Franceis curteis ameinent le chevalier,
1370 Gentement l'arment desuz un oliver.
Rollant li vest un bon halberc dublier.
Apris lui lascent le healme al rei Alier,
Qui Bibilonie conquist par guerreier.
De Cureçuse le ceint le fiz Reiner.
1375 Al col li pendent la targe de sirer.
Estult li done l'enseinie al rei loier —
Li fer fu bon, la hanste de lorier.
Uns espuruns pur sun cheval brocher
Li a chaucié Droun de Munt d'Isoier.
1380 Belesent tient sun arabi cursier;
Treis feiz la beise, puis salt el destrier.
"Bele," dit il, "jo irrai la lei Deu vengier,
Cristienté lever e eshaucier,
Paiene gent hunir e vergunier.
1385 La vostre amur comparunt il mult chier."
fol. 219rb "Amis," fait ele, "Deu vus pusse aider!"
Al erceveske se fait li ber seinier,
Eue beneité sur ses armes geter.

Del ost se part quant il fu adubez,
1390 Sa hanste leve si passe ultre les guez.
Li reis Clarel est encontre alez,
En halt s'escrie, "Traitre, defiez!
Mar i passastes ultre les guez,
Kar ja esteras a grant hunte liverez,
1395 E detrenchiez, occis, e demenbrez.
Ja ni valdra rien li parentez.
Es tu uncore nule rien purpensez
Que Maḥumet deit estre Deu clamez,
De tut le siècle serviz e honurez?
1400 Qui en lui creit james ni ert afolez!
Mais cil Deu a ki tu es turnez
Ne valt vers lui uns esperuns dorrez!"
"Par Deu," fait Otes, "Culvert, vus i mentez.

Whoever's in that place will gain such a reward
1360  That he'll go unquestionably to paradise.
But that God who has the name Jesus
Was taken and placed in prison
As a traitor and felon in Tartarus,
And you yourself will go to the pit of hell,
1365  Into the great inferno where thieves lie.
Never ever will you be redeemed!
Go, take up your arms, for I call you a traitor!"
Otinel replies, "I will never fail you."

The worthy French lead the knight away,
1370  They arm him nobly beneath an olive tree.
Roland dresses him in a good double-mesh hauberk.
Next they lace on him the helmet of King Alier,
Who conquered Babylon as a warrior.
Renier's son girds Corçuse upon him.
1375  Around his neck they hang a cherrywood shield.
Estult gives him the standard of the renowned King —
The iron was good, the grip made from laurel.
Spurs by which to prick his steed
Were placed on his feet by Droun of Mont d'Isere.
1380  Belisant holds his Arabian charger;
He kisses her three times, then leaps on his horse.
"Beautiful one," he says, "I go to avenge God's law,
To uphold and exalt Christianity,
And to shame and disgrace the pagan race.
1385  For your love, they will pay very dearly."
"Sweetheart," she says, "May God assist you!"
The warrior goes to the archbishop to be blessed,
To have holy water sprinkled on his arms.

Once he's been armed, he leaves the army,
1390  Raises his lance and crosses the ford.
King Clarel went to meet him,
Crying out loudly, "Traitor, I defy you!
You crossed the ford in an evil hour,
For now you'll be delivered to great shame,
1395  And cut to pieces, killed, and dismembered.
Your kinsmen won't be able to help you.
Have you still not reconsidered at all
How Mahomet must be proclaimed God,
To be served and honored by all the world?
1400  He who believes in him will never be deceived!
And that God to whom you've turned
Isn't worth a gilded spur compared to him!"
"By God," says Otinel, "Villain, in this you lie.

Si jo combat, tu esteras matez,
1405       Kar de Jhesu averai la poestez;
N'autre de lui n'en iert Deu apelez.
Dehez en ait Mahun e fiertez,
E vus meinie, que par lui vus clamez,.
De mun espee vus ferrai neelez.
1410       Par cel Seingnur qui en croix fu penez,
Tumber vus frai s'a cest colp m'atendez!"

Otinel broche sun arabi curant,
E Clarel broche sun destrier Turnevent.
Sur les escuz se fierent durement;
1415       Parmi se passent amdui li fer trenchant
Desk'as halbercs que de mort lur defent.
Il sient ferm e enpeinent forment,
A lur estrius s'afichent reddement.
Li uns vers l'altre del abatre cuntent,
1420       Rumpent lur cengles e les peitrals devant;
Amdui s'abatent li chevaler vaillant.
Rodlant s'en rist e dit a Belisent,
"Si m'ait Deus, cest butier valt un chant!"
Dit la pucele, "Or ai le quor dulant.
1425       A seinte Marie, mun ami vus comant!"
Paient glatissent pur Clarel d'armant;
Mahumet prient e crient haltement
fol. 219va Ke vers Otun li sert de mort garant.
Treit a Mellee, s'espee la trenchant,
1430       E Otinel s'est salli en estant,
Tint Curçuse al punt d'or luisant.
Si se requerent amdui irrement,
Grant colps se donent amdui meintenant
Amunt es healms, u li or resplent.
1435       Le feu en salt, ke l'erbe s'esprent!

Li Sarazin fu mult bon chevaler.
Leve mellee dunt li brant fu s'ascer
E fiert Otinel sur le healme le rei Alier,
Tant par est dur nel pot mie trenchier,
1440       Meis par le colp, lestut un poi pleier,
Tant l'estima kil le fist agenuiller.
"Seinte Marie!" dist Charle al vis fier,
"Garissiez, Dame, tun curteis chevaler,
Ki se combat pur sa lei eshaucier."
1445       Otes relieve, si ot corage fier
L'escu enbrace si fait un salt plener,
De Cureçuse li dune un colp plener,
Del healme a or li abat un quarter,

If I fight, you'll be defeated,
1405    For I will have strength from Jesus;
No one other than He should be called God.
A curse on anyone who trusts in Mahomet,
And on you yourself, who speak in his name.
With my sword I will etch it upon you.
1410    In the name of the Lord who suffered on the Cross,
I'll make you fall if you await my blow!"

Otinel spurs the swift Arabian steed,
And Clarel spurs his warhorse Turnevent.
They hit each other forcefully on their shields;
1415    Both sharp-edged blades pass through
As far as the hauberks protecting them from death.
They sit firmly and strike powerfully,
Fixing themselves stoutly in their stirrups.
They continue to cut against each other,
1420    Splitting saddle girths and front breastpieces;
Both valiant knights are knocked down.
Roland laughs about it and says to Belisant,
"God help me, this buffeting's worthy of a song!"
The maiden says, "My heart's frightened by it.
1425    Blessed Mary, I commend my sweetheart to you!"
The pagans bellow like cattle for Clarel;
They pray to Mahomet and cry out loudly
That he protect him against death from Otinel.
He draws Mellee, his keen-edged sword,
1430    And Otinel stands erect on his feet,
Holding Corçuse with its shining gold point.
Then they angrily seek each other out,
Quickly dealing mighty blows on the other
Upon their helmets' crowns, where gold shines.
1435    Sparks flash, causing the grass to shimmer!

The Saracen was a very fine knight.
He raises Mellee with its steel blade,
And strikes Otinel on King Alier's helmet,
Which is so hard he can't cut through it,
1440    But because of the blow, he had to bend slightly,
Making it seem that he kneeled down.
"Blessed Mary!" says Charles fervently,
"May you protect, Lady, your courteous knight,
Who fights to exalt his faith."
1445    Otinel gets back up, and with a fierce heart
Grasps his shield and makes a full leap,
Dealing him a full blow with Corçuse,
Breaking off a quarter of his golden helmet,

Trenche la coife del jacerant dublier.
1450     La jowe enprent od trestut le jower,
         Si que les denz en vit blanchoier.
         "Par Deu," dit Otes, "issi deit l'um chanchier
         Colp pur colee, maille pur dener!
         Bien semblez humme qui voillie eschiner.
1455     Ne t'avera mes Alfamie mester —
         James pucele ne te voldra baiser!"

         Li Sarazin est durement nafrez;
         Bien set que james en curt n'ert honurez.
         Tient Mellee dunt li punt fu dorrez,
1460     Ja ert a Otes si ruiste cops dunez
         Si Deu n'en pense e la sue buntez,
         Dunt Charles ert dolenz e si iriez!
         Li bon convers n'est pas espuntez —
         Ainz est plus fiers que liuns esfrenez.
1465     Sur sun chief met sun fort escu listez,
         Clarel i fiert cum humme forsenez,
         Parmi le trenche, si n'a l'esclos ostez.
         Le healme li fent, que a or bendez,
         Desk'a la coife est li brant avalez.
fol. 219vb  Ne fust le halberc, que tant est serrez,
1471     James pur juste ne serreit demandez.
         Mes nepuroec, si forment est quassez
         Parmi les mailles est li sanc volez.
         "Par fei," fet Otes, "trop est cist colp alez.
1475     Ore vei jo bien que de rien ne m'amez!
         Par seint Denis, ja tiert guerdunez
         Par tel mesure, si bien ne vus guardez,
         James pur mire ne serrez bien sanez."

         Otinel ruille les oilz de maltalent.
1480     De Cureçuse li dune un colp pesant,
         Vers la senestre li a jeté le brant,
         De juste le col desur le halberc luisant,
         Trenche les mailes e tut le quor en fent;
         Desk'en la terre fait culer le brant.
1485     Cil ne se poet mes tenir en estant;
         Mort chiet a terre. L'alme s'en veit criant,
         E Mahumet sun seingnur maldiant.
         Otes escrie "Munjoie!" passe avant,
         Paiens defi, pur amur Belisent.
1490     Franceis sunt lé e sarazins dolant.

         Li reis Garsie a mult tost entendu
         Ke li paien est mort e abatu;

Splitting the top of the double-mesh mail.
1450    He slices off the cheek with the whole jawbone,
So that one might see his white teeth.
"By God," says Otinel, "thus may one exchange
A blow for a tap, a farthing for a denier!
You resemble a man who'd want to grin.
1455    Alfamie won't have any more business with you —
Never will a girl want to kiss you!"

The Saracen is badly wounded,
And knows well he'll never be honored in court.
He holds Mellee with its gilded tip,
1460    And strikes Otinel with such savage blows
That if God in His goodness doesn't pay heed,
Charles will be sad and distressed by them!
But the good convert isn't afraid —
Instead he's fiercer than a frenzied lion.
1465    Otinel holds his strong-edged shield above his head,
While Clarel strikes like a man gone mad,
Cleaving it in the middle, removing a layer.
He splits the gold-adorned helmet,
So that the blade cuts down to the headpiece.
1470    Were it not for the tight hauberk,
He would never again be invited to joust.
Nonetheless, so thoroughly was it crushed
That his blood flowed through the linked mail.
"In faith," says Otinel, "this blow went too far.
1475    Now I see well you don't love me at all!
By Saint Denis, I'll pay you back
In such a manner that, if you don't defend yourself,
A doctor will never heal you at all."

Otinel rolls his eyes in anger.
1480    With Corçuse he gives him a mighty blow,
Thrusting the blade into his left side,
Near his neck, above the shiny hauberk,
Slitting the chain mail and slashing his heart;
He makes the blade glide down to the earth.
1485    Clarel can stand up no longer;
He falls to the ground. His soul departs, crying out,
Cursing his lord Mahomet.
Otinel shouts "Mountjoy!" and advances;
He defies the pagans for the love of Belisant.
1490    The French rejoice and the Saracens grieve.

King Garsie has soon heard
That the pagan is dead and defeated;

Tant est dulant, unques mes si ne fu:
"Oi, Clarel, cum jo t'ai perdu!
1495 Cil qui t'a mort m'a el quor feru!
Fillie Alfamie, james n'averas tel dru.
Si ui nel venge, ne me pris un festu."
Prent Dulcejoie sil sone par vertu.
Set milie gredles li respunent menu;
1500 Vint millie sunt a primer chief eissu
(Ni ceus deriere n'en est nul cunte tenu)
Ki tuit manacent Charle le vielz chanu,
Rollant le cunte, e Oliver sun dru.

Nostre enperere a sa gent avistee,
1505 Fist duze escheles de sa gent honuré,
Ki de bataille est tut dis aprestee.
A vint mile hummes est li menur aesmee.
Rollant est la primere liveré —
De ses de France, de combatre s'agree.
1510 Paien averunt mult male destinee!

Le fiz Pepin a ordané sa gent,
fol. 220ra Bien sunt armé, chascun a son talent.
Li reis chevalche sur un destrier ferant,
Par grant vertu as estrius sestent.
1515 Naimun apele si li dit en riant:
"Duc debonaire, m'enseinie te cumant,
De tels servises m'avez fait, plus de cent.
Porte le, sire, si vus durrai Volant,
Mun bon destrier, que vus cuveitez tant.
1520 De set chasteall vus vest hui, par cest guant;
A testmonie, pernez Guinemant,
Rotolt de Perche, e Gefrei le Normant."
"Sire," fait il, "tut a vostre cumant.
Pur bien porter n'i perdrez nient."

1525 Franceis se vont, lur ost conreer.
Otes se veit desuz un arbre armer;
Desçu de healme, l'estoet renuveler.
Mes Belisent li feit aporter.
Od lui se veit Gerin de Seint-Omer,
1530 Fromund d'Artois, e Garin de Muntcler;
Adubez est, si remunte li ber.
Prist un enseinie pur Franceis comforter,
Lores comande ses olifanz soner,
E cil si font, mult haltement e cler;
1535 Vers la batalle comencent a crier.
Ja esmuevent serré a paen assembler,

He was more sorrowful than ever he'd been:
"Alas, Clarel, now I have lost you!

1495     Your killer has struck me in the heart!
Daughter Alfamie, you'll never again have such a lover.
If I don't avenge him today, I'm not worth a straw."
He takes up Sweetjoy and sounds it with force.
Seven thousand trumpets answer in succession;

1500     Twenty thousand remain in the front ranks
(Of those in the rear, no count was taken)
To endanger Charles the old graybeard,
Count Roland, and his beloved Oliver.

Giving thought to his army, our Emperor

1505     Prepared twelve ranks within his famed host,
Which is always ready for battle.
The smallest has about twenty thousand men.
Roland is assigned to the first —
Those of France, equipped for battle.

1510     The pagans will have a very bad fate!

Pepin's son has organized his army
So that each is armed according to his skills.
The King rides on a galloping horse,
Standing up vigorously in the stirrups.

1515     He calls for Naimes and laughingly says to him:
"Noble duke, I entrust my standard to you,
For services you've given me, more than a hundred.
Bear it, lord, and I give you Volant,
My good warhorse, which you desire so much.

1520     Today, with this glove, I grant you seven castles;
As witnesses to this, take Guinemant,
Rotolt of Perche, and Geffrei the Norman."
"Lord," he says, "just as you command.
I'll bear it well, and you will lose nothing."

1525     The French set about preparing their army.
Otinel stands under a tree to be armed;
Having lost his helmet, he must replace it,
But Belisant has one brought to him.
With him go Garen of Saint-Omer,

1530     Fromund of Artois, and Garin of Muntcler.
The brave one is armed, and he remounts,
Taking a standard to support the French,
And commanding that trumpets be sounded.
And this is done, loudly and clearly;

1535     Advancing to battle they begin to shout.
The pagans gather tightly together,

E lur compaingnies vers nos Franceis urner —
Tant en i a ne sai le numbre conter!
Lur estandart fait Garsie lever.
1540          Dient paien, "Alum a cels juster,
Faisum nos lances en lur escuz hurter."
Viengent avant cil leger bacheler,
Cil que de France se voldrunt enheriter,
As branz d'ascer la viengent aquiter:
1545          "Nostre est le champ! Bien les poum mater!"

Noz Franceis chevalchent fierement,
E li paien mult orguillusement.
De l'ost s'en par un Turc privément,
Al rei Garsie a demandé le guant,
1550          Del primer coup pur occire Rollant,
U Oliver, u Ote le vaillant.
Quel k'il encontre — n'irra altre querant —
Seit chier morut que li veit a talant.
fol. 220rb          De cheres armes est armé gentement;
1555          De cunuissans semble bien Normant,
D'un drap de seie ke firent suliant
A tut cuvert sum halber reluisant,
E sis chevals, si qui ni piert nent
Li aligod vont a terre ferant.
1560          Porte une mace en sun braz pendant,
K'il li duna al matin en riant
La fillie al rei Cursable d'Amiant.
Pur la pucele a pris tel hardement,
Dunt il murra devant midi sonant.
1565          La hanste a reddé, e fer ja trenchant,
E gunfanun qui ventel al vent
Si est fermé a quatre clos d'argent.
Le cheval broche, li cheval se destent,
Envers le noz se vait espurunant.
1570          En halt s'escrie, "Di va, u est Rollant?
Hui en cest jur vus frai mult dolant.
Cumbatrai, par mun cors sulement,
Que France est nostre e a Garsie apent,
Ne Charlemanie ni deit aver nient.
1575          A tort est rei! Ore vien si le defend!"
Rodlant l'entent si a muetalent.
Envers le paien, se veit espurunant,
Lance lieve e trait l'escu avant.
Ja ert la juste de eus dous certeinement.
1580          De nos Franceis vunt les reines fremissant,
Li plus hardi voldreit estre avant.

And their companies turn toward our French —
So many that I can't count the number!
Garsie has their standard raised.
1540 The pagans say, "Let's go fight them!
Let's make our lances strike their shields."
The agile young men proceed in front,
Those who desire to inherit France,
Hoping to acquit themselves with steel swords:
1545 "The field is ours! We can easily defeat them!"

Our French knights ride courageously,
While the Saracens ride too pridefully.
A Turk removes himself from the army,
Asking King Garsie for the gauntlet,
1550 That he might kill Roland with the first blow,
Or Oliver, or the valiant Otinel.
Whoever he finds — he'll not seek any others —
Will fall down dead when he meets his goal.
He's armed nobly with precious weapons;
1555 In bearing he looks much like a Norman,
With a Syrian-made silk cloth
That covers all of his shiny hauberk,
And his horse, which is as fast as
The greyhound that speeds along the ground.
1560 Carrying a mace that hangs from his arm,
Laughingly given to him that very morning
By the daughter of King Cursable of Amiant.
Because of this girl, he's now brave,
And thus he'll die before sext has sounded.
1565 His lance is stiff, the iron always sharp,
And the banner fluttering in the wind
Is fastened with four silver pins.
He pricks his horse, and it rushes forward,
Galloping fast toward our men.
1570 He calls out loudly, "Tell me, where's Roland?
On this very day I'll bring you trouble.
I'll assert by fighting, by my body alone,
That France is ours and belongs to Garsie,
And that Charlemagne doesn't possess it at all.
1575 Your king is wrong! Come and defend him!"
Roland hears him and flushes with anger.
He swiftly advances toward the pagan,
Raises his lance, and draws his shield forward.
Now battle has begun decisively between them.
1580 Among our French, bridle-reins are shaking,
The strongest want to be at the front to see it.

Martoires fiert Rollant en sun escu,
Desuz la bucle li a freint e fendu,
Trenche les mailles al fort espé mulu.
1585    Pres del coste le li a abatu,
Suz la chemise de desur la charnu;
Sun destre escriu li a del pié tolu —
Enpeint le bien, mes ne li valt un festu.
La hanste brise, le quons l'a si feru
1590    Desur l'arcel k'il le porte par vertu;
Ultre s'en passe li bon fer agu;
Mance d'armur ne halberc qu'ait vestu
Ne li valt mie encontre mort un festu.
Le piz li pierce, le quor li a fendu,
1595    Enpeint le bien. Mort l'at abatu.
fol. 220va   "Munjoie!" escrie. Paien l'unt entendu.
Dous moe li dit: "Bien vus ai conu,
James en France ni ert par vus plai tenu.
Charles a dreit! Vus l'avez perdu!"
1600    Dist l'almuafle, ki maragunde fu,
"Par Mahumet, cesti avum perdu!
C'est Rollant ki'l nus a tolu.
Si jo nel veng mult serrai confundu!"

L'almuafle se leisse a Oliver,
1605    E li quons broche Fauvel, sun bon destrier.
Li Sarazin fiert le fiz Reiner,
L'escu li pierce, si fait les espleier;
Cent mailles trenche del bon halberc dublier,
Que del costé li fait le sanc raier.
1610    E li druz Charle le fiert par tel irrer
Ke sis escuz ne lui valt un denier,
Ne sis chevals la reinie d'un prunier.
E cors li met l'enseine de sirier,
Mort l'abatu deliez un rochier.
1615    "Munjoie!" escrie. "Fierez i, chevaler!"
Des ore i fierent Franceis e Beiver,
E Loerenc, Aleman, e Puier,
Normans e Francs, Flemengs e Berrvier —
Mult ot grant bruit as enseignes-bessier.
1620    Avant se traient cil lu, curage ont fier,
Mes li cuart n'orent il vet mester;
Li hardi funt les escuz piercer,
E les halbercs rumpre e desmailer;
Les hanstes reddes el vermeil sanc banier;
1625    Murent e versent cil barun chevaler;
Estrae fuient cil auferant destrer.

Martoires strikes Roland on his shield,
Cracking and splitting it beneath the boss,
And cutting mail-rings with his sharp sword.
1585      He struck him upon the side,
Beneath the skirt, above the flesh;
He tore the right stirrup from his foot —
Though he hit well, it wasn't worth a straw.
His lance breaks, and the count strikes him
1590      Upon the armband he bears for good luck;
Strong pointed iron passes right through;
Both armored sleeve and hauberk shirt
Weren't worth a straw in the face of death.
The point pierces him, splitting his heart,
1595      And pinning him well. He has struck him dead.
"Mountjoy!" he shouts. The pagans hear him.
He says a few words: "I've met you well!
Never in France will you win a plea!
Charles is right! You have lost!"
1600      Says the emir, greatly distressed,
"By Mahomet, we've lost this one!
Roland has taken him from us.
May I be cursed if I don't avenge him!"

The emir rushes upon Oliver,
1605      And the count spurs Fauvel, his good horse.
The Saracen strikes Renier's son,
And pierces the shield, causing it to split open;
He cuts a hundred bits from his double-ring hauberk,
Causing blood to flow from his side.
1610      Charles' favorite strikes back so angrily
That his shield's not worth a penny to him,
Nor his horse the value of a plum tree.
Into his body he places his cherrywood standard,
Throws him down dead next to a rock.
1615      "Mountjoy!" he shouts. "Strike at them, knights!"
Then the French and Bavarians attack,
Lorrains, Germans, and men of Puy,
Normans, Franks, Flemings, and Bavarians —
They loudly roar their battle cries.
1620      Those with brave hearts draw to the front,
But the cowards don't have the same desire;
The hardiest ones proceed to pierce shields,
And break and crumble hauberks.
Stiff lances are bathed in red blood;
1625      Brave knights fall and die;
Swift warhorses scatter and flee.

   Assez en prennent, cil curteis escrier.
   Puis fu tel ure qu'il orent grant mester!

   Quant ces fiers osz se furent a justees,
1630 Fruissent ces hanstes e ces targes roees.
   Aprés les lances, si sachent les espees,
   Demaintenant dunent grant colees;
   Trenchent ces healmes e ces bruinies afrees;
   Morent e versent e crient ahees.
1635 Dunc sunt del cors les almes deseverees,
   Ki pur nul mire ni erent meis assemblees.

   Del estandut ke out lievé Sarazin,
fol. 220vb Sunt departi dis mile barbarin;
   Celui n'i a n'ait halberc dublentin,
1640 E sen e healme e gunfanun purprin,
   Vermail u blanc u vert u samin.
   Alfan les guie, un duc de Palestin.
   Porte l'enseinie al rei Alepantin.
   Manseis les fierent e mettent el chimin.
1645 As arcs turkeis i treient Sarazin,
   Lacent lur guivres e darz teint en venim.
   Otes s'afiche a ses estrius d'or fin,
   Par les en armes, prent l'escu belveisin,
   Brandit sa lance al gunfanun sanguin,
1650 Fait une puinte al rei de Palestin.
   Parmi la targe fiert Alfan sun cusin,
   Le halberc descire al bon fer ascerin,
   Parmi le cors li met le fust fresnin,
   Mort le tresturne, a la terre suvin.
1655 E suus a justés Gefrei e Morin,
   Huge de Seies e Boue le fiz Gauvin.
   Gefrei a mort le fel de barbarin.
   Huge de Seies a mort Balsadrin;
   O de prist vengance d'un felun barbarin
1660 K'a mis a mort Guineman de sa lin,
   Mort le tresturne devant Alepantin.
   "Munjoie!" escrie. "Ore a . . . . . . . .
   Ni guarra mes, paien ne Sarazin!"

   D'un munt avale li reis Corsabrez,
1665 Une batalle ameine d'Atropez,
   Dis mille sunt sis guie barbarez.
   Desk'al ferir les meine tuz serrez.
   Li quons Elins li est encontre alez
   A quatre cent de Bretuns adurez.
1670 Neel de Nantes vient tut afeltrez.

Many are captured who cry for mercy.
In that hour they had great need!

When the fierce armies clash in battle,
1630 They shatter spears and round shields.
After using lances, warriors pull out swords,
And immediately deal ferocious blows;
They slice helmets and rip coats of mail;
They kill, destroy, and shout with delight.
1635 Thus are souls severed from their bodies,
Never to be united by any doctor.

Of the forces raised by the Saracens,
There are ten thousand pagans left;
They've never had double-ring hauberks,
1640 Or helmets or banners either, whether purple,
Vermilion, white, green, or salmon.
Leading them is Alfan, a Palestinian duke.
He carries the standard of King Alepantin.
They strike the Mansians and send them running.
1645 The Saracens draw their Turkish bows,
And shoot their javelins and poison darts.
Otinel puts on stirrups of pure gold,
From those in arms, he seizes a Beauvaisian sword,
And brandishes his red-bannered spear,
1650 Taking a stab at the king of Palestine.
He strikes his cousin Alfan mid-shield,
Ripping the hauberk with a good steel spearhead,
Then thrusting his ash-shaft into the body,
Twisting him dead, prone on the earth.
1655 Now do Geffrei and Morin joust,
And Hugh of Soissons and Boue son of Gawain.
Geffrei has killed a wicked pagan.
Hugh of Soissons has killed Balsadrin;
Now he takes vengeance on the wicked pagan
1660 Who had killed Guineman with his sword,
Twisting him to death in front of Alepantin.
"Mountjoy!" he shouts. "Now . . . . . . . .
Pagans and Saracens, you'll never succeed!"

King Corsabrez heads down a hill,
1665 With a battalion led by Atropez,
Six thousand pagans under his command.
He leads them to the fight in tight ranks.
Count Eleins goes to meet them
With four hundred hardened Bretons.
1670 Neel of Nantes comes fully equipped.

           "Mallo!" escrie. "Francs chevalers, fierez!"
           Gui de Custances i a Bigoz menez,
           A set cent healmes les gunfanuns levez.
           Ja i avera d'uns e d'altres palmez.
1675     Troias li bers est a Malfruit justez;
           Li paienz porte quatre darz enpennez,
           Del un lance que plus est alcemez.
           Par grant vertu la escus li malfez
           A Troians treit mult bien l'at assenez,
fol. 221ra  Ke tut le fent si a les quirs severez;
1681     Del bon halberc at les pleiz descloez,
           Parmi la quisse est li darz volez.
           Troiais le fiert cum vassal adurez;
           Nel pot garir escu n'auberc saffrez,
1685     Li fer de la hanste li est el cors entrez,
           Mort l'abati. Si est ultre passez.
           Meis al travers, l'a feru Corsabrez
           Suz la mammele e parmi les costez,
           Li a l'espleiz del gunfanun butez;
1690     Le quor li fent, le vassal est versez.
           Deus en ait. L'alme a la fin est alez.
           Li quons Eleins vient, tut effreez —
           Forment le pleint kar de sa soer esteit nez.
           Ja le vengast bien del rei Corsabrez,
1695     Mes a la traverse est venu Barbez.
           Li quons Eleins s'est a lui turnez,
           Brandist sa lance, dunt le fer est quarrez.
           L'escu li perce k'est entur listez
           A riches pieres e a or neelez.
1700     Mort le tresturne si li dist, " Ore tenez!
           Mielz vus venist k'ariere ussez estez!"
           Bens est li jurs. Si est mult passez.
           De la pudrere en est li airs trublez.
           Paiens complissent si est . . . tez,
1705     Cornent e crient si sunt grant taburez.
           Je k'en dirai les noz ont fort quassez,
           Plus d'un arpent, les noz ont si menez,
           K'unques n'i out halberc n'escu turnez!
           Lambert d'Averenches i est a mort liverez,
1710     E Raul de Bleives de dous parz enpennez,
           Ne vivera gueres, kar il en est pasmez.
           Gui de Custances i a le chief colpez;
           Tebald de Rues e del altres assez.
           Ja cist damage n'en iert restorez!
1715     Uns esquiers, qui a nun Amirez —
           Vavassur est si est de Paris nez,
           Fiz a Droun li Riche des fossez —

"Mallo!" he shouts. "Hit them, French knights!"
Gui of Custances has led Bigoz there,
With banners raised upon seven hundred helmets.
Each one has been on pilgrimage to Jerusalem.

1675    The mighty Troias jousts with Malfruit;
The pagan carries four poison darts,
From which he hurls the most poisonous one.
With great vigor the evildoer deals
A rough blow against Troias' shield,

1680    Splitting it entirely and severing the leather;
The dart splits open the good hauberk's layers,
And has flown into his thigh.
Troias strikes him like a hardened warrior;
Neither shield nor adorned hauberk can save Malfruit

1685    When the spearpoint enters his body,
And he strikes him dead. He's passed beyond.
But meanwhile Corsabrez attacks Troias
Under the breast and between the sides,
Successfully thrusting forth his pennon;

1690    It splits his heart, and the warrior falls.
God takes him; the soul goes to its end.
Count Eleins intervenes, deeply upset —
He grieves loudly, for he was born of his sister.
Soon he'll be avenged on King Corsabrez,

1695    But meanwhile Barbez has arrived.
Count Eleins turns toward him,
Brandishing his spear with its squared-off head,
And piercing the shield ornately decorated
With rich gems and embellished with gold.

1700    He throws him down dead, saying, "Now be still!
You'd have been better off if you'd stayed behind!"
The day has gone well. Most of it has passed.
With dust has the air been disturbed.
Pagans come forth, and it is . . . . . . . . . . . .

1705    They blow trumpets, shout, and bang large drums.
With this, I can say they've overwhelmed our men,
Driving our men back more than an arpent,
None has a hauberk or shield that's not turned around.
Lambert of Avranches was sent to his death there,

1710    And Raoul of Bleives, pierced by two arrows,
Won't live long, for he's already lost consciousness.
Gui of Custances had his head cut off there;
So did Tebald of Rouen, and others as well.
Never can such a loss be remedied!

1715    A squire, whose name is Amirez —
A vavasour born in Paris,
Son of powerful Droun of the Moat —

Cent damisals a od sei a justez,  
Tut li plus viel n'a ke vint anz passez.  
1720 Armes ont prises des morz qu'il ont trovez,  
De lur bliauz unt gunfanuns lievez.  
fol. 221rb Veient les noz venir tut effreez;  
Passent avant sis ont returnez.  
Par grant efforz ont paiens reculez  
1725 Quatre arpenz de terre mesurez.  
Des abatuz e des acervelez  
Est tut li champ plein e encombrez.  
Lez un parei s'aresteit Corsabrez,  
S'enseinie escrie, "Paien a mei estez!"  
1730 L'escu enbrace, vers les noz est alez.  
Par grant vertu est as estrius fermez,  
Ja eust les noz gravment desturbez,  
Quant en l'escu l'a feru Amirez  
Par teu vertu k'en sun frunt l'at entrez  
1735 Desuz le halme. A l'un des oilz quassez.  
Li paien est del colp espontez;  
N'en a sucurs — tut est abandunez!  
Ignelement le saisist Amirez,  
Treis bons vassals a l'emfes apelez:  
1740 Ço est Galdin e Fauchet li hastez,  
E d'Aigremunt Baldewin la fiez.  
"Franc esquier, icest rei me pernez.  
Gardez ni mure ne ne seit afolez.  
A Charlemeine, mun seingnur, le rendez,  
1745 E de ma part mult bel le presentez."  
E cil respunent, "Sicum vus comandez."  
Mult justent bien les noz as Atropez.  
Desore est li travei tut mellez  
Par le sucurs des novels adubez.  
1750 Cent i sunt i a des abatuz muntez,  
Ke puis i ferent des bons branz ascerez.  
Hue de Nevers est a Podras turnez,  
C'est un paien fier e desmesurez —  
De feluns est trestut si parentez.  
1755 Mesk'as dames est li fel acuntez;  
Des puceles fu pleint e regretez.  
En la cité fu grant doel demenez,  
Assez a vi nos franceis empeirez.  
Hues les fiert cum vassal espruvez;  
1760 Amunt el helme que fu a or bendez,  
Desk'as espalles li est li branz alez;  
Li cors chiet, i us ci faillent ses buntez.  
"Mallo!" escrie les Bretuns aturnez.  
fol. 221va "Deus aidez ore a Otes le senez!"

Has a hundred young men to fight with him;
The oldest is merely twenty years old.
1720  They've taken the arms found among the dead,
And raised banners made from their tunics.
They see our men arrive, terrified,
And step in front of those who retreat.
With great effort they push back the pagans
1725  The length of four arpents of ground.
Bodies of the fallen and maimed
Fill and clutter the battlefield.
Corsabrez pauses along a defensive wall,
And shouts his war cry, "Pagans, stand with me!"
1730  He grips his shield and charges at our men.
He has skillfully locked in his stirrups
And already stopped many of our men,
When Amirez strikes him on the shield
So forcefully that it enters his forehead
1735  Below the helmet. He has crushed one eye.
The pagan is terrified by the blow,
But receives no help — all have fled!
Amirez seizes him at once,
And the youth calls three good vassals:
1740  They are Galdin, swift Fauchet,
And loyal Baldwin of Aigremunt.
"Noble squires, take this king for me.
Don't allow him to die or be injured.
Deliver him to Charlemagne my lord,
1745  And graciously present him on my behalf."
And they answer, "As you command."
Our men fight very well against Atropez.
From this point on, the battle's fully engaged
With the help of those newly knighted.
1750  Of those knocked down, a hundred arise,
And then strike with their good steel swords.
Hugh of Nevers turns toward Podras,
A ferocious and wild pagan —
All his kinsmen are evildoers.
1755  The villain is well regarded by ladies;
He'll soon be mourned and grieved by damsels.
Those in the city suffer great pain,
For they witness our French injure many.
Hugh strikes Podras like a proven warrior;
1760  From the top of his gold-banded helmet,
The sword descends to his shoulders;
The body falls, its powers failing him there.
"Mallo!" shout the armed Bretons,
"May God now help wise Otinel!"

1765    Ja seiserunt l'enseine barbarez
De ceste part fu li cham tut liverez,
Mes ne pot estre il est aliurs mellez:
Ja est al estandard treis feiz alez,
A quatre reis a les chefs colpez.

1770    Li reis Garsie en a dit a Parant,
Un fel paien que Deu n'aime nient.
"Frere," fait il, "mult m'esta malement.
De mes baruns dunt ai le quor dolent,
Ke Otes at occis, mes oilz veant.
1775    Murrai de doel si jo mult halt nel pent,
Cil Charlemeine me meine malement,
Ke tient ma terre estre mun talent,
Corune porte sen mun comandement!
Si en bataille ne'l faz ui recreant,
1780    James en France ne voil aver nient."

"Sire," fait il, "manacez ore forment:
Charles est pris! Veez le ci devant!
La sue flambe, vus veit mult aspresmant.
Grant pour ai de sun nevu Rollant,
1785    Jo'l vi ui matin, tut aceleement,
U il feri sur le healme Balant —
Tut purfendi l'umme e l'auforant!
Tel pour oi ke m'en alai fuiant!"
Li reis apele Belduit d'Aquilant:
1790    "Pernez des Turcs tant ke seiez cent;
Gardez les Turcs que nul n'alge fuiant.
Cil qui finera si li feites itant,
Que i a honur n'ait mes a sun vivant."
Grant est la noise, mult sunt li cop pesant,
1795    E la bataille mene estreitement.
Li quons Rollant veit les Persses cerchant;
A Durendal veit les reues deperçant.
K'il consuit, malveis luer li rent.
Mult fierent bien Beiver e Alemant,
1800    E Burguniun e Flemeng e Normant.
Granz colps i rendent Franceis demeintenant,
Li puer fierent desmesurement
Al estandard — n'unt de fuir talant;
N'en aiment pas triwe n'acordement,
1805    Ki entr'els chiet, mal li est cuvenant.
fol. 221vb  Ore espurune qui at hardement grant,
Garde sur destre, s'a véu Guinemant,
Qui ont abatu treis forz reis Persant —
Les dous a morz, li tierz se vait fuiant.

1765    They seize the pagan standard
In a space where the field was open,
But Otinel's not there; he's engaged elsewhere:
He's already charged thrice at the standard,
And cut off the heads of four kings.

1770    King Garsie speaks about this to Parant,
A wicked pagan who thoroughly hates God.
"Brother," he says, "it goes badly for me.
My heart's aggrieved on account of my barons,
Killed by Otinel before my very eyes.
1775    I'll die of sorrow if I can't stop him,
And Charlemagne will wrongfully take me —
He who holds my lands against my will,
And wears a crown without my leave!
Unless I see him surrender today in battle,
1780    I'll never possess anything in France."

"Lord," says Parant, "now you're in danger:
Charles is nearby! See him before you!
What's yours is burning, as you bitterly know.
I'm frightened by his nephew Roland,
1785    Whom I secretly spied this morning
As he struck Balant on the helmet —
He cleaved through the whole man and steed!
I'm so very afraid that I'll run away!"
The King summons Belduit of Aquilant:
1790    "Gather the Turks while a hundred remain;
Watch over the Turks so that no one deserts.
Do whatever's needed to any who do,
So they'll lose honor for the rest of their lives."
The din is great, many heavy blows are dealt,
1795    And the battle is pursued rigorously.
Count Roland goes looking for the Persians;
With Durendal he searches the streets.
To any he overtakes, he delivers a cruel reward.
The Bavarians and Germans strike very well,
1800    And so do Burgundians, Flemings, and Normans.
The French strike great blows swiftly,
And the young men attack without restraint
At the standard — they don't intend to leave;
They love neither truce nor accord,
1805    Whoever falls there receives a bad fate.
A very brave one now spurs forth,
And looks to his right, seeing Guinemant,
Who's struck down three tough Persian kings —
Killing two, and the third one fled.

1810     Prent un destrier si'l rent a Guinemant,
    Li quons i salt k'arçun ne se prent.
    "Sire," fait il, "servise m'as feit grant.
    Mar acointerunt paien tun hardement.
    Vostre merci del bon destrer curant —
1815     Mult m'unt tenu icil en destreit grant."
    Treit a l'espee dunt le punt fu d'argent,
    Si fiert un Turc, ke la teste en prent.
    Otes s'en vait "Munjoie" escriant,
    A Curuçuse, les paens detrenchant.
1820     Alsi les sent cum feit la nue le vent!
    Trove Oliver e Estult e Rollant,
    E Engeler e Garin le Normant,
    Gefrei d'Anjou et Rotold l'Alemant,
    Qui se combatent mult adurement.
1825     E "Deu," dist Otes, "Pere Omnipotent,
    Tels compaingnuns aloue jo querrant!"
    Ore sunt ensemble li chevaler vaillant.
    Roillent lur armes cume fuldre qui fent.
    As branz d'ascer funt tel marcelement
1830     Cum l'um n'oreit Deu del ciel tonant.
    Forment les dutent Arabi e Persant,
    Les Melians e Turc e Affricant.
    Li reis Garsie tremble entre sa gent.

    Nostre emperere est as degrez alez
1835     Pur sa grant gent k'entur li veit hertez.
    Sore eust Ogier, ne feust mes irrez
    En prisun est de chaenes liez.
    Meis les mains a deliverés e les piez,
    Parmi le gros del cors est atachiez,
1840     Set chevalers le gardent bien preisez.
    Ço dist Ogier, "Ces chaenes m'alaschiez —
    En quor me blescent! Dehez ait qui en est lez!"
    Ço dist li uns, "De folie parlez.
    Kar, par Mahun, si vus nies en parlez,
1845     Nus destreindrum e les mains e les piez,
    Ja en ta vie mes leals ne serrez."
    Ogier l'oi, si en est mult irrez.
fol. 222ra     Prist une hastele, si se leva en piez,
    Quatre at occis — par eus ne serra mes liez!
1850     De la tur halte a les treis trebuchiez;
    Quant aval vindrent, les cols orent brisez.
    Brise les chaines si s'en est deliverez.

    Quant est deliveré li bon Deneis Oger,
    Al einz ke pot est venu al destrier,

1810      He grabs a horse and hands it to Guinemant,
              Who leaps up without touching the bow.
              "Lord," he says, "you've done me much service.
              The pagans are unhappily feeling your power.
              Thank you for this swift warhorse —
1815      They've held me here in great distress."
              He draws his sword with its silver tip,
              And strikes a Turk, whose head he takes.
              Otinel goes off, shouting "Mountjoy!"
              And slicing up pagans with Corçuse.
1820      He senses them like a cloud does the wind!
              He finds Oliver, Estult, and Roland,
              Engeler and Garin the Norman,
              Geffrei of Anjou and Rotolt the German,
              Who all fight ferociously.
1825      "God," says Otinel, "Omnipotent Father,
              How long have I sought such companions!"
              Now the valiant knights are all together.
              Their weapons flash like bolts of lightning.
              Their steel blades create such a clatter
1830      That none might hear God's thunder in the sky.
              Arabs and Persians utterly fear them,
              The Melians, Turks, and Africans too.
              King Garsie trembles amid his army.

              Our Emperor is overtaken by joy
1835      As he watches his large army fighting.
              Ogier was upset and couldn't be angrier
              Because he's in prison tied with chains.
              He's now freed his hands and feet,
              But the center of his body is bound up,
1840      While seven knights guard him closely.
              Ogier says, "Loosen these chains —
              My heart hurts! Damn him who's glad about that!"
              One of them says, "You talk like a fool.
              By Mahomet, if you're not quiet,
1845      We'll tighten your hands and feet,
              And you'll never feel any better."
              Ogier hears this and grows angrier.
              Grasping a woodblock, he rises to his feet,
              And kills four of them — they'll bind him no longer!
1850      The last three he tossed from the tower;
              When they hit the ground, their necks were broken.
              He breaks the chains and is free of them.

              As soon as good Ogier was free,
              He went to his horse as fast as possible,

1855     En frene la (k'il n'i a esquier),
        Bien est armé a lei de chevaler.
        Quant munté fu, si cumence a huchier:
        "A l'estur vois mes compaingnuns aider,
        Désoremes dei les granz colps enpleier,
1860     Demein vendrai tant m'en poiez preier.
        Deu m'en defende de mal e d'encombrer!"
        Ist de la porte, si broche le destrer,
        Veit al estur tut un chimin plener.
        Quant vint al champ, si i truva Garnier,
1865     Rollant e Naimes e Otes e Galtier.
        Grant joie funt, trestut le vout beiser.
        Puis li demandent s'il est sein e entier.
        Il lur respunt que sein est e legier —
        Unques ni ert plus prest de ferir chevaler.

1870     Quant sunt ensemble li justur,
        Pur amur Ogier, fut un trestur.
        Cent en ont mort a glaive e a dolur.
        Veit s'en Garsie, al quor en a irrur —
        Ne pot garir kar n'i a defendur.
1875     Veit s'enfuiant senz vie de suiur,

        Otes l'enchasce par un grant valee,
        En sa main porte Curecçuse s'espee
        En l'altre main la grant targe bendee.
        E veit Garsie que se fuit a celee —
1880     Pur encontrer a sa resdue tiree.
        Quant il aprosme, si li dit sa pensee.

        "Pur Deu," dit il, "dite mei, sire reis,
        Devez a nuit conreer ces Franceis,
        Alez vuz querre le cras lard as peis?
1885     Nel mangereient pur mil mars d'Orkeneis.
        Altre mes feites: ço est manger a burgeis!"

        Li reis Garsie est forment curuciez
        Pur les paroles qu'il li a afichiez.
        Le destrier broche des espuruns dorez,
fol. 222rb   Ja se feust bien d'Otinel vengez,
1891     Quant le destrier cesta de quatre piez.
        Volsist u nun, a terre est versez,
        E sun braz destre parmi li est brisez.
        Ainceis k'il peust relever en ses piez,
1895     Li quons Rollant est a li aprosmez,
        K'as mains le prent, unkes ne fu si lez!

1855       Harnessed him (for there was no squire),
And armed himself well in a knightly way.
Once he was mounted, he began to shout out:
"I'm going to help my comrades in battle,
I now must deliver mighty blows,
1860       But tomorrow I'll return to plunder as much as I can.
May God protect me from evil and harm!"
He issues out of the gate, spurs the warhorse,
And heads to the battle by a wide road.
When he comes to the field, he finds Garnier,
1865       Roland and Naimes and Otinel and Gautier.
They rejoice, each wanting to kiss him.
Then they ask whether he's sound and whole.
He answers that he's well and able —
Never was he more ready to behave like a knight.

1870       When the fighters are all together,
For love of Ogier, they pause a bit.
They've killed a hundred by sword and for sorrow.
Meanwhile Garsie retreats furiously —
He can't guard himself for he has no defenders.
1875       He flees without any means of safety.

Otinel chases him through a long valley,
Bearing his sword Corçuse in one hand
And a large banded shield in the other.
He sees Garsie trying to flee secretly,
1880       And pulls up his reins to intercept him.
Approaching him, he speaks his mind.

"By God," he says, "explain to me, lord king,
If you were to prepare something tonight for the French,
Would you look for peas in fat lard?
1885       They'll not eat that for a thousand Orkney marks.
Make something else: that's townsfolks' food!"

King Garsie is deeply insulted
About the taunt directed at him.
Prodding his horse with gilded spurs,
1890       He wants revenge against Otinel,
But his horse stumbles on its four hooves.
Like it or not, he's thrown to the ground,
And his right arm's broken in the middle.
Before he can stand up on his feet,
1895       Count Roland approaches him,
And seizes him by the hand, overjoyed!

Li reis s'escrie, "Baruns, ne mi tuchiez!
A vus me rent! La vie me dunez!"

Li dui barun ont le rei mené,
1900    A Charles l'ont sempres presenté;
Il leva a Paris, sa cité, mené.
Francs ne s'ublient li vassal aduré.
Ainz ke feust vespre, u li solei culchie,
Urent le champ e prise la cité.

1905    Quant l'um orra de itel messagier,
Bien deivent tuit pur s'alme prier —
Ke si aida paiens a traverser.

The king cries out, "Barons, don't touch me!
I yield to you! Spare my life!"

The two barons lead the king away,
1900     And present him at once to Charles,
Who had him led to Paris, his city.
The French do not forget the honored warrior.
Before it was vespers, before sunset,
They possess the field and take the city.

1905     When people hear about this messenger,
They all ought to pray for his soul —
He who did so much to defeat the pagans.

**ABBREVIATIONS**: *AND*: *The Anglo-Norman Dictionary*; *DMF*: *Dictionnaire du Moyen Français (1330–1500)*; *DR*: *Duke Roland and Sir Otuel of Spain*; **Hassell**: Hassell, *Middle French Proverbs, Sentences, and Proverbial Phrases*; *OK*: *Otuel a Knight*; *OR*: *Otuel and Roland*; *Otinel*: Anglo-Norman *Otinel*; *Pseudo-Turpin*: *The Chronicle of Pseudo-Turpin*, ed. and trans. Poole; *RV*: *Roland and Vernagu*; *Song of Roland*: *The Song of Roland: An Analytical Edition*, ed. and trans. Brault.

Chart: Comparative passages in the Anglo-Norman *Otinel* and the English Otuel Romances

This chart is designed to aid comparisons among the romances and the *chanson de geste* as it survives in the Cologny manuscript (the text of *Otinel* presented in this volume). Each of the English romances is an adaptation of the French *chanson*. The Cologny *Otinel* is not, however, the exact version used by each English poet, nor is the Vatican City *Otinel* (ed. Guessard and Michelant). All surviving copies of *Otinel* are incomplete and exhibit much variation among themselves. The *chanson de geste* no doubt circulated in a range of versions, subject to scribal variation.

| *Otinel* | *Otuel a Knight* | *Otuel and Roland* | *Duke Roland* |
|---|---|---|---|
| line 25 | — | — | 49–54 |
| lines 33–44 | 79–114 | 64–84 | 71–105 |
| lines 59–99 | 129–76 | 88–93 | 121–68 |
| lines 130–36 | 255–58 | — | 232–46 |
| lines 165–67 | — | 151–59 | 273 |
| lines 204–08 | 346–49 | — | 313–14 |
| lines 327–28 | — | 349–50 | 397–98 |
| lines 454–65 | 521–34 | 512–28 | 518–31 |
| lines 636–42 | — | 658–63 | 703–17 |
| lines 655–60 | — | 679–84 | 733–38 |

| *Otinel* | *Otuel a Knight* | *Otuel and Roland* | *Duke Roland* |
|---|---|---|---|
| lines 696–702 | 725–32 | 721–23 | 784–92 |
| lines 848–51 | 857–74 | 884–88 | 866–75 |
| lines 1000–17 | 1017–40 | 1039–47 | 1009–27 |
| lines 1043–47 | 1061–64 | 1058–74 | 1043–54 |
| lines 1195–1234 | 1151–1212 | 1165–1203 | 1137–64 |
| lines 1311–52 | 1231–82 | 1267–1350 | 1233–69 |
| lines 1445–56 | 1314–28 | 1454–85 | 1315–26 |
| lines 1836–69 | 1629–78 | 1616–45 | 1543–60 |
| lines 1873–1901 | 1696–1734 | 1652–81 | 1565–80 |

6      *duze pers.* "Twelve peers." According to legend, Charlemagne recognized twelve knights as his greatest, noblest warriors. See also the note to lines 630–34 below.

17      *le jor . . . li innocent.* Holy Innocents' Day (December 28), the feast day commemorating Herod's slaughter of the infants (Matthew 2:16). Two of the Middle English poets borrow this detail. Compare *OK*, line 55; and *OR*, line 48.

17–44      *Seingnurs . . . . desk'al talun.* These two *laisses* are in alexandrines, not decasyllabic lines. According to Hardman and Ailes, "It raises the possibility that there was second source manuscript, now lost, which had a version of the narrative in alexandrines" (*Legend of Charlemagne*, p. 365).

18      *Paris en France.* Although the poet identifies Paris as the location of Charlemagne's court, this is historically inaccurate. The Roman town of Lutetia Parisiorum did not develop into the administrative center of France until the eleventh and twelfth centuries. Hugh Capet, count of Paris and duke of the Franks, was elected king of the Franks in 987, and subsequent Capetian kings expanded the city's size and influence. During the Carolingian age, Aix-la-Chapelle, also called Aachen, was where Charlemagne lived and ruled. The Middle English Otuel romances also set this scene in or near Paris. In *OK*, Charlemagne appears to arrive from Saint-Denis to hold court in Paris (lines 57–58). In *OR*, the situation is the opposite: he appears to dwell in Paris and hold court in Saint-Denis (lines 50–51). In *DR*, Charlemagne dwells in Paris (line 39).

     *Clermunt.* This place-name apparently refers to what is today Clermont-Ferrand in central France, one of the oldest of French cities. Beyond its rich Roman and Carolingian history, the city is famous as the starting point of the First Crusade (1095–99).

36      *fluri gernun.* "white moustache." On Charles' iconic white beard, see the explanatory note to *DR*, lines 80 and 82. See also *RV*, line 664; and *OR*, line 71.

68    *Curçuse*. Corçuse is Otuel's famous sword. In *OK*, it is Corsouse; in *OR*, Cursins; in *DR*, Corsu. On named swords, see the note to lines 873–77 below.

124   *ne valt une alie*. "Une alie" is a sorb-apple, an acidic, gritty-textured fruit. The *AND* notes that it is "used to designate a worthless object." Proverbial. See Hassell A78. See also line 1225.

129–31  *Il te dorra . . . . e la navie*. On the historically inaccurate notion that Charlemagne controlled Normandy and England, see Hardman and Ailes, who comment that "Charlemagne's actual empire has long since disappeared from sight" (*Legend of Charlemagne*, p. 364). It is typical in *chansons de geste* (as in the *Song of Roland*) that Charlemagne is depicted as the ruler of all Christendom.

165–67  *Une cité . . . . Atelie*. Lombardy, a region in north Italy, figures prominently in many of the Otuel-cycle romances. Medieval Lombardy bordered on France. In *The Siege of Milan*, the central conflict between Saracens and Christians is over the city of Milan and the surrounding Lombard region. In *Otinel, OK, OR*, and *DR*, the Saracen Emperor Garcy has conquered many key Christian cities and made Lombardy his command center. The location of Atelie as a major Lombard city situated between two rivers makes it likely that the poet is referencing Pavia, the capital of Lombardy in the seventh and eighth centuries, which is located on the Ticino River three miles upstream from its confluence with the Po River. The Ticino (which the *Otinel* poet names "Ton River" in line 668) rises in the Swiss Alps, descends into Italy through Lake Maggiore, and is the largest left-bank tributary of the Po. It is over the Ton/Ticino that Charlemagne builds the bridge over which the French will pass to attack the city; see the notes to lines 664–68 and 674–80 below. Pavia is named only at line 578.

175   *K'escufle n'i entre ne corneile ne pie*. This line refers to birds (crows and magpies) that scavenge the dead left lying on a battlefield.

199   *Charle de Seint-Denis*. Saint-Denis, located near Paris, is the site of the Basilica of Saint-Denis, housing the relics of the martyred first bishop of Paris. It has long been connected to the royal line, and was the burial site for almost all French kings from the tenth century until the French Revolution. Charlemagne's parents — Pepin le Bref and Bertrada of Laon — were interred in the basilica at Saint-Denis, the construction of which was begun by Pepin and completed by Charlemagne.

226   *Seint-Omer*. Saint-Omer is a place in northern France named for Saint Audomarus (Omer), a seventh-century bishop and founder of the monastery alluded to here. The *OR* and *DR* poets borrow this detail; see *OR*, line 239, and *DR*, line 329.

230   *Durendal*. Durendal is the name of Roland's famous sword. In Rocamadour, France, one may see a chapel with a sword embedded in its outside wall. By local legend, this sword is Durendal. De Veyrières notes the claim (found in l'abbé Cheval's 1862 guidebook, *Guide du Pélerin à Roc-Amadour*) that the real Durendal was stolen in 1183 when Henry II pillaged the chapel, and he includes a drawing of the current sword ("L'Épée de Roland," pp. 139–41).

245        *cel apostle ki que rent penant.* The reference could be to any of the twelve disciples of Jesus who suffered martyrdom. A good guess would be Saint Peter, whose legend reported that he was crucified upside-down.

255–75    *L'unze per . . . . feite d'un Almant.* On the arming of Roland, compare *OR*, lines 280–324; the shield there depicts a "lyon . . . raumpande" (line 301). In *DR*, see lines 349–72, where it is merely "a schelde of faire coloure" (line 364).

259–60    *Ço fu le healme . . . . il occist Brachant.* Hardman and Ailes, *Legend of Charlemagne*, p. 357, note that the detail of Goliath's helmet, previously won by Charlemagne, is perhaps the most interesting of several enhancements found in the Anglo-Norman scene of Roland's arming, compared to the French version.

267–73    *Peint a azur . . . . par grant estudiement.* The cosmological grandeur of Roland's shield adds an ambitious heroic touch to *Otinel.* On it are depicted the four winds and the heavens, with the twelve zodiacal signs, as well as earth and ocean, sky and sun. Symbolically, it sets Roland at the center of the universe. The description is reminiscent, on a lesser scale, of Aeneas' massive shield forged for him by Vulcan (Virgil, *Aeneid*, 8.788-955; trans. Mandelbaum).

276        *Puis li aportent un fort espé trenchant.* Roland seems to receive here a second sword; see Hardman and Ailes, *Legend of Charlemagne*, p. 358.

280        *Bruiant.* In addition to Roland's steed Bruiant, other warhorses named in *Otinel* include: Otinel's Migrados (line 350) and Flori (line 1029); Clarel's Turnevent (line 1279); Volant, gifted by Charlemagne to Naimes (lines 1518–19); and Oliver's Fauvel (line 1605). Roland's killing of Migrados and Otinel's consequent killing of Bruiant begin their duel in an exceptionally brutal way (lines 403–19).

283        *arpent.* A French measure of length, equal to about 64 yards or 71.5 meters, largely archaic, but still used in Quebec.

327–63    *Belisent apele . . . . n'en ert tenu citez.* This scene of Otinel armed and tended to by three ladies is balanced later with one of Ogier healed by three ladies; see the note to lines 978–84 below.

369        *Les duze pers.* At this moment there can be only nine of the "twelve peers" with Charlemagne because Roland, Ogiers, and Naimes are in the meadow. This line shows how loosely the term *duze pers* is used. Compare the note to lines 630–34 below.

516–18    *A ices parole . . . . descent.* The dove that alights upon Otuel is the Holy Spirit ("Sainz Espiriz"), hence his immediate conversion. Compare *OK*, lines 585–88; *OR*, lines 568–73; and *DR*, lines 578–79.

528–29    *Mahun . . . . Jovin le puant.* Middle English romances often misrepresent Muslims as polytheists who worship idols, naming three or four gods as central to their fictionalized faith: here, Mahomet, Tervagant, Apolin, and Jove. See the discussion in the General Introduction, p. 16, and compare the notes to lines 1209–10, 1265–1305, and 1292–96 below.

551      *un mul amblant.* Here, Otinel rides an ambling mule. Belisant will later ride a swift Hungarian mule (lines 656–58).

555      *Turpin de Reins.* Archbishop Turpin is a key militant and ecclesiastical character in the *Song of Roland* and other Charlemagne romances. In *Otinel*, his role is limited to episcopal duties: performing Mass and baptizing the converted Otuel. In *OR*, lines 40–41, Turpin is named as an eyewitness chronicler of events, as in *Pseudo-Turpin*. On Turpin's role in the *Song of Roland*, see the explanatory note to *OR*, line 2114.

562      *Le nun li leissent.* Otinel keeps his Saracen name despite the common practice of a convert adopting a Christian name when baptized ("christened") — as instanced in the famous conversion of Saul to Paul (Acts 9:16–20, 13:9).

565      *bele que la rose.* Proverbial. See Hassell R69.

630–34      *Li duze pier . . . . Daneis Ogiers.* This passage offers the only instance in *Otinel* and the Middle English Otuel romances where there is an attempt to list the twelve peers in total. Here, they are: Roland, Oliver, Ansels, Girard, Engeler, Estult of Lengres, Turpin, Girier, Bertoloi, Otinel, Duke Naimes, and Ogier the Dane. The names vary in different accounts. As named by Charlemagne in his plaint for their deaths in the *Song of Roland*, they are Roland and Oliver, Gerin and Gerier, Oton and Berenger, Yvoire and Yvon, Engelier, Duke Samson and Anseis, and Gerard of Roussillon (*Song of Roland*, lines 2402–10). That list is confused, however, because Charlemagne also names Archbishop Turpin. See also the note to line 369 above.

645      *Munmartre.* Montmartre is a hill in what is now the northern part of Paris, and the location where Saint Denis was purportedly beheaded by Romans. According to legend, after he was decapitated, he picked up his head and carried it some distance away before he died on the site thereafter known as Saint-Denis. For more, see "St. Denis" in the *Catholic Encyclopedia*.

656–58      *Belisent munte . . . . nef ne galie.* Here, Belisant rides a swift Hungarian mule. Earlier, Otinel had ridden an ambling mule (line 551). The detail of Belesent riding a mule is retained in *OR*, lines 679–81, and *DR*, line 736.

664–68      *Desuz Versels . . . . en la praerie.* These lines describe the final stages of Charlemagne's journey to his encampment outside Atelie. "Versels" is Vercelli, a city on the Po River around forty-five miles west-northwest of Pavia, in the province of Piedmont on the border with Lombardy. An ancient site, settled around 600 BCE, Vercelli became an independent commune in 1120, and in the years that followed was a member of the first and second Lombard leagues. The city housed the University of Pavia from 1228 to 1372. "Muntferant" suggests Casale Monferrato, which lies on the Po River between Vercelli and Pavia, around forty-five miles due west of Pavia, at the foot of the Monferrat Hills from which one can see across the Po Valley to Pavia (as specified in line 665). It was originally a Roman town. The "Ton" River is most likely the Ticino, on the left bank of which lies Pavia. "Atelie" almost definitely refers to Pavia. The historical Charlemagne laid siege to Pavia, then the Lombard capital, in the winter and spring of 773–74, after which he had himself crowned king of Pavia and its surrounding territories. "Munpoun" is likely a name made up by the poet: while Pavia itself is situated on a small hill, the plains surrounding Pavia are quite flat, with no significant heights between the Monferrat Hills and Pavia. The plain where the French army encamps is across the Ton/Ticino from Pavia, around five miles from the city. See the notes to lines 165–67 and 674–80; and compare *OR*, lines 688–93, and *DR*, lines 742–46.

674–80       *Le fiz Pepin . . . . hum passer*. The bridge that Charlemagne orders that his men build over the Ton/Ticino helps to locate Pavia as the site of Atelie. When Roland, Oliver, and Ogier cross the bridge to seek Saracens, they meet Clarel and his companions "a good league" from Atelie, that is, about three to four miles from the city. See the notes to lines 165–67 and 664–68 above. Compare *OK*, lines 697–706; *OR*, lines 697–702; and *DR*, lines 754–56.

691          *une liue*. The length of a league is more than three miles.

766          *ne . . . valt un peis*. Proverbial. See Hassell P218. The phrase reappears at line 769.

793          *Naimant!* Clarel's war cry means "For Naimant!," referring to his birth city. See lines 1142–43, where he shouts it again, riding next to the Turk Arapater from Floriant, who shouts "Floriant!"

807          *Mellee*. This is the name of Clarel's sword. Compare *OR*, line 1240, where it is named "Melyn"; and *DR*, lines 847 and 1207, where it is named "Melle" and "Modlee." On other named swords, see the note to lines 873–77 below.

814–17       *Seingnurs . . . . Rollant la prent*. The ritual of Clarel giving his sword to his captors as a guarantee of his safety is reproduced in *OK*. See the explanatory note to *OK*, line 834.

860          *Munjoie*. "Mountjoy," the war cry of the French. See *MED mon-joie* (n.) and Godefroy, *Dictionnaire de L'Ancienne Langue Française*, 5:400 ("ancien cri de guerre des chevaliers français"; an ancient war cry of French knights). Compare *DR*, lines 881, 1067, and 1476.

863          *Qui plus . . . neir que mure*. "blacker than a mulberry." Proverbial. See Hassell M246. The simile emphasizes the black skin of the pagan, perhaps an African.

873–77       *Halteclere . . . . Curteine*. Oliver's sword is named "Halteclere," and Ogier's is "Curtein." Like Roland's Durendal and Otinel's Corçuse, the mightiest warriors' swords in *chansons de geste* often acquire names that associate them with their owners. Oliver's sword is also named in *OR*, line 904 ("Haunchecler"), and in *DR*, line 914 ("Haunkclere"). Ogier's sword is named Cursable in *OR*, line 900.

890          *ne . . . valt une fie*. Proverbial. The *AND* (*fie*[1], sense 2) notes that a figurative meaning of a fig is "a worthless object."

900–01       *Alfamie . . . . li promist druerie*. Oddly, this maiden (kinswoman of Alfage and seemingly also his beloved) bears the same name as Clarel's sweetheart Alfamie (King Garsie's daughter), an important female Saracen character in *Otinel* (see line 949).

919–22    *Oi Curteine . . . . vus voil esprover.* Ogier's speech to his sword is reminiscent of Roland's famous dying speech to Durendal in the *Song of Roland*, lines 2297–2354, which is adapted in the Middle English *OR*, lines 2326–49 (see explanatory note).

978–84    *Ces treis puceles . . . . sil mettent culchier.* The scene of Ogier with the three Saracen ladies, led by Alfamie, nicely balances the earlier scene of Otinel's arming by three Christian ladies, led by Belisant (lines 327–63). Both episodes depict women softly touching a warrior's flesh as they dress or undress him, in order to heal or protect him. These two scenes of a warrior among ladies provide brief relief from the all-male violence of war, and they also inject the text with moments of mild eroticism. Their balanced presence indicates the poet's artfulness.

1012    *Trop se volt faire sur tuz hummes loer!* Otinel raises here the most common fault attributed to Roland: that he is too eager for fame and therefore prone to behave bravely but rashly, without careful deliberation. This paradoxical virtue-as-flaw is characteristically featured in legends about Roland. Here, he is faulted by Otinel for leading himself and his comrades Oliver and Ogier into danger unnecessarily. The accusation echoes Oliver's criticism of Roland's refusal to summon Charlemagne in the *Song of Roland*, especially at lines 1100–05, 1170–73, and 1715–18.

1056    *Ne li valt mie . . . un denier.* Proverbial. See Hassell D28.

1142–43    *Naimant! . . . . Floriant!* See the note to line 793 above.

1191    *complie.* "compline," approximately 9 pm. This time reference uses a term from the seven liturgical hours — matins, lauds, prime, terce, sext, none, vespers, compline — which marked a day's moments for regular prayer. See also lines 1564 and 1903.

1209–10    *Fai dreit Mahun . . . . ta lei k'as guerpie.* In *Otinel*, Clarel is consistently shown to be earnestly pious in his devotion to Mahomet; the Middle English poets all adhere to this depiction of Clarel's character as well. Here, Clarel's argument that Otinel should "make amends" with Mahomet illustrates how Western authors often painted the Muslim faith as an inverted mirror to Christianity: its basic tenets of belief were similar (repent and be forgiven), but their worship was idolatrous and misdirected toward false gods. The *Otinel* poet uses Clarel's character as a devout Saracen as a foil to Otinel's denunciation of pagan belief. See also the note to lines 1265–1305 below.

1225    *ne valt un alie.* See the note to line 124 above.

1265–305    *El chief li lacent . . . . al quor dolent.* This passage accentuates Clarel's devotion to Mahomet and loyalty to Garsie, beginning with his arming — etched on his helmet is a trinity of his gods — and ending with his prayer. On the snake's-head helmet as a sign of Clarel's pagan "alterity," see Hardman and Ailes, *Legend of Charlemagne*, pp. 358–59, and compare *OR*, lines 1225–36, and *DR*, lines 1201–04. See also the note to lines 1209–10 above.

1292–96   *Mahumet levent . . . . n'ariere n'avant.* This passage depicts the great lengths that the pagans go to in order to erect a statue of Mahomet to oversee the battle and bring victory. Corresponding scenes occur in *OR*, lines 1249–60, and *DR*, 1213–21. To a medieval Christian audience, the care taken to secure the statue with chains would have emphasized how inert, unstable, and false this idol was. In *chansons de geste*, Muslims, as Saracens, are typically depicted inaccurately as idol-worshipers. On Western Christian beliefs about Muslim idolatry, see Strickland, *Saracens, Demons, and Jews*, pp. 166–69; and the discussion in the General Introduction, p. 16.

1299      *besant.* A bezant is a Byzantine coin of gold or silver (*DMF besant*).

1307      *l'eue del col.* Charlemagne and his knights are at the fork or confluence of the Ticino and Po Rivers when Clarel shouts to them from across the Ticino.

1344      *ne valt . . . oefs.* Proverbial. See Hassell O17.

1363      *Tartarun.* Clarel is saying that upon his death Jesus was sent to Tartarus, the pit or abyss in which Greek mythology assigns the wicked to suffer eternal punishment. In 2 Peter 2:4, Tartarus appears as the place of punishment for the angels who joined Lucifer in rebelling against God.

1464      *fiers que liuns.* Proverbial. See Hassell L68.

1497      *festu.* "straw." The *AND* (*festu*[1], sense 2) notes that the word is used figuratively to connote a "worthless object." See Hassell F59. The idiom reappears at lines 1588 and 1593.

1498      *Dulcejoie.* "Sweetjoy" is the name of King Garcy's horn.

1503      *Rollant le cunte e Oliver sun dru.* These lines epitomize the legendary close friendship between Roland and Oliver, brothers-in-arms. While, in *Otinel*, Otinel and Clarel both have female love interests, and Ogier experiences some flirtation with Clarel's paramour, the bond between Roland and Oliver exists mainly without women. In its brash, brave heroics, it stands for the masculine strength of Charlemagne's army. The companionship of Roland and Oliver is central to the *Song of Roland*, as appears notably in Roland's tearful eulogy upon Oliver's death (lines 2021–30).

1554–64   *De cheres armes . . . . devant midi sonant.* This passage epitomizes the grim irony of war, common to all war literature, and yet notable amid a *chanson de geste* poet's glorification of battle. The gallant Turk who wants the honor of defeating Roland has only just departed from his girlfriend, who lovingly and laughingly armed him, and he will be dead by noon.

1559      *aligod.* Instead of this otherwise unknown word, the Vatican City *Otinel* has the reading *levrier* (greyhound), adopted here for the translation.

1564      *midi.* "sext," approximately noon, here sounded by the ringing of church bells. On time marked by the seven liturgical hours, see the note to line 1191 above.

1600      *almuafle.* The word here in the Vatican City *Otinel* is *amirans* (emir).

1612    *Ne . . . la reinie d'un prunier.* Proverbial. See Hassell P290.

1618    *Berrvier.* It seems odd that the Bavarians are named twice in this list (first at line 1616). This word may refer to occupants of another region, but no other solution presents itself. Compare, too, line 1799.

1644    *Maneis.* Inhabitants of Le Mans.

1660    *Guineman.* This French warrior is apparently not the more important Guinemant (line 1521), who remains alive for later action (lines 1807, 1810).

1671    *Mallo!* This is the war cry of the Bretons, meaning something like "Onward!" It is repeated at line 1763. For another example, see Godefroy, *Dictionnaire de L'Ancienne Langue Française*, 5:125. Compare Clarel's war cry of "Naimant!" at lines 793 (see note above) and 1142.

1693–94  *Forment le pleint . . . . del rei Corsabrez.* That is, Count Eliens is the uncle of Troias. His revenge against King Corsabrez will occur a few lines later, when Amirez crushes one of his eyes and sends him as a captive to Charlemagne (lines 1728–45).

1763    *Mallo!* See the note to line 1671 above.

1836–69  *Sore eust Ogier . . . . ferir chevaler.* In this scene, Ogier frees his hands and feet, kills four guards with a woodblock and throws three others down from the tower, breaks his remaining chains, finds his horse and arms himself, and shouts out threats as he gallops off. For alternate scenarios, see *OK*, lines 1629–78; *OR*, lines 1616–36; and *DR*, lines 1543–60.

1870–907  *Quant sunt . . . . paiens a traverser.* The rhyme pattern indicates that these lines divide into six short *laisses*, even though the scribe has not marked them with large initials. The short *laisses* seem to bring a new tempo to the poem — either a quickening up or a quieting down — as it draws to a close.

1882–86  *Pur Deu . . . . manger a burgeis.* Otinel's insult is certainly about the aristocratic class and refined tastes of the French. It may also contain an anti-Muslim slur about dietary laws that forbid pork and lard. On this passage, see Hardman and Ailes, *Legend of Charlemagne*, pp. 362–63. On the possibility of a proverbial or medical sense, compare Hassell L15 and *AND lard*.

1899–904  *Li dui barun . . . . prise la cité.* In this ending, unique to the Cologny manuscript, Garsie is captured and then the *chanson* is over. The ending of the Cologny *Otinel* is more abrupt than that in the Vatican City version, which extends the ending to include another eighty lines. There, the following events occur in rapid succession: Ogier kills a fleeing pagan; Garcy dies in prison; the French capture Atelie and slaughter its inhabitants; Otinel and Belisant wed; Otinel takes control of the country surrounding Atelie; Charlemagne returns to Paris; Otinel protects his kingdom and exalts Holy Christianity to the end of his days. On the different endings, see Hardman and Ailes, *Legend of Charlemagne*, pp. 363–64. At the end of *OK*, Garcy does homage to Charles, without conversion being specified. At the end of *OR*, Garcy is taken to Paris, converts to Christianity, and is blessed by Turpin. At the end of *DR*, Otuel weds Belesent and becomes a peer.

1903     *vespre*. "vespers," approximately 6 pm. On time marked by the seven liturgical hours, see the note to line 1191 above.

1905–07    *Quant l'um . . . . a traverser*. The final three lines of *Otinel* offer an epitaph for the titular Saracen hero of the *chanson de geste*. Readers are asked to pray for Otinel's soul; he should be remembered as both messenger and warrior for Christians. The term "messagier" seems now to rise to a new meaning: cross-cultural ambassador. Otinel brought a message to Charlemagne's court, where he received a message (God's Word), and then he heroically delivered it back, with holy vengeance, to the community that initially sent him.

# TEXTUAL NOTES TO THE ANGLO-NORMAN *OTINEL*

**ABBREVIATIONS: MS**: Cologny, Fondation Martin Bodmer Cod. Bodmer 168, fols. 211ra–22rb; **OF**: Old French.

| | |
|---|---|
| 121 | *Rucie*. MS: *bucie*. |
| 138 | *tant*. MS: *tarat*. |
| 157 | *duc*. MS: *dur*. |
| 252 | *Fait Oliver Mult parlez haltement*. MS: *laisse* opening not marked. |
| 309 | *Oriant*. MS: *Becliant*. |
| 312 | *cunterai*. MS: *curterai*. |
| 382 | *mult*. MS: *ment*. |
| 398 | *ki les*. MS: *kis*. |
| 411 | *fuerre*. MS: *suerre*. |
| 639 | *Flamenes*. MS: *Framenes*. |
| 652 | *Lumbardie*. MS: *lurbardie*. |
| 662 | *compaingnie*. MS: *compaingine* (second *i* dotted). |
| 664 | *Versels*. MS: *Vergels*. |
| 683 | *duze*. MS: *virze*. |
| 691 | *Defors Hatillie a une liue grant*. MS: *laisse* opening not marked. |
| 700 | *Forz*. MS: *Fozz*. |
| 727 | *vent*. MS: *veno*. |
| 770 | *penun*. MS: *penuer*. |
| 840 | *juste*. MS: *iute*. |
| 848 | *est*. MS: omitted. An abbreviation of unknown meaning occurs here. |
| 849 | *al rei*. MS: omitted. |
| 852 | *Sire*. This word is marked with a large initial, but the rhyme matches the preceding *laisse*. |
| 862 | *Rollant feri un paien Berruier*. MS: *laisse* opening not marked. |
| 879 | *Atant est venu Carmel de Tabarie*. MS: *laisse* opening not marked. |
| 892–93 | *ki ke peist u rie . . . . ki ke peist u ki rie*. The similarity of these lines could be a copying error. |
| 918 | *Lores*. MS: *Loes*. |
| 958 | *en estur*. MS: *en' estur* (apostrophe-type mark inserted). |
| 996 | *enhacier*. MS: superscript *r* above *ha*. |
| 1009 | *prover*. MS: *proue*. |
| 1018 | *Nostre emperere a fait un corn soner*. A large colored initial marks this line as the opening of a new *laisse*, even though the rhymes match the preceding *laisse*. The initial indicates a transition in narrative action, so the manuscript's *laisse* break is retained. |

| 1066 | *escuz*. MS: *escur*. |
|---|---|
| 1074 | *A batu la* . . . . MS: words obscured by fold; this *laisse* is not found in the OF *Otinel*. |
| 1077 | *sun*. MS: *su*. |
| 1135 | *Arepater*. MS: *Arepairer*. |
| 1217 | *Satanie*. MS: *Gatanie*. |
| 1227 | *Dist li convers Diable sunt en tei*. MS: *laisse* opening not marked. |
| 1242 | *Belisent*. MS: Letter *B* obscured by fold; the lower portions of other letters are visible. |
| 1314 | *dit*. MS: *eit*. |
| 1368 | *Ja ne*. MS: words obscured by fold; compare OF *Otinel*, line 1405. |
| 1397 | *purpensez*. MS: *purpensez* (*ur* abbreviated), with abbreviation for *ur* repeated in the right margin. |
| 1409 | *espee*. MS: letters *pe* obscured by fold. |
| 1412 | *Otinel broche sun arabi curant*. MS: *laisse* opening not marked. |
| 1431 | *Curçuse*. MS: *curcecesu*. |
| 1451 | *blanchoier*. MS: word obscured by fold; compare OF *Otinel*, line 1489. |
| 1462 | *iriez*. MS: *barnez*. |
| 1511 | *Le fiz Pepin a ordané sa gent*. MS: *laisse* opening not marked. |
| 1536 | *esmuevent serré*. MS: words obscured by fold; compare OF *Otinel*, line 1613. |
| 1568 | *se*. MS: *ge*. |
| 1577 | *le paien*. MS: words obscured by fold; for other words in this line, the upper halves of the letters are visible. Compare OF *Otinel*, line 1657. |
| 1579 | *de eus*. MS: *deeus* (second *e* marked for deletion). |
| 1604 | *L'almuafle se leisse a Oliver*. MS: *laisse* opening not marked. |
| 1610 | *par*. MS: *par* with letter *p* canceled. |
| 1619 | *enseignes-bessier*. MS: words obscured by fold; compare OF *Otinel*, line 1696. |
| 1621 | *vet*. MS: *vec*. |
| 1629 | *Quant ces fiers osz se furent a justees*. MS: *laisse* opening not marked. |
| 1662 | *Munjoie escrie Ore a* . . . . MS: words obscured by fold; this *laisse* is not found in the OF *Otinel*. |
| 1704 | *Paiens complissent si est* . . . *tez*. MS: words obscured by fold; this *laisse* is not found in the OF *Otinel*. |
| 1734 | *entrez*. MS: *entez*. |
| 1768 | *treis*. MS: *treis* (*s* superscript) or *treier*. |
| 1799 | *Beiver*. MS: letters obscured by tear; compare OF *Otinel*, line 1819. |
| 1830 | *n'oreit Deu*. MS: words obscured by fold; compare OF *Otinel*, line 1859. |
| 1876 | *Otes l'enchasce par un grant valee*. MS: *laisse* opening not marked. |
| 1882 | *Pur Deu dit il dite mei sire reis*. MS: *laisse* opening not marked. |
| 1899 | *Li dui barun ont le rei mené*. MS: *laisse* opening not marked. |
| 1905 | *Quant l'um orra de itel messagier*. MS: *laisse* opening not marked. |

# BIBLIOGRAPHY

MANUSCRIPTS

Cologny, Fondation Martin Bodmer Cod. Bodmer 168.
Edinburgh, National Library of Scotland MS Advocates 19.2.1 (Auchinleck).
London, British Library MS Additional 31042 (London Thornton).
London, British Library MS Additional 37492 (Fillingham).
Paris, Bibliothèque nationale de France MS f. fr. 25408.
Paris, Bibliothèque nationale de France MS nouv. acq. fr. 5094.
Vatican City, Biblioteca Apostolica Vaticana Reg. lat. 1616.


FACSIMILES

Burnley, David, and Alison Wiggins, eds. *The Auchinleck Manuscript*. National Library of Scotland, 2003. Online at https://auchinleck.nls.uk.

"Cologny, Fondation Martin Bodmer, Cod. Bodmer 168." e-codices — Virtual Manuscript Library of Switzerland, 2005. Online at https://www.e-codices.unifr.ch/en/fmb/cb-0168/211r/0/Sequence-887.

Pearsall, Derek, and I. C. Cunningham, eds. *The Auchinleck Manuscript: National Library of Scotland Advocates' MS. 19.2.1*. London: Scolar Press, 1979.


PRIMARY SOURCES

*Alliterative Morte Arthure*. In *King Arthur's Death: The Middle English Stanzaic Morte Arthur and Alliterative Morte Arthure*. Ed. Larry D. Benson. Rev. Edward E. Foster. Kalamazoo, MI: Medieval Institute Press, 1994. Pp. 129–284.

*An Alphabet of Tales: An English 15th Century Translation of the* Alphabetum Narrationum *of Etienne de Besançon*. Ed. Mary Macleod Banks. 2 vols. EETS o.s. 126–27. London: Kegan Paul, Trench, Trübner, and Co., 1904–05.

*Ami and Amile: A Medieval Tale of Friendship*. Trans. Samuel N. Rosenberg and Samuel Danon. Ann Arbor: University of Michigan Press, 1996.

*Amis and Amiloun*. In *Amis and Amiloun, Robert of Cisyle, and Sir Amadace*. Ed. Edward E. Foster. Second Edition. Kalamazoo, MI: Medieval Institute Publications, 2007. Pp. 1–74.

*The Anglo-Norman* Pseudo-Turpin Chronicle *of William de Briane*. Ed. Ian Short. Oxford: Blackwell, 1973.

*An Anonymous Old French Translation of the Pseudo-Turpin Chronicle*. Ed. Ronald N. Walpole. Cambridge, MA: Medieval Academy of America, 1979.

*Bevis of Hampton*. In *Four Romances of England: King Horn, Havelok the Dane, Bevis of Hampton, Athelston*. Ed. Ronald B. Herzman, Graham Drake, and Eve Salisbury. Kalamazoo, MI: Medieval Institute Publications, 1999. Pp. 187–340.

*Le Bone Florence of Rome*. Ed. Carol Falvo Heffernan. Manchester: Manchester University Press, 1976.

*The Book of John Mandeville*. Ed. Tamarah Kohanski and C. David Benson. Kalamazoo, MI: Medieval Institute Publications, 2007.

*La Chanson de Guillaume (La Chançun de Willame)*. Ed. and trans. Philip E. Bennett. London: Grant & Cutler, 2000.

365

*La Chanson de Roland — The Song of Roland: The French Corpus*. Gen. Ed. Joseph J. Duggan, with Karen Akiyama, Ian Short, Robert F. Cook, Annalee C. Rejhon, Wolfgang van Emden, and William W. Kibler. 3 vols. Turnhout: Brepols, 2005.

*Charlemagne: An Anglo-Norman Poem of the Twelfth Century*. Ed. Francisque Michel. London: William Pickering, 1836.

*The Chronicle of Pseudo-Turpin: Book IV of the Liber Sancti Jacobi (Codex Calixtinus)*. Ed. and trans. Kevin R. Poole. New York: Italica Press, 2014.

*The Complete Harley 2253 Manuscript*. Ed. and trans. Susanna Fein, with David Raybin and Jan Ziolkowski. 3 vols. Kalamazoo, MI: Medieval Institute Publications, 2014–15.

Dante Alighieri. *The Divine Comedy. Vol. 1: Inferno*. Ed. and trans. John D. Sinclair. New York: Oxford University Press, 1939.

Einhard. *The Life of Charlemagne*. In *Einhard and Notker the Stammerer: Two Lives of Charlemagne*. Ed. and trans. David Ganz. London: Penguin, 2008. Pp. 1–44.

Ferrante, Joan M., trans. *Guillaume d'Orange: Four Twelfth-Century Epics*. New York: Columbia University Press, 1974.

*Firumbras*. In O'Sullivan, *Firumbras and Otuel and Roland*. Pp. 3–58.

*Floris and Blancheflour*. In *Sentimental and Humorous Romances: Floris and Blancheflour, Sir Degrevant, The Squire of Low Degree, The Tournament of Tottenham, and The Feast of Tottenham*. Ed. Erik Kooper. Kalamazoo, MI: Medieval Institute Publications, 2006. Pp. 1–52.

*Fragment of the Song of Roland* [the Middle English *Song of Roland*]. In Herrtage, *The English Charlemagne Romances. Part II*. Pp. 107–36.

*Gormont et Isembart: Fragment de Chanson de Geste du Xiie Siècle*. Ed. Alphonse Bayot. Third edition. Paris: H. Champion, 1931.

Herrtage, Sidney J. H., ed. *The English Charlemagne Romances. Part I: Sir Ferumbras*. EETS e.s. 34. London: Oxford University Press, 1879. Rpt. 1966.

———. *The English Charlemagne Romances. Part II: "The Sege off Melayne" and "The Romance of Duke Rowland and Sir Otuell of Spayne," Now for the First Time Printed from the Unique MS. Of R. Thornton, in the British Museum, MS. Addit. 31,042, Together with a Fragment of "The Song of Roland."* EETS e.s. 35. London: N. Trübner & Co., 1880. Rpt. 2002.

———. *The English Charlemagne Romances. Part VI: The Taill of Rauf Coilyear with the Fragments of Roland and Vernagu and Otuel*. EETS e.s. 39. London: Oxford University Press, 1882. Rpt. 1969.

*John Mirk's Festial. Edited from British Library MS Cotton Claudius A.II*. Ed. Susan Powell. 2 vols. EETS o.s. 334–35. Oxford: Oxford University Press, 2009, 2011.

*The Journey of Charlemagne to Jerusalem and Constantinople*. Ed. and trans. Jean-Louis G. Picherit. Birmingham, AL: Summa Publications, 1984.

*The King of Tars*. Ed. John H. Chandler. Kalamazoo, MI: Medieval Institute Publications, 2015.

Lupack, Alan, ed. *Three Middle English Charlemagne Romances*. Kalamazoo, MI: Medieval Institute Publications, 1990.

*Lybeaus Desconus* (Lambeth Palace, MS 306). In *Lybeaus Desconus*. Ed. Eve Salisbury and James Weldon. Kalamazoo, MI: Medieval Institute Publications, 2013. Pp. 30–82.

Malory, Thomas. *Malory: Complete Works*. Ed. Eugène Vinaver. Second edition. Oxford: Oxford University Press, 1971.

Newth, Michael A. H., trans. *Heroes of the French Epic: A Selection of Chansons de Geste*. Woodbridge: Boydell Press, 2005.

———, trans. *Heroines of the French Epic: A Second Selection of Chansons de Geste*. Woodbridge: D. S. Brewer, 2014.

O'Sullivan, Mary I., ed. *Firumbras and Otuel and Roland*. EETS o.s 198. London: Oxford University Press, 1935. Rpt. 2007.

*Octavian*. In *Four Middle English Romances: Sir Isumbras, Octavian, Sir Eglamour of Artois, Sir Tryamour*. Ed. Harriet Hudson. Second Edition. Kalamazoo, MI: Medieval Institute Publications, 2006. Pp. 39–95.

*Octovian Imperator*. Ed. Frances McSparran. Heidelberg: Carl Winter, 1979.

*Otinel, Chanson de Geste*. Ed. M. M. F. Guessard and H. Michelant. Paris: Maison A. Franck, 1859. Rpt. Nendeln: Kraus Reprint, 1966.

*Otuel*. In Herrtage, *The English Charlemagne Romances. Part VI*. Pp. 65–116.

*Otuel a Kniȝt*. In *The Auchinleck Manuscript*. Ed. David Burnley and Alison Wiggins. National Library of Scotland, 2003. Online at https://auchinleck.nls.uk.

*Otuel and Roland*. In O'Sullivan, *Firumbras and Otuel and Roland*. Pp. 59–146.

*The Pseudo-Turpin: Edited from Bibliothèque Nationale, Fonds Latin, MS. 17656, with an Annotated Synopsis*. Ed. H. M. Smyser. Cambridge, MA: Medieval Academy of America, 1937.

*Richard Coer de Lyon*. Ed. Peter Larkin. Kalamazoo, MI: Medieval Institute Publications, 2015.

*Roland and Vernagu*. In *The Auchinleck Manuscript*. Ed. David Burnley and Alison Wiggins. National Library of Scotland, 2003. Online at https://auchinleck.nls.uk.

*The Romance of Duke Rowlande and of Sir Ottuell of Spayne*. In Herrtage, *The English Charlemagne Romances. Part II*. Pp. 55–104.

*Rouland and Vernagu*. In Herrtage, *The English Charlemagne Romances. Part VI*. Pp. 37–61.

*The Siege of Milan*. In Lupack, *Three Middle English Charlemagne Romances*. Pp. 105–60.

*Sir Eglamour: A Middle English Romance*. Ed. Albert S. Cook and Gustav Schleich. New York: H. Holt, 1911.

*Sir Ferumbras*. In Herrtage, *The English Charlemagne Romances. Part I*. Pp. 1–189.

*Sir Gawain and the Green Knight*. Ed. and trans. James Winny. Peterborough: Broadview Press, 1992.

*Sir Perceval of Galles and Ywain and Gawain*. Ed. Mary Flowers Braswell. Kalamazoo, MI: Medieval Institute Publications, 1995.

*The Song of Roland*. Trans. Glyn S. Burgess. London: Penguin, 1990.

*The Song of Roland: An Analytical Edition*. Ed. and trans. Gerard J. Brault. 2 vols. University Park: Pennsylvania State University Press, 1978.

*The Song of Roland: Translations of the Versions in Assonance and Rhyme of the Chanson de Roland*. Ed. and trans. Joseph J. Duggan and Annalee C. Rejhon. Turnhout: Brepols, 2012.

*The Sultan of Babylon*. In Lupack, *Three Middle English Charlemagne Romances*. Pp. 1–103.

*The Tale of Ralph the Collier*. In Lupack, *Three Middle English Charlemagne Romances*. Pp. 161–204.

*Turpines Story: A Middle English Translation of the* Pseudo-Turpin Chronicle. Ed. Stephen H. A. Shepherd. EETS o.s. 322. Oxford: Oxford University Press, 2004.

*La Vie de Saint Alexis*. Ed. T. D. Hemming. Exeter: University of Exeter Press, 1994.

Virgil. *The Aeneid of Virgil*. Trans. Allen Mandelbaum. Berkeley: University of California Press, 1982.

*Le Voyage de Charlemagne a Jérusalem et a Constantinople*. Ed. Paul Aebischer. Geneva: Librairie Droz, 1965.

Wace. *Le Roman de Rou de Wace*. Ed. A. J. Holden. 3 vols. Paris: Éditions A. & J. Picard, 1970–73.

———. *The History of the Norman People: Wace's Roman de Rou*. Trans. Glyn S. Burgess. Woodbridge: Boydell Press, 2004.

SECONDARY SOURCES

Aebischer, Paul. *Études sur Otinel: De la Chanson de Geste á la Saga Norroise et aux Origines de la Légende*. Berne: Francke, 1960.

Ailes, Marianne. "Chivalry and Conversion: The Chivalrous Saracen in the Old French Epics *Fierabras* and *Otinel*." *Al-Masaq* 9 (1996–97), 1–21.

———. "What's in a Name? Anglo-Norman Romances or *Chansons de Geste*?" In Purdie and Cichon, *Medieval Romance, Medieval Contexts*. Pp. 61–75.

———. "*Otinel*: An Epic in Dialogue with the Tradition." *Olifant* 27 (2012), 9–39.

Ailes, Marianne, and Phillipa Hardman. "How English Are the English Charlemagne Romances?" In Cartlidge, *Boundaries in Medieval Romance*. Pp. 43–55.

Akbari, Suzanne Conklin. "Incorporation in the *Siege of Melayne*." In McDonald, *Pulp Fictions of Medieval England: Essays in Popular Romance*. Pp. 22–44.

———. *Idols in the East: European Representations of Islam and the Orient, 1100–1450*. Ithaca, NY: Cornell University Press, 2009.

*The Anglo-Norman Dictionary*. University of Aberystwyth and University of Swansea. Online at http://www.anglo-norman.net/gate/index.shtml?session=L2TA11002T1539963822.

Armstrong, Dorsey. "The (Non-)Christian Knight in Malory: A Contradiction in Terms?" *Arthuriana* 16.2 (2006), 30–34.

———. "Postcolonial Palomides: Malory's Saracen Knight and the Unmaking of Arthurian Community." *Exemplaria* 18.1 (2006), 175–203.

Auerbach, Erich. "Roland Against Ganelon." In *Mimesis: The Representation of Reality in Western Literature*. Trans. Willard R. Trask. Princeton: Princeton University Press, 1953. Pp. 96–122.

Barbero, Alessandro. *Charlemagne: Father of a Continent*. Trans. Allan Cameron. Berkeley: University of California Press, 2004.

Beal, Rebecca. "Arthur as the Bearer of Civilization: The *Alliterative Morte Arthure* ll. 901–19." *Arthuriana* 5.4 (1995), 32–44.

Berlings, Elizabeth. "The *Sege of Melayne* — A Comic Romance; or, How the French Screwed Up and 'Oure Bretonns' Rescued Them." In Cartlidge, *Boundaries in Medieval Romance*. Pp. 57–70.

Best, Debra E. "Monstrous Alterity and Christian Conversion in the Middle English *The Sowdone of Babylone*." *Medieval Perspectives* 19 (2004), 42–63.

Boscolo, Claudia. "Two Otinel Frescoes in Treviso and Sesto al Reghena." *Francigena* 2 (2016), 201–18.

Breiding, Dirk H. "Famous Makers of Arms and Armors and European Centers of Production." *Heilbrunn Timeline of Art History*. New York: The Metropolitan Museum of Art, 2002. Online at https://www.metmuseum.org/toah/hd/make/hd_make.htm.

Calin, William. *The Epic Quest: Studies in Four Old French Chansons de Geste*. Baltimore, MD: Johns Hopkins Press, 1966.

———. *A Muse for Heroes: Nine Centuries of the Epic in France*. Toronto: University of Toronto Press, 1983.

Calkin, Siobhain Bly. "The Anxieties of Encounter and Exchange: Saracens and Christian Heroism in *Sir Beves of Hamtoun*." *Florilegium* 21 (2004), 135–58.

———. "Violence, Saracens, and English Identity in *Of Arthur and of Merlin*." *Arthuriana* 14.2 (2004), 17–36.

———. "Marking Religion on the Body: Saracens, Categorization, and *The King of Tars*." *Journal of English and Germanic Philology* 104.2 (2005), 219–38.

———. *Saracens and the Making of English Identity: The Auchinleck Manuscript*. New York: Routledge, 2005.

———. "The Man of Law's Tale and Crusade." In *Medieval Latin and Middle English Literature: Essays in Honour of Jill Mann*. Ed. Christopher Cannon and Maura Nolan. Cambridge: D. S. Brewer, 2011. Pp. 1–24.

———. "Romance Baptisms and Theological Contexts in *The King of Tars* and *Sir Ferumbras*." In Purdie and Cichon, *Medieval Romance, Medieval Contexts*. Pp. 105–19.

———. "Saracens." In *Heroes and Anti-Heroes in Medieval Romance*. Ed. Neil Cartlidge. Cambridge: D. S. Brewer, 2012. Pp. 185–200.

Cannon, Christopher. "Chaucer and the Auchinleck Manuscript Revisited." *Chaucer Review* 46.1–2 (2011), 131–46.

Cartlidge, Neil, ed. *Boundaries in Medieval Romance*. Cambridge: D. S. Brewer, 2008.

*Catholic Encyclopedia*. Gen. ed. Kevin Knight, 1995–2018. Online at http://www.newadvent.org/cathen/.

Cawsey, Kathy. "Disorienting Orientalism: Finding Saracens in Strange Places in Late Medieval English Manuscripts." *Exemplaria* 21.4 (2009), 380–97.

Cecire, Maria Sachiko. "Barriers Unbroken: Sir Palomydes the Saracen in 'The Book of Sir Tristram.'" *Arthurian Literature* 28 (2011), 137–54.

Cohen, Jeffrey Jerome. *Of Giants: Sex, Monsters, and the Middle Ages*. Minneapolis: University of Minnesota Press, 1999.

———. "Green Children from Another World, or the Archipelago in England." In *Cultural Diversity in the British Middle Ages: Archipelago, Island, England*. Ed. Jeffrey Jerome Cohen. New York: Palgrave Macmillan, 2008. Pp. 75–94.

Connolly, Margaret, and A. S. G. Edwards. "Evidence for the History of the Auchinleck Manuscript." *The Library: The Transactions of the Bibliographical Society* 18.3 (2017), 292–304.

Cook, Robert Francis. *The Sense of the Song of Roland*. Ithaca, NY: Cornell University Press, 1987.

Cowen, Janet M. "The English Charlemagne Romances." In *Roland and Charlemagne in Europe: Essays on the Reception and Transformation of a Legend*. Ed. Karen Pratt. London: King's College Center for Late Antique and Medieval Studies, 1996. Pp. 149–68.

Czarnowus, Anna. *Fantasies of the Other's Body in Middle English Oriental Romance*. Frankfurt am Main: Peter Lang Edition, 2013.

Daniel, Norman. *Heroes and Saracens: An Interpretation of the Chansons de Geste*. Edinburgh: Edinburgh University Press, 1984.

*Database of Middle English Romance*. Ed. Nicola McDonald, with Chloe Morgan and Catherine Nall. University of York, 2012. Online at https://www.middleenglishromance.org.uk.

De Veyrières, Louis. "L'Épée de Roland." *Bulletin de la Société Scientifique, Historique, et Archéologique de la Corrèze* 14 (1892), 139–43.

Dean, Ruth J., and Maureen B. M. Boulton. *Anglo-Norman Literature: A Guide to Texts and Manuscripts*. London: Anglo-Norman Text Society, 1999.

*Dictionnaire du Moyen Français (1330–1500)*. Analyse et Traitement Informatique de la Langue Française, Université de Lorraine, 2015. Online at http://www.atilf.fr/dmf.

*DIMEV: An Open-Access, Digital Edition of the Index of Middle English Verse*. Ed. Linne R. Mooney and Daniel W. Mosser, and Elizabeth Solopova, Deborah Thorpe, and David Hill Radcliffe. Virginia Polytechnic Institute and State University, 1995. Online at www.dimev.net.

Dinshaw, Carolyn. "Pale Faces: Race, Religion, and Affect in Chaucer's Texts and Their Readers." *Studies in the Age of Chaucer* 23 (2001), 19–41.

Duggan, Joseph J. *A Guide to Studies on the Chanson de Roland*. London: Grant & Cutler, 1976.

Ellis, George. *Specimens of Early English Metrical Romances*. Rev. J. O. Halliwell. London: Henry G. Bohn, 1848.

"Explore Archives and Manuscripts." British Library Catalogue. Online at http://searcharchives.bl.uk.

Fein, Susanna. "Twelve-Line Stanza Forms in Middle English and the Date of *Pearl*." *Speculum* 72.2 (1997), 367–98.

———. "The Contents of Robert Thornton's Manuscripts." In Fein and Johnston, *Robert Thornton and His Books: Essays on the Lincoln and London Manuscripts*. Pp. 13–65.

———, ed. *The Auchinleck Manuscript: New Perspectives*. Woodbridge: Boydell and Brewer, 2016.

Fein, Susanna, and Michael Johnston, eds. *Robert Thornton and His Books: Essays on the Lincoln and London Thornton Manuscripts*. Woodbridge: York Medieval Press, 2014.

Fenster, Thelma, and Carolyn P. Collette, eds. *The French of Medieval England: Essays in Honour of Jocelyn Wogan-Browne*. Cambridge: D. S. Brewer, 2017.

Field, Rosalind, ed. *Tradition and Transformation in Medieval Romance*. Cambridge: D. S. Brewer, 1999.

Friedman, John Block. *The Monstrous Races in Medieval Art and Thought*. Syracuse, NY: Syracuse University Press, 2000.

Ganz, David. "Introduction." In *Einhard and Nother the Stammerer: Two Lives of Charlemagne*. Ed. and trans. David Ganz. London: Penguin, 2008. Pp. 3–13.

Godefroy, Frederic. *Dictionnaire de L'Ancienne Langue Française et de Tous Ses Dialectes du IXe au XVe Siècle*. Volume 5. Paris: Librairie des Sciences et des Arts, 1938.

Goodrich, Peter H. "Saracens and Islamic Alterity in Malory's *Le Morte Darthur*." *Arthuriana* 16.4 (2006), 10–28.

Guilfoyle, Cherrell. "Othello, Otuel, and the English Charlemagne Romances." *Review of English Studies*, n.s. 38.149 (1987), 50–55.

Haidu, Peter. *The Subject of Violence: The Song of Roland and the Birth of the State*. Bloomington: Indiana University Press, 1993.

Hanna, Ralph. "Auchinleck 'Scribe 6' and Some Corollary Issues." In Fein, *The Auchinleck Manuscript: New Perspectives*. Pp. 209–21.

Hardman, Phillipa. "Dear Enemies: the Motif of the Converted Saracen and *Sir Gawain and the Green Knight*." *Reading Medieval Studies* 25 (1999), 59–74.

———. "The *Sege of Melayne*: A Fifteenth-Century Reading." In Field, *Tradition and Transformation in Medieval Romance*. Pp. 71–86.

———. "Roland in England: Contextualising the Middle English *Song of Roland*." In Purdie and Cichon, *Medieval Romance, Medieval Contexts*. Pp. 91–104.

Hardman, Phillipa, and Marianne Ailes. *The Legend of Charlemagne in Medieval England: The Matter of France in Middle English and Anglo-Norman Literature*. Cambridge: D. S. Brewer, 2017.

Hassell, James Woodrow, Jr. *Middle French Proverbs, Sentences, and Proverbial Phrases*. Toronto: Pontifical Institute of Mediaeval Studies, 1982.

Heng, Geraldine. *Empire of Magic: Medieval Romance and the Politics of Cultural Fantasy*. New York: Columbia University Press, 2003.

———. "Jews, Saracens, 'Black Men,' Tartars: England in a World of Racial Difference." In *A Companion to Medieval English Literature and Culture, c. 1350–c. 1500*. Ed. Peter Brown. Malden, MA: Blackwell Publishing, 2007. Pp. 247–69.

———. *The Invention of Race in the European Middle Ages*. Cambridge: Cambridge University Press, 2018.

Higgins, Iain Macleod. *Writing East: The "Travels" of Sir John Mandeville*. Philadelphia: University of Pennsylvania Press, 1997.

Hindley, Alan, and Brian J. Levy. *The Old French Epic: An Introduction. Texts, Commentaries, Notes*. Louvain: Peeters, 1983.

Houlik-Ritchey, Emily. "Rewriting Difference: 'Saracens' in John Gower and Juan de Cuenca." *ES. Revista de Filología Inglesa* 33.1 (2012), 171–89.

Huot, Sylvia. "Others and Alterity." In *The Cambridge Companion to Medieval French Literature*. Ed. Simon Gaunt and Sarah Kay. Cambridge: Cambridge University Press, 2008. Pp. 238–50.

———. *Outsiders: The Humanity and Inhumanity of Giants in Medieval French Prose Romance*. Notre Dame, IN: University of Notre Dame Press, 2016.

Jones, Catherine M. *An Introduction to the Chansons de Geste*. Gainesville: University Press of Florida, 2014.

Kay, Sarah. *The Chansons de Geste in the Age of Romance: Political Fictions*. Oxford, Clarendon Press, 1995.

Kelly, Kathleen Ann. "'Blue' Indians, Ethiopians, and Saracens in Middle English Narrative Texts." *Parergon* 11.1 (1993), 35–52.

Kibler, William W., and Leslie Zarker Morgan, eds. *Approaches to Teaching the Song of Roland*. New York: Modern Language Association of America, 2006.

Kinoshita, Sharon. "'Pagans are Wrong and Christians are Right': Alterity, Gender, and Nation in the Chanson de Roland." *Journal of Medieval and Early Modern Studies* 31.1 (2001), 79–111.

———. *Medieval Boundaries: Rethinking Difference in Old French Literature*. Philadelphia: University of Pennsylvania Press, 2006.

———. "Political Uses and Responses: Orientalism, Postcolonial Theory, and Cultural Studies." In *Approaches to Teaching the Song of Roland*. Ed. William W. Kibler and Leslie Zarker Morgan. Pp. 269–80.

Klein, Andrew W. "Romancing Islam: Reclaiming Christian Unity in the Middle English Romances of Otuel and Ferumbras." M.A. Thesis: University of Saskatchewan, 2009.

Klein, Holger A. "Arm Reliquary of the Apostles." *Treasures of Heaven: Saints, Relics, and Devotion in Medieval Europe*. Cleveland Museum of Art, the Walters Art Museum, Baltimore, and the British Museum, London, 2011. Online at http://projects.mcah.columbia.edu/treasuresofheaven/relics/Arm-Reliquary-of-the-Apostles.php.

Leitch, Megan G. *Romancing Treason: The Literature of the Wars of the Roses*. Oxford: Oxford University Press, 2015.

Lejeune, Rita. "La Naissance du Couple Littéraire 'Roland et Olivier.'" In *Pankarpeia: Mélanges Henri Grégoire*. Vol. 2. Brussels: Secrétariat des Éditions de l'Institut, 1950. Pp. 371–401.

Leverett, Emily Lavin. "Holy Bloodshed: Violence and Christian Piety in the Romances of the London Thornton Manuscript." Ph.D. Dissertation: Ohio State University, 2006.

Libbon, Marisa. "The Invention of *King Richard*." In Fein, *The Auchinleck Manuscript: New Perspectives*. Pp. 127–38.

Loomis, Laura Hibbard. "The Auchinleck Manuscript and a Possible London Bookshop of 1330–1340." *PMLA* 57.3 (1942), 595–627.

Malo, Robyn. *Relics and Writing in Late Medieval England*. Toronto: University of Toronto Press, 2013.

Mandach, André de. *Naissance et Développement de la Chanson de Geste en Europe: Vol 1. La Geste de Charlemagne et de Roland*. Geneva: Droz, 1961.

Manion, Lee. *Narrating the Crusades: Loss and Recovery in Medieval and Early Modern English Literature*. Cambridge: Cambridge University Press, 2014.

McDonald, Nicola, ed. *Pulp Fictions of Medieval England: Essays in Popular Romance*. Manchester: Manchester University Press, 2004.

Mehl, Dieter. *The Middle English Romances of the Thirteenth and Fourteenth Centuries*. London: Routledge and Kegan Paul, 1969.

Melick, Elizabeth. "Saracens, Graves, and the Formation of National Identity in Sir Thomas Malory's *Le Morte Darthur*." *Enarratio* 19 (2015), 50–67.

Metlitzki, Dorothee. *The Matter of Araby in Medieval England*. New Haven: Yale University Press, 1977.

Mickel, Emanuel J. *Ganelon, Treason, and the 'Chanson de Roland.'* University Park: The Pennsylvania State University Press, 1989.

*Middle English Dictionary*. Ann Arbor: University of Michigan Press, 2001–. Online at http://quod.lib.umich.edu/m/med/.

*NIMEV: A New Index of Middle English Verse*. Ed. Julia Boffey and A. S. G. Edwards. London: The British Library, 2005.

*The Oxford English Dictionary*. Third edition. Oxford University Press, 2018. Online at http://www.oed.com/.

Paris, Gaston. *Histoire Poétique de Charlemagne*. Paris: Librairie A. Franck, 1865.

Pastan, Elizabeth. "Charlemagne as Saint? Relics and the Choice of Window Subjects at Chartres Cathedral." In *The Legend of Charlemagne in the Middle Ages: Power, Faith, and Crusade*. Ed. Matthew Gabriele and Jace Stuckey. New York: Palgrave Macmillan, 2008. Pp. 97–135.

Porcheddu, Fred. "Edited Text and Medieval Artifact: The Auchinleck Bookshop and 'Charlemagne and Roland' Theories, Fifty Years Later." *Philological Quarterly* 80.4 (2001), 465–500.

Purdie, Rhiannon. *Anglicising Romance: Tail-Rhyme and Genre in Medieval English Literature*. Cambridge: D. S. Brewer, 2008.

Purdie, Rhiannon, and Michael Cichon, eds. *Medieval Romance, Medieval Contexts*. Cambridge: D. S. Brewer, 2011.

Ramey, Lynn Tarte. *Christian, Saracen and Genre in Medieval French Literature*. New York: Routledge, 2001.

———. *Black Legacies: Race and the European Middle Ages*. Gainesville: University Press of Florida, 2014.

Raybin, David. "*The Song of Roland*." *Oxford Bibliographies Online*. Oxford University Press, 2016. Online at http://www.oxfordbibliographies.com/view/document/obo-9780195396584/obo-9780195396584-0207.xml.

Rouse, Robert. "Expectation vs. Experience: Encountering the Saracen Other in Middle English Romance." *Selim* 10 (2000), 125–40.

———. "Walking (Between) the Lines: Romance as Itinerary/Map." In Purdie and Cichon, *Medieval Romance, Medieval Contexts*. Pp. 135–47.

Russell, Delbert. "Admiring Ambivalence: On Paul Meyer's Anglo-Norman Scholarship." In Fenster and Collette, *The French of Medieval England*. Pp. 241–56.

Rychner, Jean. *La Chanson de Geste: Essai sur l'Art Épique des Jongleurs*. Geneva: Librairie E. Droz, 1955.

Sikorska, Liliana. "Malevolent Visitors: On Hosts and Hostiles in Medieval Romances." In *Phases of the History of English: Selection of Papers Read at SHELL 2012*. Ed. Michio Hosaka, Michiko Ogura, Hironori Suzuki, and Akinobu Tani. Frankfurt: Peter Lang, 2013. Pp. 69–92.

Smyser, H. M. "*Charlemagne and Roland* and the Auchinleck MS." *Speculum* 21.3 (1946), 275–88.

———. "Charlemagne Legends." In *A Manual of the Writings in Middle English, 1050–1500*. Vol. 1. Ed. J. Burke Severs. New Haven: Connecticut Academy of Arts and Sciences, 1967. Pp. 80–100, 256–66.

Speed, Diane. "Translation and Conversion in *The Romance of Duke Rowlande and Sir Ottuell of Spayne*." *Medieval Translator* 8 (2003), 235–44.

Strickland, Debra Higgs. *Saracens, Demons, and Jews: Making Monsters in Medieval Art*. Princeton: Princeton University Press, 2003.

Taylor, Andrew. *Textual Situations: Three Medieval Manuscripts and Their Readers*. Philadelphia: University of Pennsylvania Press, 2002.

———. "The *Chanson d'Aspremont* in Bodmer 11 and Plantagenet Propaganda." In Fenster and Collette, *The French of Medieval England*. Pp. 100–15.

Thompson, John J. *Robert Thornton and the London Thornton Manuscript: British Library MS Additional 31042*. Cambridge: D.S. Brewer, 1987.

Vance, Eugene. *Reading the Song of Roland*. Englewood Cliffs, NJ: Prentice-Hall Inc., 1970.

Vincent, Diane. "Reading a Christian-Saracen Debate in Fifteenth-Century Middle English Charlemagne Romance: The Case of *Turpines Story*." In *The Exploitations of Medieval Romance*. Ed. Laura Ashe, Ivana Djordjević, and Judith Weiss. Cambridge: D. S. Brewer, 2010. Pp. 90–107.

Walpole, Ronald N. *Charlemagne and Roland: A Study of the Source of Two Middle English Metrical Romances, Roland and Vernagu and Otuel and Roland*. Berkeley: University of California Press, 1944. In *Modern Philology* 21.6 (1944), 385–451.

———. "The Source MS of Charlemagne and Roland and the Auchinleck Bookshop." *Modern Language Notes* 60.1 (1945), 22–26.

———. "The *Nota Emilianense*: New Light (But How Much?) on the Origins of the Old French Epic." *Romance Philology* 10 (1956), 1–18.

Warm, Robert. "Identity, Narrative and Participation: Defining a Context for the Middle English Charlemagne Romances." In Field, *Tradition and Transformation in Medieval Romance*. Pp. 87–100.

Whiting, Bartlett Jere, and Helen Wescott Whiting. *Proverbs, Sentences, and Proverbial Phrases from English Writings Mainly before 1500*. Cambridge, MA: Belknap Press of Harvard University Press, 1968.

Wiggins, Alison. "Importance." *The Auchinleck Manuscript*. National Library of Scotland, 2003. Online at https://auchinleck.nls.uk/editorial/importance.html.

Wilcox, Rebecca. "Romancing the East: Greeks and Saracens in *Guy of Warwick*." In McDonald, *Pulp Fictions of Medieval England: Essays in Popular Romance*. Pp. 217–40.

Williamsen, Elizabeth A. "The Quest for Collective Identity in the Middle English Charlemagne Romances." Ph.D. Dissertation: Indiana University, 2009.

# GLOSSARY

**abayste** *embarrassed, abashed, upset*

**abien** *to pay for; to pay a penalty for an offense*

**ac** *but, yet, however, nonetheless*

**acquellen** *to slay, kill*

**agramen** *to get angry, annoyed, or provoked*

**agrisen** *to tremble with fear*

**(h)aketon** *a padded jacket worn under armor*

**algate** *in all ways, in every manner, entirely*

**alswa** *also*

**amorwe** *in the morning, the next morning*

**anour** *dignity, honor*

**apaien** *to be satisfied or pleased*

**aplight** *in faith, truly*

**appayrayle** *clothing; armor or martial equipment*

**arblaster** *crossbowman*

**arere** *to build, raise up*

**arowe** *one by one, in succession*

**arso(u)n** *a saddle*

**asleped** *sleepy, tired, drowsy*

**aspien** *to find, discover, seek out*

**astonen** *to stun, stupefy*

**at(w)o** *in half, in pieces*

**aught(e)** *a possession, a belonging*

**avaunten** *to boast or brag*

**aventale** *a piece of chain mail used to cover the neck and upper chest*

**awede** *enraged*

**awreken** *to avenge*

**bacinet** *a type of helmet*

**bai(y)lie(y)** *a district under control of a bailiff; custody, governance*

**beden** *to request, ask for, pray, proclaim*

**bihesten** *to promise, make a pledge*

**bihoten** *to promise*

**bilien, bilai(y)** *to besiege, attack*

**binimen** *to take away, deprive; to take hold of*

**bitaken** *to bestow, give; to commend to God or condemn to hell*

**bithinken** *to reflect, ponder*

**bitoknen** *to symbolize, mean*

**ble** *countenance, expression; hue*

**blith(v)e** *joyful, quickly*

**blo** *discolored, bruised, bloody*

**bon(e)** *a prayer, request, petition*

**bote** *relief, healing, salvation, redemption*

**bo(w)un** *ready, prepared, eager*

**bour(e)** *a bedroom, a lady's chamber*

**burdour** *a minstrel, story-teller, entertainer*

**busken** *to prepare, make ready, clothe*

**braisten** *to harm, injure*

**bra(o)nd** *a torch, firebrand; sword*

**bre(a)i(y)d** *a sudden movement, like a jerk; a blow*

**breme** *fierce, cruel, savage*

**britten** *to slash, slay; to shatter, demolish*

**burde** *a shield*

**c(h)ano(u)n** *a clergyman*

**cas** *an event, occurrence, incident*

**caytyf** *a wretch, wicked man, coward*

**certes** *certainly*

**chaumberlein** *a king's personal attendant*

**chere** *facial expression*

**clepen** *to call, to name*

**clerk** *a clergyman*
**co(u)lver** *a dove*
**connen** *to have an ability; to know*
**coupen** *to fight, exchange blows, engage in battle*
**couthe** *known, familiar with*
**craft** *strength, power; ingenuity, cleverness*

**delen** *to have dealings with; to rule or reign over*
**deray** *trouble, suffering, harm*
**deren** *to hurt, damage, injure; to dare, have the courage to do something*
**de(i)scrien** *to rebuke, criticize, condemn*
**deserd(t)** *a barren area, either uninhabitable or sparsely inhabited, a wasteland*
**despisen** *to disparage; to feel contempt for*
**dighten** *to condemn, arrange, prepare for*
**dingen** *to beat, strike; to overcome, defeat*
**dint** *a sword stroke, blow*
**dolour** *pain, suffering; grief, lamenting*
**doth** *to act against, fight*
**dou(g)hti** *valiant, brave, strong*
**do(w)un(e)** *a hill or elevation*
**dounright(es)** *downward*
**d(th)urren** *to dare to*

**ei(y)e** *fear, respect, reverence*
**eke** *also*
**eme** *an uncle, family member*
**entayle** *shape, cut, form, or character*
**entent(e)** *purpose, will*
**erd** *a region, area of land*
**everidel** *completely, utterly*

**fa(e)l(le)** *wicked, cruel; strong, bold*
**faren** *to travel, depart, journey*
**fauchoun** *a type of sword*
**fayn(e)** *eager, joyful, glad*
**fellen** *to vanquish; to slay*
**felon** *hostile, wicked; fierce, dangerous*
**fend(e)** *a demon, fiend, evil spirit*
**fer** *fierce, bold, proud*
**ferd** *an army, military force*
**fere** *a companion;* **in fere** *together*

**fetten** *to retrieve something, bring something out*
**firmament** *the heavens, the sky*
**flytte** *the passage of a weapon through a body, a wound*
**follaut** *baptism*
**fomen** *enemies, foes*
**fonden** *to test one's strength*
**for the nones** *for the occasion*
**forleten** *to yield, give up, desert*
**forsothe** *truly*
**forto** *in order to*
**fothot** *quickly, speedily, suddenly*
**fre** *of noble social status*

**game(n)** *amusement, merriment*
**gerth** *a strap passing below a horse's belly to secure a saddle or harness*
**gesseraunte** *a jacket or coat of scale armor*
**gilden** *glorious, blessed; made of gold or overlaid with gold leaf*
**gin** *talent, ingenuity, skill*
**gi(e)nge, gines** *group of people, warriors*
**ginne** *a siege machine*
**girden** *to strike, hit; to rush, charge; to buckle on a sword and belt*
**girdilstede** *waist, midsection*
**gnede** *lacking, scarce*
**gome** *a man, warrior*
**gonfa(y)noun** *a battle standard, banner*
**gramaungere** *an overambitious undertaking*
**gredden** *to cry out, shout*
**greven** *to wound, injure, cause physical damage*
**grot** *a part, bit, fragment*
**grym** *stern, fierce*
**grythe** *governance, control, counsel; shelter, refuge*

**haberion** *a coat or jacket of scale armor*
**hap(e)** *a person's lot, luck, or fate*
**hau(w)berk(e)** *a coat of mail*
**heigheing** *exaltation, praise*
**hele** *good health, sound physical condition*
**hem** *them*

**hend(e)** *noble and courtly; (of God and the Virgin Mary) graciousness, mercy*
**henten** *to sieze, capture*
**her** *their, her*
**herberwen** *to take shelter, lodge, dwell*
**herken** *to listen, pay attention*
**heued** *a head*
**hien** *to go quickly*
**hi(e)ghten** *to call someone, to name someone*
**holt(e)** *a wood, grove*
**hone** *delay, hesitation*
**ho(a)re(e)** *grayish white hair*
**hynder arson** *the back part of a saddle*

**ich** *I; each, every*
**i(y)fere** *each other, together*
**ilke** *those same*
**imelle** *among, amid, between*
**i(y)nowe** *enough, an abundance*
**iwis** *truly, certainly*

**juels** *jewels*

**kene** *fierce, sharp*
**kennen** *to know, be aware of*
**kerven** *to cut, trim*
**ki(y)then** *to perform, do; to make known*
**kydd(th)en** *to know or learn something; to proclaim something*

**la(o)ugh(w)en** *to laugh*
**lef(e)** *a beloved person, friend, sweetheart*
**lei(y)** *a set of laws; a religious faith*
**lel** *loyal*
**leman** *a lover, paramour*
**lend(e)** *loin, hip, buttocks, lower back*
**leren** *to know; to teach; to learn*
**lesing(e)** *lying; losing; destroying*
**lett** *to delay*
**leve** *religious beliefs, faith*
**levedi** *a lady*
**leven** *to believe, trust, rely on*
**li(y)veré** *heraldic clothing, uniform*
**louerd** *a lord, master*
**loth** *hateful, unwilling, reluctant*
**lyst** *hearing, listening*

**mai(y)n** *physical strength, vigor, force*
**maugré** *shame, blame, culpability*
**maumete** *idols*
**meden** *to reward or bribe*
**mei(y)ne** *power, authority, military might*
**menestrausie** *minstrelsy, musical performance, merriment*
**menske** *honor*
**mervail** *a marvel, astonishing act*
**meten** *to measure, as in distance; to measure out, as to dispense*
**mi(u)chel** *many, much*
**mi(y)schau(w)nce** *injury, harm, mishap*
**mi(y)ssaunter** *misadventure, misfortune*
**misseien** *to insult, slander*
**mode** *temperament, character, emotion*
**mo(u)n** *might, may; must*
**mone** *a complaint, cry*
**morwen** *morning*
**moten** *must, to be compelled*
**mounde** *power, strength, prowess*

**nevenen** *to tell, explain, call upon*
**neveradel** *nothing at all; not a bit*
**nimen** *to take, seize*
**noblay(e)** *of high rank; worthy of respect, honorable; of good quality, pleasing*

**oftaken** *to overtake, apprehend, capture*
**ord** *the point of a spear*
**ordenaunce** *battle array, arrangement of troops*
**ori(y)so(u)n** *a prayer, petition, request*
**ost** *a host, military force, army*
**overhien** *to overtake*

**paien** *to please*
**pan(i)er** *a basket*
**pa(i)nim** *pagan, Saracen*
**pas** *a way, path, passageway*
**passen** *to go, leave*
**pei(y)trel** *a breastplate for a horse*
**pingen** *to pierce, spur a horse*
**pli(y)ghten** *to promise or pledge*
**pousté** *power, strength, control*

**pover** *poor*
**priken** *to urge a horse with spurs, gallop*
**priour** *head of a monastery*
**purveia(u)nse** *preparations, a plot or plan*
**pusesoun** *poison*

**quede** *sinful, wicked*
**qui(y)ck(e)** *living, alive*

**rapen** *to hurry, hasten, rush*
**rappen** *to strike, hit*
**rathely** *quickly, hastily, immediately*
**raumpen** *(of an animal, like a lion or bear) to stand up on hind legs in a threatening manner*
**rec(k)reyande** *cowardly, defeated*
**reden** *to read; advise, counsel; to command*
**reuen** *to regret; to have pity for*
**reven** *to steal, rob, take*
**rode** *the cross on which Christ died*
**ro(u)t(e)n** *to bellow, cry out, roar*
**roum** *a room, chamber*
**route** *a company or troop*

**sadde** *mighty, powerful, strong*
**sale** *a great hall*
**sau(w)e** *a number, tally*
**saughtillynge** *reconciliation*
**saunfayl** *without fail, assuredly*
**sauter** *a psalm*
**scomfit(e)** *defeated in battle, overcome*
**seg(g)en** *to besiege, to attack*
**seightnesse** *reconciliation*
**sely** *remarkable, unusual, strange*
**semble** *a gathering; battle*
**semely** *splendid, pleasant, worthy*
**s(c)henden** *to injure, harm, overcome*
**s(c)hene** *bright, splendid, beautiful*
**s(c)heren** *to pierce, cut off*
**s(c)hiveren** *splintered, broke to pieces*
**s(c)hond** *disgrace*
**s(c)hriven** *to administer the sacrament, hear confession, absolve of sin*
**s(sc)henden** *to harm, injure, ruin*
**siker** *true, trustworthy; secure, safe*

**skil(le)** *intelligence, knowledge*
**sle(n), slo(w)(en)** *to kill, slay*
**slo(ugh), slewe** *slew (past tense of sle(n))*
**slone, islein** *slain (past participle of sle(n))*
**smiten** *to hit, strike, deal a blow*
**smothirly** *menacingly, grimly*
**snel(le)** *quick, valiant, fierce*
**sond(e)** *a message, a mission; divine intervention*
**sond(e)r(e)** *in pieces, broken apart*
**soth(e)** *truth, facts*
**soun** *sound, music made by an instrument*
**speden** *to fare, prosper, thrive, succeed*
**spillen** *to die, to kill*
**stede** *a place, area, location*
**steven** *a voice*
**sti(y)nten** *to cease, stop*
**stiren** *to move oneself, set into motion, move about*
**stounde** *a short period of time, a particular moment*
**stoute** *valiant, bold, stern*
**stripen** *to strike with a weapon, thrust*
**stro(u)i(y)en** *to overcome, conquer, slaughter*
**su(w)i(y)the** *swiftly, vigorously*
**swein(e)** *a knight's attendant, squire*
**swete** *sweat, perspiration; lifeblood*
**sweven** *a dream vision*
**swi(y)re** *neck, throat*
**swith(e)** *such, so much, an excessive amount*

**targe** *a shield*
**tene** *suffering, injury, wrath*
**thennes** *thence, from there*
**ther(e)of** *because of, as a result of*
**thider** *to that place, there*
**thilke** *this, that, those (pointing to a particular person or thing)*
**tho** *then*
**thonwange** *cheeks, temples*
**thro** *bold, valiant, fearless*
**ti(y)d(th)ing(nd)e** *message, news, information*

**tinen** *to suffer a loss, lose footing in stirrup while riding*

**tite** *quickly, soon, immediately*

**todreven** *to scatter, disperse*

**tofore** *before, in front of*

**toteren** *to break into fragments*

**tour** *a tower, tall building, fortress or stronghold*

**travayle** *toil, effort, exertion; suffering; knightly competition*

**treu(w)the** *promise, oath*

**unconnande** *foolish, imprudent, unwise*

**underfongen** *to host, accept, provide hospitality for*

**unwrest** *wicked, immoral*

**venou** *an onslaught, attack*

**verrai(y)** *true, legitimate*

**verrament** *truly*

**vestement** *liturgical garment*

**warde-cors** *an attendant, squire, bodyguard*

**wede** *clothing, garments, armor*

**wede** *mad, senseless, insane*

**wem** *sin, guilt, moral impurity*

**wenden** *to leave, pass through or from; to fall*

**wenen** *to believe, suppose, conclude*

**werken** *to make, cause*

**whylome** *at one time, formerly*

**wight** *an unnatural creature, demon*

**wight** *brave, valiant*

**wi(y)ssen** *to instruct, teach*

**witen** *to know, be certain about*

**witherling** *an enemy, foe*

**wo(o)** *woe, dismay*

**wod(e)** *insane, foolhardy, amazed*

**wonen** *to be present in a location; to remain*

**wonnynge** *territory, country, habitation*

**wowynges** *courting, seducing*

**wroth(e)** *angry, irate*

**wrotherhele** *having an evil or misfortunate outcome*

**yare** *ready, prepared*

**yede** *to walk, travel, depart*

**yeven** *to give*

**ywis** *truly, certainly*

# MIDDLE ENGLISH TEXTS SERIES

*The Floure and the Leafe, The Assembly of Ladies, The Isle of Ladies,* edited by Derek Pearsall (1990)

*Three Middle English Charlemagne Romances,* edited by Alan Lupack (1990)

*Six Ecclesiastical Satires,* edited by James M. Dean (1991)

*Heroic Women from the Old Testament in Middle English Verse,* edited by Russell A. Peck (1991)

*The Canterbury Tales: Fifteenth-Century Continuations and Additions,* edited by John M. Bowers (1992)

Gavin Douglas, *The Palis of Honoure,* edited by David Parkinson (1992)

*Wynnere and Wastoure and The Parlement of the Thre Ages,* edited by Warren Ginsberg (1992)

*The Shewings of Julian of Norwich,* edited by Georgia Ronan Crampton (1994)

*King Arthur's Death: The Middle English Stanzaic Morte Arthur and Alliterative Morte Arthure,* edited by Larry D. Benson, revised by Edward E. Foster (1994)

*Lancelot of the Laik and Sir Tristrem,* edited by Alan Lupack (1994)

*Sir Gawain: Eleven Romances and Tales,* edited by Thomas Hahn (1995)

*The Middle English Breton Lays,* edited by Anne Laskaya and Eve Salisbury (1995)

*Sir Perceval of Galles and Ywain and Gawain,* edited by Mary Flowers Braswell (1995)

*Four Middle English Romances: Sir Isumbras, Octavian, Sir Eglamour of Artois, Sir Tryamour,* edited by Harriet Hudson (1996; second edition 2006)

*The Poems of Laurence Minot, 1333–1352,* edited by Richard H. Osberg (1996)

*Medieval English Political Writings,* edited by James M. Dean (1996)

*The Book of Margery Kempe,* edited by Lynn Staley (1996)

*Amis and Amiloun, Robert of Cisyle, and Sir Amadace,* edited by Edward E. Foster (1997; second edition 2007)

*The Cloud of Unknowing,* edited by Patrick J. Gallacher (1997)

*Robin Hood and Other Outlaw Tales,* edited by Stephen Knight and Thomas Ohlgren (1997; second edition 2000)

*The Poems of Robert Henryson,* edited by Robert L. Kindrick with the assistance of Kristie A. Bixby (1997)

*Moral Love Songs and Laments,* edited by Susanna Greer Fein (1998)

John Lydgate, *Troy Book Selections,* edited by Robert R. Edwards (1998)

Thomas Usk, *The Testament of Love,* edited by R. Allen Shoaf (1998)

*Prose Merlin,* edited by John Conlee (1998)

*Middle English Marian Lyrics,* edited by Karen Saupe (1998)

John Metham, *Amoryus and Cleopes,* edited by Stephen F. Page (1999)

*Four Romances of England: King Horn, Havelok the Dane, Bevis of Hampton, Athelston,* edited by Ronald B. Herzman, Graham Drake, and Eve Salisbury (1999)

*The Assembly of Gods: Le Assemble de Dyeus, or Banquet of Gods and Goddesses, with the Discourse of Reason and Sensuality,* edited by Jane Chance (1999)

Thomas Hoccleve, *The Regiment of Princes,* edited by Charles R. Blyth (1999)

John Capgrave, *The Life of Saint Katherine,* edited by Karen A. Winstead (1999)

John Gower, *Confessio Amantis,* Vol. 1, edited by Russell A. Peck; with Latin translations by Andrew Galloway (2000; second edition 2006); Vol. 2 (2003); Vol. 3 (2004)

*Richard the Redeless and Mum and the Sothsegger,* edited by James M. Dean (2000)

*Ancrene Wisse,* edited by Robert Hasenfratz (2000)

Walter Hilton, *The Scale of Perfection,* edited by Thomas H. Bestul (2000)

John Lydgate, *The Siege of Thebes,* edited by Robert R. Edwards (2001)

*Pearl,* edited by Sarah Stanbury (2001)

*The Trials and Joys of Marriage,* edited by Eve Salisbury (2002)

*Middle English Legends of Women Saints,* edited by Sherry L. Reames, with the assistance of Martha G. Blalock and Wendy R. Larson (2003)

*The Wallace: Selections,* edited by Anne McKim (2003)

Richard Maidstone, *Concordia (The Reconciliation of Richard II with London),* edited by David R. Carlson, with a verse translation by A. G. Rigg (2003)

*Three Purgatory Poems: The Gast of Gy, Sir Owain, The Vision of Tundale,* edited by Edward E. Foster (2004)

William Dunbar, *The Complete Works,* edited by John Conlee (2004)

*Chaucerian Dream Visions and Complaints,* edited by Dana M. Symons (2004)

*Stanzaic Guy of Warwick*, edited by Alison Wiggins (2004)

*Saints' Lives in Middle English Collections*, edited by E. Gordon Whatley, with Anne B. Thompson and Robert K. Upchurch (2004)

*Siege of Jerusalem*, edited by Michael Livingston (2004)

*The Kingis Quair and Other Prison Poems*, edited by Linne R. Mooney and Mary-Jo Arn (2005)

*The Chaucerian Apocrypha: A Selection*, edited by Kathleen Forni (2005)

John Gower, *The Minor Latin Works*, edited and translated by R. F. Yeager, with *In Praise of Peace*, edited by Michael Livingston (2005)

*Sentimental and Humorous Romances: Floris and Blancheflour, Sir Degrevant, The Squire of Low Degree, The Tournament of Tottenham, and The Feast of Tottenham*, edited by Erik Kooper (2006)

*The Dicts and Sayings of the Philosophers*, edited by John William Sutton (2006)

*"Everyman" and Its Dutch Original, "Elckerlijc,"* edited by Clifford Davidson, Martin W. Walsh, and Ton J. Broos (2007)

*The N-Town Plays*, edited by Douglas Sugano, with assistance by Victor I. Scherb (2007)

*The Book of John Mandeville*, edited by Tamarah Kohanski and C. David Benson (2007)

John Lydgate, *The Temple of Glas*, edited by J. Allan Mitchell (2007)

*The Northern Homily Cycle*, edited by Anne B. Thompson (2008)

*Codex Ashmole 61: A Compilation of Popular Middle English Verse*, edited by George Shuffelton (2008)

*Chaucer and the Poems of "Ch,"* edited by James I. Wimsatt (revised edition 2009)

William Caxton, *The Game and Playe of the Chesse*, edited by Jenny Adams (2009)

John the Blind Audelay, *Poems and Carols*, edited by Susanna Fein (2009)

*Two Moral Interludes: The Pride of Life and Wisdom*, edited by David Klausner (2009)

John Lydgate, *Mummings and Entertainments*, edited by Claire Sponsler (2010)

*Mankind*, edited by Kathleen M. Ashley and Gerard NeCastro (2010)

*The Castle of Perseverance*, edited by David N. Klausner (2010)

Robert Henryson, *The Complete Works*, edited by David J. Parkinson (2010)

John Gower, *The French Balades*, edited and translated by R. F. Yeager (2011)

*The Middle English Metrical Paraphrase of the Old Testament*, edited by Michael Livingston (2011) *The York Corpus Christi Plays*, edited by Clifford Davidson (2011)

*Prik of Conscience*, edited by James H. Morey (2012)

*The Dialogue of Solomon and Marcolf: A Dual-Language Edition from Latin and Middle English Printed Editions*, edited by Nancy Mason Bradbury and Scott Bradbury (2012)

*Croxton Play of the Sacrament*, edited by John T. Sebastian (2012)

*Ten Bourdes*, edited by Melissa M. Furrow (2013)

*Lybeaus Desconus*, edited by Eve Salisbury and James Weldon (2013)

*The Complete Harley 2253 Manuscript*, Vol. 2, edited and translated by Susanna Fein with David Raybin and Jan Ziolkowski (2014); Vol. 3 (2015); Vol. 1 (2015)

*Oton de Granson, Poems*, edited and translated by Peter Nicholson and Joan Grenier-Winther (2015)

*The King of Tars*, edited by John H. Chandler (2015)

*John Hardyng Chronicle*, edited by James Simpson and Sarah Peverley (2015)

*Richard Coer de Lyon*, edited by Peter Larkin (2015)

*Guillaume de Machaut, The Complete Poetry and Music, Volume 1: The Debate Poems*, edited and translated by R. Barton Palmer (2016)

*Lydgate's Fabula Duorum Mercatorum and Guy of Warwyk*, edited by Pamela Farvolden (2016)

*The Katherine Group (MS Bodley 34)*, edited by Emily Rebekah Huber and Elizabeth Robertson (2016)

*Sir Torrent of Portingale*, edited by James Wade (2017)

*The Towneley Plays*, edited by Garrett P. J. Epp (2018)

*The Digby Mary Magdalene Play*, edited by Theresa Coletti (2018)

*Guillaume de Machaut, The Complete Poetry and Music, Volume 9: The Motets*, edited by Jacques Boogart (2018)

*Six Scottish Courtly and Chivalric Poems, Including Lyndsay's Squyer Meldrum*, edited by Rhiannon Purdie and Emily Wingfield (2018)

Gavin Douglas, *The Palyce of Honour*, edited by David John Parkinson (2018)

*Guillaume de Machaut, The Complete Poetry and Music, Volume 2: The Boethian Poems, Le Remede de Fortune and Le Confort d'Ami*, edited by R. Barton Palmer (2019)

*John Lydgate's "Dance of Death" and Related Works*, edited by Megan L. Cook and Elizaveta Strakhov (2019)

## 🖋 COMMENTARY SERIES

Haimo of Auxerre, *Commentary on the Book of Jonah*, translated with an introduction and notes by Deborah Everhart (1993)

*Medieval Exegesis in Translation: Commentaries on the Book of Ruth*, translated with an introduction and notes by Lesley Smith (1996)

*Nicholas of Lyra's Apocalypse Commentary*, translated with an introduction and notes by Philip D. W. Krey (1997)

Rabbi Ezra Ben Solomon of Gerona, *Commentary on the Song of Songs and Other Kabbalistic Commentaries*, selected, translated, and annotated by Seth Brody (1999)

John Wyclif, *On the Truth of Holy Scripture*, translated with an introduction and notes by Ian Christopher Levy (2001)

*Second Thessalonians: Two Early Medieval Apocalyptic Commentaries*, introduced and translated by Steven R. Cartwright and Kevin L. Hughes (2001)

*The "Glossa Ordinaria" on the Song of Songs*, translated with an introduction and notes by Mary Dove (2004)

*The Seven Seals of the Apocalypse: Medieval Texts in Translation*, translated with an introduction and notes by Francis X. Gumerlock (2009)

*The "Glossa Ordinaria" on Romans*, translated with an introduction and notes by Michael Scott Woodward (2011)

Nicholas of Lyra, *Literal Commentary on Galatians*, translated with an introduction and notes by Edward Arthur Naumann (2015)

*Early Latin Commentaries on the Apocalypse*, edited by Francis X. Gumerlock (2016)

*Rabbi Eliezer of Beaugency: Commentaries on Amos and Jonah (with selections from Isaiah and Ezekiel)*, by Robert A. Harris (2018)

*Carolingian Commentaries on the Apocalypse by Theodulf and Smaragdus*, edited and translated by Francis X. Gumerlock (2019)

## 🖋 SECULAR COMMENTARY SERIES

*Accessus ad auctores: Medieval Introduction to the Authors*, edited and translated by Stephen M. Wheeler (2015)

*The Vulgate Commentary on Ovid's Metamorphoses, Book 1*, edited and translated by Frank Coulson (2015)

Brunetto Latini, *La rettorica*, edited and translated by Stefania D'Agata D'Ottavi (2016)

## 🖋 DOCUMENTS OF PRACTICE SERIES

*Love and Marriage in Late Medieval London*, selected, translated, and introduced by Shannon McSheffrey (1995)

*Sources for the History of Medicine in Late Medieval England*, selected, introduced, and translated by Carole Rawcliffe (1995)

*A Slice of Life: Selected Documents of Medieval English Peasant Experience*, edited, translated, and with an introduction by Edwin Brezette DeWindt (1996)

*Regular Life: Monastic, Canonical, and Mendicant "Rules,"* selected and introduced by Douglas J. McMillan and Kathryn Smith Fladenmuller (1997); second edition, selected and introduced by Daniel Marcel La Corte and Douglas J. McMillan (2004)

*Women and Monasticism in Medieval Europe: Sisters and Patrons of the Cistercian Reform*, selected, translated, and with an introduction by Constance H. Berman (2002)

*Medieval Notaries and Their Acts: The 1327–1328 Register of Jean Holanie*, introduced, edited, and translated by Kathryn L. Reyerson and Debra A. Salata (2004)

*John Stone's Chronicle: Christ Church Priory, Canterbury, 1417–1472*, selected, translated, and introduced by Meriel Connor (2010)

*Medieval Latin Liturgy in English Translation*, edited by by Matthew Cheung Salisbury (2017)

*Henry VII's London in the Great Chronicle*, edited by Julia Boffey (2019)

.

Typeset in 10/13 New Baskerville
and Golden Cockerel Ornaments display

Medieval Institute Publications
College of Arts and Sciences
Western Michigan University
1903 W. Michigan Avenue
Kalamazoo, MI 49008-5432
http://www.wmich.edu/medievalpublications

 WESTERN MICHIGAN UNIVERSITY